SHOOK OVER HELL

Post-Traumatic Stress, Vietnam, and the Civil War

ERIC T. DEAN, JR.

HARVARD UNIVERSITY PRESS
Cambridge, Massachusetts
London, England
1997

Library of Congress Cataloging-in-Publication Data

Dean, Eric T.
Shook over hell : post-traumatic stress, Vietnam, and the Civil War /
Eric T. Dean, Jr.
p.   cm.
Revision of the author's thesis.
Includes bibliographical references and index.
ISBN 0-674-80651-4 (alk. paper)
1. Post-traumatic stress disorder.
2. United States—History—Civil War, 1861–1865—Veterans—Mental health.
3. Vietnamese Conflict, 1961–1975—Veterans—Mental health.   I. Title.
RC552.P67D434   1997
616.85'212—dc21   97-9737

Designed by Gwen Nefsky Frankfeldt

All visible objects, man, are but as pasteboard
masks. But in each event—in the living act, the
undoubted deed—there, some unknown but still
reasoning thing puts forth the mouldings of its
features from behind the unreasoning mask.
If man will strike, strike through the mask!
How can the prisoner reach outside except
by thrusting through the wall?

HERMAN MELVILLE, *MOBY-DICK*

Contents

Illustrations follow page 114.

Acknowledgments

This book began as a seminar paper which I wrote at Purdue University in 1987, when I was practicing law in Indiana and studying history in my spare time for intellectual stimulation. The topic of Civil War veterans, however, caught my attention and eventually led me to close my law office and embark on the full-time study of history at Yale University. At Purdue, I would like to thank Harold D. Woodman, Robert E. May, John J. Contreni, Lois N. Magner, and Donald J. Berthrong. Hal Woodman helped show me how history should be studied and written, and I have kept his high standards in mind while working on this book. I still regard Bob May's seminar on the Old South as one of the most enjoyable and stimulating academic experiences of my life; over the years, Bob has kept in touch and offered insightful criticism as well as enthusiastic support, for which I am most grateful.

At Yale University, I would like to thank David Montgomery, John Harley Warner, David Brion Davis, John Demos, Ruth Wedgwood, and Peter Schuck. David Montgomery in particular offered detailed comments on my dissertation, and had an uncanny ability to detect fault lines where critical points needed to be rethought and reworked. Beyond faculty members at Purdue and Yale, I have benefited from the time and advice of a number of historians, archivists, and physicians. Daniel A. Pollock, M.D. (Centers for Disease Control), read and commented on an early version of Chapter 7; Pete Maslowski (University of Nebraska) read and commented on Chapter 9 and the Conclusion; Susan M. M. Tainsh, M.D. (McMaster University), offered comments on Chapter 7; Jack Talbott (University of California, Santa Barbara) read and commented on Chapter 2; and David C. Brown (M.D., Univ. of Pennsylvania), a fellow history graduate student and friend from Yale, read and commented on Chapters 7 and 8. I have also profited greatly from comments on the entire manuscript made by Steve Towne of the Indiana State Archives and from discussions with my brother, Jonathan R. Dean, concerning military history.

Research for this book was supported by the following grants or fellowships: Mellon Research Fellowship (awarded by the Yale University Graduate School for research travel during the academic year 1992–1993); Albert J. Beveridge Grant for Research in the History of the Western Hemisphere (awarded by the American Historical Association for dissertation research in the academic year 1993–1994); Mark C. Stevens Researcher Travel Fellowship (awarded by the Bentley Historical Library at the University of Michigan, for research in the academic year 1993–1994); Indiana Historical Society Graduate Fellowship in History (awarded for research in the academic year 1993–1994); John F. Enders Fellowship (awarded by the Yale University Graduate School for research travel during the summer of 1994); and a Whiting Fellowship in the Humanities (Dissertation-Year Fellowship awarded by the Yale University Graduate School for preparation of the dissertation in the academic year 1995–1996).

I conducted research for this book in nine different states and the District of Columbia, and received generous assistance from librarians and archivists at the Connecticut State Archives (Hartford), the Florida State Archives (Tallahassee), the P. K. Yonge Library of Florida History at the University of Florida (Gainesville), the Georgia State Archives (Atlanta), the Illinois State Archives (Springfield), the Indiana State Archives (Indianapolis), the Indiana State Historical Library (Indianapolis), the Indiana Historical Society (Indianapolis), the Bentley Historical Library at the University of Michigan (Ann Arbor), the Ohio State Archives (Columbus), the South Caroliniana Library (Columbia), the South Carolina State Archives (Columbia), the Tennessee State Archives (Nashville), the Television News Archives at Vanderbilt University (Nashville), the Library of Congress (Washington, D.C.), the National Archives (Washington, D.C., and College Park, Maryland), and the National Library of Medicine (Bethesda, Maryland). In particular, I would like to thank Michael Musick of the National Archives, and I am also most indebted to Bob

Horton and Steve Towne of the Indiana State Archives. At a time when I was contemplating a ninety-county search for records in local courthouses in Indiana, Bob Horton unearthed a remarkable cache of inquest papers in the basement of the Central State Hospital in Indianapolis, which (thankfully) made my county-by-county search unnecessary; indeed, I am convinced that Bob discovered records which for the most part—owing to fire, flood, and neglect—no longer exist at the county level.

With the permission of the relevant journals, portions of the following articles of mine were used in the preparation of this book: " 'We Will All Be Lost and Destroyed': Post-Traumatic Stress Disorder and the Civil War," *Civil War History*, 37(2) (June 1991): 138–153 (with permission of the Kent State University Press); "The Myth of the Troubled and Scorned Vietnam Veteran," *Journal of American Studies*, 26(1) (April 1992): 59–74; "War and Psychiatry: Examining the Diffusion Theory in Light of the Insanity Defence in Post–World War One Britain," *History of Psychiatry*, 4(1) (1993): 61–82: "Rethinking the Civil War: Beyond 'Revolutions,' 'Reconstructions,' and the 'New Social History,' " *Southern Historian*, 15 (Spring 1994): 28–50; and " 'A Scene of Surpassing Terror and Awful Grandeur': The Paradoxes of Military Service in the American Civil War," *Michigan Historical Review*, 21(2) (Fall 1995): 37–61.

Last of all, I would like to mention my father. He passed away in 1989, and over the years I have missed his sympathetic ear and wise counsel. I dedicate this book to his memory.

January 1997

SHOOK OVER HELL

INTRODUCTION

"Terbacker Out"

Owen Flaherty had migrated to the United States from his native Ireland, and before he enlisted in Company C of the 125th Illinois Regiment of Volunteers in the Civil War, he was by all accounts a well-adjusted and normal person. His comrades in the service regarded him as a quiet but good soldier, one upon whom they could rely; on social occasions, he would talk, laugh, and drink with his companions.[1] During the course of his service with the Union Army against Confederate forces in Tennessee and Georgia from 1862 to 1864, however, Flaherty seemed to undergo a strange and disturbing transformation. Following the Battle of Stones River near Murfreesboro, Tennessee, in December of 1862, a vicious engagement during the dead of winter in which both sides suffered casualty rates of almost one third of available manpower, Flaherty requested a furlough, which was denied by his superior officers. This refusal weighed heavily upon his mind, and those who observed him at this time reported that he seemed "homesick," had a "far away, Melancholy look," and wanted to be alone. A fellow soldier noted that he seemed quiet, appeared to be in a "deep study all the time," and would not answer questions when asked, unless spoken to two or three times, and then only when he was spoken to in a very loud tone of voice, at which point he would start as though excited or surprised.[2]

Owen Flaherty's bunkmate, John McVey, noticed that Flaherty had a "wild scared look," was very restless and wakeful at night, and when he did manage to fall asleep, began to talk and mumble in his sleep about his family. He would tremble and toss about so much during these nightmares that he would pull the blankets off, forcing McVey to go elsewhere and sleep by himself. Flaherty seemed to believe that his family would never see him alive again, and this worry preyed on his mind; he eventually began to talk to himself.[3] The situation deteriorated further after the Battle of Resaca, Georgia, in May of 1864, when Flaherty's company was thrown into the thick of the battle and eight of his fellow soldiers were killed in action. On a skirmish line in a valley between two hills, the regiment was subjected to an extended artillery barrage, the constant concussion of which actually knocked down several men. This exposure to the unrelenting blasting of the artillery seemed to further unnerve Flaherty, and fellow soldiers noted afterward that he acted as if he were lost. He would wander off and had to be watched, and began to take his rations separately and sleep alone in his own tent away from the main camp. Some noted that he had a "wicked look in his eyes," and at one point he threatened to kill one of his best friends.[4] When the Union Army under William Tecumseh Sherman finally reached Bentonville, North Carolina, near the end of the war, Flaherty was placed on picket duty on the camp perimeter. Suddenly he came running in, saying that the enemy was coming, when in fact no one was in sight. A fellow soldier noted that Flaherty was very frightened, and had to be forced to resume his post. This soldier saw a "bad look" in Flaherty's eye, and was convinced that he had become entirely insane.[5]

After the war Flaherty returned to his home at Terre Haute, Indiana, but his friends immediately noticed that something was terribly wrong with him. He was hired to work at a blast furnace, but couldn't concentrate on the work; his employer noted that Flaherty always seemed to be thinking of something else, and "appeared to be wild. [He] always appeared to want to be on the go." Irritable and angry at life in general, he drove his son away from home, and the police were called to his house several times during his periods of violence. On one occasion during the winter of 1865–1866, Flaherty woke up during the night, remarked that "they have moved camp—by golly," got up, dressed himself, left home, and was gone four or five hours. His wife, Mary, noticed that Owen would take "flighty spells," when he would "imagine they were firing on him with guns." At any mention of the war or politics Flaherty would become furious, and his friends and family learned to avoid these topics. One acquaintance noted: "Whenever anything is said to [Flaherty] about the army life,

[he] would get very angry. [You] dare not mention anything about the army to him." To his wife and others, Owen explained that his condition was due to "those cannon balls," and on another occasion when one of his friends asked him what was the cause of his problems, he "laughed at me finally, got mad at me, walked away."[6]

Owen Flaherty eventually quit work and spent his days wandering the streets. Finally, in 1876, he was sent to the Indiana Hospital for the Insane in Indianapolis, where he was diagnosed as having acute mania. The asylum generally did not have room for long-term commitments (so-called chronic cases) in the late nineteenth century, so, after a short stay, Flaherty was placed at the poorhouse in Vigo County, where he lived from 1877 to 1885. His guardian, alleging that Flaherty's insanity was caused by his service in the Civil War, applied on his behalf for a federal veteran's disability pension. The medical board which examined him wrote: "He is almost constantly in motion his eyes are restless, his movements quick & energetic, his speech laconic and abrupt." These doctors noted that he was suspicious of strangers, became angry and violent at the slightest provocation, and suffered from delusions: "As far as noticed his delusions consist in fear from imaginary persons who intend to kill him and he plans to hide or defend himself . . . the cause due to some mental shock probably sustained in the service." The Pension Bureau granted Owen Flaherty's claim at the highest rate available, $72 per month, a category reserved for men who were totally disabled and in fact helpless, requiring the care and attendance of another.[7]

As opposed to the case of Owen Flaherty, we know very little concerning what happened to James P. Green during the Civil War. Available military and pension records indicate that Green enlisted in the 69th Indiana Regiment on July 19, 1862, and that he served with the unit throughout the remainder of the war. The 69th Indiana Infantry fought in the Battle of Richmond, Kentucky, and participated in Sherman's assault on Chickasaw Bayou near Vicksburg as well as Grant's siege of Vicksburg and the attack on Jackson, Mississippi, during 1863. At various times, the unit sustained substantial battle casualties as well as numerous deaths from diseases contracted by the men in the swamps of Louisiana, Mississippi, and Florida.[8] Military records indicate that James Green was taken prisoner and held briefly by the Confederates after the Battle of Richmond, but little else is known. Did he shoot and kill any Rebel soldiers? Was he present when Rebel "bushwhackers" were caught and summarily hanged? Did he witness the death or maiming of any of his fellow soldiers? Did he participate in burial details to inter the shattered bodies of men in his unit who had been killed during the fight for Vicksburg? What was his reaction to the stifling heat, the unrelenting mosquitoes, the swamp fevers and chronic diarrhea that were rampant in the ranks, the chaos, din, and terror of battle as Union forces stormed the Rebel fortifications at Vicksburg? The historical record is silent.

What is known is that James P. Green returned to Indiana after the war and was unable to settle down or readjust to civilian life. His father tried to get work for him, but Green was unable to engage in any gainful activity owing to his unstable and deteriorating mental condition. In 1878 he was committed to the Indiana Hospital for the Insane in Indianapolis, and the records there indicate a diagnosis of acute mania; the recording clerk noted that Green had suffered from a great loss of sleep for some time, and that he had made attempts to commit violence upon himself. It is unclear how long he was held at the asylum, but in 1893, his family applied for a veteran's pension on his behalf, and Green was examined by a board of pension doctors. These doctors could not get him to utter a sound or to acknowledge their presence. Green's family explained that this was his usual condition: he could feed and dress himself without assistance, kept his person clean, and never left the yard, but for years had never spoken to or taken any notice of anyone coming or going; he had never at anytime, for years, spoken to any member of the family, except to say "terbacker out," when his chewing material was exhausted. Yet he would frequently pet and talk to dogs, the family reported. It seemed that James Green had given up on the human race and had withdrawn into the safety of his own narrow mental world, where he could block off disturbing memories of the outside.[9]

To anyone familiar with military psychiatry and the concepts of "shell shock" from World War I or "combat fatigue" from World War II, the cases of Owen Flaherty and James P. Green should not be completely surprising, and yet these cases do tend to register in one's mind as atypical and novel, probably for two reasons. First, in the more than 50,000 books which have been written on the American Civil War over the past 130 years, the focus has usually been on great generals rather than on bleeding and bewildered soldiers. In any bookstore, one is much more likely to encounter biographies of famous generals such as William Tecumseh Sherman, Ulysses S. Grant, and Robert E. Lee, assessments of political leaders such as Abraham

Lincoln and Jefferson Davis, or unit and battle histories that emphasize tactics and the meritorious or flawed leadership of key commanders, rather than explorations into delayed stress and the turmoil that veterans experienced in the postwar years. Although more attention has been paid to the common soldier of the Civil War over the past forty years, this interest has tended to translate into a passion for reenactments rather than a focus on trauma, pain, and tragedy. In addition, historians have more recently tended to portray the Civil War as a righteous crusade to end slavery and initiate the civil rights revolution, culminating eventually in the "Second Reconstruction" of the 1950s and 1960s—the era of *Brown vs. Board of Education*, Selma, and the landmark Civil Rights Act of 1964. In sum, whatever one's view of the current state of Civil War historiography (the Civil War as righteous or merely heroic in stature), the concept of the Civil War soldier and veteran as a psychiatric victim (with attendant antiwar tones) does not resonate; the idea has not been extensively explored.[10]

Second, much of our current thinking on the American veteran has been shaped by the image of the troubled and scorned Vietnam veteran that has emerged over the past thirty years in the United States. In this view, psychologists regard Vietnam veterans as having suffered serious, lingering, and debilitating mental problems, centering around the phenomenon of Post-Traumatic Stress Disorder (PTSD), a delayed stress syndrome which is caused by exposure to combat and can produce symptoms of rage, guilt, flashbacks, nightmares, depression, and emotional numbing, and can lead to a variety of grave social and psychiatric problems—from unemployment to suicide. This medical view of the psychologically disturbed Vietnam veteran finds an analogue in popular culture with such novels as *Going After Cacciato* or *Paco's Story*, which tend to view the Vietnam War as absurd and as having led to unprecedented mental stress for the American participants. Central to these interpretations has been the suggestion or outright assertion that Vietnam veterans have been unique in American history for their psychiatric problems. In this construction of the past, previous American veterans either didn't suffer from serious psychological problems or, if they did, their problems were ameliorated by a warm homecoming at war's end (something that eluded the Vietnam veteran). The stories of Owen Flaherty and James Green, then, run counter to the many claims of the singularity of the Vietnam War and its veterans.[11]

Hence the image of the Civil War with its dashing generals, stoic soldiers, and legendary campaigns persists in stark contrast to the image of Vietnam as a surreal quagmire from which only damaged men managed to escape. How can one reconcile these two divergent views of war? Is it possible that these two realities are indeed so far apart, or can the stories of Owen Flaherty and James Green open up a new window through which to reconsider the veterans of both wars? A reexamination of the Civil War veteran through the lens of the Vietnam experience promises new perspectives and challenges, regarding not only the assumption that Civil War veterans readjusted well after their war owing to parades in the North and sectional adulation through the Lost Cause in the South, but also the idea that all Vietnam veterans came home in a dazed, unstrung condition, with any psychological difficulties due in some measure to the war.

Consideration of these issues immediately leads one to a series of questions: How widespread were psychiatric problems in the Civil War veteran population? What caused these problems, and can one correlate cases of psychopathology among the approximately 3 million Civil War veterans to either cumulative exposure to combat or to particularly shocking or horrific war experiences? What was the profile of disturbed Civil War veterans—did they suffer from the classic symptoms of PTSD, including flashbacks and sleeplessness? Did they experience the same sense of alienation concerning which Vietnam veterans have testified at length? If the evidence indicates that Civil War veterans as well as Vietnam veterans experienced post-traumatic stress problems in substantial numbers, should we then also assign a primary identity to the Civil War veteran as a psychiatric victim, or is the matter more complicated than that? Can one perhaps conclude—contrary to the post-Vietnam tendency to view war as a negative, toxic substance—that there was, in spite of, in addition to, or as part of the mental suffering, something positive and invigorating in the experience of war for the Civil War generation—and perhaps for individual Vietnam veterans as well? Ultimately a study of Civil War veterans and a reevaluation of Vietnam veterans offers the opportunity to challenge orthodox views and to seek wisdom on the topic of war and the American veteran—knowledge and insights that transcend time and place.

"Unwelcome Heroes": The Agony of Vietnam

From the late 1960s, Americans have been subjected to a steady stream of books, motion pictures, and newspaper and magazine articles that have portrayed Vietnam veterans as unique in American history for having suffered in substantial numbers from the psychological syndrome now known as Post-Traumatic Stress Disorder.[1] According to this view, the Vietnam veteran's problems began in Vietnam where he was forced to participate in a brutal and disturbing war in which he was under fire twenty-four hours a day. The enemy, the wily and tenacious Vietcong and North Vietnamese regulars, were not always clearly defined nor were they above using civilians as shields or assassins, leading to the unintentional—and sometimes intentional—killing by American forces of noncombatants, including women and children. Because of the military's policy of limiting the tour of duty in the war zone to one year, combat groups lacked cohesion and suffered from low morale, the results of which included the excessive use of marijuana and heroin and an eventual breakdown of discipline.

When the Vietnam veteran returned to the United States, he did not come back slowly on a troop ship with his comrades (as had been the practice in World War II, allowing time to unwind, "decompress," and assimilate the experience), but was flown back quickly by himself, moving from the blood and gore of the combat zone to his hometown in the space of twenty-four hours. Once at home again and trying to deal with the shocking transition, he was either totally ignored by the civilian population or, worse, spit upon and blamed for losing the unpopular war. He was given no parade or welcoming celebrations. These factors were thought to cause a number of readjustment problems, including high unemployment, drug addiction, divorce, suicide, crime, ill health due to exposure to Agent Orange, and lingering psychological problems that manifested themselves in the form of flashbacks, nightmares, depression, guilt over atrocities and dead buddies who did not come back, and "psychic numbing." The experience of the Vietnam veteran has been contrasted with that of American veterans from Valley Forge to World War II, who were supposedly older and more mature, coped better, derived strength from unit cohesion throughout the war, fought a clearly defined enemy in conventional warfare, and, because the United States won the war, returned home to exuberant parades, offers of jobs, and, after World War II, a generous G.I. Bill that provided a wide array of benefits from guaranteed education expenses to low-interest home mortgages.[2]

The strong impression has thus emerged that earlier American veterans, including those from the Civil War, may have developed psychological problems due to exposure to combat during their war, but that these problems were "washed away" by the ritual of acceptance and celebration by appreciative civilians that came in the wake of a successful military effort by American armed forces. In the one prior major episode of defeat for Americans in combat—the experience of Confederate troops in the Civil War—historians have suggested that the phenomenon of the Lost Cause, which celebrated and deified the Southern fighting man even in defeat, served to prevent the development of psychological and social problems.[3]

This view of the Vietnam veteran as troubled and prior American veterans as well-adjusted first emerged in the popular media in the late 1960s, acquired additional definition from 1971 to 1974, and has taken on a life of its own as the years have passed. By the 1980s, it became common in the United States to view the Vietnam veteran as beset by a wide range of problems and betrayed by his fellow citizens and government. As a result the Vietnam veteran has acquired an almost mythic stature, that of the "survivor-as-hero," who fought under insane conditions in Vietnam and then rebuilt his life in an ungrateful America; some critics even see the Vietnam veteran—because he lost the most, because he did it seemingly for nothing—as the most romanticized war hero in American history.[4] Through the powerful image of the Vietnam veteran, the Vietnam experience has shaped, redefined, or even invented our current view of war, our concept of military service, our ideas of risk and citizenship, our view of the American soldier and veteran, and the very category of Post-Traumatic Stress Disorder itself.

Have Vietnam veteran advocates been correct in arguing that Vietnam produced unprecedented levels of psychiatric casualties? Is it true that parades and celebrations can wash away the disturbing memory of combat? Can there be true unity and understanding between civilian and soldier (as Vietnam veterans have contended)? Have the problems of Vietnam veterans been overstated and, if so, why? Any examination of these issues must begin with a thorough consideration of the shaping of the image of the troubled and scorned Vietnam veteran and how he has come to dominate and condition our thinking on the matter of the psychological repercussions of warfare.

Oddly enough, during the height of American participation in the Vietnam War in the 1960s, most accounts of the Vietnam veteran returning from the war zone presented him as readjusting quite well to civilian life. The *New York Times* noted in 1968 that returning servicemen were finding jobs faster than at any time in the past ten years. Numerous efforts had been made by the Ford Foundation, the Veterans Administration, the United States Post Office, and other private and public groups to see that returning vets received jobs. Some were even worried that the Vietnam veterans would not utilize the G.I. Bill for education because jobs were so easy to find. The state of affairs was such that the *New York Times,* in an editorial entitled "Veterans' Lobby Outdoes Itself," protested this lavish treatment, and noted that military service was an obligation of citizenship, and that continued efforts to give the veterans preferential treatment would create a permanent privileged class of veterans, "a postwar mercenary class uncongenial to the national heritage."[5]

The print media reported a public reaction in which strangers on the street would approach the Vietnam vet to thank him for his service, or, in a restaurant, a stranger would pick up the check in gratitude. The first American troops to be withdrawn from Vietnam (in 1969) were greeted by a parade in Seattle at which the crowd yelled "Thank you! Thank you!" and "flags waved, ticker tape showered down on the troopers, and pretty girls pressed red roses into the men's hands." Comparisons with the veterans of previous American wars tended to favor the Vietnam veteran who was described as "knowing exactly what he wants" in contrast to the veterans of the Korean War who were characterized as "quiet, apathetic young men who shuffled aimlessly about," with a "glassy faraway look . . . staring nowhere."[6]

Another view emerged in the late 1960s, however, and it began with concern over the ability of the Vietnam veteran to bridge the psychological gulf between war in East Asia and his return to peaceful vocations in America. Writers were struck by the stark contrast between a war zone of napalm, body counts, and killing and the relatively tranquil domestic scene where civilians were largely ignorant of or indifferent to the war. On the basis of these shocking and anomalous images of war, the view of the Vietnam War as unique emerged, and, accordingly, the Vietnam veteran also came to be seen as unique. He returned quickly with no reorientation period and appeared to be jolted to discover that his society was not deeply committed to the war. As a result, he experienced a feeling of "strangeness and helplessness" in encountering the "uncommitted."[7]

Given that most veterans of past wars have experienced some readjustment problems, including a feeling of alienation from the civilian population, the Vietnam veteran might not have seemed unusual in this regard. But by 1971, popular culture, without any reference to historical context, began to regard the Vietnam veteran as alone in American history in allegedly being unappreciated, troubled, rejected, and blamed for the war. Four factors contributed to this increasingly prevalent view. First, the domestic opposition to the war significantly shaped the image of the Vietnam veteran. Particularly after the Tet Offensive of early 1968 and the revelation of the Mylai Massacre of 1969, the Vietnam veteran came to symbolize everything that was wrong with the war. On the one hand, he seemed to be an instrument of mass destruction; on the other hand, he appeared to be a victim himself, perverted by this strange war. The idea that American soldiers could commit atrocities shocked and disappointed the American public, which began to oppose the war in increasing numbers. By pointing to its veterans as corrupted, tarnished, and ruined innocents, critics could condemn the war, demand full American withdrawal, and pursue a related agenda of reform, which included (after disengagement from Vietnam) an attempt to change military and foreign policy, achieve greater access to health care, and secure equal rights at home.[8]

Second, the massive demobilization from 1970 to 1972 created a short-term crisis and the perception of serious and continuing problems. With the withdrawal of American forces from Vietnam, approximately one million soldiers were released from military service in 1970; this coincided with President Nixon's effort to "cool down" the economy. As a result, unemployment increased at the exact time that the greatest number of new veterans were entering the job market. As opposed to earlier fears that few Vietnam veterans would use the G.I. Bill because they were being actively pursued by employers, the concern suddenly shifted to a disproportionately high unemployment rate for these veterans. *Business Week* concluded: "Back home, [the Vietnam veteran] is primarily a job problem." Numerous magazine and newspaper articles trumpeted the fact that 12.4 percent of Vietnam vets between twenty and twenty-four were unemployed, compared with a national unemployment rate of 6 percent. Television news programs highlighted the protests of jobless, disgruntled Vietnam veterans.[9] By 1973 returning vets had been reabsorbed into the economy and their unemployment rate was essentially the same as that for the general civilian population, but the indelible impression had been created that Vietnam veterans were unemployed or even unemployable. Articles in the late 1970s cited fantastic (and incorrect) unemployment rates of 39 percent for Vietnam vets, and print media coverage in the 1980s continued to claim serious unemployment problems for these veterans, characterizing such difficulties as "common." Television news also continued well into the 1980s to portray the Vietnam veteran as suffering from persistent unemployment.[10]

Third, there had been a "heroin epidemic" in Vietnam from 1970 to 1972, in which somewhere between 25 percent and 50 percent of the American forces used heroin. Particularly in the television news, drug problems of soldiers in Vietnam and returning Vietnam veterans received a great deal of attention. At the outset, in 1969, television news did not view drug abuse as a problem exclusive to Vietnam, but, after it was revealed that the American soldiers involved in the Mylai Massacre had smoked marijuana the night before, the issue came to be viewed in a different light. Walter Cronkite reported on November 13, 1970, that the army's marijuana problem in Vietnam was soaring and, eleven days later, that Vietnam veterans were bringing heroin into the United States. Television reports eventually described the drug problem in the military as an "epidemic" and "out of hand," and by March of 1972 the Vietnam veteran himself was seen as importing his habit back to the United States. On March 2, 1972, David Brinkley attributed a number of problems, including Vietnam drug usage and the alienation of young Americans, to the

Vietnam War, which he called the biggest blunder in U.S. history. Although studies showed that returned vets were not primarily using heroin, that their usage of drugs was similar to that of civilians, and that their drug use had dropped to pre-Vietnam rates or lower, the "drug addict" component of the "troubled Vietnam veteran" became embedded in the national conscience.[11]

Fourth, with the return of the Vietnam POWs in 1973 to parades and national celebration, the myth-making process was complete. Vietnam vets were described as the "Forgotten Veterans" who, despite their sacrifices in Vietnam, had never received "their parade" or any recognition or appreciation from their society.[12] Media reports of the early 1970s commonly described Vietnam veterans as the newest "minority." Mere teenagers, they had been forced by their government to fight in an unpopular war where they had committed atrocities, and came home psychologically disturbed and addicted to drugs, facing future unemployment and neglect. Articles such as "Will Somebody Please Welcome This Hero Home?," "The Vietnam Vet: 'No One Gives a Damn,' " and "Vietnam Veterans: A Shocking Report on Their Damaged Lives" became typical. Vietnam veterans were called "unheralded, even unwanted," and "the most alienated generation of trained killers in American history."[13]

In response to the perceived crisis of the Vietnam veteran in the early 1970s, the military developed drug screening and treatment programs, Congress raised the level of G.I. Bill benefits, the head of the Veterans Administration (VA), Donald Johnson (who was supposedly responsible for red tape and delays), was sacked, and efforts were made to "welcome home" the Vietnam veteran. President Nixon proclaimed a "Vietnam Veterans Day" on March 29, 1974. President Ford's Veterans Day speech in 1974 centered on the Vietnam veteran, whom he described as the "forgotten hero." Veteran unemployment, which had stood at 4.5 percent in 1969 and increased to 11 percent in 1971, returned to 4.4 percent in 1973.[14] Subsequent studies have demonstrated again and again that American veterans have higher median income levels than their civilian peers, and some researchers argue that men who have been in the military acquire skills and motivation (a "premium") which serve them well in civilian employment after discharge from the military. The most thorough study of Vietnam veterans, *Legacies of Vietnam: Comparative Adjustment of Veterans and Their Peers*, demonstrated that as of 1977 these veterans had a higher median income than their civilian peers, and that the unemployment rate was similar for veteran and nonveteran groups.[15] By 1977 over 64 percent of Vietnam vets had used the G.I. Bill (compared with 55 percent by World War II veterans and 43.4 percent by Korean War veterans) and a greater percentage of these Vietnam veterans used the G.I. Bill to pursue higher education than ever before (60 percent, compared with 51 percent of Korean veterans utilizing the bill and 30 percent of World War II veterans). By 1976 the source of the largest amount of federal aid for the nation's college students was not the Office of Education but the Veterans Administration.[16]

Because the major problems of the Vietnam veteran had apparently been solved, he was the subject of few articles or programs in the print or television media in 1975 and 1976. President Ford declared an end to the Vietnam era and developed programs of clemency and amnesty for Vietnam-era draft-dodgers and deserters. In 1977, however, the Vietnam veteran suddenly became a focus of renewed interest. Newspapers and magazines again routinely described the treatment of the Vietnam veteran as a "national disgrace," and accounts of this neglect varied from poetic descriptions of men who had battled grimly in leech-infested rice paddies (despite the fact that only about 15 percent of soldiers in Vietnam had been assigned to combat) and were now unwanted like volunteer corn in a soybean field, to the vitriolic "veteran testimonial," with angry tales of abuse and rejection. These testimonials excoriated America for not "coming to terms" with Vietnam.[17] From this point forward, the predominant theme of the Vietnam veterans' movement was that the United States would have to come to terms with and welcome home its Vietnam veterans before there could be reconciliation and healing concerning what had been a most divisive war.

This reemergence and amplification of the idea of the Vietnam veteran as a scorned and troubled person focused less on concrete problems of unemployment or supposedly inadequate levels of funding for the G.I. Bill[18] than on three new issues: "delayed stress syndrome" (later to become Post-Traumatic Stress Disorder); Agent Orange; and a supposedly high rate of suicide in Vietnam veterans. Common to all three concerns was an inability to quantify the magnitude of the problem, but with a steady barrage of media stories and recriminations from Vietnam vets, the impression emerged that Vietnam veterans were in a crisis and that the government was largely to blame, both for sending them to Vietnam to start with and for ignoring them upon their return. In addition, as had been the case with the 1973 repatriation of the American POWs from Indochina, the return of the Iranian hostages to national exultation in 1981 strengthened the perception that Vietnam veterans were being neglected. The *New Republic* noted that year: "Few topics have received as much anguished attention lately as our national inattention toward Vietnam veterans."

PTSD had its genesis in the "post-Vietnam syndrome" of the late 1960s and early 1970s, when observers noted that some veterans seemed nervous, irritable, and jumpy, suffered from insomnia, had a "short fuse," and felt guilty over surviving the war when comrades had been killed. During the 1970s, accounts of a variety of crimes committed by Vietnam vets kept the issue of possible psychological damage to these veterans alive. Headlines such as "Vietnam Veteran Releases Hostages and Gives Up in Ohio After 9 Hours," "Vietnam Vets Seize Statue of Liberty," or "Vietnam Veteran Held in Boston After Firing on Imaginary Enemy" became standard fare in American newspapers. Murder, kidnapping, and the illegal use of weapons were frequently the crimes involved, and many incidents had political content. Examples ranged from a sit-in at the local VA hospital to the sensational case of James Hopkins, who crashed his Jeep through the doors of a VA hospital and fired nine rounds.[19] The image of the veteran as disoriented, neglected, and a victim of war's madness was reinforced by motion pictures such as *Apocalypse Now* and *Taxi Driver*, which portrayed the Vietnam War as surreal, grotesque, and absurd and the Vietnam veteran as psychotic and ready to commit mayhem at the drop of a hat;[20] these themes also appeared in the book *Dispatches*, which attempted to show the utter senselessness of the Vietnam conflict. The typical Vietnam vets in the public mind in the 1970s were the ultimate victims and survivors of war, the paraplegics and the POWs, and, indeed, paraplegic veterans such as Ron Kovic and Robert Muller became leading spokesmen for the cause of Vietnam veterans in the 1970s and 1980s. Tom Wicker referred to the psychological problems of Vietnam vets as the "Vietnam Disease."[21]

In the late 1970s the American Psychiatric Association officially recognized PTSD as a psychological disorder, and this syndrome became the centerpiece of descriptions of the problems of Vietnam veterans; estimates of its incidence among Vietnam veterans soared. The psychologist John P. Wilson, frequently quoted on the subject, estimated that as many as 500,000 Vietnam vets were victims of PTSD, and Dr. Cherry Cedarleaf's estimate of an incidence of 50 percent (1,500,000 Vietnam veterans) was also cited. Most articles concluded that between 700,000 and 800,000 Vietnam vets suffered from PTSD, although only 94,630 had been deemed disabled for psychiatric or neurological reasons by the Veterans Administration as of 1978. (As of 1946, 454,699 World War II veterans were receiving disability benefits for neuropsychiatric diseases, constituting an overall rate similar to that for Vietnam veterans.) Although PTSD's exact incidence has remained a topic of great uncertainty—recent studies have placed the current incidence in Vietnam veterans in a range from a low of 2 percent to a high of 15 percent—PTSD has formed a perfect bridge between the horror of combat in Vietnam and the supposedly widespread readjustment problems of its veterans.[22] Nor was the concept of PTSD in 1970s America limited to Vietnam veterans. The fascination with Post-Traumatic Stress Disorder and guilt over the war reached the point in the early 1980s where several magazine articles described the traumatic aftereffects for those who dodged the draft and felt that they had missed an important *rite de passage* in not participating in the war; readers were reminded that women veterans, too, suffered from PTSD. As PTSD seemed to become the "disorder du jour," the possibility was raised that practically the entire population of the United States was suffering from some sort of PTSD or associated guilt syndrome related to the Vietnam War.[23]

Vietnam veteran advocates in the 1970s frequently presented PTSD as not just a psychological condition along the lines of shell shock, that is to say a condition which one could find in earlier American veterans. Rather, PTSD was presented as something unique to the circumstances of Vietnam and the Vietnam vet, and hence something that required special treatment. Therefore, the politics of PTSD—the issue of whether it should be recognized as a new category of mental illness, and whether the VA system was capable of dealing with the special needs of the Vietnam veteran pertaining to this psychological syndrome—became particularly heated in the early 1980s and in part revolved around the issue of storefront "vet centers," informal counseling centers established to deal with psychologically disturbed Vietnam vets who distrusted the VA and would not seek conventional psychiatric treatment at VA facilities. Approximately 90 centers were opened in 1980, and 250,000 veterans had been counseled by 1984. The original program was to expire on September 30, 1981, but was extended and even expanded to 189 centers. Attempts by the Reagan administration to close the centers (with the intent of funneling these patients into the regular VA hospital system) were characterized as "another betrayal," "disgraceful," and "devastating," and provided further evidence of the Vietnam veteran as neglected and persecuted—despite the fact, of course, that many vets had already taken full advantage of the panoply of veterans' benefits under the G.I. Bill (funds for education and vocational training, low-interest home mortgages, veterans' preferences in federal employment, health care through the VA system).[24]

The second new issue which emerged in the late 1970s concerned Agent Orange, a herbicide containing dioxin which, in the so-called Operation Ranch Hand, was sprayed from airplanes as a defoliant to clear extensive areas of jungle in Vietnam to prevent the enemy from concealing his operations. Agent Orange (so named for the orange bands around each drum of chemicals) was a 50–50 combination of two artificial plant hormones, 2,4-D and 2,4,5-T, and an unintentional byproduct in the manufacture of 2,4,5-T is dioxin, often known as TCDD, an acutely toxic and potent carcinogen. In 1978 a twenty-eight-year-old Connecticut Vietnam veteran named Paul Reutershan died of cancer, and before his death he suspected that his terminal disease had been caused by his earlier exposure to Agent Orange during the war. This led to the formation of the Vietnam Veterans Agent Orange Victims Inc., a group which began collecting an ever-lengthening list of veterans with a broad spectrum of medical problems. As anecdotal evidence accumulated, Vietnam veterans claimed that their exposure to Agent Orange in the war zone was causing high rates of cancer in the veterans themselves and birth defects in their children. Accordingly, Vietnam veterans filed a class action suit against the United States government in addition to the seven chemical companies which had manufactured Agent Orange; the case resulted in a judgment of $180 million against the chemical companies. An additional Agent Orange issue has concerned whether the U.S. government through the VA service-based disabilities program should compensate Vietnam veterans suffering from several forms of cancer (especially non-Hodgkins lymphoma and soft-tissue sarcomas, in addition to chloracne, a severe skin condition), which Vietnam veteran advocates argued were caused by Agent Orange exposure.[25]

Over the years, the Agent Orange issue has been a source of extraordinary acrimony and continuing uncertainty; the more dramatic media coverage has claimed that the United States government "poisoned its own army in Vietnam," and the rhetoric of the issue routinely has included allegations of a government cover-up in which key scientific data was supposedly "rigged," "suppressed," or "sabotaged." Rhetoric to the effect that Vietnam veterans were being "stalked by an enemy more insidious than the Vietcong" became typical, and the title of one account is revealing: "Agent Orange Furor Continues to Build: For Vietnam Veterans, the Herbicide Has Become a Symbol for Everything That Was Wrong About the War."[26]

However, contrary to the sensational and dramatic rhetoric, government studies by the Centers for Disease Control have consistently demonstrated that Vietnam veterans and their children are not at risk for elevated rates of birth defects, and that added risk of cancer in this population is nonexistent or slight (only 3,800 of 3 million Vietnam vets were affected by the extension of service-related benefits based on the presumption that non-Hodgkins lymphoma, soft-tissue sarcoma, and chloracne resulted from Agent Orange exposure), but Vietnam veteran advocates have not accepted these conclusions. There has even been complete disagreement on whether the issue of Agent Orange exposure in Vietnam veterans can be effectively studied: the CDC concluded that military records did not offer specific enough information to assess individualized risk for every Vietnam veteran. This conclusion has been attacked in an alternative study funded by the American Legion, which maintained that on the basis of retrospective self-reporting by Vietnam veterans themselves (that is, their recollection of exactly where they were in Vietnam at specific times twenty years ago), investigators could pinpoint the location of each American soldier during the war so as to assess exact Agent Orange exposure, and proceed with epidemiological studies on that basis. After almost twenty years, the anger and recriminations continue, and in popular culture, the idea of the Vietnam veteran as suffering from mysterious skin ailments in addition to cancer as a result of Agent Orange exposure has taken firm hold. In the motion picture *In Country*, for instance, a Vietnam veteran has strange rashes on his body—seemingly attributable to Agent Orange exposure.[27]

One of the most sensational aspects of the reenergized image of the troubled Vietnam veteran of the late 1970s and early 1980s, and an issue closely tied to PTSD, has been the question of suicide and the Vietnam vet. This issue first emerged in 1980 as newspapers reported under headlines such as "Horror Festers in Viet Nam Veterans" that of the approximately 3 million Vietnam veterans, more (60,000 or even as many as 100,000) had committed suicide after the war than had died in Vietnam during the war itself (58,000). Assertions of this rather astonishing suicide rate (at least 6.6 times the rate for a comparable civilian peer group) were used to bolster a number of contentions concerning the Vietnam veteran: that unique circumstances in Vietnam (guerrilla warfare, constant exposure to danger, the widespread commission of atrocities, lack of unit cohesion) produced a high rate of Post-Traumatic Stress Disorder; that these problems only became worse (or frequently first manifested themselves) after the end of the war since soldiers were repatriated quickly without counseling; that civilians in the United States further aggravated these psychological problems by either ignoring or reviling (rather than welcoming home) Vietnam veterans; and that as a result of all this Vietnam veterans, desperate and abandoned, were committing suicide in unprecedented numbers, and were, to say the least, in a continuing crisis.[28]

In response to this perceived emergency, researchers conducted a number of careful studies and concluded that either there was no difference between the suicide rates in Vietnam veterans and their civilian peers, or that, if there was a difference, it was slight (less than 25 percent higher) and was part of a generally increased risk of mortality during the first five years following the return from Vietnam, after which suicide rates for Vietnam vets and the comparable civilian population were essentially identical. Daniel A. Pollock of the Centers for Disease Control concluded in 1990 that fewer than 9,000 Vietnam veterans had committed suicide through the early 1980s, and that the suicide rate for this veteran population was similar to that for civilians.[29] In spite of this meticulous research, however, one notices again and again in media reporting from the 1980s and 1990s assertions such as the statement of one Vietnam veteran advocate that 159,000 Vietnam vets had committed suicide since the end of the war, Tom Wicker's claim (later retracted) of 500,000 suicide attempts by Vietnam vets, or repeated anecdotal reports of Vietnam veterans committing suicide—in one case at the Vietnam Veterans Memorial in Washington, D.C.[30]

Upon investigation these inflated numbers have been revealed to be entirely without merit. When Tom Wicker reported that 500,000 Vietnam vets had attempted suicide, for example, it turned out that he had obtained the statistic from an article in *Penthouse Magazine*, which was relying on a pamphlet issued by "Twice Born Men," a veterans' group in San Francisco, defunct by 1975. That organization's former director, Jack McCloskey, said he got the figure from the National Council of the Churches, but the council disavowed any knowledge of the statistic. This idea that as many (or even twice as many) Vietnam veterans committed suicide after the war as died in the war zone during the war itself appears to be a rumor that turned into a myth that has become legend and now is being quoted as the truth. Despite the careful research by CDC scientists, the impression lingers that suicide remains a major problem for Vietnam veterans, and that these men are unique in the history of American veterans for this persistent and serious problem.[31]

In addition, various newspapers and magazines in the late 1970s and early 1980s reported that as many as 125,000 Vietnam veterans were in jail, and that "one third of the Federal prison population is made up of vets," the implication being that a disproportionate number of veterans were in jail as a result of readjustment and PTSD problems that had forced them to commit criminal acts: "There is a pretty strong belief out there that a lot of these men were incarcerated because they were in Vietnam—because of problems they had 'in country.'" Television has also presented the matter of the incarcerated Vietnam veteran, sometimes in very dramatic fashion, implying that even veterans convicted of armed robbery or rape were acting out as a result of their war experience, or that the involvement of these men with crime was a circuitous way of attempting suicide, in that they expected to be shot and killed by armed clerks or by police officers who caught them in the act.[32]

Because the perceived crisis of the Vietnam veteran centered on the assertion that he had either been actively reviled or had never been properly welcomed home, and that this neglect and abuse had led to substantial psychological problems, something of a national obsession to "welcome home" the Vietnam vet developed in the late 1970s. This manifested itself primarily in various declarations, lavish parades for the Vietnam veterans, and the construction of the monument to the Vietnam war dead in Washington, D.C. President Carter followed the example of Presidents Nixon and Ford of honoring the Vietnam vets by declaring a Vietnam Veterans Week to coincide with Memorial Day in 1979. In addition, Veterans' Day on November 11, 1979, was dedicated to the Vietnam veterans, and Congress declared April 26, 1981, to be "Vietnam Veteran Recognition Day."[33]

On May 7, 1985, 25,000 Vietnam veterans marched in a New York City ticker-tape parade attended by one million people, many of whom held signs saying: "You're Our Heroes, Vietnam Vets." On June

13, 1986, 200,000 veterans in Chicago participated in a "Welcome Home, Vietnam Veterans" parade, at which General Westmoreland served as parade marshal and Playboy bunnies, clad in military costumes, walked with the vets. General Westmoreland led another group of 200,000 in a parade in Houston on May 23, 1987, where parade-goers waved American flags, yelled "Thanks," and held "Welcome Home, Vietnam Vets" signs despite the fact that the last veteran had returned fourteen years prior to that date. Smaller parades and tributes were held in a variety of places, including Modesto, California; Anderson, Indiana; Northfield, Vermont; and Kalamazoo, Michigan. With each new event, some veteran would inevitably be quoted as saying that the Vietnam veterans had never received such recognition before and were "finally being welcomed home."[34]

Another central landmark in the 1980s "Welcome Home, Vietnam Vets" phenomenon was the Vietnam Memorial constructed in Washington, D.C. The dedication ceremony in 1982 drew a crowd of 150,000. On November 10 of that year a four-day tribute to Vietnam veterans commenced in Washington, D.C., during which the names of all 57,939 servicemen who died in Vietnam were read at the Washington Cathedral. Television coverage focused on weeping veterans and survivors at the monument itself, interviews with veterans who still claimed they had been betrayed and rejected by society, or interviews with family members who commented that the war was a waste and that the men (and women) had died for no good reason. Despite the post-Vietnam emphasis on "reconciliation," "healing," and "closure," the centrality of the Vietnam Veterans Memorial in American culture and consciousness along with the continuing emphasis on loss, grief, suffering, and persistent pain raised the possibility that there would never be anything remotely approaching closure concerning the Vietnam War.[35]

This effort to "welcome home the Vietnam veteran" and to "come to terms with Vietnam" marked yet another shift in representations of the Vietnam War and the Vietnam veteran. In the 1960s and early 1970s, most images of the Vietnam War had been of domestic protest and Vietnamese pain. The nightly footage of Vietnamese parents stricken with grief and children charred by napalm provided striking images, but the plight of American soldiers in Vietnam was not equally evident. In the mid-1970s, though, media accounts and motion pictures such as *Heroes, Taxi Driver, Rolling Thunder,* and *The Ninth Configuration* shifted the emphasis by presenting Vietnam veterans as battle-scarred, disturbed, and out to create havoc. The Vietnam veteran was seen as a junkie, emotional cripple, or ticking time bomb.

In the 1980s, with the rehabilitation of the image of the military under the Reagan administration, the veteran as victim of war's madness was transformed into the veteran as a kind of "survivor-hero," one who endured not only the madness of war, but the perfidy of his own government that sent him to fight a meaningless war on terms which guaranteed defeat. Sylvester Stallone as Rambo, Chuck Norris in *Missing in Action,* and Tom Selleck as Magnum, P.I., revealed the Vietnam veteran as a "hunk" and a hero, a "cannier, sharper, braver guy" than before he went to Vietnam; while still a type of a victim, the Vietnam vet was transformed from a villain into a real-life "stud."[36] Motion pictures such as *Platoon, Full Metal Jacket,* and *Hamburger Hill,* however, continued to depict the madness, violence, and pointlessness of the Vietnam War. Despite the goal of "promoting national healing," much of the continued focus on Vietnam perpetuated earlier stereotypes.[37]

After the upheavals of the 1980s—both the blistering recriminations made by Vietnam veterans and the extensive and effusive efforts made by individuals, cities, and the U.S. government to make amends for perceived earlier neglect—one might think that the issue of the troubled and scorned Vietnam veteran would have been laid to rest, but this has not proved to be the case. The image of the Vietnam veteran as a spurned, neglected, and troubled individual has refused to die; it is a concept that has proved to be highly resilient and that has continued to manifest itself in a number of forms throughout the 1990s. Three factors account for this phenomenon: a refusal of the media to cease and desist; a new emphasis on the psychological problems of women veterans, which has restated many of the problems of male veterans first discussed in the 1970s; and the close association of the Vietnam veteran with the concept of PTSD, which has become a widely utilized psychiatric diagnosis for a variety of psychological ills in post-Vietnam America.

First, despite the parades, adulation, and the Vietnam Veterans Memorial, media stories have continued to present the Vietnam veteran as suffering from significant social and psychological problems —the genesis and continued existence of which can be explained by neglect. For instance, a number of stories into the 1990s have focused on the "bush" or "tripwire vets," Vietnam veterans who have shunned society and have chosen to live in the wilds of the Pacific

Northwest or in other isolated, often mountainous regions of the United States. Some stories have estimated that there are as many as 35,000 to 45,000 of these veterans, and indicate that their problems are often attributable to PTSD.[38] Other stories have presented the dilemma of homeless Vietnam veterans (this condition is also usually represented as attributable to PTSD and consequent alcohol and drug abuse), and estimates of the number of these veterans have gone as high as 500,000. The homeless, of course, cannot be counted with any certainty, and widely divergent figures between one study and another suggest the unsystematic nature of and political agendas driving such research. Despite these problems, stories on homeless Vietnam veterans have tended to characterize their treatment as a "disgrace" and have denounced the ingratitude of the American people, while condemning the Veterans Administration for failing to respond adequately to the situation (despite the extensive VA program of providing shelters for homeless veterans).[39] Although a recent CDC study put the figure of Vietnam veterans suffering from PTSD at 2 percent (about 60,000 men and women out of approximately 3 million Vietnam veterans), media reports continue to present estimates of the past and present incidence of PTSD throughout the Vietnam veteran population as in excess of 1 million, and as high as 1.5 million; media reports continue to assert that over 100,000 Vietnam veterans have committed suicide.[40]

Second, the image of the Vietnam veteran as abused and psychologically tormented has been reinforced by the tendency in the 1990s to focus on female Vietnam veterans as a separate population, which similarly has never been welcomed home or appreciated, and which has developed a wide array of psychological problems as a result of this neglect. The focus on women vets has tended to repeat all of the allegations of mistreatment made in the late 1970s, and has shifted attention away from the issue of whether the parades, welcomes, and attention of the 1980s actually did any good for male Vietnam veterans. Approximately 11,000 women served in the armed forces in Vietnam, and although only 8 died in combat-related incidents, stories on women vets have focused on the psychological trauma involved in their exposure to gruesome and upsetting scenes when they tended to the wounds of the men who were shot up in combat. Some media presentations have suggested that female Vietnam veterans were worse off than male veterans in that they were never treated as returning warriors, but were simply forgotten.[41]

Finally, in the past ten years, the image of the Vietnam veteran as a troubled individual has resisted modification because the Vietnam vet has become the quintessential "stressed-out" American and a reference point whenever the subject of PTSD is considered in any context. Almost any discussion regarding stress and PTSD in contemporary America will refer to the Vietnam veteran to legitimate and clarify the matter: witness discussions of pro football players ("in some cases, players developed post-traumatic stress disorders comparable to those experienced by some Vietnam veterans"), farmers in rural Iowa ("mental-health workers say that psychologically rural Iowa resembles a Vietnam veteran with post-traumatic stress disorder"), victims of airplane crashes ("Airborne calamities . . . claim a psychological toll months, years and possibly decades afterward—in a manner comparable to the post-traumatic stress syndrome common among Vietnam veterans"), the homeless ("nearly half of the homeless people . . . exhibited many of the symptoms of post traumatic stress disorder, a condition most often linked with Vietnam veterans"), those in the vicinity of oil spills ("it found a high level of post-traumatic stress, the same diagnosis made of some Vietnam veterans"), workers exposed to an industrial accident ("like Vietnam veterans who can't cope with recurring visions of the war, Phillips employees who saw their co-workers die are struggling with emotional troubles"), the problems of traveling salesmen ("they suffered symptoms of post-traumatic stress disorder—a condition often associated with Vietnam veterans"), victims of auto accidents ("motorists involved in fatal accidents experience what mental-health experts define as post-traumatic stress syndrome. Most commonly associated with Vietnam veterans. . ."), incest and rape victims ("when victims finally find their way into therapy, they are often diagnosed as having Post Traumatic Stress Syndrome, the same diagnosis given to Vietnam veterans who suffer debilitating flashbacks years after coming home from the war"), rescue personnel ("they must deal with the dead, the mangled, the bewildered and stunned . . . it could lead to post-traumatic stress disorder, the delayed reaction first widely identified among Vietnam veterans"), victims of earthquakes ("In disaster research, we're starting to look at such things as post-traumatic stress disorder, which has been experienced by Vietnam veterans"), hostages ("like some Vietnam veterans, hostages are apt to show evidence of what professionals call Post-Traumatic Stress Disorder"), teenage drug abusers ("among teen-agers who sought help at Samaritan Village, the drug-related experiences were so devastating that 44 percent suffered from post-traumatic stress syndrome similar to that of Vietnam veterans"), young adults who are pushed too hard ("A large number of young adults who had the hothouse style of up-bringing are now suffering post-traumatic stress syndrome like Vietnam veterans"), children exposed to violence ("the children he interviewed suffer from the same kind of post-traumatic stress as Vietnam veterans"), battered women ("[their behavior] is similar to that demonstrated by Vietnam veterans who suffer from post-traumatic stress disorder"), and African-Americans exposed to racial prejudice ("the African-American community is suffering from post traumatic stress syndrome caused by years of oppression and insensitive treatment. It is similar to that diagnosed for Vietnam veterans").[42]

Over the past twenty years, a number of commentators—often Vietnam veterans themselves—have protested this regnant image of the Vietnam veteran as a maladapted and permanently scarred psychiatric victim. One vet condemned all of the "ludicrous blubbering and psychobabble" about the Vietnam veteran as a misfit and tormented loser, and pointed out that the Vietnam vets he knew were proud to have served their country and didn't whine or complain about life. Another commented: "[E]nough is enough already. Not stepping on anyone's toes, but it's kind of gotten out of hand." An exasperated movie reviewer, on encountering yet one more motion picture about a psychologically disturbed Vietnam veteran, titled his column "Another Vietnam Vet Goes Haywire" and noted: "Just when you thought you'd seen the last suspense thriller to feature as its chief villain a deranged Vietnam veteran, along comes 'Fear' . . . to keep the asinine cycle rolling along." A second weary film reviewer, called upon to review a movie dealing with Vietnam veterans, concluded: "So familiar has this story become that I have started to think of it as a brand new film genre—the PTSD (Post-Traumatic Stress Disorder) genre."[43]

Despite the welcomes of the 1980s, repeated efforts to respond to Vietnam veteran concerns, and an occasional skeptical comment or assessment, the Vietnam veteran has come to be regarded in American society as a psychiatric victim and as the least-honored and most-abused veteran in American history. This image emerged from the antiwar movement of the early 1970s, centered on a temporary crisis in reintegration into American society during the early 1970s, and then shifted to controversial issues such as PTSD, suicide, and Agent

Orange—issues on which incontrovertible scientific data is lacking. Advocates of Vietnam veterans, fueled by anger against the U.S. government and particularly against the Veterans Administration, have created and maintained the presumption of crisis, detriment, and singularity. The stories of Owen Flaherty and James P. Green, however, suggest that the conventional wisdom on Vietnam veterans should be reconsidered.

"Every Man Has His Breaking Point": War and Psychiatry

The predominant view by the late 1970s was that the Vietnam veteran was exceptional in the history of American veterans. His experience was believed to largely contrast with that of veterans of earlier American wars, who, as a result of acceptance and adulation, were able to shake off disturbing memories of violence and settle down to peaceful and productive lives. Over the past twenty years, however, the continued study of the phenomenon of PTSD and the associated readjustment problems in Vietnam veterans has led to a reassessment of veterans of earlier American wars, including those from World War II. One reads less and less about how earlier American veterans had trouble-free periods of readjustment, and increasingly of the way in which PTSD is only the most recent incarnation of the psychological problems that earlier American veterans experienced under the rubric of "combat fatigue," "shell shock," or in the Civil War era, "nostalgia" and "irritable heart." As a result of this reevaluative trend, the Korean War in particular has received special attention: a drive was established in the 1980s to build a memorial for these veterans, and standard reports of the number of American fatalities in Korea were revised from the commonly accepted figure of 33,629 (combat deaths), which had been used for several decades, to 54,000, a figure that includes all soldiers who died in the war zone. It seems that Korea is on the verge of displacing Vietnam as being the "forgotten war," with veterans who never received their just due from society.[1]

Hence, in the 1990s, one sees two somewhat inconsistent post-Vietnam paradigms at work concerning the American veteran, the first of which regards the Vietnam veteran as unique for the anguish associated with post-traumatic stress, and the second of which tends to view all American veterans as victims for having endured psychological suffering or for having been underappreciated in the same way as was allegedly the case with Vietnam veterans—in this second view the suffering of the Vietnam veteran becomes an archetype for the experience of American veterans throughout history. These conflicting paradigms raise a number of questions regarding the issue of war and psychiatry: What are the classic symptoms of PTSD? To what extent are these symptoms novel, and to what extent is PTSD simply a restatement of earlier concepts of shell shock or combat fatigue? If PTSD is largely a restatement, why did psychiatric reformers in the 1970s demand with great urgency that it be recognized as a new concept in psychopathology, necessary to respond to the unique problems of returning Vietnam veterans? What is the relationship between military and civilian psychiatry? Why is it that the prevailing methods of describing mental illness seem to shift every twenty to thirty years as old concepts are jettisoned in favor of new ideas, from "shell shock" and "combat fatigue" to "PTSD," or from "neurasthenia" and "hysteria" in the nineteenth century to the "neuroses" and "psychoses" of the twentieth century, which in turn have been abandoned by the psychiatric profession in the 1990s?

Post-Traumatic Stress Disorder first came into existence as an officially recognized psychiatric syndrome in 1980, when the American Psychiatric Association adopted it as a disorder contained in its third *Diagnostic and Statistical Manual* (DSM-III), but the roots of this concept go back at least to the nineteenth century when physicians first encountered what came to be known as "railway spine" (also known as "traumatic neurosis," "railroad shock," "Erichson railway spine," "railway brain," "nervous shock," "physical shock," "neurasthenia following shock and accident," or "accident neurosis"). Medical men[2] in the early to mid-nineteenth century examined and described perplexing cases of injuries to the spine, frequently the result of accidents on the newly emergent railway systems in the United States and Britain. Patients experienced "nervous shock" and "hysteria" that was sometimes quite extreme and seemingly completely out of proportion to the severity of the physical trauma incurred. Symptoms could include fear of the place of the accident, sleeplessness, mental depression, loss of energy, stuttering, loss of sexual desire, contraction of the visual field, and sleep disturbances. The cause seemed to be psychic shock:

[M]ore than the physical injury in these cases, there seems to be psy-
chical effect, either immediately accompanying the accident, such as
horrible sight of suffering, the cries of the injured, the agony of the
mangled bodies, and all sorts of horrible scenes; in addition to that, even
if not injured himself, come the terror of personal danger, the mental
agony, the fright, etc., affecting the victim profoundly.

The question that physicians began to address was whether the resulting dysfunction and the psychological sequelae associated with
these traumatic episodes were "organic" and "structural" in nature,
literally caused by some underlying, physical changes in the nervous
system (owing to concussive changes—"lesions"—or inflammation
of some kind), or whether ensuing physical problems and mental
neuroses were purely psychological, that is to say "functional" in
nature, with no underlying (or at least not readily discernible) somatic basis.[3]

This dilemma was particularly critical and perplexing to late
nineteenth-century medical investigators because of the state of contemporary psychiatric theory, which was dominated by the rise of
"scientific medicine," neurology, modern hospitals, and modern research universities, and accordingly emphasized materialistic, strictly
scientific explanations of diseases and disease processes. Earlier psychiatric theory had been pragmatic or even religious in orientation,
more concerned with "moral reform" and the creation of a supportive
environment in asylums for mental patients than with the construction of a rigorous, coherent, and internally consistent theory of insanity. This earlier approach, typical of that of the giants of the moral
reform movement, Pinel, Tuke, and Rush, was replaced in mid-
century, however, by German "university psychiatry," with its conviction (inspired by allopathic medicine's discovery of germ theory
and disease localization) that the brain was the seat of mental illness,
and that psychopathology could ultimately be explained by "mecha-
nistic principles."[4]

In addressing the issue of "railway spine" in the late nineteenth
century, psychiatry thus struggled to find, consistent with its quest
for exact, scientific principles, the supposed physical changes in the
nervous system that would account for hysterical reactions in trauma
patients. Dozens of articles in scientific journals at that time admitted
that no actual changes could be identified in the nervous systems of
those experiencing "nervous shock," but hypothesized nonetheless
that there was "an acutal degeneration of the nerve-substance," "mo-

lecular jarring," "fine granular degeneration of the ganglion cells," that mental shock impaired the nutrition and normal function of neurons in the human nervous system, or that nervous conditions resulted from the improper circulation of organic substances from the surrounding "vital fluids" to neurons in the spine. However, theory concerning these traumatic neuroses remained highly speculative and inconclusive; one exasperated physician concluded:

> In the study of traumatic neurosis, tracing its evolution from its first description up to the present time, no elements will impress the neurological student more than the diversity of theories presented: their wide range of interpretation, their multiplicity of symptomatology, incongruities of description, lack of definite detail, their subjectivity presenting in its evolvement vagaries difficult of comprehension and seemingly full of contradiction.[5]

The whole subject of post-traumatic shock was given added urgency and propelled further by the experience of World War I and the "discovery" of shell shock. War was declared in mid-1914, and when the first military thrusts and counter-thrusts of the antagonists failed to produce victory in the summer and fall of 1914 (at the cost of 900,000 casualties), static trench warfare ensued thereafter along the entire Western Front in which massed armies of hundreds of thousands of men confronted each other at a distance of several hundred yards. Each army was securely dug into a series of mutually reinforcing trenches, which constituted a practically invincible defensive position protected by barbed-wire, obstacles, machine guns, and massive high-powered artillery that could focus devastating fire on any attacking force. Despite the overwhelming odds against a successful offensive, each side in turn would launch all-out assaults in which thousands of men in wave after wave were sent "over the top" into the surreal, bombed-out, blasted, barbed-wire and obstacle-strewn hell referred to as "no man's land," where they were systematically slaughtered by the firepower of the defenders. Robert Kee has characterized the trenches as the concentration camps of World War I, in which long docile lines of young men, shoddily uniformed, heavily burdened, numbered about their necks, plodded forward across a featureless landscape to their own extermination.[6]

At the Battle of the Somme in 1916, in the first hour of the battle, the British suffered over 60,000 casualties with 20,000 men killed; before the end of the offensive, the Allies had incurred 500,000 casualties. That same year, at the Battle of Verdun, the Germans and French engaged in a conscious war of attrition, which resulted in total casualties of approximately 700,000. The Germans preceded their attacks with concentrated artillery bombardments, which frequently buried French defenders alive in collapsed trenches; indeed, long-range artillery bombardment could be the most nerve-wracking experience for the World War I infantryman, who, huddled in his underground shelter, could hear "aerial torpedoes" enter the ground with a thud, and would then have to wait for several agonizing seconds for the explosion, which might or might not collapse his bomb shelter, turning it into a grave, whose occupants would be smothered in darkness under tons of earth.[7]

Exposed to such a horrific environment ruled by the machine gun, poison gas, the artillery barrage, and the smell of rotting human flesh, a world in which one's comrades were routinely cut down, decapitated, or blown to bits before one's eyes, many World War I soldiers seemed to go mad. They fell victim in epidemic numbers to a wide variety of symptoms of post-traumatic stress. This condition was first characterized as "shell shock," because it was thought to be caused by physical lesions of the brain brought about in some way by carbon monoxide or changes in atmospheric pressure resulting from the commotional effects of artillery explosions. The symptoms associated with "shell shock" were varied, from vague anxiety, depression, startle reactions, an inability to concentrate one's thoughts, loss of memory, insomnia, nightmares, intense fear, "trotting heart," and panic attacks to uncontrollable shaking, aphonia, mutism, hysterical blindness, amnesia, partial or total paralysis, and hysterical fits, in which the subject might scream and blindly thrash about in desperation. One observer described breakdown on the battlefield as follows: "It is difficult to describe the clinical appearance of the man who broke down suddenly. The man looked obviously out of control; he gave way to involuntary movements, wringing his hands, his eyes became staring, and he got the look of a hunted animal—you cannot mistake it. When the crash does come he loses all shame and cringes."[8]

The first cases of shell shock began to filter into forward military hospitals in the fall of 1914, and by the winter of 1914–15, these casualties were appearing in large numbers; by 1916 as many as 40 percent of casualties were shell-shocked men. The British Army Medical Service treated at least 80,000 cases of shell shock, and 200,000 soldiers stricken by this condition were discharged from the service during the war. By 1918 there were over twenty army hospitals for shell-shock casualties in the United Kingdom, and private and public asylums well as spas had been commandeered for treatment of the shell-shocked. Attitudes toward the psychiatric casualties of the war varied widely over time: initially, many disoriented men at the front were treated as deserters and shot; others were cared for in the manner of late nineteenth-century therapeutics and given the "rest cure" (of isolation, rest, and food) or treated with electricity—either mild faradization or substantial electrical current intended, essentially, to coerce a man to talk, walk, or act normally. Eventually, innovators in the ranks of the military medical service such as Charles S. Myers and W. H. R. Rivers developed rudimentary techniques of psychotherapy to investigate and treat these mental disorders; Rivers and one of his most famous patients, Siegfried Sassoon, have become the subjects of a stream of fictional and nonfictional books dealing with shell shock and the World War I experience.[9]

World War I resulted in three major changes in the theory and practice of psychiatry and psychology: first, military psychiatry was changed (or, in some sense, invented) as innovators in Europe and their American adherents such as Maj. Thomas Salmon developed new "front-line" methods of treatment for shell-shocked soldiers in accordance with the principles of "proximity, immediacy, and expectancy" (P.I.E.). In this approach, the affected soldier was treated immediately and as close to the front (and his unit) as possible, with the expectation that he would return to his unit as soon as possible to help maintain manpower levels at the front. The Russian Army in the Russo-Japanese War (1904–1905) was apparently the first army in modern times to establish a system of forward psychiatric clearing hospitals equipped with its own specialists, who were prepared to recognize and treat war neuroses, but the primary objective of the Russian system was to evacuate men back to Moscow by means of the trans-Siberian railroad, about a thirty-day trip. In fact, the clearing hospital in Harbin had only fifty beds, and something like 3,500 men went through the system, forcing Russian Army officials to place mental patients in regular military hospitals and to turn to the Red Cross Society of Russia for assistance.[10]

By contrast, military psychiatric methods in World War I (particularly as developed by the French and copied by the Americans) avoided at all costs quickly removing men to the rear, on the theory that such rapid evacuation would lead to the symptoms of their neuroses becoming "fixed," preventing forever a man's return to combat. On the surface, the policy has been justified as humane ("He may become a permanent casualty unable to function in any other role than as a psychiatric patient the remainder of his life"), but an alternative explanation for the necessity of forward-area treatment is that few psychiatric casualties who actually made it to the rear could be convinced or even coerced to return to the hellish conditions of combat. By the time the United States entered the war, the U.S. Army was well aware of the problem of psychiatric casualties on the Western Front, and created a Division of Neurology and Psychiatry in the Office of the Surgeon General, which was charged with examining recruits and setting up adequate facilities and plans for the care of "nervously and mentally sick" soldiers. Field hospitals were established to treat men for three to ten days with rest, good food, sleep, and encouragement, during which time an effort was made to convince or shame them into returning to their unit at the front. Those who resisted were not technically "punished," but were given distasteful work, such as policing the grounds or digging latrines: "No one was permitted to impugn their motives, yet on every side they were confronted by a questioning attitude. . . . About 90 per cent of this group were eventually reached by such a simple method." Again, the primary emphasis of this approach was to preserve military manpower levels.[11]

The second innovation inspired by the World War I experience was related primarily to psychiatric practice, and saw the treatment of mentally ill people shift in some degree from inpatient care at insane asylums toward outpatient care and the use of "mental hygiene teams" in the community. Prior to the war, treatment for mental disorders in both Britain and the United States tended to be controlled by asylum doctors with their generally antique ideas that mental illness was caused by hereditary factors rather than by nurture or environmental forces. After the end of the war, those army doctors who had pioneered brief treatment at the front, as a kind of "outpatient care" that could cure the incipient mental problems of shell-shocked soldiers, carried their innovative treatment methods over into civilian psychiatry. Various asylum reforms were accompanied by a more profound transformation of psychiatry's role in society, which entailed an expansion of the field of mental medicine, the incorporation of other professions (psychologists, psychiatric nurses, psychiatric social workers) under psychiatry's medical umbrella, and the opening up of new sites of practice outside the asylum.[12]

The third consequence of World War I was a reorientation of psychiatric theory from a "materialist" basis, which sought to explain abnormal psychological behavior by positing actual physical changes in the brain or nervous system, toward the recognition that neurotic behavior might be primarily "psychogenic" in nature—resulting from shock, fright, or mental conflict rather than physical trauma or rigidly physicalist processes. Freudian constructs, such as the topographical model of id, ego, and superego, and Freud's idea of drives, conflicts, psychic energy, fixations, complexes, and dream analysis, along with the methods of psychotherapy, seemed to be more useful in understanding and attempting to treat neurotic behavior. What occurred, in essence, was one of psychiatry's many "paradigm shifts" as the profession moved from a biological, rigidly "scientific" outlook (as evidenced by the late nineteenth century's fixation on examining brain tissue at post mortems) toward a more "psychological" attitude, which paid attention to accounts of feelings, thoughts, and life as expressed and reported by the patient.[13]

But despite this general shift in attitude and approach, there was no new consensus among psychiatrists and physicians concerning the phenomenon of shell shock. In interpreting the World War I experience, argument ensued regarding the nature of trauma, the role of predisposition (the old "nature versus nurture," "heredity versus environment" debate), the possibility of malingering, and the meaning of recurrent nightmares in which the victim relived the war experience that had caused the breakdown. Although psychiatry as a whole had scored a triumph in the acknowledgment that breakdowns were psychological in origin, the idea that these breakdowns could be caused by the traumatic events of warfare challenged the prevailing Freudian notion that all neuroses had an origin in sexual experience and trauma. Repetitive nightmares of combat also had to be reconciled with Freud's belief that wish fulfillment was the motivating force behind dreams. Allowing that the traumatic neuroses of war might not be sexual in origin, Freud developed a new view of trauma and concluded that this behavior was the result of fright, and that repetitive dreams were an attempt to be prepared after the fact, to dissipate by repetition the anxiety generated by the experience. Other psychiatrists continued to insist that there was a sexual basis of the disorder, which could be characterized as "wounded self-love," or that those who fell prey to war neuroses had suffered an arrest of development at the oral or anal libidinous stage, and the subsequent trauma of war forced the soldier to regress to the original state of the arrest.

Abram Kardiner, in contrast, suggested that these traumatic neuroses might be more "conditioned" behavior—a "physioneurosis," a mental disorder with both psychological and physiological components—than the result of internal conflict, unresolved stages of development, relations with parents, or fixations. Regarding this lack of consensus pertaining to the theory of the traumatic neuroses of war, Kardiner observed:

> In general there is a vast store of data available . . . but it is hard to find a province of psychiatry in which there is less discipline than this one. There is practically no continuity to be found anywhere, and the literature can only be characterized as anarchic. Every author has his own frame of reference—lengthy bibliographies notwithstanding.[14]

Did an officially recognized psychiatric syndrome or disorder along the lines of PTSD emerge from the experience of World War I? Although the postwar psychiatric literature generally centered on the concept of "traumatic neurosis" or the "traumatic neuroses of war," there was no contemporary equivalent to the American Psychiatric Association's *Diagnostic and Statistical Manual* (first issued in 1952) that could serve as a kind of Bible for the profession. The history of psychiatry has, in a sense, been the history of various medical men and theoreticians attempting to understand mental pathology by means of rigorous classification: sometimes these efforts have centered on theoretical and speculative system-building with little attention paid to clinical observation (as in the eighteenth century), and at other times the emphasis has been on meticulous observation of actual mental patients on a case-by-case basis with classification built slowly from the ground up (as in the nineteenth century under the influence of French clinical medicine). By most accounts, modern classification in psychiatry and psychology began in the late nineteenth century with Emil Kraepelin, the German alienist, credited with first describing schizophrenia ("dementia praecox"). Kraepelin (1856–1926) attempted to describe "disease courses" rather than symptom clusters, and his series of textbooks on mental pathology from 1883 on were both exhaustive and influential, spreading to the

United States after 1896. A *Statistical Manual* was issued by the American Medico-Psychological Association and the National Committee for Mental Hygiene in 1918, but it had nothing like the influence later exerted by the DSM.[15]

A recurrent theme in the history of military psychiatry is that the lessons of the last war are almost always ignored in the next war, at least initially, and this certainly proved to be the case for American forces at the outset of World War II. Rather than establish front-line treatment strategies for shell-shocked soldiers in accordance with the lessons of World War I, American military authorities in 1941 adopted the theory that if "defectives" were adequately screened out at induction, then those men who had passed muster and remained in the ranks would be resistant to or immune from psychological breakdown. Accordingly, about 1.6 million draftees (of 20 million men examined) were rejected at army induction centers for psychiatric reasons; this rejection rate was 7.6 times the rejection rate in World War I. The policy of admitting only "resilient" men into the army proved to be a failure, however, as soldiers and sailors, despite initial screening, suffered from psychiatric problems—before battle, in battle, and in noncombat situations. The military's initial response was simply to discharge these men, on the theory that they were "ineffective" and could not be cured or salvaged: approximately 438,000 men were discharged for psychiatric reasons during the war, and the rate of discharge for emotional or mental problems was five times the rate for such discharges in World War I. Yet these induction and discharge policies proved to be so disastrous that in 1943, the number of psychiatric discharges from the army exceeded the number of new enlistees. This loss of manpower led eventually to the reinstitution of the principles of preventive military psychiatry from World War I. As always, military authorities displayed a skeptical attitude toward the practice of front-line psychiatry, fearing undue sympathy for malingerers. This view held until commanders were faced with the reality of psychiatric breakdown on the battlefield, as throngs of disturbed, shaking, stuttering, terrified men flocked to the rear.[16]

The U.S. Army finally initiated its program of forward psychiatric treatment in the Tunisian campaign in April of 1943, and these procedures became fully functional in the Italian campaign later that year; programs were also established for the Army Air Corps. The approach was similar to that of World War I: casualties were purposely treated as close to the front as possible (P.I.E.), labeled "ex-haustion" cases, and given rest (often being administered narcotics for twenty-four hours or longer), good food, and a warm place to sleep. The idea was to restore a man quickly in the vicinity of his unit (where he would still have a sense of loyalty and obligation to his buddies), and to return as many men as possible to combat as quickly as possible. As in World War I, the symptoms of what was termed, in the effort to avoid an official psychiatric diagnosis, "combat ex-haustion" were varied; one report noted that "dreams and night-mares of killing and catastrophe were common," and as had proved to be the case in World War I, artillery fire could be the most devas-tating cause of this mental breakdown:

> Continued and severe shellfire and "screaming meemies" [mortar fire] produced an anxiety that was not easily cured as long as the threat of returning remained. These patients were tremulous and tense. They would jump at slight stimuli, be dazed, mentally confused, with feelings of intense anxiety and apprehension, and their sleep was disturbed with battle dreams and persistent recollections of traumas. They would de-velop crying spells, lose their appetites, and have severe heart palpita-tions, or become depressed and oblivious of everything.[17]

The "psychotherapy" utilized in World War II seemed at times to vary slightly from that employed in World War I: along with sleep and encouragement, some patients were subjected to what was called "Pentothal abreaction," in which the medical staff would administer pentothal and then lead the patient through a reenactment of the battle scene that had produced the breakdown. The problem was that some men, even under the influence of these drugs, would insist during these reenactments that they be assured they would not be returned to combat:

> It is electrifying to watch the terror exhibited in the moments of supreme danger such as at the imminent explosion of shells, the death of a friend before the patient's eyes, or the absence of cover under a heavy dive-bombing attack. The body becomes increasingly tense and rigid; the eyes widen and the pupils dilate while the skin becomes covered with perspiration. The hands move about convulsively, seeking a weapon or a friend to share the danger. Breathing becomes incredibly rapid and shallow. The intensity of emotion sometimes becomes more than they can bear and frequently at the height of the reaction, there is a collapse; Some patients return over and over again to one short traumatic scene,

living it through repeatedly as if, like a needle traveling around a cracked record, they could not get past this point.[18]

The idea of "abreaction" or "catharsis" goes back at least as far as Freud and the use of hypnosis in the late nineteenth century. The intent is to uncover a repressed memory, deal with and banish or neutralize it, and thereby achieve mental balance; it would seem that this objective was not accomplished in these sessions during World War II. Because the goal of military psychiatry was to return as many men as possible to duty of some sort (front-line or otherwise), treatment in World War II tended to focus on patching up problems, on "covering things up" and "salvaging" the man so that he could quickly be returned to his unit on the front lines. Rates varied: when men were evacuated to the rear, only about 15 percent were ever returned to combat; with front-line treatment, the rate of return to duty exceeded 50 percent.[19]

One of the most enduring lessons of World War II psychiatry was that "every man has his breaking point." Although initial policy had been intended to insulate the army from psychiatric problems by careful screening, the army soon discovered that environmental stress put every man at risk. Hence it was important not to overexpose troops to combat, and to afford men periodic relief from battle by means of relaxation and leaves away from the front lines. Psychiatric staff determined that American troops would lose their effectiveness after a hundred days of intermittent exposure to battle, and that breakdown could be expected after about two hundred aggregate days in battle. These findings held even in experienced and battle-tested men, as witnessed in the "old sergeant's syndrome," when men who had exercised excellent leadership on the line turned up at psychiatric treatment centers, saying they felt "all burned out" and apathetic. The experience of World War II revealed that the age group which experienced the fewest problems were those aged eighteen to twenty-five; with age, there was a sharp rise in psychoneurosis, for instance from 6 per thousand in eighteen- and nineteen-year-olds to 45 per thousand in thirty-six- and thirty-seven-year-olds.[20]

As was the case after World War I, experience during World War II had profound effects on the theory and practice of civilian psychiatry. First, the war witnessed the rise of clinical psychology as a major force in the mental health professions. Academic psychology first originated in the laboratories of such German luminaries as Wilhelm

Wundt in the 1880s, and earned a niche of social power and influence with its mastery and successful promotion of intelligence testing early in the twentieth century. Until World War II, the field of psychology was dominated by academic psychologists; clinical psychologists were limited mostly to testing. Especially with the influence of the Veterans Administration, which demanded and legitimized the use of psychologists in therapy roles, by 1950 almost 70 percent of psychologists were involved in treatment. Although psychiatrists generally adhered to methods of psychotherapy that attempted to clarify psychic conflict and promote personal insight, most clinical psychologists tended to favor behavioral theories and were largely interested in the modification of behavior.[21]

Second, the practices of World War II military psychiatry with its eventual widespread use of "front-line" methods of "outpatient" treatment, which posited that mental illness was the result of environmental stress (the battlefield) and could be successfully treated with early and brief psychotherapeutic intervention, spilled over into civilian psychiatry and reinforced trends established after World War I. Before World War II, most mental patients were cared for in asylums, and the majority of the membership of the American Psychiatric Association was employed in these (mostly state) hospitals; during the war, however, more psychiatrists were trained by the military (2,400) than had even belonged to the American Psychiatric Association before the war. The war experience revolutionized the thinking of these psychiatrists, whose advocacy was largely responsible for reforms leading eventually to the Community Mental Health Centers Act of 1963 and the phenomenon of "deinstitutionalization," as patients were released from huge state insane asylums and sent back to the community—supposedly for outpatient or outreach care. The idea was that civilian psychopathology could be effectively treated in the same manner as military psychopathology had been dealt with at "front-line" stations during the war; in a civilian setting, it was thought, community outreach centers utilizing brief psychotherapy could eliminate or quickly cure most mental illness. As mental health care delivery systems changed, so did the nature of mental health care personnel, which—as had begun to be true after World War I—came to include increasing numbers of psychologists, psychiatric social workers, and psychiatric nurses.[22]

Granted that soldiers suffered during both world wars, what about the matter of delayed stress, which seems so central to interpretations of the experience of American soldiers and veterans from the Vietnam War? Did these earlier veterans suffer from lingering psychological problems, persisting after the end of the war or first manifesting themselves years later? Veterans of the world wars did indeed suffer from delayed stress: in England in the wake of World War I, numerous newspaper articles focused on the war-related problems veterans were experiencing in readjusting to civilian life. A *London Times* article of March 1, 1920, entitled "Friends of the Shell-Shocked" was typical in describing the World War I veteran as alienated, rejected in the labor market, and in need of "local centres" (reminiscent of the Vietnam veteran's "vet centers") for specific treatment:

> Of the many problems calling for solutions, one of the most urgent is that of the man disabled in the war or suffering from shell-shock or neurasthenia. There exists a great army of men suffering from varying degrees of mental instability, and in the ordinary labour market, and particularly in the employment bureaux, such men are at a serious disadvantage. Employers have come to look askance at them.[23]

Other articles chronicled individual cases of despondency, suicide, and unemployment related to shell shock.[24] In the United States, the number of veterans receiving hospital care for neuropsychiatric disorders stood at 7,499 in 1921 and increased over the subsequent ten years to 11,342 in 1931. The amount of money spent on service-connected disability awards to World War I veterans for neuropsychiatric diseases increased from $28,256 in 1923 to $67,916 in 1932. In 1944, almost half of the 67,000 beds in VA hospitals were occupied by the psychoneurotics of World War I. Particularly critical were certain innovations in federal law pertaining to veterans' benefits: subsequent to World War I, a veteran was presumed to have been in good health at induction, and the occurrence of certain conditions or diseases, such as a neuropsychiatric disease within two years of discharge (or for some conditions, onset as late as January 1, 1925), was presumed to have resulted from conditions in the service. The law recognized and accepted the fact that the onset of some neuropsychiatric problems could be delayed in nature.[25]

For the World War II veteran, the situation was similar. One group of researchers tracked a set of veterans over a twenty-year period and discovered persistent symptoms of tension, irritability, depression, diffuse anxiety symptoms, headaches, insomnia, and nightmares; they labeled this clinical picture "veteran's chronic stress syndrome" and concluded: "These particular veterans cannot blot out their painful memories." Investigators in a 1960 study played a tape of combat sounds to several target groups, and the group of combat veterans suffering psychiatric disorders displayed "near-psychotic disturbed behavior" that required that the experiment be terminated immediately in their case. These service-related psychological conditions were often delayed in onset: for instance, R. R. Grinker noted in 1945, "[the] majority of psychiatric admissions among returnees are not men who have returned with war neuroses, but those who develop signs of illness after completing a full term of duty"; a study of 955 veterans from 1951 discovered that combat was a factor in 50 percent of the breakdowns and that 13 percent of the subjects broke down after returning to the United States from service overseas.[26]

By the time of the Vietnam War, then, the army had extensive experience in dealing with "combat fatigue" and the psychological consequences of warfare. In order to minimize adverse reaction to combat, it limited the infantryman's tour of duty in the combat zone in Vietnam to one year (thirteen months for Marines) unless soldiers chose to extend their service, offered rest and recreation to alleviate the stress of combat, and provided immediate medical treatment if problems developed. The "front-line" methods of treatment in Vietnam were similar to those of the world wars: men experiencing psychiatric problems were treated at or near the front and were only evacuated out of country if "salvage" appeared impossible. As a result, American troops in Vietnam had a very low incidence of psychiatric casualties: about 12 such cases per thousand men, as compared with 37 per thousand in the Korean War and 28–101 (depending on assignment) per thousand during World War II. Combat itself generated only a small number of these cases; boredom, loneliness, and interpersonal conflicts experienced by rear-echelon troops seemed to account for most psychological problems. Researchers suggested that these lower rates were due to a number of factors: the intermittent nature of combat in Vietnam, the relative lack of sustained indirect fire (from artillery and aircraft), helicopter mobility (which allowed raids to be made from secure bases, at which material comforts were available), the screening of men at induction, a support troop:combat troop ratio of 7:1, the yearly rotation of troops, rest and recreation, an unprecedented high educational and training level in the soldiers, and the implementation of well-planned preventive psychiatric programs and network of mental health services.[27]

The rate of psychiatric breakdown in American troops in Vietnam actually did rise in the latter stages of the war, from 10.8 per thousand in 1965 and 9.8 per thousand in 1967, to 15 per thousand in 1969 and 24.1 per thousand in 1970.[28] Early in the war, psychiatric cases had accounted for only 5 percent of all medical evacuations out of country (compared with average rates of 6 percent in Korea and 25 percent in World War II), but by 1972 the rate was 61 percent, with the majority of these cases involving heroin dependency. The rate of psychiatric disorders (defined to include substance abuse) in U.S. troops thus actually increased as fighting wound down for the Americans as President Nixon's "Vietnamization" policy (which placed ARVN troops on the front line and relegated American forces to primarily a support role) took effect during 1969–1970. The data on Vietnam seemed to indicate, at least initially, that rates of psychiatric breakdown were low by historical standards, and that what breakdowns did occur were related more to boredom and drug abuse than to terror and anxiety produced by combat. A leading psychiatrist concluded: "As a result [of increasingly sophisticated knowledge of military psychiatry] there is reason to be optimistic that psychiatric casualties need never again become a major cause of attrition in the United States military in a combat zone."[29]

In the late 1960s, however, the whole issue of the psychological repercussions of the Vietnam War on its combatants came to be viewed in a different light. Leading critics such as Robert Jay Lifton and Chaim Shatan began to reinterpret what had been thought of as advantages for the Vietnam vet as actual disadvantages (for instance, a limited one-year tour of duty was seen as leading to a lack of unit cohesion and less resistance to psychological breakdown).[30] They argued that Vietnam was, in fact, worse than World War II in that the soldiers were younger and less resilient, were subjected to a surreal guerrilla conflict unknown to prior generations of American soldiers, suffered from low morale owing to a lack of public support, were haunted by guilt because of the widespread commission of atrocities in the war zone, and were further traumatized upon their return home when they were abused by antiwar demonstrators.[31]

This new critique functioned on two levels: first, it suggested that the rate of traditional psychological breakdown in American troops in Vietnam was higher than previously thought. The armed forces, it was charged, had "faked" low rates of combat fatigue by treating many cases of mental breakdown as disciplinary problems and simply releasing these men from the military with dishonorable or "less than honorable" discharges.[32] Second, it argued that because of all the factors that made the Vietnam War unique, Vietnam vets were also suffering from a new type of delayed stress disorder, first labeled the "Vietnam Syndrome," "Post-Vietnam Syndrome (PVS)," "Vietnam-Veteran Syndrome," "Re-Entry Syndrome," or "Post-Viet Nam Psychiatric Syndrome (PVNPS)."[33] As a result of the efforts of Lifton, Shatan, and other antiwar psychiatrists and psychologists such as John Wilson and Charles Figley, the diagnostic category of Post-Traumatic Stress Disorder was eventually accepted as an official psychiatric disorder by the American Psychiatric Association in 1980. Although the definition of PTSD has changed from DSM-III to DSM-III-R and DSM-IV, it includes the basic elements of a history of trauma, reexperiencing of trauma ("intrusion"), avoidance phenomena ("numbing"), and hyperarousal/hyperreactivity, which can all involve elements of depression, anxiety, panic attacks, flashbacks, startle reactions, and survivor guilt. Onset can be immediate or delayed. In the drive to have PTSD recognized, many psychiatrists functioned as unabashed advocates rather than neutral scientists: "Out of kinship with the veterans, some professionals have moved beyond therapy alone, and toward advocacy; we have entered actively into public affairs. Our goal is to give the widest publicity to the unique emotional experiences of these men; to do so, we go—together with the veterans—wherever we will be heard: conventions, war crimes hearings, churches, Congress, even abroad."[34]

Although PTSD has been recognized by the American Psychiatric Association and although Vietnam veterans have acquired a primary identity as psychiatric victims, the whole matter of PTSD, the Vietnam vet, and the idea of PTSD as a "scientific concept" has been plagued by two problems. First, approximately 3.14 million American troops served in or around Vietnam during the war (they are known as "theater" Vietnam veterans as opposed to the overall number of 8,269,881 Vietnam "era" veterans), and estimates of the number of theater veterans affected by PTSD have varied wildly. Early studies based on "convenience samples" indicated an incidence of from 250,000 (under 10 percent) to 1.5 million (50 percent); more thorough epidemiological studies have produced rates as far apart as 2 percent and 26 percent.[35] Second, reminiscent of the conceptual anarchy described by Abram Kardiner regarding "shell shock," researchers have also been unable to agree on conceptual paradigms in describing and studying the phenomenon of PTSD. Approaches vary widely from the "biological" (PTSD as resulting from structural changes in the nervous system), the "cognitive" (problem as one of information-processing), "behavioralist" (focus on "conditioned responses"), "psychoanalytic" (internal conflict between self and society), and "developmental" (interaction between war stress and early adult development). Accordingly, ideas of appropriate treatment for PTSD also vary widely. The DSM itself is regarded as "atheoretical," which essentially allows any researcher to superimpose his or her conceptualization on the disorder.[36]

As was the case following the world wars, psychiatric diagnoses and treatment methods first developed in studying Vietnam War soldiers and veterans have eventually been extended to the practice of civilian psychiatry. PTSD, first developed as an official diagnosis in the 1970s and closely identified with the Vietnam veteran at that time, has become a popular diagnosis for the condition of millions of Americans, as suggested in the last chapter, from the survivors of natural disasters to victims of domestic violence, traveling salesmen, and stressed-out overachieving adolescents.

In sum, although the practice of positioning mental health specialists near the battlefield began with the Russo-Japanese War, modern military psychiatric techniques of treatment involving the principles of proximity, immediacy, and expectancy emerged in the First World War, and have been used thereafter in some modified form by many modern armies. Studies on military psychiatry have usually revealed that elite units have lower rates of psychiatric breakdown, that duration in combat is critical, that indirect fire such as World War I's horrific artillery barrages produce higher rates of breakdown, and rapidly advancing troops experience low psychiatric casualty rates (as opposed to troops in a defensive or stationary posture, who experience feelings of helplessness).[37] The terminology to describe adverse psychological reactions to combat and war has shifted, but the core elements and the underlying reality of these different descriptive and diagnostic concepts seem to be similar. Delayed stress reactions to combat have been noted in the veterans of twentieth-century wars prior to the Vietnam War.

In considering twentieth-century military psychiatry, three major themes emerge: first, a dynamic relationship has developed between military psychiatry and the mental health professions in that psychiatry and psychology have used war to expand their influence, and in turn have been changed by their discoveries and experiences in warfare; ideas and treatment methods developed in wartime to treat soldiers, sailors, and airmen are later applied to the practice of civilian psychiatry and psychology.[38] Second, in its relationship with the military and the conduct of war, psychiatry has usually had a "political agenda": prior to the 1970s, this agenda involved colluding with the military in order to "salvage" and return agitated soldiers to combat; W. C. Menninger described this as a "dirty job," and other psychiatrists have written of the ethical dilemma involved in trying to convince anxious and depressed young men to return to battle.[39] With Vietnam, however, one sees a change in emphasis as psychiatry moved away from serving the manpower needs of the military, toward increased concern for the welfare of the individual and, accordingly, a more skeptical or pronounced antiwar stance, in which many mental health professionals essentially became the adversaries of the military. This is all to say that politics play a role in psychiatry's approach to war— sometimes in a subtle, sometimes in an overt manner.[40]

Third, despite decades of study, psychologists and psychiatrists have not yet been able to determine in advance with any certainty which men will be able to withstand the stress of combat and which will fall victim to psychiatric breakdown. They are also uncertain of the exact process by which impressions of danger and death are translated into traumatic memory, an aroused sympathetic nervous system (rapid heart beat and respiration, perspiration, increased blood pressure), and, eventually, psychopathology. Debate still occurs over the relative roles of genetics, predisposition, and environment in causing breakdown in soldiers and veterans. These uncertainties and disputes are symptomatic of larger issues and problems throughout the history of psychiatry. As Erwin Ackerknecht and others have demonstrated, the history of psychiatry has been the story of a frustrating (and continuing) attempt to understand the nature of mental illness, and has revolved around such questions as whether abnormal, "insane" behavior is a form of divine inspiration, demonic possession, creative genius, a "cultural construct," or an illness. If an illness, can "abnormal" psychological behavior best be understood as a disease of the brain or the nervous system as a whole or, given that underlying physical changes in brain structures and brain chemistry often cannot be detected in "mentally ill" people, would it be preferable to think of mental illness less as a "disease" and more as the failure to adjust to one's social surroundings, or an inability to move successfully from one developmental stage in life to another (say, from adolescence to adulthood)? Should somatic explanations and "disease constructs" be abandoned in favor of Freudian dream analysis, somewhat imprecise discussions of "ego strength," and Jungian ideas of the religious consciousness of mankind? The continuing lack of consensus within the professions of psychiatry and psychology regarding the conceptualization and treatment of mental pathology are a testament to the difficulty of the issues engaged. Psychiatry is concerned with the most complex medico-physiological problem, that of the body-mind relationship, which has remained unsolved to the present day.[41]

This reexamination of Civil War and Vietnam War psychiatric casualties seeks to reconsider the two dominant post-Vietnam ideas concerning American veterans: the idea of the Vietnam veteran as unique in his suffering, and the somewhat contradictory concept of all American veterans as psychiatric victims of one sort or another. Given the similarities between the experience of the world wars and Vietnam, how is it that the idea has emerged of the Vietnam veteran as unique in American history for his or her delayed stress problems? Regarding the diametrically opposed emerging paradigm that sees the Vietnam veteran as typical of all twentieth-century veterans in his experience as a psychiatric victim, can a reexamination of the Civil War experience in the nineteenth century shed additional light on the matter—to either substantiate or refute these ideas?

"Dangled over Hell":
The Trauma of the Civil War

In post-Vietnam America, the key word in considering the psychological state of returning veterans is "trauma." Specifically, what hardships and trials did the veteran undergo during his service in the military? Was he placed in situations in which he experienced anxiety and fear? Was he exposed to combat, to the death and mutilation of his fellow warriors, or to the spectacle of enemy soldiers being slaughtered in battle or, as prisoners, being summarily executed? Did he encounter disease or discomforts that might have weakened his psychic defenses or exacerbated his sense of alienation and unease about being sent far from home and given the anomalous task of killing other human beings? Did his bonds to fellow soldiers or to civilians at home somehow ameliorate his problems and prevent psychological breakdown? Did an eventual warm homecoming "wash away" disturbing memories of pain and death?

In comparing the trauma experienced by the Civil War soldier with that of the Vietnam veteran or any combatant in modern twentieth-century armies, one is struck first of all by the physical hardships that soldiers encountered in what one man characterized as a "destroying manner of living." Although the Civil War has been portrayed as the first modern or industrial war in which machinery such as locomotives and rifled muskets or ironclad warships and naval torpedoes were engaged, the infantryman in this war moved from one place to another mainly on foot. He sometimes covered ten and twenty miles a day, or even more in the case of a forced march when troops had to be maneuvered quickly to come to the aid of embattled and endangered comrades or to defend or seize key positions. During the Civil War, the 11th Indiana Infantry marched a total of 9,318 miles; during a key three-and-a-half-month period, the 44th Indiana Infantry marched over 725 miles, an average march of 10 miles per day when on the move. One Northerner noted in a letter home: "Walking ten or twelve miles a day will hurt no one, but walking 12 miles and carrying a knapsack full of clothing, a blanket, half tent, several days rations, gun, ammunition, &c, is the hardest kind of work, and makes many a man wish he was not a soldier." Civil War soldiers quickly learned to jettison everything from their packs that was not absolutely essential, and still the task of marching over long distances could be crushing.[1]

Men were frequently marched through suffocating dust and under the blazing sun throughout the day, with minimal and sometimes seemingly no breaks allowed. A New York volunteer remembered that on a forced march of thirty miles in the fierce heat of summer, the men had thrown away overcoats, blankets, and even their knapsacks. Nonetheless many became violently ill from the exertion, some having convulsions and others dying from heatstroke. Another soldier recalled that during such a forced march he had to stop and vomit "every once in a while and my head ached dreadful." He vomited eight or ten times during the day, and the last time threw up blood. An overcome Indiana volunteer fell unconscious, with his eyes jerking and his tongue protruding out of his mouth in a type of epileptic fit induced by the heat. Nor were these torturous marches necessarily merely one- or two-day ordeals; an Alabama infantryman wrote to his mother: "I am not very well at this time. We have been on a march for about nine-teen days. . . . I am so near marched to death that I cannot write with any degree of intelligence, and having lost so much sleep too." The scenery on these marches was not always calculated to lighten the mental burden consequent to such physical exertion, as is demonstrated by the letter of one Rebel soldier to his wife: "i am well as common except for a bad cold and march most to death. . . . Mi dear wife i want you to pray for me i hop i will se you agin. . . . I have walked over more ded yankes than i ever want to do agin." Within two weeks this man was killed at the Battle of Antietam.[2]

Confederate troops in particular also had to deal with the problem of inadequate (or no) footwear. One Rebel surgeon lamented in a letter to his wife that she could hardly believe what the army had recently endured: "Most of our marches were on graveled turnpike roads, which were very severe on the barefooted men and cut up their feet horribly. When the poor fellows could get rags they would tie them around their feet for protection." Sometimes these forced marches lasted into or throughout the night, and soldiers literally learned to walk while asleep or would sometimes collapse from fatigue and sleep at that spot for hours, oblivious to all attempts to rouse them and force them to continue. A Massachusetts volunteer wrote: "I doubt if our ancestors at Valley Forge suffered more from cold than we did. . . . [I] often found that I had been sound asleep while my legs were trudging along."[3] Accounts of marching three hundred miles in the rain and mud, with inadequate rations and rest, only to be thrown immediately into a deadly battle are not at all unusual in Civil War letters and diaries. When the health of the Civil War soldier deteriorated to the point that he could no longer keep up with the unit on the march, he might become part of a pack of what became known as "stragglers." One account of such men described the following:

> We met hundreds of stragglers in squads of from two to fifty—indeed enough to make in themselves, if consolidated, a large army. The majority of them were sick, however, or miserably worn. Their countenances are sunken and melancholy and indifferent almost to stolidity. When left to themselves they progress very slowly, cooking their own food and sleeping upon the ground. . . . They are all thoroughly disgusted with the life they lead and swear that if ever they get out of the army they will commit suicide almost before entering it again.[4]

Such was the centrality of marching to the experience of the Civil War soldier that when some men were eventually issued disability discharges, it was not uncommon for the examining surgeon to give as the reason for such separation the fact that the man was no longer able to carry a knapsack or keep up with the army on the march. In the years following the war, Union veterans frequently claimed "sunstroke" and "hard marching" as the basis for military disability pensions—and these claims were often granted. All who had been through the experience knew exactly how trying and destructive it could be.[5]

When the hard-marching Civil War soldier reached his destination, conditions did not improve, for a constant fact of life in the Civil War era was that all soldiers, Northerners as well as Southerners, were routinely exposed to the elements. These men were expected to sleep out in the open on the ground in the middle of winter or in the midst of a driving rainstorm, oftentimes with only one blanket or the equivalent of a pup tent to fend off the damp and cold or the frost and snow. One Indiana soldier wrote in his diary: "Rained nearly all last night, woke up two or three times before day, the water was running under us so that we had to get up and sit shivering around the fire until morning." Another Hoosier volunteer's diary revealed similar circumstances: "Last night very cold, did not sleep well . . . woke from a dream crying. . . . Day rainy and gloomy. . . . Have the blues." As a Michigan volunteer reflected: "We had atuf time Last night. it rained all night and when I got up this morning my bed was wet thru this is what a soldier has got to stand." Regarding winter conditions, in letters and diaries, Civil War soldiers frequently mention waking up covered with frost or snow, and with both their boots and clothes, and even their very bodies, seeming to be frozen, requiring several hours to thaw out. Under such circumstances, a Confederate who was called to fall out in the middle of the night recalled: "I had gotten chilled and my teeth were glued together and a feeling of complete wretchedness came over me as I took my place in the ranks to march to the front." One irony was that when railroad cars were made available to transport Civil War troops, the conditions could be all the more difficult, as when men were transported on open cars throughout the night in a driving rainstorm: "We have bin shiped several hundard miles and we have done the most of it of nights right through the rain and cold on top of freitcars I have bin allmost chilled to death & have shook for hours & worse than if I had ague . . . then when we got to lay down we had to lay down wet through and cover up with a wet blanket." In pension claims after the war, one frequently encounters the expression "exposure in the army" as the claimed basis of a disability such as rheumatism or mental prostration. In reviewing the conditions that these men had to endure, one begins to understand exactly what this "exposure" was and how it shattered men's constitutions and health—a situation from which many never recovered.[6]

Soldiers shivering in the rain or snow had the added anxiety, of course, resulting from the ever-present danger of being killed by the enemy. One Confederate assigned to protect Missionary Ridge as Federal troops massed for an attack in the vicinity of Chattanooga during the winter of 1863 recalled later that he would never be able to forget the hard fight itself or the suffering endured by his comrades in the three or four weeks preceding the battle. Because the men had no tents, they had to use their blankets stretched on poles to keep the rain off; since few had more than one blanket, this left the Confederate soldiers nothing with which to cover themselves or to place over the freezing ground. They suffered intensely: "You could hear the boys praying and wishing for the fight to come if it was coming, anything to get out of the suspense and suffering caused by lack of rations and shelter." He noted that at night the only fire allowed was a few coals over which the men would warm their fingers and toes, because the light from any more substantial fire would inevitably attract the attention of enemy snipers. Undergoing a similar experience, a Union soldier wrote home to his wife that civilians could never imagine the suffering and hardships that had to be endured by the men in the ranks: "All last night they lay right out in the rain in line of battle without even their rubber blankets. May this cruel rebelion soon be crushed is the wish of every soldier."[7]

In light of the frequent rain, mud was another of the elements with which Civil War soldiers had to contend, and memoirs and letters are filled with depressing accounts of men, animals, and equipment mired in the muck. On occasion the situation was so bad that equipment sank halfway into the ooze, and had to be abandoned. One Hoosier infantryman characterized camp at Cheat Mountain in West Virginia as "this infernal mountain which is the meanest camping ground that I have ever seen," noting that the mud was not less than shoe-top deep. Another Hoosier volunteer, sent to the front shortly after the Battle of Shiloh in April of 1862, was appalled by the stench of dead bodies, and struggled with his comrades to move an artillery piece up to a bluff. The men were literally masses of sticky mud moving around, and were so tired that they were ready to lie down in the mud to sleep, which they had to do eventually anyway: "There was not a dry spot in the Country about to make camp on. Mud mud *every* where." A Confederate reminisced: "Space forbids my describing the length, depth and breadth of the mud." It seemed that both armies were usually foundering in the mud to some degree, and that the discomfort associated with wet feet was the usual state of affairs for Civil War soldiers. Sherman's men during the Carolinas campaign late in the war were described as follows: "Uniforms, worn threadbare and in rags, from head to foot were covered with mud. Their shoes were in the last stage of existence, many being held together with strings tied around them."[8]

Although the marching, rain, snow, damp, and mud clearly had a depressing effect on the spirits and health of men in Civil War armies, the psychological and physical effect of these conditions probably did not compare with the impact of infectious disease. Paul Steiner has noted that the Civil War was a form of "biological warfare" in which several hundred thousand men died of disease; because accounts of the Civil War often focus on the dash and verve of famous commanders, it is easy to forget the basic pedestrian fact that for every battle death, two men died of disease in the Civil War. Exact statistics are not available, but by most estimates about 164,000 Confederates and 250,000 Federals died of disease during the war. In the absence of a sound understanding of public health or effective medical therapies, diseases such as cholera, typhoid, malaria, smallpox, measles, mumps, scurvy, and tuberculosis, in addition to a variety of "camp fevers" and chronic diarrhea, were prevalent, frequently spread without restraint, and took a substantial toll. Although diseases such as typhoid and smallpox killed large numbers of men, dysentery and diarrhea were the great nuisance, affecting 78 percent of the soldiers annually. At times, up to two-thirds of a regiment might be on sick call at the same time, and historians have estimated that there were approximately 10 million cases of sickness (6 million for the Union Army and 4 million for the Confederates) during the Civil War, with every participant falling ill an average of four to six times.[9]

Medicine was still in its dark ages during the Civil War era, and the great advances in sanitation, germ theory, medical education and medical training, as well as the emergence of the hospital as the modern technological palace of healing, were all in the future. Of all the great advances of the nineteenth century, only anesthesia was available at this time; Koch and Pasteur were still conducting experiments in their laboratories, and Lister's precepts regarding the use of disinfectants were not yet established. Asepsis was almost half a century away, meaning that Civil War surgeons operated with germ-infested instruments; the infectious agents of disease were unknown, with the result that there was no conception that certain diseases could be communicated by air, water, or in the case of inadequate cleanliness, by touch. Moreover, tragically, the Civil War was marked by an almost total absence of any significant medical discovery or addition to existing knowledge. Civil War medical men operated in ignorance, and continued to make the same mistakes throughout the war, which often led to unnecessary suffering and death. Writing in 1905, a Civil War veteran recalled that in his youth a doctor had—astonishingly

—denied him any water during his bout with typhoid; of this ignorant and dangerous treatment, the veteran observed: "Darkness &
fog surrounded the medical profession. The doctors were then feeling
their way thru their duties, as a blind man gropes his way along a
strange street." Confidence in the medical profession was not great
in the Civil War era, as indicated by the comment of one soldier: "Dr.
seems to have been the executioner indirectly."[10]

Civil War doctors' ministrations to their troops consisted mainly
of dispensing drugs such as opium to kill pain or control chronic
diarrhea, or calomel and other purgatives to purge the system when
deemed appropriate. One physician recalled of his work in the Civil
War: "In one pocket of my trousers I had a ball of blue mass [mer-
curial ointment], in another a ball of opium. All complaints were
asked the same question, 'How are your bowels?' If they were open,
I administered a plug of opium; if they were shut I gave a plug of
blue mass." The common soldier's lack of understanding concerning
the risk of infectious disease is demonstrated by one man's account
of filling his canteen: "Nearby was a ditch that had some stagnate
water in it we poaked the Skum one side with our cups then gave
the water a spat to scare the bugs and wiglers to the bottom then
filled our canteens and returned to our Regiment."[11]

It is no shock, then, that Civil War letters and diaries report the
frequent deaths in camp of soldiers from disease (in one man's words,
the "fangs of disease") and the depressing effects of illness and death
on the troops. One soldier wrote home: "Sickness causes more deaths
in the army than Rebel lead. . . . A man here gets sick and unless he
has a strong constitution he sinks rapidly to the grave." A typical
diary of a Union soldier reported: "June 1, 1862: Sunday, On guard.
Had the tooth ache. Thomas Shepherd died. June 2, 1862: In camp.
very warm. Harry Arnold died." Another Federal noted that the unit
was losing a man a day on average, and that the roll of the muffled
drum and the blank discharge of a dozen muskets served as a solemn
reminder to the entire camp that another soldier had gone to his last
bivouac. Civil War soldiers could be haunted by the deaths of comrades, especially when they died far from home and did not receive
decent burials. Years after the war, Ben R. Johnson of the 6th Michigan
Infantry wrote of the disease and death he had witnessed in the
swamps of Louisiana, something that he would never forget:

> The enemy [was swamp fever]. . . . His slimy, cold, and merciless hand
> bore down upon us until we moaned in our anguish and prayed for

mercy . . . many comrades were stricken down in the midst of life and laid away under the accursed soil of the swamp. . . . Ask any living member of the old 6th if they remember Camp Death, and ten chances to one he will tell you its fearful perils are engraved upon memory's tablet as with a pen of iron. I wonder when I look back how any of us boys from the clime of Michigan ever escaped from the doom that hung over us in that hades of the swamp.[12]

Also hardly calculated to ease the mental stress and anxiety of Civil War soldiers was the fact that pay was often in arrears, and that, especially for Confederate soldiers, food was chronically in short supply. As one Southerner wrote his wife: "The main topic of conversation among the men is what they could eat if they had it."[13]

As devastating as marching, exposure to the elements, and disease could be, the major psychological trauma that Civil War soldiers encountered related to the terror of battle. One of the ironies of the experience of fighting men in the Civil War was that green recruits were often terribly worried that the war would end before they had a chance to experience combat; as one Confederate recalled: "I was tormented by feverish anxiety before I joined my regiment for fear the fighting would all be over before I got into it." In a similar vein, a Hoosier volunteer reminisced: "We really conceived the idea that if we could only get to the front with our six guns the whole affair would soon be settled to the entire satisfaction of our side. . . . A horrible fear took possession of all of us that the war would be over before we got to the front." Veterans, however, assured one Union Army novice that there would be sufficient action ahead: "They always advised us not to worry about not having plenty of chances to meet the enemy as we would soon get enough and plenty when spring came."[14]

Indeed, the glories of war regarded from afar were one thing, but as troops were assembled and moved to the front to enter combat, men began to experience the worst sort of nerve-wracking anxiety, fear, and tension imaginable. It was particularly difficult for men—especially new recruits—to be within earshot of the battlefield, to hear the bullets, exploding shells, and screams of the combatants, without yet being engaged. One Union man commented: "The real test comes before the battle." Rice Bull depicted the terrific anxiety of the moment as his unit awaited the order to move forward at the Battle of Chancellorsville and, while waiting, witnessed terror-stricken Union troops fleeing from the battlefield for the rear. These men had thrown away everything that was loose—guns, knapsacks, caps, and coats: "Nothing could stop them. They were crazed and would fight to escape as though the enemy were close to them. We were ordered to stop them but we might as well have tried to stop a cyclone, . . . One can hardly conceive of the terror that possessed them . . . their panic was nerve-wracking to troops new to the service." An Ohio veteran recalled his experience directly before the Battle of Winchester in 1864:

> [O]ne second you want to dash forward; the next, you want a rock or a tree to dash behind; men think by seconds and part of a second; minutes are too long to dwell on; . . . One second you are filled with anxiety; the next with fear; one second you want to, and the next you dont. At times your heart is jumping a thousand times a minute; at other times it dont seem to move at all; your knees begin to tremble; your hair to stand up so stiff that you are unable to tell if you have hair or hazel brush on your head . . . the suspense is awful . . . you have no conception of time under such conditions. You are chained; riveted to the spot; . . . we waited on and on; every minute appeared to be a full century.[15]

Some men on the line before battle could look merely solemn or even calm, but the reaction of another Union soldier seemed more typical when he recalled that a feeling of horror, dread, and fear came over him: "I was faint. . . . A glance along the line satisfied me that I was not alone in my terror; many a face had a pale, livid expression of fear." A Michigan volunteer remembered: "Some may say they never had any fear that may be true but it was not so with me I was scared . . . I was scared good and sure." Sometimes this fear was so intense that men would fall to the ground paralyzed with terror, bury their face in the grass, grasp at the earth, and refuse to move. Officers would scream and cajole and beat on these men, even striking them with bayonets, or, in extreme instances, resort to shooting them—but with no effect. Before one battle, a Union soldier noticed one man who was trembling so badly that he could not stay on his feet or hold his gun, and another who had great beads of sweat on his forehead and a fixed stare on his face. A third man threw his head back and, with mouth wide open, sang a hymn at the top of his lungs; it was understood that he was simply trying to steady himself under the well-nigh unendurable strain. Instances of men being so terrified before a battle that they lost control of their bowels were not unknown.[16]

Once men actually entered combat and began to fire their weapons, however, there was a radical transformation as fear and anxiety evaporated and gave way to rage, anger, and a sense of disembodiment. One Federal soldier recalled: "As soon as the first volley was fired all dread and sense of personal danger was gone." As the line surged forward in one assault, a Union officer noted great hysterical excitement, the eagerness to go forward, and a reckless disregard of life: "The soldier who is shooting is furious in his energy. . . . The men are loading and firing with demoniacal fury and shouting and laughing hysterically." Another Union soldier participating in such an attack heard his comrades shrieking like demons. Standing on a defensive line, Rice Bull of the 123rd N.Y. Infantry recalled that a feeling of fearlessness and rage took the place of nervousness and timidity; as the Rebel attackers approached to within twenty yards of the Union line, one soldier accidentally fired his ramrod: "He looked a good deal surprised, and shaking his fist in the direction of the Johnnies yelled, 'Take that you —— and see how you like it.' " Another Northerner observed a hellish scene: "Some of the men, with faces blackened by the powder from the tearing open of cartridges with the teeth in the act of loading their rifles, looked like demons rather than men, loading their guns and firing with a fearful, fiend-like intensity; while others, under an intense, insane excitement, would load and fire without aim." Seeing one of his comrades killed, one Union soldier remembered that a savage desire for revenge and retaliation drowned out the finer emotions, and he was eager to put this new desire into execution.

Commenting on this rage as well as an obliviousness to personal danger, Franklin H. Bailey of the 12th Michigan Infantry wrote to his parents: "Strange it may seam to you, but the more men I saw kiled the more reckless I became; when George Gates . . . was shot *I was so enraged* I could have tore the heart out of the rebal could I have reached him."[17] These wild emotional extremes could push some men to the breaking point on the battlefield itself, as in the case of one young Confederate: "I witnessed a sight I have never forgotten a member of the 14 Miss, a young boy looked to be about 15 was calling on his regt for Gods sake to reform and charge the Yankees again the tears were rolling down his face and I think he would have gone alone if an officer had not taken him to the rear."[18]

Numerous Civil War soldiers testified to the sense of disembodiment they felt during battle: when the firing began, they became oblivious of their own bodies and needs, and focused entirely on the action at hand in the battle. The matters of food, water, and comfort were forgotten, and one Northerner described what almost appeared to be an out-of-body experience. He seemed to be living out of and beyond himself, with all sympathy for suffering, all sense of bereavement having been obliterated: "Through all this din of danger I was both spectator and actor . . . there was steadily with me another feeling—a sort of double self-consciousness. This new and higher self was watching the old one I had known so long, criticising its thoughts and acts, and expressing one continual astonishment that this enthusiastic fellow, fond of ease, of home and all its peaceful joys, should be found an active participant in any deadly strife." When men were wounded, it frequently came as a complete surprise: in memoirs or letters they would describe the feeling of a sting, a "strange sensation," a feeling of being struck with an axe or a board, or of being inexplicably whirled around or knocked off their feet; sometimes the realization of having been hit came only when a soldier was no longer able to lift an arm, or when his vision was suddenly blurred by his own blood flowing into his eyes from a head wound:

> By far the larger number felt, when shot, as though some one had struck them sharply with a stick, and one or two were so possessed with this idea at the time, that they turned to accuse a comrade of the act, and were unpleasantly surprised to discover, from the flow of blood, that they had been wounded. About one-third experienced no pain nor local shock when the ball entered. A few felt as though stung by a whip at the point injured. More rarely, the pain of the wound was dagger-like and intense; while a few, one in ten, were convinced for a moment that the injured limb had been shot away.[19]

Such shell or gunshot wounds could quickly bring a man back to the reality of his own body and a sense of vulnerability, leading in some cases to panic, terror, and the fear of dying: "When hit, he thought his arm was shot off. It dropped, the gun fell, and, screaming that he was murdered, he staggered, bleeding freely, and soon fell unconscious." Those who fought on rarely experienced such vulnerability, however, and in some cases, men became so engrossed in the action that they refused to leave the front when their unit was relieved. A Confederate soldier recalled the scene after one battle: "[O]n every living face was seen the impress of an excitement which has no equal here on earth."[20]

The demoniacal appearance of the men—enraged, blackened faces, screaming, firing their rifles in a frenzy, grappling in hand-to-hand combat—was matched by the surreal aspect of the battlefield, its smoke, smell, noise, confusion, and havoc. Smokeless gunpowder had not yet been developed, so after the firing began, the Civil War battlefield was frequently enshrouded in a pall of smoke and sulphurous vapor, which severely limited one's field of vision and added to one's sense of confusion and disorientation. Appalling sounds assaulted one's senses from all directions in what one man described as the "awful shock and rage of battle," and others characterized as "that howling acre," a "portrait of hell," or a "rumbling, grinding sound that cannot be described." One veteran recalled pandemonium, and another that his ears were deafened by noise from the "crash of worlds," the "dreadful, tremendous cannonading," often compared to the sound of an earthquake or being engulfed in and having one's life threatened every moment by the most fearsome storm one could imagine. The Battle of Chancellorsville "was like two wrathful clouds had come down on the plains, rushing together in hideous battle with all their thunders and lightnings. . . . The timber was literally torn to pieces . . . with grape, canister, shot and shell." The dreadful pounding and concussion from the cannonading was such that blood gushed out of the nose and ears of one Indiana infantryman at the Battle of New Hope Church in Georgia, and numerous Civil War soldiers were permanently deafened from exposure to the concussion of cannon fire.[21]

At Chickamauga, the "rattle of musketry was dreadful and to see the men lying dead and dying on the field and being run over by artillery and lines of men it was perfectly appalling." At Spotsylvania Courthouse, "it was an awful din. The air seemed full of bullets." The cacophony of zipping bullets and bursting shells created such a maelstrom that it was impossible to shout orders so that one could be heard. An Ohio soldier recalled an atmosphere hideous with the shrieks of the messengers of death at the Battle of Franklin: "The booming of cannon, the bursting of bombs, the rattle of musketry, the shrieking of shells, the whizzing of bullets, . . . the falling of men in their struggle for victory, all made a scene of surpassing terror and awful grandeur." Of the sights and sounds of battle, one Northerner concluded: "The half can never be told—language is all too tame to convey the horror and the meaning of it all."[22]

Nor should one overrate the ability of men infuriated and obsessed with battle to screen out all horror of death. Although men concentrated on the task at hand and put personal safety aside, they still witnessed and reacted to—even if belatedly—horrific scenes of slaughter, and these sights and memories took an eventual toll. In the Civil War, innovations in weapons (particularly the rifled musket and an array of antipersonnel artillery charges) had extended the range of deadly fire on the battlefield and allowed defenders, ensconced in trenches or behind abatis and breastworks, to mercilessly shred the ranks of assaulting troops; in spite of this, however, Civil War commanders still frequently attempted to storm enemy fortifications by means of frontal assaults. The results could be deadly as attacking columns were torn and blasted by the defenders: "Brains, fractured skulls, broken arms and legs, and the human form mangled in every conceivable and inconceivable manner.... At every step they take they see the piles of wounded and slain and their feet are slipping in the blood and brains of their comrades."[23] Soldiers who participated in these scenes of slaughter would never be able to forget what they had seen. Elbridge Copp recalled that at the Battle of Deep Bottom a man standing near him was struck by a piece of a shell: "The sickening thud as it entered his body, sent a chill of horror through me, such as those only who have heard can know." In a similar vein, another soldier recalled seeing a man in the ranks in front cut down by rifle fire: "I heard the bullets chug into his body; it seemed half a dozen struck him. I shall never forget the look on his face as he turned over and died." At times the horror and shock overwhelmed men, who would flee from the battlefield in terror, for sights of the wounded could be devastating:

> A wounded man begged piteously for us to take him to the rear; he was wounded in the neck, or head, and the blood flowed freely; everytime he tried to speak the blood would fill his mouth and he would blow it out in all directions; he was all blood, and at the time I thought he was the most dreadfull sight I ever saw. We could not help him, for it was of no use, for he could not live long by the way he was bleeding.[24]

The Civil War has sometimes been portrayed as almost gentlemanly, an unfortunate war between brothers in which Union and Confederate soldiers routinely chatted with each other and exchanged newspapers or tobacco for coffee. Such incidents surely did take place, but not on the battlefield. There frenzy drove and impelled soldiers to commit acts of violence and cruelty toward their fellow men. Participating in the assault on Confederate positions at Spotsylvania Courthouse on May 12, 1864, Robert S. Robertson of the 93rd New York Infantry recalled a scene of violent chaos when the Rebel line was finally broken:

The 26th Mich. was the first to reach the breastworks, and as the line scaled the bank it was met by a volley from close quarters & recoiled with fearful loss, but only for an instant, for we pushed on, and the works were ours. The men, infuriated and wild with excitement, went to work with bayonets and clubbed muskets, and a scene of horror ensued for a few moments. It was the first time I had been in the midst of a hand to hand fight, and seen men bayonetted, or their brains dashed out with the butt of a musket, & I never wish to see another scene.[25]

On another occasion a Confederate fleeing before a Union attack at the Battle of Antietam was frantically trying to climb over a fence to escape when he was brought down by rifle fire; so infuriated were the pursuing Northerners that numerous men in their band continued to shoot or bayonet the body of the doomed Rebel, even after he was already dead.[26]

In other recorded incidents, Confederates took aim at a Federal running for his life on a battlefield several hundred yards away, and shot the man in the back, watching calmly as the stricken soldier stopped in his tracks and dropped to his knees. In another such episode, a Confederate trapped an unarmed Union soldier, who, with tears running down his cheeks, pleaded for his life while attempting to hide behind a tree; the Rebel calmly took aim and prepared to shoot and kill the Union man until he was restrained by a comrade. And, of course, once battle lines were established—whether in campaigns in Georgia or in siege warfare in the vicinity of Richmond and Petersburg, Virginia—snipers from both sides would shoot and kill any soldier who was careless enough to expose his head above the parapet: "As soon as a man showed himself during daylight a bullet would come. Not more than one shot in fifty hit its mark, but it was nerve-wracking. . . . Every day someone in the Regiment was hit."

Cases of atrocities in which prisoners of war were killed in cold blood, furthermore, were certainly not unknown in the Civil War: in some instances, the motivation was racial as Confederates killed captured African-Americans, or Northerners retaliated by killing captured Rebels. In one such instance, Union men took a Confederate prisoner only to notice a "Fort Pillow" tattoo—Fort Pillow having been the scene of the Confederate massacre of dozens of Union troops, who had surrendered, but were nonetheless slaughtered: "As soon as the boys saw the letters on his arm, they yelled, 'No quarter for you,' and a dozen bayonets went into him and a dozen bullets were shot into him. I shall never forget his look of fear." In describing the Battle of Gettysburg, Wladimir Krzyzanowski wrote that the men with their powder-blackened faces and fierce expressions looked more like animals than human beings and that they indeed had an animal-like eagerness for blood and the need for revenge. He concluded that this "portrait of battle was a portrait of hell. This, indeed, must weigh heavily on the consciences of those who started it. Terrible, indeed, was the curse that hung over their heads."[27]

The vicious disregard for human life evident at pitched battles such as Shiloh, Gettysburg, and Spotsylvania Courthouse was particularly pronounced in the guerrilla warfare that raged constantly behind the lines in Tennessee, Kentucky, Missouri, and Kansas; this guerrilla warfare is particularly relevant in assessing the claims of some that the Vietnam War was singular in the history of American warfare. Rebel guerrillas routinely blew up trains and destroyed Union property throughout the war, and in early 1865, Franklin H. Bailey of the 4th Michigan Cavalry wrote to his mother that "bushwhackers" would kill any Union soldier who strayed from his unit. Another Michigan man observed that his camp—despite being "behind the lines"—was every bit as dangerous as a battlefield: "Our lives are in danger every moment without having the satisfaction of even defending ourselves. Those Bushwhackers fire on you as they would on sparrows." In innumerable incidents, guerrillas would single out and murder African-American soldiers or shoot and kill Union troopers out foraging; they would place dead animals in ponds to poison the water and then threaten to kill anyone who removed the carcasses; utilizing their spies, they would take care not to attack an adequately guarded train, but would strike and kill unsuspecting Union soldiers and civilians on trains, boats, and elsewhere when the opportunity permitted. In Missouri and Kansas, atrocities were all too common, such as the incident in Lawrence, Kansas, in August of 1863, when marauding Rebels under the leadership of William C. Quantrill shot and killed over 150 civilian Union men and boys in cold blood. The legendary James brothers, Frank and Jesse, got their start as Confederate "raiders" or guerrillas—"murderers" in the Union Army's lexicon—in the Civil War.[28]

Under such circumstances, reprisals were common in which entire towns were shelled and destroyed or plundered in retaliation for guerrilla activity. As was the case in Vietnam, Union soldiers were frequently fired upon, but the guerrillas would scatter before they could be engaged; in these cases, Northern infantrymen would burn and pillage all houses and towns within reach: "[W]e burned all their houses & everything they had & we boys hooked everything we could carry & some things we could not." When Union soldiers found army mail in a house, they burned down the house in which they found the mail in addition to adjacent houses, and "throwd women and childern out of dores and plaid hell Generaly." In other instances, when the Union Army determined that a house had been used to harbor guerrillas or if Union men were killed in the vicinity, these houses, or even all houses within a certain radius, would be torched and the occupants ordered to leave the district. Union retaliation went beyond the destruction of property; when guerrillas were captured, they were frequently hanged with or without a trial. In some cases there would be some measure of due process, as was the case in one instance when seven Rebels were caught and held under guard pending a trial: "i think we will see them shot i could shoot them myself and would like to have the chanse." In other instances, Union men did not bother with judicial forms: "Yesterday morning a citizen came in & Sayed he had just cut the ropes & let down 3 rebles that he found hanging by the neck about one mile out of town on the Shelbyville Pike. You see our 4th Tenn boys take no prisoners, but when they come acrost the rebs they make a clean job of it." A Confederate soldier commented on the Union Army's employment of such drastic measures: "That was their way!"[29]

Did Union soldiers feel guilt over such acts of violence committed during the war? Regarding the mere observation of these executions, one notes occasional comments in letters and diaries such as "entirely beyond the pale of civilization" or "awful." Regarding the feelings of Union men who actually did the hanging or shooting, the case of John A. Cundiff of the 99th Indiana Infantry is suggestive of an answer. Cundiff had apparently been detailed to shoot a Confederate prisoner during the war, and in the years after the war, he was convinced that Rebel spies or relatives of the dead Confederate were after him. Affidavits taken by Pension Bureau officials in 1893 and 1894 revealed the following behavior:

> He has always claimed that the rebels had spies out to kill him, and would take his gun and blanket and stay in the woods for days and nights at a time, and would leave the house at night and sleep in the

fence corners. . . . He told me one day that two or three of his neighbors
were rebels from the south (there were some new people came in then)
& that they were going to kill him but that he put his axe under his bed
at night to defend himself.[30]

Cundiff's troubling memories of having shot Rebel prisoners calls to
mind the atrocities and "abusive violence" that psychologists frequently discuss in reference to Vietnam veterans.

In addition to the adverse impact on soldiers, civilians were also
affected by guerrilla violence. In Ohio, George W. Campbell was committed to the insane asylum because of fright over Morgan's Raid;
the asylum ledger noted: "When Morgan in his raid passed through
Harrison this patient was found in an upper room of his house
'wringing his hands and crying, and saying that the soldiers were
going to take and kill him. Since then most of the time he has been
indisposed to talk. He says little on any subject. The supposed exciting cause is fright.' " In Illinois, Emma D. Lawrence, a teenager, was
committed to the Jacksonville asylum in 1863 with the following notation: "Caused by a severe fright in Sept 1861. Was in a house in
Morristown Cass Co., Mo., which was attacked by Guerrillas. A nervous fever followed & insanity soon began to show itself." In addition, in considering the psychological impact of the war on civilians,
one should not overlook what foraging meant in reality, for when
Union or Confederate troops went out to collect supplies, they frequently for all intents and purposes took all a family's available food
and livestock, with or without compensation:

> I have just returned from a forage expedition across the Cumberland. . . .
> Our labors lasted three nights and days and resulted in the capture of
> one hundred and fifty loads of corn and oats. I'm afraid you wouldn't
> be so fierce if you could see us taking all the property in the world from
> heartbroken women whose husbands have been forced by circum-
> stances into the Secesh Army. A man had been taken from his bed three
> weeks ago and carried South leaving a beautiful woman, looking very
> much like Aunt Catharine twenty years ago, and five children under
> ten years old to our mercy. Of course we took her food and horses and
> left her weeping over coming starvation.[31]

Historians have often claimed that World War I was the watershed
in psychological casualties during warfare, that such casualties were
minimal before 1914 and epidemic in numbers thereafter. This argument is based on two assertions. First, soldiers of World War I,

compared with soldiers from the nineteenth century, had less training and regimentation to shield them from the horrors of war: they are viewed as industrial, "deskilled" workers/soldiers. Second, and more important, the advent of high-powered explosives shifted the nature of warfare to a situation in which as many as 70 percent of casualties resulted from artillery fire, and this killing occurred at long range, leading to a sense of dread and helplessness in infantrymen subjected to this type of bombardment. An army surgeon commented on the eve of World War I: "[T]he mysterious and widely destructive effects of modern artillery fire will test men as they have never been tested before. We can surely count then on a larger percentage of mental diseases, requiring our attention in a future war." In considering the experience of soldiers in the Civil War era, attention must therefore be paid to the attitude of infantrymen to artillery fire. A review of the evidence quickly reveals that Civil War soldiers were indeed terrified at the prospect and actuality of such bombardment, and experienced considerable psychological fear and anxiety as a result.[32]

In his first exposure to combat, Rice Bull noted the terrifying noise of a shell overhead, which, "hissing and shrieking," tore through the branches and leaves of a tree; Bull noted that the shell made everyone jump and duck. This was a nervous habit few ever fully overcame, and perhaps the basis of what may have become startle reactions, a classic symptom of PTSD, in some of these men. Other Union soldiers who witnessed artillery duels wrote of "screaming metal," which made the earth groan and tremble; one recalled that through the murk, he heard hoarse commands, the bursting of shells, and cries of agony:

> We saw caissons hit and blown up, splinters flying, men flung to the ground, horses torn and shrieking. Solid shot hit the hill in our front, sprayed battalions with fountains of dirt, and went plunging into the ranks, crushing flesh and bone. . . . The shock from a bursting shell will scatter a man's thoughts as the iron fragments will scatter the leaves overhead.[33]

The Union cannonading at Fredericksburg was so awful that the ground shook and even rabbits left their dens in the earth and came into the camps, trembling with fright. A Federal at the Battle of Chickamauga was stunned at the carnage wreaked by Union artillery on Confederate ranks, as a cannonball wiped out four lines of Rebels, making a space large enough to drive and turn around a six-mule team: "It was terrible to behold. It seemed like they had almost annihilated them." Predictably, a Confederate wrote that men subjected to artillery bombardment never forgot how to hug the ground. In addition to solid shot, Civil War soldiers particularly feared what was called canister, a load of antipersonnel shrapnel (three-quarter-inch iron balls) fired from cannons at close range on charging infantry; these projectiles frequently dismembered or disemboweled attacking soldiers.[34]

Men subjected to long-range bombardment lost the ability to calculate time objectively. Recalling a seemingly interminable Rebel artillery bombardment at Gettysburg, one Northerner commented that the thunder of the guns was incessant as the whole air seemed to be filled with rushing, screaming, and bursting shells: "Of course, it would be absurd to say we were not scared. . . . How long did this pandemonium last? Measured by our feelings it might have been an age. In point of fact it may have been an hour or three or five. The measurement of time under such circumstances, regular as it is by the watch, is exceedingly uncertain by the watchers." Another Union soldier reflected that in the space of a mere two seconds on the approach of a shell, thoughts and images of all types of possible mutilation and death occupied the minds of men, and that if one wrote for an entire day afterward, one could not completely express these myriad fears and terrors as they had run through the mind the instant before impact.

These horrific scenes and emotions were forever burned into the memories of the men who huddled in their trenches or "bombproofs" praying that they would not be annihilated by a direct hit. During Sherman's Atlanta Campaign, one Northerner commented that if he lived a hundred years, he would never forget the fearful night in which "all the earth and sky semed on fire and in a struggle for life or death. . . . The earth seems crashing into ten thousand atoms . . . the world about us seem[ed] like a very hell. . . . The cries of the wounded and dying murdered all sleep for me that night." Terrified men wrote of the "death dealing cannon," of cannons "belching forth their deadly contents," of "villainous" artillery, of artillery as a "messenger of death." As happens with men subjected to such terror (and is perhaps instructive regarding the attitude toward Vietnam), some soldiers were convinced that what they were experiencing was completely unprecedented. They claimed, for instance, that the barrage at Gettysburg surpassed anything in ancient or modern history. A Rebel subjected to artillery bombardment during the siege of Vicksburg characterized the situation as desperate and talked of certain death. He noted that the troops had behaved nobly, but couldn't stand it much longer: "Night is almost as bad as day. The air is filled with missiles of destruction." Of a Union artillery barrage, another Rebel wrote: "O Sister I can not pertend to discribe it."[35]

Aside from dead soldiers or mangled bodies, what were the psychological repercussions of this horrific cannon fire? Artillery and high explosives produced a number of psychiatric casualties in the Civil War that seemed at times almost identical to the hysterias, mutism, and uncontrollable shaking produced by the barrages on the Western Front in World War I. One nurse recounted the case of a man buried alive in the terrific explosion of a Union mine at Petersburg in 1864, when Union sappers had attempted to breach the Confederate defenses by placing a huge load of high explosives in a mine shaft under the Rebel lines: "[He] was buried alive in the explosion of the mine at Petersburg and has lost hearing, speech and almost all sensation. He has a piteous expression of face and makes signs, as best he can, of gratitude for even a look of sympathy." Another man almost struck by a shell fragment which narrowly missed his head "went all to pieces, instantly" and was described as completely "demoralized, panic-stricken and frantic with terror." In a similar incident, a man who had been chattering away before a shell shrieked overhead and landed nearby was left completely speechless. When shelling began in another instance, an officer begged a companion: "For Gods sake dont leave me."

Perhaps the most striking case, however, is that of Albert Frank. Sitting in a trench near Bermuda Hundred in the vicinity of Richmond, Virginia, Frank offered a drink from his canteen to a man sitting next to him. Frank kept the strap around his own neck and extended the canteen to the other man's mouth for him to take a drink, but at just this moment a shell decapitated the other man, splattering blood and brain fragments on Frank. The shell continued on, exploded to the rear of the trench, and in no way directly injured Frank. That evening, Albert Frank began to act strangely, and a fellow soldier advised that he go to the bomb shelter; once there Frank began screaming, ran out the other door, and went over the top of the breastworks toward the enemy. His fellow soldiers, alarmed, went looking for him, and eventually found him huddled in fear. On the way back to Union lines, he seemed to go mad: "[H]e would drop his gun, and make a noise like the whiz of a shell, and blast and say 'Frank is killed.' " Because he had completely lost control, his comrades tied him up that night to restrain him and took him to the doctor the next day. There he was declared insane, and sent to the Government Hospital for the Insane in Washington, D.C.[36]

Also deeply affected after artillery fire was John Bumgardner of the 26th Indiana Light Artillery. At Dalton Hill, Kentucky, he was knocked down by the concussion of an exploding shell, and other soldiers at the scene noticed that he was shaken and pale; after returning to camp, he was morose and sullen and continued to tremble for weeks. He talked constantly about fighting when there was no enemy in sight, and would suddenly start yelling: "There they come men run boys run they are after us." He was eventually sent to the insane asylum at Lexington, Kentucky.[37] The Civil War experience seems to confirm the theory that soldiers in a passive position of helplessness—such as those subjected to artillery bombardments—feel intense terror and anxiety, and may be at great risk for psychological breakdown. Although the experience of World War I might have intensified this phenomenon, it certainly did not originate it.

While exposure to artillery fire and the sights and sounds of a battle in progress could be unnerving in the extreme, perhaps the most horrific aspect of the Civil War experience was the scene of the battlefield after the firing had subsided. Mangled men, dead and dying, littered the landscape; the wounded would frequently plead for water and medical attention, and an occasional man, terminally wounded, would beg to be shot and put out of his misery. One North Carolina soldier wrote that after the heat and excitement of the battle ended and the smoke cleared away, the battlefield presented a harrowing scene that beggared description: "The grim monster death having done its terrible work leaves its impress on the faces of its unfortunate victims . . . now wrapt in the cold embrace of death." A Confederate described the scene at Chickamauga as ghastly, with hundreds of dead on the field, their faces upward and some with their arms sticking up as if reaching for something. According to a Maine volunteer, the dead were lying about as thickly as if they were slumbering in camp: "[T]he sight was most appalling . . . the horror of such a picture can never be penned." A Rebel recalled that after the Battle of Seven Pines in 1862 many Union wounded were too weak to pull themselves out of ditches, which were full of water because of inordinately heavy rains; judging by the sounds he heard, these men seemed to be drowning and strangling to death: "The cries of the wounded Yankees sound in my ears yet."[38]

After fierce fighting in Georgia in 1864, a Rebel walked over the field and saw the dead piled four deep. Some guns were still standing on end, their bayonets having been driven through the bodies of victims, giving ample evidence of the awful conflict that had gone before. Of the field at Shiloh, a Hoosier noted that dead men seemed to be everywhere: "You could find them in every hollow, by every tree and stump—in open field and under copse—Union and Rebel, side by side—in life foes, in death, of one family." The psychological effect of these scenes could be devastating, as evidenced by one Confederate, who characterized the battlefield at Franklin, Tennessee, as one vast slaughter pen: "After gazing on it I felt sick at heart for days afterwards. . . . The men were so disheartened by gazing on that scene of slaughter that they had not the nerve for the work before them." In a similar vein, a Northerner wrote: "It was a scene that I wish never again to behold. I have had enough of War." Nor did these impressions fade with time; a Union soldier wrote decades after the war that the Shiloh battlefield had shocked and disheartened him: "Tho it now lacks but two days of forty two years since that morning, the picture has not faded in the least . . . it was a rude awakening to the realities of an active War Service." He characterized this scene as the "real stuff good & strong." After attempting to describe such a scene, a Michigan volunteer ended a letter to his sister: "I cannot comment more, nor dwell on the subject. *I am so unwell.*"[39]

As with recruits aching for a fight, Civil War soldiers had a great curiosity to see what a battlefield looked like. One such experience was usually satisfactory, as indicated by the account of Calvin Ainsworth of the 25th Iowa Infantry:

> I went over the field of battle as soon as possible after the surrender. At some points it was terrible. My eyes never beheld such a sight before. I hope they may never again. In some places the dead lay very thick, not more than 3–5–10 feet apart; some were shot in the head, others in the breast and lungs, some through the neck, and I saw 3 or 4 torn all to pieces by cannon balls; their innards lying by their side, ... It is indeed a sickening sight, . . . I had often wished that I could be in one battle and go over a battle field. My curiosity has been gratified. I never wish to see another.[40]

Twentieth-century research into psychiatric disorders associated with military service has indicated that soldiers attached to the Graves Registration Detail (that is, those who handle dead bodies) often experience psychological problems related to this work, and, in the Civil War era, duty with burial details could indeed produce psychological distress. One man noted that he helped to bury the dead after a battle, and it was, to say the least, a disagreeable job: "i helped to bury Some that was tore in pieces and throwed in every direction one leg here and another there wee Just had to gather up the pieces and fix them away the best wee could wee caried a hundred and fifty together and dug a big ditch. . . . i never want to See another battle field." The bodies of the dead would sometimes lie on the field for several days before they were buried, creating an unbearable stench. Particularly during the summer, this would result in scenes of sun-baked and putrefied bodies: "These corpses were so black that we, at first glance, thought they were negroes; but they had lain in the hot August sun all the day before and all this day and had been burned black and were in a state of loathsome corruption and covered with living vermin. . . . Our task of burying these poor fellows was loathsome and disgusting."[41] The attempts of Civil War soldiers to describe the carnage of the battlefield seemed time and again to end with phrases such as "pen cannot properly describe this valley of death, it was too horrible"; "the horrors of a battle field cannot be described, they must be seen"; "[t]he most shocking sight I ever saw"; "ghastly"; "O what a sight, it almost makes me shudder to think of it"; "I am shure I would not want you to witness the sight I did."[42]

Last of all, in assessing the psychological trauma to which Civil War soldiers were exposed, one should consider the ritual execution of deserters. In the Vietnam era, executing deserters would have been an utter impossibility—completely unthinkable. In the Civil War, however, hundreds of such men were shot to death by the military, and these executions were staged in ceremonies calculated to terrify the men remaining in the ranks, so as to discourage others from engaging in such behavior. The temptation to desert did, of course, exist, as one might imagine after considering the situation regarding marching, exposure to the elements, lack of adequate clothing and food, the prevalence of disease, and the horrors of battle.[43]

When executions were staged, the men in the regiment were lined up on three sides, and the condemned man was placed on top of his coffin and brought to the grounds by wagon; after the man was shot to death by the firing squad, the entire company of men was paraded by the bullet-riddled body. At times, the man executed would then be buried on the spot and the ground above smoothed over with no marker, to further terrify onlookers with the prospect not only of death, but eternal oblivion. On most occasions, men who were forced to witness these executions were appalled and deeply disturbed. One Confederate soldier witnessed an execution at which the condemned man begged piteously for his life, but was nonetheless tied to a stake and shot; the Rebel observer called it "one of the most sickening scenes I ever witnessed . . . [it] looked more like some tragedy of the dark ages, than the civilization of the nineteenth century." A Union soldier who witnessed such an execution wrote in his diary: "I call it murder in the first degree in taking his life. I don't think I will ever witness another such a horror if I can get away from it. I have seen men shot in battle but never in cold blood before." A New Hampshire volunteer was equally stunned: "I venture to say it was [a scene] never to be forgotten while life lasted, with any who witnessed it. There the body lay, the clothing stripped from the breast revealing it perforated with bullets." Writing forty years after the end of the war, a Hoosier veteran remembered that it had taken him a long time to mentally recover from the shocking sight of an execution he had witnessed so many years before: "To me it was a dreadful thing to see a human being sat on a box, blindfold & his life taken in such a savage barbarous manner. I have long since disbelieved in capital punishment, & this affair was, I think, the forerunner of this disbelief." Another Civil War soldier summed up the entire experience: "War is horrid beyond the conception of man."[44]

"A Gizzard Full of Sand":
Reactions to Violence

Civil War historians have often pointed out that green troops were the most likely to flee in terror at the beginning of a battle, but that once these men had been "blooded," or hardened through exposure to combat, they performed steadily and coolly under fire, for the most part seeming immune to panic. Other writers have asserted that enthusiastic welcoming parades at the end of the war for Union soldiers, or the Lost Cause's continuing adulation for Confederate veterans, minimized any troubling memories of combat: "How quickly in victory is atrocity forgotten! In one great victory parade, all death and filth and thieving were painted over with the brush of glory." Could it be, then, that although the Civil War involved a significant amount of trauma from physical hardship, disease, and the shock of battle, its soldiers and veterans escaped the kind of post-traumatic stress experienced in the Vietnam era? A close review of available evidence concerning Civil War soldiers and veterans indicates that they did not escape this misfortune, and that these men did indeed suffer from what we would today think of as PTSD, of both the acute and the delayed type.[1]

It is certainly true that after their first exposure to death and battle, many Civil War soldiers testified that while initially shocked they were now "getting used to it," and horrific sights, sounds, and smells no longer bothered them. An Illinois volunteer was so used to men dying in camp of disease that he commented on one funeral that there was a mere prayer but no volleys at the grave: "The boys were anxious to get back to pitching quoits even [the deceased soldier's] own mess. It is a little strange how dull a man's sensibilities will get &

this war will do it so quick"; a Hoosier remembered that irreverent and wicked remarks at such ceremonies were not unusual. A Michigan soldier noted that after men had been in the service for six months, the death of a comrade made little change in their conversation or thoughts.[2]

Regarding exposure to combat, the undeniable reality of the Civil War was that after the tedium of camp, with men sitting around watching their comrades die of disease one by one, most soldiers were initially enthusiastic at the prospect of starting a campaign: "Our men are getting sick, and the surgeons say better advance and take the chances of battle than wait here for a certainty of death by disease. . . . Active campaigning in pleasant weather is certainly more agreeable than inactive Camp life. The same old routine day after day is a great bore." Once in battle, veterans did seem to handle the stress better than newcomers; the conscripts and raw recruits seemed to be apprehensive and fearful while the veterans had already accustomed themselves to combat. Astonished by the nonchalance of troops directly before the disastrous Union attack at the Crater near Petersburg in 1864, an army surgeon wrote with some wonder that the men were lying down in the line of battle with their guns at their sides, cartridge boxes and belts on: "They were all sleeping soundly, sleeping as if they did not know that at daybreak they were to charge the enemy and that for many of them it was to be their last sleep on earth. The men had become used to the near presence of death." Seemingly inured to the sights and sounds of battle, a veteran bragged to his parents that he did not mind seeing human blood anymore than that of animals, and that as he was running through the field on one occasion he had seen a man directly in front get his brains shot out, and he had not found this upsetting. After the firing had subsided, observers frequently noted that soldiers would camp on a battlefield in the midst of dozens of dead bodies without being bothered, even going so far in one instance to use corpses as head rests: "One of our regiments had camped in some woods there and the men were lying among the dead Yankees and seemed unconcerned." Noting the result of this phenomenon of hardening, Rice Bull characterized Sherman's men as "hard as iron, toughened by an active campaign of more than three years. This is a feeble description of them as they marched with no attempt to make a show."[3]

In their own minds, men would reach an accommodation with the cruelty and carnage of warfare, and persevere sometimes through prayer ("I uttered a short prayer leaving my safety with Him who can save and again brought my mind to common temperance"), a belief in divine protection ("[t]he Lord has been with me in the hour of danger. On the battle field His strong arm has been my protector and my shield"), religious fatalism ("I feel as though if I am cut down all will be well with me.... I am ready to go"), belief in the odds ("[o]ut of 100 who go to battle maybe 10 are killed or wounded. Of those 10 wounded ones one dies"), a sense of invulnerability ("[the soldier believes] he is immune. It is the buoyancy of youth, ... To him, it is always the man in the next rank who is to be the victim"), or simple devotion to one's comrades ("ties of affectionate friendships were formed that bind us into one brother-hood by an invisible chain").[4]

The bluster and apparent ruggedness of the veteran should not always be taken at face value, however; when one carefully examines accounts of men professing to be unconcerned about the dangers and terrors of war, one often discovers that these stoic declarations of indifference hid a deeper fear and horror, held at bay for the time being, but lurking within nonetheless. Washington Ives of the 4th Florida Infantry noted that he shot twenty men in one battle, saw men slaughtered without experiencing any shock or dread, and felt that he had been hardened and was oblivious to fear or emotion; yet, after a year of this, he wrote to his sisters that it made him sad to see an old warrior regiment on the march with its battle flag frayed and full of holes from many hard engagements, and with only fifty men (rather than the original thousand) marching in the ranks. Another Confederate who had seen and endured years of death felt a stab of sorrow on contemplating the fate of men, many of whom he knew would soon be dead:

> While waiting at Corinth, some of Hood's infantry, some Texas troops, were aboard a train of flat cars, headed eastward, which stood for sometime on the track and I watched them from a seat near by. They were a very hardened, ill-clothed, dirty-looking set of fellows—but were laughing and jeering and cursing as if there were nothing serious in life—or death.
>
> As I stood and looked at these poor fellows, so hardened, so Godless, and probably so soon to die, I felt oppressed with a feeling of pain and sadness, which comes back to me in some degree even to this day [1901] when I think of them.

A Rebel declared in a letter to his aunt that he had become accustomed to the sights of war, which no longer bothered him, but, in describing the Seven Days' Battles in the same letter, he wrote of a field strewn with dead Northerners: "It was a sight that I never shall forget!" Even Wade Hampton, the legendary Confederate cavalry commander and Reconstruction leader in South Carolina, who showed no lack of bravery or verve in leading his men, wrote at one point that the Civil War was the most atrocious and unnatural war ever waged, and if it did not soon cease, its horrors would exceed those of any previous war recorded in history: "It is fearful. And the sights after a battle are too horrible to think of. I want to see no more of them." Another Rebel who had fought successfully throughout the war without breakdown, recalled years later that whenever he thought of the bloody Battle of Perryville, "the tears roll down my cheeks and I cannot force them back now while writing this article. . . . Some claimed that they never dreaded a battle and some claimed to have a gizzard full of sand."[5]

Although hardened Civil War soldiers frequently adjusted to combat to the point where they could watch without apparent emotion while others were cut down in battle, the situation might be radically different if the victim were a close friend or comrade. As one soldier remembered: "Who can describe the feeling of a soldier on going into battle. I do not fear for myself but dread seeing others shot down . . . for whom I have a feeling of a brother and we know some of us must die the death of a soldier." A Michigan infantryman came across a close friend from his unit, seriously wounded on the battlefield, and stopped to help the stricken man:

I soon found myself with my dying Brother. I stooped to his ear & called his name, but no answer. . . . Taking my handkerchief from my pocket I wiped his brok forehead washing it with my tears. All this time I was unconscious of the dangers I was in[.] a shell buzzed close to my head from one of the rebble guns brought me to my sences. I curled myself down close to the ground & stayed some time with my Dying Brother When I left him the last spark of life seemed to have gon. I was obliged to leave him amidst the rore of battle. Here was a trying time for me; To leave one I Loved with a most tender & brotherly affection Leave him on the battle field in the cold embrace of death & in an enamyes land I bid farewell to him for this world Hoping to meet him at the judgemant seat of Christ with his sins washed & made white by the blood of the lamb.[6]

A Confederate on a scouting party witnessed the death of his younger brother, who was killed instantly and never spoke, "but looked straight at me, with a silent understanding reflected in his eyes, and I caught him as he fell." He carried his brother's body sixty miles back to camp, and then to his home in Mississippi for burial. Even decades later, this veteran wrote: "[H]is tragic and pathetic passing from life left in my heart a burning scar which the long years, with their submerging floods of joy and sorrow, have never wiped out." Sometimes the most difficult time came in burying one's slain comrades after a battle. Civil War soldiers would often inter the dead of the enemy in one large trench, but tried when possible to bury their own dead in individual graves, frequently with pine boughs at the bottom of the grave, a rolled blanket under the head, and a handkerchief over the face of each dead soldier to lend a shred of dignity, no matter how meager, to the scene. One Northerner recalled intense sadness at witnessing such an event, and another Union man wrote of burying men from his own company, men he had known, respected, and loved as fellow soldiers: "We have looked upon such scenes before; but then the faces were strange to us. Now they are the familiar faces of intimate personal friends, to whom we are indebted for many kindly acts. We hear convulsive sobs, see eyes swollen and streaming with tears."[7]

American military experts observed in World War II that there is no such thing as "getting used to combat": "Each moment of combat imposes a strain so great that men will break down in direct relation to the intensity and duration of their exposure . . . psychiatric casualties are as inevitable as gunshot and shrapnel wounds in warfare."[8] One can see this principle operate in the Civil War, both after each battle and cumulatively over time. After the commotion of battle and the attendant adrenaline rush had subsided, there was frequently something akin to physical collapse as many Civil War soldiers felt completely exhausted and sometimes ached all over; they realized for the first time in hours that they had overwhelming thirst, that their clothes were muddy and drenched with sweat, or that their faces were blackened, covered with gunpowder. Sometimes men would drop on the spot and sleep in the midst of dead bodies on the field—which reflected not so much diminished sensibilities as complete physical prostration after the incredible exertion and emotional tempest of a battle.[9]

At such a time, many Civil War soldiers could feel a coincident sense of depression, sagging morale, or sudden vulnerability. Following the slaughter at Chickamauga, a Hoosier volunteer wrote: "[T]hat night I never shall forget. the remnant of us gathered in that low dark valley, with but little fire, little grub & less than little appetite to eat what we had. solemn was the theme of our conversation." For some, the physical effects of fear would register for the first time: "[W]hen the firing ceased, I was unaware of the strain and excitement I had been under, until we were ordered to move, when I found that I was in a tremble all over." Others experienced an acute sense of vulnerability: "[I]t almost makes me shudder to think of [the Battle of Shiloh], although at the time, I did not think any more of seeing a man shot down by my side than you would of seeing a dumb beast kiled." Another soldier reflected:

> The survivor . . . cannot but wonder for the rest of his life how or why he did not go with the unfortunate instead of being a survivor of it all. When the fire is heavy, one forgets the danger and instinctively follows his call for duty. When he has time to think is the time of greatest danger of running away . . . in every campaign or rather every battle there comes a time when the bravest may say I can do no more.[10]

In reading the memoirs or letters of these soldiers, one often sees a progression in each life from an initial carefree optimism about "soldiering" to a growing weariness and sense of vulnerability. Samuel Merrill, a colonel in the 70th Regiment of Indiana Volunteers, who initially was highly critical of the enlisted men who seemed to be shirking duty, himself turned up sick, seeking a medical discharge. In one of his letters, he noted that even if one remained quiet, the constant firing and the continued waiting exhausted every fiber of one's body and spirit: "Scarcely a night passes without an attack and no words coined on earth can describe the terrific nature of such affairs. . . . When will this horrible noise cease?" Aden G. Cavins, a captain with the 59th Regiment of Indiana Volunteers, in his early service reviled men running from the battlefield, but after exposure to combat noted "there is a point beyond which few can go." While on duty with Sherman in Georgia, after two years of service, he wrote, "it seems almost strange that I am alive" and later "[t]hose that have stood by me in these conflicts do not believe that many of us will see the end of this campaign." Also participating in the campaign through Georgia, General Alpheus S. Williams wrote to his family that for more than a month he had been literally under fire day and night, and the din of war had ceaselessly gone on: "Early in the war I had a curiosity to ride over a battlefield. Now I feel nothing but sorrow and compassion, and it is with reluctance that I go over these sad fields."[11]

This increasing sense of vulnerability in the troops by 1864 coincided tragically with a new way of fighting. The pattern early in the war had been for the two sides to meet briefly in a one- or two-day clash, such as the battles of First Bull Run, Antietam, or Chickamauga, and then step back to lick wounds and reassess the strategic position. By 1864, however, in what most Civil War historians characterize as a shift to "total war" methods, Union forces under both Ulysses S. Grant in the East and William Tecumseh Sherman in the West embarked on extended campaigns to wear down the Confederate armies; unlike earlier methods, the Union forces now remained engaged from day to day with their Rebel foes and attacked constantly. In the West, Sherman favored a strategy of swinging his army around the Confederate flanks to maneuver the Rebels out of one position after another in what the military theorist B. H. Liddell-Hart referred to as the "indirect method." Sherman, however, also engaged in a fierce frontal assault against well-entrenched Confederates at the Battle of Kennesaw Mountain, Georgia, and fended off the suicidal lunges of the Rebel general John Bell Hood in a series of desperate and bloody battles in the vicinity of Atlanta. A Union general described the sheer difficulty of the drive toward Atlanta in the West:

> From our crossing the Etowah, the Rebs. have entrenched themselves every five miles. Driven from one line, they would fall back to another and each one seemed stronger than the last. If you could see the obstructions they place in front of their strong lines of dirt and log breast works you would wonder that any attempt should be made to carry them. The country is all woods, deep ravines, muddy creeks, and steep hills, the most defensible positions by nature I have ever seen, and they most skillfully bring art to aid nature . . . making a network through which a man could hardly crawl in an hour. Just imagine a line of armed men making their way through and thousands of rifles firing upon it![12]

Grant's frontal assaults in the East at the Wilderness, Spotsylvania Courthouse, and Cold Harbor are legendary, and resulted in 65,000 casualties in seven weeks. In the trenches at Spotsylvania at a salient which came to be known as the "Bloody Angle," a close-range struggle in the mud began on May 12, 1864, before dawn and lasted until nearly midnight; dead bodies were trampled out of sight in the sodden ground as the conflict raged on. Men were literally driven insane in this battle, and over one hundred cases were recorded by Union surgeons of soldiers who shot off their own fingers or toes, seeking a medical discharge to escape the slaughter. A Confederate who experienced the chaos and slaughter at the Bloody Angle at Spotsylvania Courthouse wrote to his wife:

> The musketry and cannon continued from daybreak until night. Nothing that I have ever before heard compared with it. We were behind breastworks, but the Yankees charged into them in many places, fighting with the greatest determination, and it strained us to the utmost to hold our own. Such musketry I never heard before, and it continued all night, . . . It was perfectly fearful. I never experienced such anxiety in my life. It was an awful day, and it seemed to me as if all the "Furies of Darkness" had come together in combat. Everybody who was not firing was pale with anxiety, but our noble soldiers stood their ground, fighting with the utmost desperation. . . . I will try to write you a longer letter when my mind gets settled.[13]

Later, at Cold Harbor, in an infamous frontal assault, Grant threw his men at well-entrenched Rebel formations and suffered almost 7,000 casualties in less than one hour.

This fighting led eventually to the environs of Richmond and Petersburg, Virginia, where Grant laid siege, developing a type of trench warfare that foreshadowed conditions on the Western Front in World War I. Both sides lived in the trenches (or in "bomb-proofs") and were subject to twenty-four-hour-a-day bombardment as well as deadly sharpshooters, who would shoot and kill any man foolish enough to stick his head above the parapet: "On neither side do the men dare show their heads above the entrenchments, for it is almost sure death to do so. . . . Death was as familiar as our rations of hard tack." One Northerner characterized Grant's men as "played out," and a Rebel diary revealed that the situation on the other side of the line was no better: "[T]he Yankey shell us evey nite [They] thro thar shls from 5 to 6 miles We go in the gun proof thar shootin . . . the solgers her is giten tired of the war they say thay cant stand ite much lounger." The necessity of charging fortified positions, the trench warfare, the constant bombardment and attacking all took a heavy toll on Union and Confederate troops in the last year of the war. It seems that the paradigm of "hardening" in the Civil War should at a minimum be augmented by the idea of the "exhausted," "played out," or, indeed, "stressed out" Civil War soldier.[14]

In considering the role of stress disorders in the Civil War, one should also consider the plight of doctors and nurses. Much of the drive since the 1980s to bring recognition to the women who served in Vietnam as nurses has been based on the fact that these women were exposed to harrowing and disturbing scenes of mutilated and dying men, rushed directly to the operating room by helicopter from the battlefield. After having performed their duties stoically, the American nurses in Vietnam took many troubling memories home with them—and then wrestled with these images in private for several decades. In examining the letters and memoirs of Civil War nurses and doctors, one discovers a similar experience of women and men who, devoted to duty, quickly responded to the medical needs of badly wounded men, but who, over time, developed symptoms of what we would today think of as PTSD.[15]

Dozens and dozens of accounts of Civil War hospitals mention horrific scenes in which wounded men in every condition conceivable—shattered and shrieking—were brought in on stretchers to be tended by the overworked medical staff. With an unendurable stench pervading the air, mangled men, some with limbs already rotted by gangrene, covered the floor and flowed out into the yard as blood-splattered surgeons hoisted the next screaming victim onto the "operating table"—frequently a door propped up on tables— and, as their assistants held the struggling patient down, sawed away furiously to amputate an arm or leg. Buckets of blood and piles of amputated arms, legs, and feet littered the ground, and the groans or haunting death appeals of the mortally wounded rang forever in the ears of all those who were there. Kate Cumming, a Confederate nurse, wrote in her diary that a colleague had tried to prepare her for the scenes which she would witness upon entering the wards: "But alas! nothing that I had ever heard or read had given me the faintest idea of the horrors witnessed here. I do not think that words are in our vocabulary expressive enough to present to the mind the realities of that sad scene." A man professing to be accustomed to the sights of a battlefield visited a hospital and declared it to be the saddest day of his life.[16]

Those men and women who ministered to these stricken soldiers often suffered from stress reactions, including flashbacks and intrusive recollections. After visiting a hospital, Mary Boykin Chesnut wrote in her diary: "Oh, such a day! Since I wrote this morning, I have been with Mrs. Randolph to all the hospitals. I can never again shut out of view the sights I saw there of human misery. I sit thinking, shut my eyes, and see it all." A man assigned the task of taking piles of amputated arms and legs to a trench for burial endured the job for one day and then fled, unable to bear another moment of such work. Rice Bull went to the hospital to care for an ill comrade from his company, and when the man had been restored to health, the surgeons asked Bull if he could stay to become a permanent member of the hospital staff; he politely declined and years later wrote in his memoirs: "Nothing could have induced me to continue in that work. . . . It made a deep and lasting impression not easily forgotten." One nurse, speaking of "overtaxed nerves," found herself overcome with tears, "which had been kept under control amid all I had witnessed for so many days."[17]

Kate Cumming would typically stay up all night tending to the soldiers, either bathing their wounds or talking with them to comfort them in their moment of anguish. She wrote that she was frequently completely worn out, and would sometimes collapse in exhaustion and finally sleep after days of labor. Although she thought herself becoming used to the scenes and routines of the hospital, she would write again and again of yet another horrible and depressing turn of events, as when a soldier was brought in with a wound to the face that startled and upset even the veteran nurses, or when another soldier was brought in with a head wound involving oozing brains that presented a "hideous spectacle." On April 23, 1862, she wrote: "I often wish I could become as callous as many seem to be, for there is no end to these horrors." On a hot day, she wrote that she was tired and bothered by the noise and confusion: "[I]t is almost impossible to collect one's thoughts." Awaiting the arrival of a trainload full of casualties from the front, she wrote: "This anxiety is enough to kill any one." She frankly discussed being depressed, melancholy, completely demoralized, and having disturbing dreams: "O, I felt so sad! visions of the terrible past would rise in review before me—the days, weeks and months of suffering I had witnessed—and all for naught. Many a boyish and manly face, in the full hey-day of life and hope, now lying in the silent tomb." Yet she persisted, and was an effective nurse; she found her work important and rewarding, and something she could not abandon.[18]

Civil War surgeons are often presented as heartless automatons, sawing limbs without mercy or feeling; one soldier commented after witnessing amputations in a makeshift hospital assembled in a barn that it required a man with a steel nerve and a case-hardened heart to be an army surgeon. The memoirs and letters of army doctors, however, make it clear that these men were constantly struggling with their emotions, and valiantly attempting to do their job effectively under miserable and depressing circumstances. Upon losing his first patient, one Union doctor wrote that he took this death very much to heart. While doctors thereafter might seem to adjust to death and suffering, stress reactions were still common.[19]

Thrown into service during the slaughterhouse of the Union Army's assault against Robert E. Lee and the Army of Northern Virginia from the Wilderness to Cold Harbor in the summer of 1864, John G. Perry, a surgeon for the 20th Massachusetts Infantry, wrote that ten days of continuous fighting had produced a stream of steady casualties into the unit hospital. He wrote: "I am so exhausted and nervous it is difficult to express myself; am operating day and night. This thing cannot last much longer." By the time the Union Army reached the South Anna River, he scribbled that he was up to his elbows in blood, that he only had time to sleep one night out of three, and that even then he found himself exhausted but too nervous to sleep. Two hours of fighting at Cold Harbor produced four days of steady operating for Dr. Perry: "I am heartsick over it all." At Petersburg, he described war as a "perfect maelstrom of horror": "I am up to my neck in work. It is slaughter, slaughter. . . . War! war! war!" Dr. Perry was eventually discharged from the army, ostensibly owing to his wife's ill health, although one suspects that he had simply reached the limits of his endurance.[20]

A Confederate surgeon recalled a time when he began operating at 3:00 P.M. in the afternoon and was not relieved until 5:30 A.M. the next morning. Characterizing it as a "horrible night," he worked without food, was sustained only by nervous energy, and finally had to stop: "I could do no more. I went out by myself and leaning against a fence, I wept like a child. And all that day I was so unnerved that if any one asked me about the regiment, I could make no reply without tears." Many surgeons were driven to use alcoholic beverages, either to dull the mental anguish or to get to sleep at night, as one Confederate surgeon recalled: "I would wake up cold during the night and reach out for a jug of whiskey and take a swallow and go back to sleep again." Civil War health care personnel, in the midst of demanding and unrelenting schedules, thus shared the risk of developing stress disorders related to witnessing disturbing scenes of death and suffering.[21]

The last group of soldiers one should consider in any examination of stress disorders in the Civil War era are the prisoners of war (POWs). Extensive studies of POWs from World War II and the Korean War have revealed that the difficult conditions of boredom, monotony, and deprivation, particularly if combined with physical cruelty, disease, and significant weight loss, could result in serious psychological problems that lingered and intensified in the years following the end of the war. There were approximately 137,000 American POWs in World War II and the Korean War, and while 99 percent of American POWs held by the Germans survived the war, only 60 percent held by the Japanese in World War II or by the North Koreans in the Korean War survived. In general, World War II POWs suffered from two types of injury: one was somatic (from, for instance, accidents, tuberculosis, and cirrhosis of the liver) and primarily short-term (the period of increased risk lasted about ten years), and the other was psychological and essentially permanent.[22]

Studies of World War II POWs have indicated postwar PTSD rates of anywhere from 46 to 90 percent, with some psychologists determining that weight loss and torture were the best predictors for the development of this psychopathology.[23] Particularly the POWs in Japanese and Korean control, who suffered significant weight loss of from 18 to 30 percent below their precaptivity weight, may have suffered from what has come to be known as the K-Z syndrome (first observed in concentration camp survivors), a persistent defective state, caused by trauma-induced weight loss and associated with cortical dysfunction and lessened intellectual efficiency. Starvation and profound weight loss can—in the opinion of some—cause structural changes in the brain, which permanently affect a person's intellectual abilities and emotional responses.[24]

During the early years of the Civil War, prisoners of war were typically kept in captivity by each side only a number of days before they were returned pursuant to what was called a prisoner of war cartel, signed and adhered to by both the North and the South. In accordance with these procedures, captured men would promptly be released, or "paroled," upon signing a pledge not to engage in further hostilities until they had been officially "exchanged." Frequently these men were returned to their own military where they would reside in camps specifically designated as holding areas for POWs who had been paroled but not yet formally exchanged. Once "exchanged" on paper, the soldier would then be free to return to his own unit and resume his military assignments. In the first three years of the war, it was somewhat unusual to see a POW held by the enemy for more than thirty days, and the typical period of captivity was generally a week or less.

In 1864, however, the situation changed radically as the POW cartel collapsed, and men were no longer quickly and routinely returned to their own side after capture. The basic impasse related to African-American soldiers: beginning in 1862 and reaching full stride in 1863, the Union actively recruited and engaged black troops in its armies; these black regiments consisted of both free black volunteers from the North and former slaves from the Confederacy who had escaped or fallen into Union hands with the capture of Southern territory and who had volunteered for military service. The Confederates insisted on continuing to treat former slaves as human chattel, and if they were captured, either returned these men to their former masters or sold them at slave auctions. President Lincoln insisted that the Confederacy accept the status of African-Americans as officially freed under the authority of the Emancipation Proclamation, or pursuant to congressional legislation authorizing the formation of black regiments in the Union Army. Confederate resistance to these demands led to the collapse of routine exchanges and the consequent emergence of the notorious POW prisons at Andersonville, Georgia, and elsewhere.

Upon initial capture, men in the Civil War were usually treated decently by the front-line enemy soldiers, who respected them as fellow warriors. The abuse began when the POWs were turned over to rear-echelon enemy troops, who frequently stole their possessions and ridiculed them. One Union POW remembered being lined up by a Confederate commander, who ordered all to remain still upon penalty of being shot: "Under the terrible mental and physical strain . . . the hours passed like so many months, it is not within my power to describe the physical and mental torture experienced that November night. . . . Discouragement and a keen sense of our condition pervaded each one." When exposed to enemy civilians, the POWs might be mocked or even stoned.[25]

At journey's end, when eventually sent to a stockade prison such as the one at Andersonville, the men entered a surreal world of unspeakable horror and despair. With inadequate tents and clothing, men passed day after day in a compound staring at the fences. At

Andersonville, a fourteen-foot stockade surrounded the compound, and twenty feet within the fence was what was called the "dead line," a pole fixed on sticks about three feet off the ground, which marked the perimeter beyond which the prisoners could not pass. If a man stepped beyond this limit, he would be shot to death. There were instances of men who accidently tripped over the line and were shot and killed anyway; in some cases, POWs who had gone mad and no longer desired to live intentionally stepped over the line and were immediately executed by Rebel sentries. These same "dead lines" were also established in Union camps for Confederate POWs.[26]

Under these conditions, some men sank into despair and apathy: homesick and disheartened, they lost all interest in everything, and would sit in the same attitude hour after hour and day after day with a fixed gaze. One Union surgeon recalled POWs as "the most abject, pitiful mass of humanity the mind could conceive; their faces vacant, cadaverous and staring and their minds gone to the verge of dementia." A Union POW recalled that while incarcerated, tormented by hunger and despair, he couldn't sleep and "my mind was become greatly impaired, and my spirits had sunk into a black midnight of despair." Another Union POW remembered that time moved slowly, and it seemed to require weeks for the sun to cross from east to west. Rapidly sinking into despair and despondency, the men told over and over all the stories they knew, read over and over every scrap of reading matter available, and then fell silent:

> A large number of those who had been in the prison over a year were now insane. They seemed to loose all power of speech and memory, and did not know whether they had been in prison one day, or one year. If spoken to, their only answer would be a far away and vacant stare or look as though they were trying to recall something beyond the reach of their memory. They wandered wildly about and kept their comrades constantly watching to keep them away from the dead line.[27]

Nor were conditions for Confederate men in Union POW camps any better. They were given inadequate tents and fuel to fend off the bitterly cold winters and, sitting and shivering in huddled masses, were reduced to mental imbecility. Writing of the long and dreary winter on Johnson's Island in Sandusky Bay, Lake Erie, one Confederate recalled temperatures that fell to 27 degrees below zero, a lack of fuel, and consequent intense misery: "[W]e suffered and endured all for the sake of a Cause, and a Nationality which was destined to be crushed." Another Rebel POW recalled that a man was executed for building a boat with an escape attempt in mind, and a second soldier who had escaped and was caught was also shot and killed. Owing to the glaring sunlight on the white ground, half of the men developed what was known as "moon blindness," night blindness. Such captives testified, as was the case with Northern POWs, that constant disappointment and loss of hope were mentally devastating. On occasion, both Confederate and Union POWs were declared to be hostages (sometimes after drawing lots) and held in solitary confinement or threatened with execution as their governments, engaged in a complicated game of intimidation, used them as pawns to achieve certain public policy objectives, such as (for the North) the cessation of guerrilla activity in certain districts, or (for the South) prevention of Union execution of captured Confederate privateers as pirates.[28]

When POWs were finally repatriated, their condition would often shock those who welcomed them home. One Northern man characterized a returning set of POWs as a "sorry spectacle": "Some had to be carried on stretchers to the ship which was to take them north. All were pale, haggard and emaciated." Indeed, many were reduced to human skeletons; afflicted with scurvy resulting from a diet of corn meal, bread, and little meat or vegetables, one Union POW recalled: "I kept getting worse until my mouth and gums became very sore. My teeth became loose & some of them dropped out. I also had bloody diarrhoea, and my body & limbs got very sore. My legs were swollen & turned a purplish color, & the flesh below the knees got caked & hard." A friend who observed this man recalled that he was of a leaden color, and had running sores on his feet and one leg, in addition to pains in his chest and joints. A doctor who examined the man declared: "He was then a horible wreck with large ulcers on extremities, spongy gums loose teeth." An acquaintance of another Union POW recalled that upon his return home, "we did not think he would live."[29]

All of these physical and mental problems had repercussions that continued to be felt in the postwar years. Jason Roberts, a veteran of the 5th Indiana Cavalry, who had been held as a POW at Andersonville and other Southern prisons during the war, came home in such a weak condition that he had to be carried on a stretcher; subsequently, scurvy caused all of his teeth to fall out, and he continued to suffer in the years after the war from chronic diarrhea and rheumatism. His wife noted that he sometimes "had peculiar actions & talked curious," and would get excited and preach about religion. He whipped the children, annoyed the neighbors, and finally frightened his wife: "I kept him a little afraid of me, by threatening him with punishment. He got so that he did not mind me, & I saw that he watched me very closely. He had a wild angry look in his eyes and I got afraid of him at last." His wife finally applied to have him committed to the Indiana Hospital for the Insane in February of 1886, for chronic mania.[30]

The request for commitment triggered the required judicial inquiry in Fayette County, Indiana, and the resulting inquest papers noted of Jason Roberts:

> Says he has been shook over hell. . . . Sometimes he is raving and excited, at others melancholly . . . Very peculiar and excentric. flying from one Subject to another, and talking incoherently on all Subjects, . . . The subject of religion and his experiences in the army being paramount in his mind . . . thinks all his enemies should be in hell.

After the commitment was approved by local authorities, the admitting clerk at the insane asylum noted of Roberts: "Suffered in Prison during war." Jason Roberts subsequently applied for a federal disability pension, and the Pension Bureau's special examiner reported to his superiors regarding this case: "He seemed all right mentally, until he began to tell his prison experience, & then he got excited, & wild in his Conversation. It will be seen from the evidence of Mrs. Roberts that the man is insane."[31]

Numerous other Indiana Civil War veterans who had been POWs in the war also continued to suffer both physically and psychologically. Erastus Holmes served as quartermaster sergeant in the 5th Indiana Cavalry, and was taken prisoner by the Confederates near Macon, Georgia, on July 31, 1864. He was held as a POW first at Florence, South Carolina, and then at Andersonville. While at Andersonville, he was affected by disease and had to sleep in holes in the ground that were damp or partially filled with water. Before the war he had weighed 160 pounds, but when finally released from Andersonville, he weighed only 85 pounds. A doctor testified that "his constitution was racked and broken down when I first saw him after the war," and his sister, with whose family he briefly lived after his release from the military, recalled that "he was the poorest looking object I ever saw" with bed sores from his stay in the hospital; "[h]e could scarcely walk at all." She noted that her brother, in telling of an escape attempt from Andersonville, would grate his teeth, with his nerves all tense, "and he seemed to be living it all over again. He also said while he was there at that time that he did not think he would live three months, and that he did not care to live; that his health was all shattered and he would never be able to do anything."[32]

Erastus Holmes's daughter, Emma, recalled that her mother had said her father was afraid to go to sleep at night; at times he was irritable, and had "worked through" difficult spells on several occasions when his mental health seemed to be particularly threatened by memories of the war. Holmes apparently never quite got over the starvation that he had experienced at Andersonville. His daughter testified to Pension Bureau officials:

> When he first came home he was so starved that it seemed that he could not get enough to eat. [He] would often get up in the night to eat. Mother often got up at night and cooked and got something for him to eat; for two years it seemed as though he could not get enough to eat, and he used to have hungry spells at times always after that. He used to say that we did not know what it was to be hungry. He would feed all the tramps he could find and worried mother a great deal. In winter he would get the pies and cakes and set them out for the birds, and if a dog came along that looked hungry he would call him in and feed him. It seemed as though he could not bear to see anything that seemed to be hungry.

His son-in-law remembered that Holmes was obsessed with his experience in the army and at Andersonville. He would break off any conversation concerning religion or politics, and begin to talk about the army. He would then become very excitable, would focus on his prison life, and "[he] bored me almost to death": "He had what he called a facsimile of the prison dug out in the ground in the yard, had the stream of water and every hill and stump. He used to take me out there and talk to me about it and when others would come would take them out and show it to them."[33]

A neighbor recalled that the Holmes family seemed quiet, and for the most part managed to keep their problems to themselves, although this neighbor thought "Mrs. Holmes herself seemed to be about half crazy—caused by so much trouble." Erastus Holmes had been able to weather periodic "spells" of mental turmoil related to memories of his ordeal at Andersonville, but eventually broke down completely and irrevocably. His daughter remembered that after her father finally went insane, he could remember events from before the war and, of course, his experience at Andersonville, but was blank on events thereafter. He was committed at the Indiana Hospital for the Insane on November 19, 1885, and remained at the asylum until his death in 1910. At the insane asylum he was generally quiet, except when he was in his room alone, and then he would chatter to himself about the war, about generals, heroic deeds, and the necessity of escaping from prison so that he could report to General Sherman.[34]

Exposure to combat and scenes of suffering could produce a variety of stress reactions in Civil War soldiers, nurses, and POWs, including intrusive recollections, flashbacks, nightmares, intense anxiety, depression, probable cognitive disorders, and, in extreme cases, what would once have been seen as psychotic episodes or permanent psychotic states. In view of the almost universal dread experienced by Civil War soldiers before combat, the exhaustion of veterans "played out" after the constant exposure to combat in 1864–1865, and the tragic plight of the POWs, can one conclude that the concept of "hardening" is invalid and misleading? Should we view Civil War soldiers as all being at risk of developing stress disorders and, with sufficient exposure or certain mental shocks, lapsing inevitably into some form of psychopathology? Before dismissing the idea of hardening and adopting the post-Vietnam outlook that tends to view soldiers as potential psychiatric victims and as little else, one must consider the somewhat strange phenomenon of the Civil War soldier's attraction to a life of hardship and danger.

Although concerned with the welfare of family and, at times, yearning to be with loved ones at home, the attitude of the Civil War soldier was also marked by a curious transformation in which he began to look at life at home as irrelevant or boring, and longed to be or remain at the front with his unit—despite the many hardships associated with life in the military. This attitude is seen most clearly in the feelings of men on home leave during the war; they were initially overjoyed to see relatives and to be at home again, but this bliss quickly gave way to tension, an eagerness for news from the front, and a desire to return to their unit to share the fate of their comrades. One sees these sentiments expressed again and again, by Union and Confederate soldiers alike. Elbridge J. Copp, of the 3rd New Hampshire Infantry, was sent home to convalesce after being wounded, and was puzzled at his own reaction; he found himself reading the papers daily to find out what had happened to his unit, and each day brought an increasing and undeniable desire to return to the front: "It may seem unaccountable that I should have this feeling to return to the dangers of the battlefield. I can not explain for I do not know —it surely was not the love of danger." Against the advice of his physician, who felt that the wound needed more time to heal, Copp started for the front to rejoin his regiment.[35]

Another Northerner, home on veteran furlough, received an enthusiastic welcome from civilians. He had a good time carousing with old friends and the other soldiers on leave, but "strange as it may sound, many of us soon became restless & more or less discontented. Time soon 'hung' on our hands & we longed to get back with the boys. I confess I shared this experience"—and this from a man who had earlier written of the sickening odor of decaying bodies on the Shiloh battlefield. In part these feelings related to unit cohesion, a devotion to one's fellow soldiers, and a "burning desire to be with one's organization and share its fortunes, whether good or bad." However, one suspects this also related, for some men, to the strange but undeniable attraction of war, to the visceral allure of excitement, danger, and death, faced and endured in the company of one's comrades: "Despite its hardships and dangers, there is a strong fascination about war life, and when a heart, especially a young heart, has once been fired by the peal of the cannon, roar of musketry and shouts of contending forces, it soon chafes under the monotonous quiet of home." Another man on home leave commented: "It appears very lonely & dull. I shall go back just as soon as my feet will allow for with all the horror and danger of war, I prefer it to this almost painful stillness that broods over one here." And, of course, for some, such as the Confederate nurse Kate Cumming, there was a tremendous sense of purpose in their work.[36]

Related to this desire of men on furloughs to return to the front is one of the strangest phenomena of war, namely that soldiers, particularly those men exposed to combat or the most difficult circumstances, can complain bitterly about their predicament, and yet, when given the chance, will choose to remain in the very situation against which they had railed. One sees this in the Civil War era especially in men who were discharged from the service for disabilities and yet reentered the service, sometimes with the same unit. Because lucrative bounties were given to those enlisting in military units, financial motives may have been involved in some of these decisions, but one suspects there was more to it than money alone. For instance, John O. Todd was granted a disability discharge from the 53rd Indiana Infantry on April 21, 1862, for rheumatism and "on account of a constitution naturally feeble and protracted illness," and yet this same man apparently subsequently enlisted with two other Indiana units, the 117th and the 148th, later in the war. While on service with Company F of the 35th Indiana Infantry, William Stoneking went insane: "[The company] was about to go into action when in going along Stoneking began hollering—saying that he would never see home again—and thus went crazy from fear." Stoneking was discharged and sent home, but when members of his old regiment came home on veteran furlough, he reenlisted with his old company and, amazingly, finished out the war with this unit. As one Hoosier infantryman wrote in his diary: "We were somewhat surprised this morning at the arrival of several of our old comrades that were discharged but have enlisted again." After considering this love-hate relationship, a Michigan officer concluded: "I occasionally hear these sick boys saying that if they were only at home once more they would bid farewell to soldiering. They undoubtedly feel most sincerely what they say yet half of them if discharged would reenlist within 3 months. A soldier's life is a hard one but those who have tried it once are the first to reenter the service."[37]

One sees these same elements of devotion to unit, fascination with exposure to battle, and expressions of satisfaction with life in the military in the ordinary day-to-day letters of many Civil War soldiers—aside from the context of home leave and reenlistment. One Union surgeon wrote: "The night was so cold that I could not sleep a wink, but sat shivering beside the fire. My hand shakes so now with the cold, I can barely write; yet, rough as this life is, I never was better." Fighting in a battle which involved the front ranks being "torn apart by shells" followed by hand-to-hand combat, Elbridge Copp wrote, "Never before had we seen such a magnificent, fearful sight—it was the greatest of all dramas—a tragedy and a horror, indescribable." Others facing battle mentioned "that thrill of fear and horror" they experienced before the first shot was fired. A veteran who in 1869 returned to the sites of Civil War battles in which he had fought recalled the fatiguing marches, chilly and sleepless nights, fierce combat, and dying comrades, and wrote of the "charm" and "fascinating interest" associated with memories of these times. One sees in these letters and countless others from Civil War soldiers and veterans an ambivalent attitude—the experience of hardship and horror, yet devotion to their unit and overpowering feelings of fascination with what they had seen and experienced; their army experience was "bigger than life itself," something of overwhelming importance and power, and not to be denied.

Some historians have suggested that positive sentiments concerning life in the military were generally expressed by veterans years after the war, well after the fact, and were a retrospective distortion of the Civil War experience, influenced perhaps by boredom with civilian life and part of a general tendency to look at the past through rose-colored glasses—to forget all the killing and to remember only the camaraderie. This would appear not to be the case. Abundant evidence demonstrates that Civil War soldiers had these feelings during the war itself, even in the midst of the carnage they were experiencing. Analysis of casualty statistics in relation to desertion rates in Indiana Civil War units suggests that there was no overall relationship between the incidence of casualties (either death alone, or death in conjunction with disability) and the rate of desertion: devotion to one's unit or a general attraction to life in the service frequently seemed to overcome fear and apprehension.[38] In sum, no simple statement or seemingly straightforward characterization concerning the attitudes, conditions, or desires of Civil War soldiers— either to say that they became hardened with exposure to battle or that they were all potential victims just waiting to break down—will suffice. The matter is much more complex, and begs a more sophisticated level of understanding than has been typical in the post-Vietnam era.

"For God's Sake Please Help Me": Post-Traumatic Stress

Although psychiatrists have long understood that soldiers in warfare will break down under certain conditions in the war zone itself, the Vietnam experience introduced the idea of delayed stress reactions, the concept that men who come back from the front looking completely normal will, over time, develop an array of psychopathological symptoms—from intrusive recollections such as nightmares and flashbacks, to disoriented thinking, startle reactions, social numbing, depression, and anxiety. Critical to this theory of delayed stress is the issue of social support: the idea expressed again and again by Vietnam veteran advocates and psychologists studying the Vietnam veteran has been that if returning veterans are greeted enthusiastically in their homeland, psychological and readjustment problems will be minimized. It has often been concluded that the troubled readjustment of the Vietnam veteran and the relatively trouble-free postwar experience of earlier American veterans can be explained by variations in the manner in which veterans have been welcomed home. One must ask, then, in considering Civil War veterans, whether they received significant social support from civilians during and after the war, and whether such support prevented or minimized psychological problems; did Civil War veterans experience post-traumatic stress, and, if so, what forms did it take?

An important point in this post-Vietnam theory, though not always fully articulated, implies that veterans can find forgiveness for having participated in brutal killing through the ritual acceptance of civilians in victory parades and similar activities. This certainly implies that veterans not only believe that civilians can understand what war is all about, but place great stock in the absolution of those who stayed at home. Contrary to this somewhat simplistic post-Vietnam idea that soldiers and civilians can ever be of one mind (and participate together in washing away disturbing memories of war through parades), however, the memoirs and letters of Civil War soldiers and veterans indicate a deeply ambivalent attitude toward those on the home front. On the one hand, soldiers were anxious to receive mail from home, and could be both jubilant and anguished when letters from loved ones arrived. Soldiers frequently chided relatives for not writing more often; one soldier complained to his sister that he had been waiting for a letter from her for two weeks, but all in vain: "I would be glad if you would write to me at least once a month for my pleasant moments, are when I receive a letter from home." Another Confederate soldier reproached his folks: "I have *waited* and *waited* for a letter from you all at home until I am so anxious to hear from home I hardly know what to do."

At mail call, soldiers would drop everything else and dash to see if they had received any letters; one Michigan volunteer reflected that the coming of the mail was looked forward to with deeper interest than almost any other experience of a soldier's life. One Indiana infantryman read over a newly arrived letter from his parents three times on the spot, and another soldier reflected that he was in a dark, despondent mood, but that a letter from home had the power to change this and revive hope, confidence, and trust. But letters from home could also fill soldiers with feelings of longing and homesickness, as in the case of one man who received a letter from home and wept as though some terrible affliction had come upon him. Such sentiments could lead to profound dissatisfaction, and one historian has estimated that 50 percent of Confederate desertions were the result of letters from wives describing the dire circumstances at home.[1]

On the other hand, even while soldiers remained in close contact with loved ones at home throughout the war and depended on their letters to sustain morale, one can also detect a growing sense of alienation—a feeling that the folks at home did not and in fact could not understand the privations and horrors of army life. This feeling sometimes evolved into a type of anger, when soldiers bitterly complained that they could never be adequately compensated for the trials they were enduring and condemned all of the "enemies of the soldier" at home. These included bounty agents ("cold blooded hell-hounds"), war profiteers ("a parcel of swindlers and scoundrels"), antiwar demonstrators ("those detestable copperheads"), politicians (knaves or fools), traitors ("the Army will fight in spite of traitors at home"), "professional patriots" ("[they] made the loudest noise to bring on the war and are now sneaking and creeping in every hole to keep out of it"), and, sometimes, seemingly all civilians—with the exception of one's immediate family. This curious sort of bitter free-floating anger is an important element with which one must come to terms in understanding both the Civil War and the Vietnam soldier and veteran.[2]

In letters and diaries of Civil War soldiers, one constantly comes across phrases such as: "how little they did know"; "[f]ew a[t] home have any idea of a soldier's hardships and privations"; "[t]o tell you how we feel is impossible"; "nobody at home can form the least idea of the hardships that a soldier has to go through." A Hoosier volunteer wrote to his mother: "People at home owe a debt to the soldiers that they can never Pay let them do what ever they may they can never cancel the obligation." And, in a similar vein, an Alabama infantryman excoriated his brother: "You speak of hard times and troublesome times. Just permit me to say that you do not know anything about trouble. Suppose you had to lie night after night and day after day in dread of your life every moment. . . . Do not talk about troubles and hard times while God and your country permits you to stay at home with your family and friends."[3]

The overwhelming mental distance that the Civil War soldier could feel between himself and his loved ones was poignantly expressed by James Stephens of the 20th Indiana Infantry:

[Indiana] has for the last three years nearly seemed as distant from and isolated to me as England. More than the Ocean with all its dangers has surged and rolled between me and my Earthly home since I left it in "61". Since then I have thought of home in the future as if I were in a dream. With a heart throbbing with a fearful hope I looked forward to the time when I might again be at home. But when I thought of that which lay before me. The hours of hellish conflict yet to come. Comrades falling all around me. The deadly minnie. The fearful shell. The screaming solid shot. The dreadful charge into the very jaws of death. Disease in a hundred forms. When I thought of all this, the faces of my friends seemed to fade to my view, and home seemed hidden by the smoke of battle.[4]

The question is whether in the months and years after the end of the war this gap between soldier and civilian could be fully bridged, whether thoughts and memories of "hellish conflict" and "fearful shells," the "jaws of death," and "disease in a hundred forms" could be washed away in celebrations.

When the news of Lee's surrender to Grant at Appomattox Court-house on April 9, 1865, was finally received, Union troops were jubilant: "The men went wild, ranks were broken, and shouting and crying, the men in their joy hugged and kissed each other. Never have I witnessed such happiness." Nelson Stauffer of the 63rd Illinois Infantry recalled that every hat flew up into the air, and every man let loose cheer after cheer until tears of joy ran down every cheek: "[I]t seemed that the dark cloud of war rolled back and vanished away. Our hearts were full, and it seemed that the scape valves were too small, and something would surely burst . . . our steps were quickened, our strength renewed, and our rheumatic akes and pains forgotten." Even Confederate soldiers on the losing side often felt a wonderful sense of relief, knowing that they could now go back to their homes and be with loved ones. James Cooper recalled that from the mirth and revelry in Rebel ranks, one would have thought that Confederate forces had prevailed in the war: "The meeting of rela-tives for the first time in years contributed much to this gayety and all went as happily as you please. . . . I am afraid if the truth were known that we were not as sorry as we should have been."[5]

When Union men finally made it back to their homes, wild scenes of jubilation and joy were repeated in countless towns and villages across the North. One Maine man arrived at his farm and found a "royal, loving welcome from my father and brothers"; his little step-sister would sit for hours, begging him to tell more stories of the war. Austin Stearns of the 13th Massachusetts Infantry arrived in Boston and was met by a large crowd that had congregated to welcome home the troops; all food and refreshments were provided free, and after the men assembled to march through the streets of Boston, they were officially welcomed home by the state at Faneuil Hall. The next day there was yet another parade after which the men finally collected their pay and were sent on to their homes. In Indianapolis, David Wiltsee of the 2nd Indiana Cavalry found a similar scene in which marching, music, crowds of appreciative citizens, and formal cere-monies abounded; when Wiltsee was finally able to proceed on to his home several hours to the north in Wabash, Indiana, he arrived at

1:00 A.M. and was greeted by his family; all were so excited that they stayed up the entire night talking and spent the next day celebrating as well. Another Union veteran from Iowa wrote: "I have been gone three years. I meet my wife and Oh, such a greeting."[6]

In Washington, D.C., the greatest military parade in American history was conducted as, on May 23 and 24, 1865, 200,000 soldiers of the Grand Army of the Republic assembled and marched for the civilians. Riding his horse, which was smothered in garlands, General George Gordon Meade, who had commanded victorious Union forces at the Battle of Gettysburg, led the parade which by all accounts was magnificent. On the reviewing stand, President Andrew Johnson and leading politicians acknowledged the waves of soldiers as they marched by. Such irresistible power made a deep impression upon the watchers and created a mood tinged with awe, "almost a terror." Signs such as "The Only National Debt We Can Never Pay Is the Debt We Owe to the Victorious Union Soldiers" draped the avenues. Crowds thronged the streets to see the men march. Here, there, and everywhere, Union veterans were welcomed home as heroes who had saved the nation.[7]

The situation for returning Confederate veterans seemed less a matter of pure jubilation and was, on balance, more bittersweet. One Southern veteran came home, and in the manner of Ulysses, decided to see if he would be recognized and meanwhile to gauge the reactions of his family. He asked for lodging at his own house without identifying himself, and his father, finally recognizing him, broke down and wept. When his mother discovered that he was home, she came running: " 'Where is he? Where is he?' ... 'My son, my son, where are you?' A moment later she was in my arms. How I rained tears and kisses on that dear, sweet face and pressed her to my bosom in ecstacy of joy and tenderness such as my heart had never known before!" Several Confederates on the way home stopped over at the house of a stranger, were surprised at all the attention they received from the young ladies, and were treated to a splendid supper, being given the seat of honor at the head of the table: "They treated us like we were *somebody* to use a common expression." Many Southern men noted general rejoicing upon their homecoming.[8]

For some returning Rebels, however, there was disappointment and heartbreak. They found that their houses had been destroyed or were occupied by others, or that they were no longer entitled to vote and that they were being ridiculed and mocked by some of the newly freed slaves. Indeed, the situation was desperate and depressing across the South for civilians as well as for veterans; one Southern lady grieved over the collapse of her plantation and lamented: "The times ahead a[re] fearful. . . . We are crushed indeed, & humiliated." Another Southern woman wrote that her family had been ruined and that words could not express her sense of desolation: "And all our poor soldiers suffering for nothing, worse than nothing. All the precious blood shed for naught. Merciful Father is this our wretched fate? It seems more than I can bear." A correspondent from the *Nashville Daily Press* claimed that people had gone mad by the dozen during the war and that an addition to the state insane asylum was now required. Indeed, commitments from the insane asylums in South Carolina and Georgia reveal many cases related to the war: women committed to the asylum after their sons or husbands had been killed in battle; POWs still suffering from the mental repercussions of their experience in Northern prisons; and Confederate veterans who were "deeply chagrined and depressed" and unable to shake off the disappointment and trauma of what they had seen and experienced.[9]

Even for Union veterans in the midst of all the victory celebrations up north, there were mixed emotions. How did Union men themselves react to all the marching and parades? A few commented approvingly on the splendor of such proceedings, but most seemed to have been bored or put off by such pageantry. One Michigan infantryman characterized a division review as "very tedious," and another commented on an early parade: "It was as usual a very fine sight for lookers on & a great bore to the actors." Regarding the "Grand Review" at the end of the war when the soldiers marched for huge crowds of civilians in Washington, the same sentiment prevailed, as indicated by one man's comment about the "much dreaded" Grand Review. A Union nurse observed similarly that the men did not like the Grand Review, and were anxious to get home rather than march around Washington. Simon B. Cummings wrote to his father: "They made us all wear white gloves and black hats but the dust soon soild this chicken fixings. It was so hot in the streets that several fell down. Sun struck and some died."[10]

Moreover, Union soldiers in the midst of these celebrations were often experiencing emotions that onlooking civilians would never have been able to discern. Soldiers who had been like brothers and endured the worst of the war together found it difficult to part. This was the case with Rice Bull, who wrote that he would never forget the last meeting of his company as they separated to go home: "The Captain in a broken voice, for he could not control his emotions, bid us farewell and Godspeed. When he had finished, we men crowded about him to shake his hand and each others." A Tennessee veteran remembered that when his unit was called together to stack arms and depart for home, the commanding officer in charge passed before the troops for a final review, but, overcome with emotion, had tears running down his cheeks as he bade his men farewell. In accord with these sentiments, Abner R. Small of the 16th Maine Volunteers recalled that it was extraordinarily difficult for him, even in the midst of wild cheering from townsfolk, to say farewell to the comrades from his unit: "That was hard; I prefer not to speak of it; I cannot." An equally difficult emotional moment for Small on this occasion was to see the faces of parents in the crowd whose sons had been killed in the war: "[T]hese unhappy ones had been drawn to us as if somehow we must have brought their dead boys back with us, alive."[11]

The inner mental turmoil of returning veterans, which was not readily apparent to civilians, is seen clearly in the memoirs of William Henry Younts, who had served with the 93rd Ohio Infantry. When Younts returned to his hometown, a church service was in session, but when the people noticed him, they immediately ended the service and came rushing out into the yard to enthusiastically greet him. Everyone wanted to shake his hand; his mother and sisters cried, and his young son jumped up into his arms. Younts recalled that he felt a lump in his throat the size of a six-pound shot. Yet as all of his friends, family, and neighbors peppered him with questions about his experiences in the army, he noticed that he was not happy, that while talking and laughing with his friends, his mind would suddenly revert to times, places, and scenes in the South. During the extended homecoming celebration, in spite of efforts of friends to keep everyone cheerful and happy, he continued to notice that his mind would drift off in this manner and that he would become oblivious of his surroundings and find himself thinking of "some comrade, who, unlike me, was not permitted to return home to his family, but his body lay moldering in some Cemetery in the south, or his bones lay bleaching on some battlefield, far from home and friends." Despite his best efforts, these thoughts would come repeatedly into his mind during this day, "unbidden," as he put it, and in spite of himself. But he also noted, remarkably, that "I felt glad in entertaining them on such occasions. I had no desire to separate myself permanently from them." Psychologists in the post-Vietnam era would characterize what was happening to Younts as the experience of "intrusive recollections" and "survivor guilt"; the interesting part of the equation, however, and something post-Vietnam psychiatry has perhaps not fully come to terms with is that Younts felt these memories were appropriate in some measure—to remember his fallen comrades, and to temper jubilation over victory in war with some measure of sober reflection.[12]

We can see that Civil War veterans—those in the North as well as some in the South—received enthusiastic welcomes and parades, but that these ceremonies did not instantly "wash away" the disturbing memories of the past four years, or necessarily result in the "healing," "reconciliation," or "closure" of popular post-Vietnam rhetoric. The matter was much more complex than that, and involved grappling with tangled emotions of devotion, horror, honor, fear, excitement, anger, and boredom. The men were thrilled to be reunited with their families, but frequently viewed parades with annoyance, as they confronted thoughts of the past and the prospect of separation from their fellow soldiers; nor did these men apparently routinely share their inner thoughts and mental conflict with the civilians who were thronging to all the parades and welcoming celebrations or, for that matter, with their immediate families. These were private reflections that centered on mourning lost comrades and determining the meaning of their war experience. As these Civil War veterans moved into the postwar years, returned to small towns and villages, migrated to the city or other states, taking up old or new trades, marrying and having children, how did they deal with these memories of the war years? Was the legacy of the Civil War a well-adjusted and content veteran?

First, as historians have noted regarding other wars, the Civil War "let the genie out of the bottle," as the violence of the war years spilled over into civilian life in the postwar era. During the war, soldiers had been trained to kill and thereby threw off the restraints of civil society and accepted a life of violence; there was no immediate way to put an end to the habit of violence and reintroduce all of these men to the industrious and peaceful vocations of life. In both the North and the South a period of turmoil followed the end of the war. In the North, two-thirds of all commitments to state prisons were men who had seen service in the army or navy, and in some state prisons, commitments were up by 400 percent. The *New York Times,* surmising that the increase in crime was probably caused by "rough material turned loose upon society by the close of the war," contained numerous accounts of disturbed veterans, including one who committed suicide, and another former Confederate charged with burglary, who was "quite insolent" and "claimed to have killed many Yankees." Among many crimes, the *Indianapolis Daily Herald* reported an attempted murder (of his wife and her mother) by a veteran as well as a murder committed by a veteran who claimed insanity but was found guilty and given a life sentence. The *Indianapolis Daily Herald* also recounted the following disturbing incident: "A soldier of the 145th, apparently very much 'fatigued,' was yesterday crossing Illinois street in front of a street car. Rather than quicken his pace he undertook to stop the car by knocking down one of the horses with the breech of his musket. The driver remonstrated, when the irate son of Mars 'presented arms' in a threatening manner, but didn't fire."[13]

The situation throughout the South was even more chaotic as newspapers reported a "frightening increase in crime," which involved bands of what appeared to be former Confederate soldiers running wild and terrorizing citizens. In various incidents, unidentified thugs (probably Confederate veterans or deserters in most instances) hanged a woman before her husband to force him to turn over all of his property, called people out of their houses at night to shoot them (either out of political motives or as part of a robbery), castrated young boys and raped women in front of their husbands, robbed and killed countless citizens at their homes, broke into the Quartermaster and Commissary stores, sacked and burned all the houses in certain villages, burned passenger trains after stealing watches and gold from the passengers, destroyed railroads just to be destructive, and shot and killed Union soldiers (oftentimes African-Americans). Newspaper headlines such as "A Night of Terror," "Disorder in Alabama," "Guerillas in Mississippi," and "Reign of Terror in East Tennessee" were common; one story deploring these atrocities darkly remarked: "Murder stalks abroad and crime of every character and grade is rife everywhere."[14]

Vigilante bands and posses were formed to control this violence, although some of these were Ku Klux Klan outfits, more interested in challenging federal rule and the empowerment of the freedman than in suppressing random violence in the countryside. Aside from this lawlessness, racial strife, and Ku Klux Klan activity in the old Confederate states, the postwar era also witnessed "regulator" or vigilante troubles in Kentucky, southern Appalachia, Texas, Kansas, and Missouri. Union and Confederate veterans were involved in much if not most of this postwar violence.[15]

But what of those veterans who returned home to their families and jobs, and did not make it onto the front page of the newspaper? Were they able to escape the aftereffects of the violence they had witnessed and settle down to function as sons, brothers, husbands, and fathers again? Did they successfully put aside the war and look forward with an optimistic spirit toward the development of a newly unified American nation? In the past, the study of the psychological problems and readjustment of veterans of the American Civil War has been hindered by the lack of data. However, a sample of 291 Indiana veterans of the American Civil War who were committed at the Indiana Hospital for the Insane (later Central State Hospital) in Indianapolis from 1861 to 1920 provides substantial information on the continuing psychological problems of these men throughout the remainder of the nineteenth century and beyond. It is important to note, however, that this group of 291 veterans, though offering intriguing data, is not a random sample (see Appendix A and Chapter 8), and may or may not be representative of Civil War veterans in general.

Although retrospective clinical analysis of men long dead is not possible, and while the engagement in the nineteenth century of different terms and concepts to describe psychopathology make retrospective diagnoses difficult, information from asylum commitments, local inquest papers, and federal pension records on these 291 men is nonetheless illuminating. These records reveal a range of behaviors and symptoms typical of the twentieth-century victim of PTSD, including elements of depression, anxiety, social numbing, reexperiencing, fear, dread of calamity, and cognitive disorders. Many of these men continued to suffer from the aftereffects of the war and, along with their families, often lived in a kind of private hell involving physical pain, the torment of fear, and memories of killing and death.[16]

One should note at the outset that most patients admitted to the Indiana Hospital for the Insane in the nineteenth century were considered to be curable; chronic cases were generally turned away. The men in this sample were therefore not (at least initially) afflicted by a profound and permanent disorder, along the lines of what we would think of today as schizophrenia or a fixed psychotic state; the median length of confinement at the asylum for this group of men was 8 months, with the most common stay being 1.5 months. All men whose behavior could be presumably attributed to organic disorders or diseases, such as epilepsy, neurosyphilis, brain tumors, and degenerative neurological diseases have been excluded from the sample. Many of the veterans in the resulting sample were committed to the asylum only during episodes when their behaviors reached extremes and provoked a crisis. The overwhelming majority were able to return home, although in many cases their nightmares and torment returned, prompting a second or third commitment.

Probably the most striking symptom that one sees again and again in this sample is fear, specifically the fear of being killed. When Elijah Boswell was committed to the insane asylum in 1872, the admitting clerk noted: "Sobbed & cried & imagined that some one was going to kill him." His brother testified that Boswell had never been normal since he had come back from the army, and that "a heap of times he would be sitting around in a deep study." His condition worsened and he eventually became violently insane and would scream that "the rebels was after him and appeared to always be in dreaded danger, and would imagine the rebels was after him and try to run away." Another Indiana veteran, Demarcus L. Hedges, imagined he was being pursued and that members of his family were trying to kill and bury him; he had the delusion that he was engaged in warfare, commanding armies at Vicksburg, a battle in which he had actually fought. Appearing wild and scared, he had a peculiar way of looking behind him as if expecting someone to approach; time and again he would suddenly drop his voice to a whisper and look behind.

This terror of being killed would often lead men to barricade themselves in their houses, particularly at night, and stay up all hours watching and waiting. Henry C. Carr, a veteran from the 22nd Indiana Infantry, had had a leg amputated after incurring a gunshot wound at the Battle of Perryville. Those testifying at his inquest hearing reported that he had a nervous and anxious expression on his face, and claimed that someone was trying to kill him. At night he was convinced that intruders would try to break into his house, and he improvised a plan of defense; he would creep around looking under the beds, and shoot at imaginary objects. Another Hoosier veteran, who could not sleep at night, declared that he was afraid of being captured and murdered, and kept the doors of the house barred, or fastened at night; during the day he would maintain a steady watch. Needless to say, exposed to this spectacle, his entire family was also unable to get any sleep. In a similar manner Leonard C. Griffith, whose commitment report read "in constant dread of being killed," was endlessly in motion and refused to sit before an open door or with his back turned to an open door or window for fear someone would take his life. He could not sleep unless sedatives were administered, as was often the practice in such cases. One veteran, for example, convinced people were trying to kill him, was in a state of frenzy and begged for protection, leading a local doctor to administer a heavy dose of sedatives. Such was the desperation of these men that they would frequently threaten to kill others to remove the supposed threat, or would make attempts on their own lives—with drug overdoses or by cutting their throats—to escape the agony and fear of their imagined predicament.[17]

Under the delusion that they would at any moment be attacked and killed, many of these Indiana veterans kept weapons at their side for protection—and this ten, twenty, and thirty years after the end of the Civil War. In a fairly benign form, this practice would lead men to carry pistols with them wherever they went, but in more serious cases resulted in veterans sleeping with axes or other weapons under their beds for self-protection: "Preparing his knife and bringing his ax in near his bed at night time. . . . Carried a revolver. slept with it &c." The inquest papers of Jacob Fink noted: "Has fortifyed his house with himself and a Navy revolver . . . delusion that he is holding a fort in state of siege. Fort being his own house." William H. Guile would carry both a revolver and a knife, and, subject to "wild spells," so alarmed local townfolk that they on one occasion sent out the sheriff to tie him up and forcibly confiscate the revolver. His niece testified that Guile would get up in the middle of the night and go through the house with a hatchet. Witnesses in the insanity inquest of Elias Hammon in 1883 recalled of him: "Gave evidence of fear by arming himself to resist attacks of imaginary enemies . . . calls for his gun & declares his enemies are seeking his life & at times talks as if the Rebels were threatening an attack."[18]

In such an agitated state, these and other veterans could not sleep at night. Anna Britton testified that her husband, John, was gloomy, morose, and cross; he was apprehensive of something happening to himself and the family, and imagined that he had enemies who were seeking to harm him in some way. He would not sleep during these times and, in fact, didn't sleep much at any time, but would walk the floor at night, sometimes all night long. When particularly agitated, he would wander out into the woods or disappear for days. Sometimes he would imagine he saw some person watching the house and would therefore sit up and maintain a vigil the whole night. Another veteran depended entirely on his wife to run the farm owing to his mental state, in which he would become excited and ramble in his speech at any mention of the war; at night he could not sleep and would get out of bed every few minutes and go out into the fields, forcing his wife to follow him to bring him back home—frequently many times in one night. The insomnia of many veterans related not to delusions or memories of the war but to chronic physical ills and continuing pain, which plagued them and made it impossible to sleep. Rufus C. Carpenter suffered from chronic diarrhea related to his service in the Civil War, which in turn produced nervous prostration and, in the words of one doctor, "paroxysms of melancholy": "If claimant performs any mental labor, his mind is unsettled, and produces sleeplessness." Suffering from intense gastric distress, Lewis Chowning walked the floor all night long, muttering to himself and threatening suicide.[19]

For many veterans, this fear, anxiety, and restlessness were accompanied by a desire to be alone, sometimes an explicit fear of strangers or a fear of going outside, and sometimes simply the desire to go off in the woods as a means of getting away from people or as a way of perfecting one's defenses against imaginary danger. Descriptions of such veterans noted that they wanted to be alone, would refuse to leave their rooms for days on end, or shunned company: "[I]t appeared like he did not want to form any acquaintances with any one . . . he imagines himself utterly alone with nobody or nothing around him." Michael Cassidy, who had suffered a gunshot wound to his shoulder at the Battle of the North Anna River, seemed to be afraid all the time and tried to keep himself hidden from other people; his commitment ledger read "fears impending danger." He would lie out in the woods, even in inclement weather, to escape these imagined dangers. Of particular interest is the record of Edwin Kellogg, which recalls the cases of Vietnam veterans living in the wilds of the Pacific Northwest, Maine, or Hawaii. Kellogg enlisted in the army at the age of sixteen, and although he was small for his age, he was sent to the front. He participated in the grueling Atlanta Campaign in which General Sherman's men grappled with stiff Confederate resistance and layer after layer of fortified defenses on their way from Chattanooga to Atlanta. Kellogg was stricken near Kennesaw Mountain with what was described as fever and sunstroke, although one wonders if this was simply a nineteenth-century variant of combat fatigue; upon his return to Indiana, he kept away from society and lived out in the woods by himself, sleeping on the ground. His inquest papers of 1886 stated: "Seclusive . . . Likes to hide away in caves . . . has lived for a long time alone in the woods and in caves and subsisted upon what he could get and what was carried to him by neighbors."[20]

One particularly striking symptom associated with the post-traumatic stress of Vietnam veterans has been the "flashback" or intrusive recollection, in which the veteran, prompted by some sight, smell, or sound, will suddenly reexperience a traumatic or horrific episode of his time in the war zone—usually related to watching men being killed or having participated in violence. For Civil War veterans in the sample, one notices this sort of flashback, sometimes brief episodes and at other times almost a descent into a kind of permanent psychotic state. John Bumgardner had been rattled by a near miss from the concussion of a shell at Dalton Hill, Kentucky, during the war; after the incident, fellow soldiers noticed his uncontrollable trembling, fear, and moodiness. Bumgardner managed to regain his composure, and after the war, he returned to Indiana, married, and engaged in farming. Several weeks after his marriage, however, his wife, Charlotte, noticed that something was terribly wrong. Her husband would sit quietly and then suddenly blurt out: "Dont speak to me; dont you hear them bombarding?" On one occasion, he came running in from the fields crying and yelling, "They are coming, they are coming. see the bombshell." He then ran up to an upstairs room, where his wife eventually found him trembling in great fear, saying, "Be still; dont you hear them." She noted that he was always going on about the war and that his idiosyncrasy was war cannonading, and breastworks: "He would grow so wild when talking of the army that I refrained from talking about the War as much as possible, which is a reason why I know so little about his military history."[21]

Equally troubling is the case of Raney Johns. In the service he had contracted typhoid fever, and one comrade recalled him thereafter as a physical wreck and altogether "played out." Another man confirmed this view: "He was what I regarded as a physical wreck at the date of his discharge, both in mind and body." When he came home, he was emaciated and at times seemed absent-minded, and the war continued to bother him. Two of his brothers had died in the service, and one neighbor remembered that Johns was completely morose and that his mind was "shattered and bad." He would sit for hours staring off into space, and when spoken to, he would be startled and turn and look at the speaker with surprise. While plowing one of his fields with his team, he would sometimes wander off and sit in the fence corners and brood, and his wife would have to go looking for him. When he came down with fever again in 1875, however, his constitution and resistance seemed to completely give way, and he lapsed into a state of mania that required several men to hold him down; his whole mind was on the service, and he ranted and raved about the army, saying that the Rebels were after him and that he could hear them digging holes to put him in. He would scream and make desperate efforts to get away. Even after he recovered from this episode of fever, he climbed up on his father's roof, and when caught, said the Rebels were after him and he was trying to get away from them. He would refuse to eat and at night would beg his wife to stay with him, saying that otherwise the Rebels would get him. The idea of a "flashback" seems almost too trivial a concept to describe what had happened to Raney Johns.[22]

Johns's condition seemed to be on the verge of spilling over into what once would have been regarded as severe psychosis, not unlike the case of John Corns. According to friends and neighbors, John Corns had been mentally and physically sound when he enlisted in the army. He served with the 10th Indiana Cavalry and, at the front, he "appeared as if he was kind of homesick like." He later was sick on at least two occasions, and was relieved of duty. On a furlough from the army, he looked pale and emaciated and appeared to be estranged from and suspicious of his relatives. When his unit was mustered out, he came back to Indianapolis with his fellow soldiers, but failed to collect his pay. He did some work on returning to his home in Vevay, but progressively sank into insanity. He would "look wild and excited and being evidently in great mental commotion," would say, "there is some one after me," "do you see them coming over the hill, we will all be lost and destroyed," and "the house will be burned up and everything will be lost and destroyed." He said his head hurt, and would put his hands over his face and cry. He would imagine he was drilling troops, or that he was an aide to some great officer. Applications on his behalf for a pension were denied since it could not be proved that the insanity was caused by military service. His family finally sent him to the poorhouse, where he was chained.[23]

Indeed, the behavior of John Corns, even if well beyond the pale of what is usually thought of as a mere "stress disorder," does contain one element typical of PTSD, and that is the fear of the recurrence of some great calamity not unlike the trauma that had precipitated the condition to begin with. In many veterans in the sample, one notices symptoms such as "he seemed to fear some impending danger. . . . In constant dread of some dire calamity"; "Thinks something horrible is going to happen to him. Has threatened suicide to end his sufferings."[24] In the area of intrusive recollections, one should also consider dreams or nightmares. Oddly, although a few references appear regarding "bad dreams" or "disturbed sleep" in commitment reports or the memoirs of Civil War veterans, the evidence is not deep. For instance, the Union veteran Abner Small spoke little of the war except to say that it gave him bad dreams, and another veteran who had returned to the Cold Harbor battlefield after the war remarked that "[s]keletons and ghosts haunt us in our dreams." Judson Austin of the 19th Michigan Infantry is the exception in that his letters during the war frequently referred to dreams, including repeated dreams that he was back at home in normal, happy circumstances with a fellow soldier, who had recently been killed in battle. Other than collections such as the Austin letters and a few scattered remarks, however, discussion or analysis of dreams is not common in Civil War materials.[25]

Aside from the fear of being killed, the fear of impending calamity, flashbacks, persistent delusions relating to the war, the fear of going outside, the tendency to isolate oneself, and insomnia, one also sees depression (melancholy), crying spells, and a wide variety of anxiety symptoms in the sample. Regarding depression, the rhetoric is of "brooding," "spells of despondency," and "very much depressed."[26] Crying was not at all unusual: "would cry at intervals"; "weep[s] bitterly"; "[s]ometimes he weeps without any cause or excitement."[27] For anxiety disorders, one sees about every condition imaginable in this sample from the diagnosis of hysteria, once thought to be limited primarily to females in the nineteenth century, to restlessness, general anxiety, "nervous" behaviors, trembling and shaking, irritability, and hyperreactivity: "I remember that his eye had a peculiar appearance as a man who is frightened, and he spoke of the damn big guns. Whenever he spoke of the cause of his trouble he said it was the constant roar of the guns in the service. . . . he was wild and very excitable and imagined persons were after him and upon the firing of a gun he was frantic." One also notices other symptoms of stress such as "smothering spells" or heart palpitations. These call to mind the diagnoses of "irritable heart," "effort syndrome," or "trotting heart" from the Civil War medical lexicon; one suspects these conditions were anxiety-related rather than organic in nature.[28]

Another peculiarity one notices regarding this sample is the occasional expression of guilt or the conviction that one has been tainted by sin. It is certainly not unknown for psychologically disturbed people to express the firm belief that they have "committed the unpardonable sin": indeed, the pathology of the matter is exactly that the person has done nothing serious, but is convinced of being doomed to eternal perdition for some imagined transgression. Yet at times it seems that the men in the sample of Civil War veterans may have in fact been reacting to events that actually occurred, acts that they committed while in the army. For instance, one veteran was operating under the delusion that he had been accused of murder and that a corpse was secreted in the house. Another thought that he was guilty of heinous crimes committed during his early life. Others were brooding over transgressions or convinced that they were hopeless sinners: "Said he was guilty of great crimes . . . he thinks he is lost for all eternity"; "delusion seems to be that he has done something terrible."[29]

One case that makes these assertions intriguing is that of William Churchill. The physician treating Churchill noted that over the past seventeen years "his mind has been badly deranged, talking about the scenes of the Civil War, seems to think at times he committed a great crime for participating in it at other times weeps over it and thinks it was all right." The matter is further illuminated by the memoirs of William A. Ketcham, a veteran of the 13th Indiana Regiment, who wrote of fighting with Grant's army in the eastern theater during the Civil War. On one occasion, Ketcham took aim at a Confederate officer, but shot too low; in his memoirs, Ketcham wrote: "I am now glad that I did not elevate the sight." In another incident, Ketcham shot a Rebel color bearer during a battle, but went up to the man's corpse after the fighting had subsided, and noticed that the dead man had multiple gunshot wounds; this seemed to ease Ketcham's conscience: "[T]hat survey of the target satisfied my mind that I was not responsible for his death and his blood was not on my hands and I have always been glad that I knew that fact. I went to war to put down the rebellion and incidentally to kill. I endeavored always to shoot as true as I could but now in my old age I am grateful that I do not know that any man's blood is on my hands." One wonders to what extent that others' concern with "crimes" and "terrible sin" may have been less a matter of delusion and related somehow to concrete memories of the war. One is reminded again of the emphasis in studies of Vietnam veterans on "abusive violence" and the effect this can have on participants years after the war has ended.[30]

The last element of PTSD symptomatology one can find in the sample of Civil War veterans relates to "cognitive disorders," that is to say problems in thinking and memory such as the inability to concentrate or remember—in such instances, one has been shaken by some traumatic experience that continues to disrupt one's ability to function in a normal manner. Again and again relatives and friends noticed that returning Civil War veterans seemed apathetic and had "lost their will power." The most common symptom observed, particularly in men who had just returned from the war, was the inability to concentrate on anything: "could not concentrate his thoughts upon any subjects"; "was in a state of kind of bewilderment"; "despondent and seemed to be wholly lacking in concentration and will power." One also notices loss of memory, not apparently related to any neurological deficit.[31]

However, more telling than any symptom profile in demonstrating the manner in which some returning veterans appeared apathetic and were unable to concentrate on anything or get their feet back on the ground is the sad case of George Wood. Wood enlisted with the 26th Indiana Infantry on August 30, 1861, and served with his unit in Mississippi and Louisiana. He fought in the Battle of Prairie Grove, Arkansas, and also participated in the siege of Vicksburg in July of 1863. During service in these conflicts, he suffered on at least one occasion from heat exhaustion and exposure. A fellow soldier remembered that when Wood was overcome by the heat, he "seemed to be unconscious like, and didn't have his full senses," and had to rest underneath a tree. Thereafter, he seemed cranky, irritable, and "off"; previously he had been an enthusiastic checkers player, but thereafter kept to himself, was excused from duty, and was even, apparently, locked up on several occasions—although it is not clear why. When George Wood finally came back from the service in 1864, he began to drink alcoholic beverages to deal with his mental state; his sister later remembered that he would tremble all over when in the sun: "I noticed something in his eyes that frightened me." Prior to the war, he had been a schoolteacher, but, because of his drinking, the county school superintendent refused to renew his teaching license. His father sent him to Franklin College, but Wood was unable to remain in school or finish the academic program there. His father also tried to set his son up in business, but this venture likewise ended in failure.

Most disappointing to George Wood was a failed love affair, in which he pursued a local girl named Harriet Diltz, but was spurned. Faced at every turn with disappointment, rejection, and failure, he began to spend more and more time alone. His father owned a house nearby that was being fixed up by workmen; George Wood would go down to the house and "would sit in that house up in the garret among the rafters for hours alone." His drinking problem grew worse, resulting in several arrests and, eventually, commitment to the asylum in Indianapolis, where, if the records are correct, he was held for fourteen years from 1880 to 1894. In 1901 Wood was examined by a pension bureau medical board, and he declared to the doctors present that he had never been insane, but was the victim of a plot. By this time he was also suffering from a form of multiple personality disorder, judging by the board's findings: "He speaks of himself & of his other self as though the two are united in one body & yet distinct." In terms of psychopathology, the George Wood case suggests a number of diagnoses—but the simple fact behind it all was that the man was unable to settle down and adjust to civilian life after his army service in the Civil War, and his somewhat fragile mental condition continued to deteriorate over time until he became completely insane and dysfunctional.[32]

At the same time, as difficult and painful as it is to imagine, the suffering of all of these veterans was magnified manyfold in that their torment also affected and disrupted the lives of their parents, wives, sisters, brothers, and children. These loved ones stood by helplessly, wanting to assist, but, in the final analysis, were unable to understand what was happening or what they could possibly do to lend comfort or reverse the course of the mental havoc wreaked by memories of violence and killing. One gets a particularly sharp picture of the disruption in the private lives of families of mentally ill Civil War veterans in the case of Allen Wiley. Wiley had served briefly as a second lieutenant with Company C of the 54th Indiana Infantry, which was sent as a contingent of fifty men into Kentucky to guard the pike south of Louisville. The unit took up a defensive position in a stockade, but was attacked by at least six hundred Rebels with artillery under the command of Confederate General Kirby Smith, who shelled the fort and forced this Union contingent to surrender.

The shelling was not intense or prolonged, but a number of rounds hit inside the fort, and at least one of these exploded near Wiley, either knocking him off his feet or sending him sprawling in fright. Comrades noticed the shell had "shocked" Lt. Wiley and that he seemed excited and badly frightened. Thereafter he could not sleep for three or four nights, and was no longer able to handle the unit's paperwork, because he could not concentrate his mind on the task. When the unit came back to Indianapolis to be mustered out of the service, a fellow soldier thought Lt. Wiley "off" in his manner and behavior. Wiley returned to his home in Indiana in Switzerland County near the Ohio River, but his family immediately noticed that something was wrong: "He did not sleep as good as he used to before [the] service. . . . Thought that someone (the neighbors) was going to shoot him. Appeared to be absent-minded and in a deep study . . . would say that someone was going to come in the night and shoot him." His sister, Almena, had always been close to him, and he would confide in her. In about 1867, while riding with her in her wagon, he suddenly seemed seized by panic and fear; as she recalled, he held his head in his hands and, in a highly distraught condition, "said for me for God's Sake to help him away from there and from that country, and . . . his face turned red, and he said he thought someone was going to shoot him." She took him toward her home in her wagon, "and on the way he would have me stop and listen and see if I couldn't hear the pistols; that some one was following him to shoot him." On other numerous occasions, Wiley, in a disturbed condition, would come to his sister's house at midnight or even later with the same terrified look and belief that he was being pursued and that his life was in danger.

Under these conditions, Wiley's marriage became a shambles, and his wife, who had filed and then dropped a similar case in 1867, finally divorced him in 1869, alleging that he had threatened and beaten her, on one occasion menacing her with a chair and on another occasion kicking her. At about that time Wiley was consulting with his lawyer, discussing possible lawsuits against a wide variety of people. In 1870 he was committed to the asylum in Indianapolis; after about seven months, he was sent home, but quickly relapsed and was back at the institution in 1871. His family finally made arrangements to take care of him at home in a "strong room," that is to say a room with bars on the windows where he could be kept so that he would not harm himself or others. Wiley would experience violent spells, and apparently was considered so dangerous that on one occasion a doctor performed a necessary operation on him through the bars in the window. A pension bureau medical board that examined him in 1887 observed: "Mentally he is insane. Talks constantly & very rapidly, incoherently, frequently repeating the words 'I cant tell.' Easily excited & when excited his language is excessively filthy, obscene & profane. His attention cannot be gained long enough to ask a question." Although Allen Wiley had pleaded with his family for help, he seemed, in fact, beyond hope.[33]

Granted that these Civil War veterans suffered from considerable mental ills in the years after the Civil War, two inevitable questions follow: To what extent were these problems caused by the war? Would not some of these men have developed mental difficulties anyway, regardless of their experience in the military? These questions have no easy answers. In some instances, one notices clear predisposition or prior indications of insanity, as when a man had been committed to the insane asylum before the war, or when neighbors testified that the individual in question had always been peculiar, even before military service.[34] For others, mental breakdown in the years following the war seemed clearly to relate to nonmilitary factors, especially in cases which involved the death of a spouse or child, which seemed to produce the most potent mental shock. The matter of Albert Gorgas would appear to be such a case. His only service during the Civil War was with the 132nd Indiana Regiment for a term of one hundred days, during which little of note took place. After the war, he was committed to the Indiana Hospital for the Insane in 1867, where the "exciting" cause of the insanity was listed as "Loss of wife and child." It is unclear how long Gorgas remained at the asylum, but he remarried in 1875, had three children from that marriage, and went on to become a successful hardware merchant in Shelbyville, Indiana. It is doubtful that one could in any way (directly, at any rate) attribute his mental problems in 1867 to his experience in the military.[35]

In many cases, however, the connection between military service and later mental problems is quite clear and undeniable, especially in three classes: cases with their origin in mental breakdown in the service itself, cases involving gunshot or shell wounds, and cases of disease incurred in the service that subsequently had psychological repercussions. Typical of the first class of case is that of William H. Smith. Smith was with the 60th Indiana Regiment, apparently at Jackson, Vicksburg, and in Louisiana. After seven days of fighting at Jackson, he said he would rather see his coffin than to go in the fight. At the Battle of Grand Coteau, he went into combat on a skirmish line. No one saw him during the battle, but afterward he "became very talkative" and acted in a peculiar manner. When his unit was moved out for further combat, he refused to go, expressing a dread of getting on the boat. He was sent to the Government Hospital for the Insane in Washington, D.C., and discharged from the military. Apparently this order did not get back to his unit, and he was arrested for desertion, but eventually released. The "disappointment and mortification because of his arrest unsettled his mind" further. He had been "sharp," participating in fun in camp, but after his release he became totally insane: "He had laughing spells with nothing to laugh at and cry for no cause. Now he plays with and seems content to sit and play with little children his mind is like a childs." He spent the rest of his life in poorhouses or insane asylums.[36]

Another class of cases of insane Civil War veterans clearly related to military service were those men who incurred gunshot wounds in the service. John Medsker of the 58th Indiana Infantry was out foraging near the Neuse River in North Carolina in March of 1865 when guerrillas attacked his party and shot him in the right side, resulting in a serious wound. For the remainder of his life, he had difficulty breathing or stooping, could not engage in manual labor, and at times would spit up blood. Worse yet were the psychological consequences of the wound, as he was in and out of the asylum in Indianapolis at least six times with recurrent mania; when he was committed to the Indiana Hospital for the Insane in 1901, thirty-six years after the date he was shot, the admitting clerk noted in the ledger: "Restless and sleepless, suicidal. Attempted suicide. Imagines he is bleeding to death from imaginary wounds." A particularly poignant case is that of James B. Farr. Farr served with the 33rd Indiana Regiment in Georgia and was shot through the neck by a rebel sniper at Kennesaw Mountain. The wound left some permanent damage to muscles in his neck and back which prevented him from moving his head forward, but, more critically, the gunshot wound rendered permanent psychological damage. The pension bureau doctors examined James Farr and found "melancholy, taciturnity, loss of memory, sleeplessness and impaired power to think." In 1871 Farr was committed to the insane asylum where the admitting ledger noted "Gets wild. thinks he will not live." A family member observed: "[He is] Often afraid he is going to die and often begging some one to remain with him to keep him from doing harm. The family and myself often sit by him quieting him and soothing him. . . . He has a wild look from the eyes,—. Talks constantly and incoherently. The Doctor has often been compelled to stay with him all night."[37]

Last of all, and this point most distinguishes Civil War veterans from the Vietnam veteran, there were those men who came back from the war suffering from the continuing repercussions of diseases such as smallpox, typhoid, malaria, measles, mumps, and a wide variety of fevers and digestive and gastrointestinal ailments. Indeed, in reviewing pension records of Civil War veterans, one discovers that one of the most common phrases employed by family, friends, and fellow soldiers to describe returning veterans was the expression "physical wreck." Various veterans in the Indiana Sample were described as follows: "broken down physically and mentally"; "a total wreck"; "he was then the most emaciated person we ever saw & appeared just ready to go to his grave"; "[h]e looked more like a dead man than anything else."[38]

While some men recovered their health and went on to lead normal and productive lives, others suffered from continuing physical and psychological consequences of disease, which could be severe and excruciating: "Cannot rest day or night . . . countenance Sad & expressionless. Eyes dull. Has been twice in the insane Assylum at Indianapolis"; "[he] was mentally unsound, . . ., a result doubtless of anaemia and debility"; "did not know what he was doing or where he was. he appeared to be perfectly crazy . . . chronic diarrhea and nervous prostration which affected his mind so much that it did not yield to treatment." A review of asylum commitment records in addition to inquest and federal pension records of the 291 men in the Indiana Sample reveals explicit mention of the military experience in some respect in 115 of these cases; in many of the other 176 cases, records are too fragmentary to reach an informed judgment as to causation of the man's psychological problems.[39]

Exuberant parades did not wash away the disturbing memories of pain and death that many Civil War veterans brought back from the war zone. Although they willingly participated in such celebrations, these men were mainly interested in being reunited with immediate family, and, moreover, they were often preoccupied with private thoughts, misgivings, and reflections that they did not immediately discuss with civilians, concerning whom they often had ambivalent feelings. The aftermath of the Civil War witnessed a proliferation of violence in both the North and the South, with incidents of crime and lawlessness in which veterans freely participated—if they were not, in fact, energizing and driving this development. Even those veterans who returned to their small towns, families, and old jobs continued to suffer from a wide range of physical and psychological ills related to the service. In the Indiana Sample, one can find a wide array of symptoms consistent with the diagnosis of PTSD (of both acute and delayed variants), although many of these veterans seemed eventually to develop more serious, chronic mental disorders that left them completely disabled and, often, totally out of touch with reality—living in a kind of personal hell in which they were constantly in fear of being killed or maimed, or in which they continued to relive the battles and horrific experiences of the Civil War. The data from this sample challenge the thesis that Vietnam veterans were unique in the history of American veterans for suffering from the delayed stress caused by traumatic experiences in the war zone.

George Alford
(6th Michigan Infantry)

Civil War soldiers and veterans were often haunted by the deaths of their fellow soldiers. George Alford of the 6th Michigan Infantry wrote to his sister Helen: "When I am alone and get to thinking over the names and numbers of my own company that are now sleeping in the Sacred Soil of Louisianna [*sic*] unbidden tears will flow in spite of my stout heart that has been hardened in the Army." (Bentley Historical Library, University of Michigan.)

Franklin Bailey
(12th Michigan Infantry)

Consumed by anger or rage in the midst of battle, Civil War soldiers could, upon reflection, later be horrified by memories of this experience. Franklin Bailey of the 12th Michigan Infantry wrote to his parents concerning the Battle of Shiloh: "It was the first battle I have seen, and I hope that it will be the last one. O what a sight, it almost makes me shudder to think of it, although at the time, I did not think any more of seeing a man shot down by my side than you would of seeing a dumb beast kiled [*sic*]." (Bentley Historical Library, University of Michigan.)

John W. Blake
(Col., 40th Indiana Infantry)

Col. John W. Blake suffered a gunshot wound to the left arm at the Battle of Stones River and, during this same battle, was accused of being drunk on the battlefield; he was subsequently exonerated at a court-martial. In the years after the war, he was committed to the Indiana Hospital for the Insane on four different occasions because of recurrent alcoholism. (Indiana State Library.)

Newell Gleason
(Lt. Col., 87th Indiana Infantry)

Gallant leadership of his unit during heavy fighting at the Battle of Chickamauga earned Lt. Col. Newell Gleason of the 87th Indiana Infantry a promotion to brevet brigadier general, but after the Atlanta Campaign of 1864, his men noticed that he seemed nervous and "rattled." After the war, Gleason's life was plagued by depression, troubled sleep, and an inability to concentrate. The Pension Bureau ruled his death in 1886 a suicide. (Library of Congress.)

Albert J. Gorgas
(132nd Indiana Infantry)

As was probably the case with Vietnam veterans, not all of the psychological problems of Civil War veterans were related to the war. Albert J. Gorgas's wife and child died in 1867, and he was committed to the Indiana Hospital for the Insane with melancholia. He remarried in 1875, had three children from that marriage, and went on to become a successful hardware merchant in Shelbyville, Indiana. (Indiana State Library.)

Eli Griffin
(Capt., 6th Michigan Infantry)

Civil War soldiers were often expected to execute frontal assaults on well-defended enemy trenches. Eli Griffin, a captain with the 6th Michigan Infantry, wrote to a friend of the "terrible slaughter of Port Hudson": "We charged on the rebel earthworks and batteries. Their fire was terrible. It was a perfect storm of bullets and grape shot. How I escaped I cannot tell." (Bentley Historical Library, University of Michigan.)

Ira G. Grover
(Lt. Col., 7th Indiana Infantry)

Lt. Col. Ira G. Grover suffered from rheumatism in addition to the aftereffects of multiple gunshot wounds incurred at the battles of Winchester and Port Republic during the Civil War; he was also held as a POW by the Confederates after the Battle of the Wilderness. After the war, he suffered from mental instability, domestic troubles, and alcoholism, which seemed to be the product of his war experience. The Pension Bureau rejected his claim for a pension, however, on the grounds that these problems were the result of his alcoholism, considered a "vicious habit" and his own fault, and not the result of illnesses or wounds contracted in the service. (Library of Congress.)

Frank M. Howard
(11th Indiana Cavalry)

Excruciating pain from gunshot wounds or chronic physical illness related to diseases contracted during the war plagued many Civil War veterans in the years after the war. Frank M. Howard, who had served with the 11th Indiana Cavalry, was a successful attorney in Rockville, Indiana, in later years. Unrelenting pain from physical illness, however, led him to attempt suicide in 1900 by cutting an artery in his leg. (Indiana State Library.)

John A. Keith
(Lt. Col., 21st Indiana Infantry)

Many Civil War veterans who had incurred gunshot or shell wounds in the war continued to suffer agonizing pain after the war because of poorly performed operations. Bone fragments sometimes worked their way out of these wounds ten and twenty years later. John A. Keith of the 21st Indiana Infantry suffered a gunshot wound to his right shoulder in 1862 that shattered bones and resulted in anchylosis, atrophy, and the recurrent emergence of bone particles. This condition caused intense pain; Keith was committed to the Indiana Hospital for the Insane twice in 1888 for alcoholism. (Indiana State Library.)

Michael Schwenk
(56th New York Infantry)

Michael Schwenk of the 56th New York Infantry was sent in 1864 to Beaufort and Morris Island, South Carolina, where his unit engaged in a series of raids and night attacks. "Sunstruck," Schwenk threatened others with an axe; he then went on a rampage at night with his gun, seeking to kill other Union soldiers. Schwenk was captured, confined, and sent to the Government Hospital for the Insane in Washington, D.C. (National Archives.)

William Collin Stevens
(Lt., 3rd Michigan Cavalry)

Despite the many difficulties of army life, Civil War soldiers often expressed a fondness for it. William Collin Stevens of the 3rd Michigan Cavalry wrote home: "Although we have seen some pretty hard fare since we left St. Louis still I like this kind of a life very well and could I only know that you were all well I should be contented." (Bentley Historical Library, University of Michigan.)

David Wiltsee
(2nd Indiana Cavalry)

Like many Union veterans, David Wiltsee of the 2nd Indiana Cavalry was greeted at the end of the war with official speeches and parades at his home state in Indianapolis as well as an exuberant welcome from his family and relatives at his home in Wabash, Indiana. In 1888, melancholy, restless, and suicidal, he was committed to the Indiana Hospital for the Insane. As is frequently the case with fragmentary nineteenth-century records, it is difficult to tell whether Wiltsee's mental breakdown was service-related. (Indiana Historical Society Library, Sub. col. neg.)

Pension Award Certificate

Many of the 1.9 million Union Civil War veterans received invalid or service pensions from the federal government. The system was established during the war and was periodically expanded thereafter; by 1893, there were 935,084 active pension awards. This certificate is for the Indiana veteran James P. Green, who was pensioned for insanity. (National Archives.)

Field-Hospital Station

In the twentieth century it has become common practice for armies to treat psychiatric casualties as near the front as possible, with the hope of returning over 50 percent of these men to combat. Although forward-area medical treatment centers became common in the Civil War, they generally did not provide care for psychologically disturbed soldiers, who were regarded as cowards or shirkers, turned over to the adjutant general, and sometimes court-martialed. (National Library of Medicine.)

Indiana Hospital for the Insane (c. 1870)

Many Civil War veterans were committed to the Indiana Hospital for the Insane in Indianapolis during the years from 1865 through 1919. Their symptoms and behaviors varied from "[he] appeared to always be in dreaded danger, and would imagine the rebels was after him" and "in constant dread of being killed" to "becomes much excited, supposes he is in battle gives commands &c." (State Archives, Indiana Commission on Public Records, Indiana State Library.)

Reunion of the 18th Indiana Battery

Despite the many hardships and dangers involved, Civil War soldiers and veterans often found their experience in the military to have been the most meaningful time of their lives, as is perhaps evident from this photograph of a reunion of members of the 18th Indiana Battery in about 1917. (Indiana Historical Society Library, neg. no. C4704.)

Union Soldiers at Rest

Civil War soldiers were frequently able to endure the war's many horrors and difficulties because of unit cohesion and devotion to their comrades. One Union soldier wrote that "ties of affectionate friendships were formed that bind us into one brother-hood by an invisible chain." (Library of Congress.)

Ward No. 4, Lincoln General Hospital, Washington, D.C.

During the Civil War, Union hospitals cared for over one million soldiers and experienced a mortality rate of only 8 percent, the lowest recorded for military hospitals to that date. Despite these favorable statistics, two-thirds of the approximately 600,000 men who died during the war succumbed to disease. This magnitude of death and suffering from physical disease has been practically unknown to twentieth-century soldiers and veterans, who have benefited from the late nineteenth-century revolution in science and medicine. (National Library of Medicine.)

"Dying of Nostalgia":
Official Diagnoses

Given the fact that acute and delayed stress disorders of a wide variety existed in Civil War soldiers, doctors, and nurses, how were these conditions conceptualized, described, and treated by soldiers and the military during the Civil War? If Civil War soldiers felt depressed, anxious, or mentally overwhelmed, what words or phrases did they use to describe their condition? What was the military policy toward stress disorders—were "shell-shocked" men excused from duty and treated for a medical condition, or punished for malingering? Indeed, did the military even have any diagnostic category along the lines of "shell shock," "combat fatigue," or "PTSD" that applied to soldiers who were no longer able to endure combat or function effectively in the ranks? Did the armies of the Civil War era have any policy akin to the twentieth century's theory of "proximity, immediacy, expectancy" in which men suffering from combat fatigue are treated briefly near the frontlines with rest, good food, and encouragement, and then returned to their units as soon as possible—if at all possible?

Although nothing resembling the American Psychiatric Association's *Diagnostic and Statistical Manual* (with its dozens of disorders and multi-axial system of diagnosis) existed in the mid-nineteenth century, Civil War soldiers still managed to engage a complex and varied terminology in describing their depressed mental state or depleted physical and mental resources. The terminology employed by Civil War soldiers for these purposes included phrases such as "the blues," "lonesome," "disheartened," "downhearted," "discouraged," "demoralized," "nervous," "played out," "used up," "anxious," "worn down," "worn out," "depressed," "rattled," "dispirited," "sad," "melancholy," and "badly blown."[1] For instance, letters frequently mentioned that Civil War soldiers or medical personnel were "blue," or "had the blues": "I am blue and homesick"; "when we remain long in one place in Camp I always get the 'blues' "; "I am about sick with Cold, Rheumatism, Blues & other ills too numerous to mention"; "one of our 'blue days' "; "[after defeat in battle] Yesterday was one of unmingled rage, hate and shame. These gradually gave way to the blues." It seemed that "the blues" were often brought on by boredom, disease, separation from home, inclement weather, or, sometimes, exposure to battle, and were nearly always interchangeable with "depressed," "gloomy" or "sad."[2]

In describing the collective or individual mental collapse of an army or an individual soldier if this condition was attributable to military reverses or exposure, the term "demoralized" was more often employed: "It is said the army is very much demoralized by the retreat from Kentucky"; "Hood's army is really demoralized"; "report says we have lost two thirds of our army and the balance demoralized"; a straggler claimed he was the "most demoralized man in the whole of the Army of the Potomac."[3] "Rattled" could also apply to a combat-induced state of mental collapse. Although "played out" and "badly blown" usually seemed to refer to man or beast that had been leveled by physical exertion or disease, this was not always the case. Some of Grant's demoralized troops, who refused to charge after the initial bloodletting during the offensive of 1864, were also referred to as "played out."[4]

When it came to the issue of determining whether men should be excused from the obligations and responsibilities of military service, however, other terms and diagnostic categories such as "insanity," "nostalgia," "irritable heart," or "sunstroke" came into play and were much more important. The first concept which must be understood is that of insanity, for if a man were determined to be insane by military authorities in the Civil War era, he would be rejected for military service or, if already in the service, would be sent to the Government Hospital for the Insane in Washington, D.C., and discharged from the army. In the nineteenth century, while the concept of insanity was in transition, the four-thousand-year-old Greek diagnostic system of "mania," "melancholia," and "dementia" was still employed.[5]

Roughly speaking, if a person were agitated and anxious and his condition were not attributable to some somatic condition such as fever, he would be diagnosed as having mania; if he were depressed or lethargic, then he would be considered to be suffering from melancholia; if there was a deterioration in the mental processes involving disordered thinking, then dementia would be diagnosed. Sometimes variations would be introduced into the system, such as the terms "senile dementia" or "paralytic dementia" (which almost always involved some sort of degenerative neurological disease), or "acute" versus "recurrent" mania; on other occasions, new terms such as "monomania" or "hysteria" entered the medical lexicon to reflect recent trends in describing and categorizing psychopathology—but, still, the classical tripartite system of diagnosis for the most part served as a sort of diagnostic and statistical manual of its day. This diagnostic system also provided for assessing "predisposing" and "exciting" causes of the insanity, which could include dozens of different types of causation—from physical disease and heredity to "religious excitement," "financial reverses," and "disappointment in love." As historians of psychiatry have pointed out, the system for the diagnosis of insanity in the early to mid-nineteenth century was primarily pragmatic, and did not take a turn to more exact and ambitious forms until the end of the nineteenth century when psychiatrists such as Kraepelin began to advance more modern, sophisticated systems of classification; it would not be until the time of World War I that more complex diagnostic systems along the lines of the modern DSM would be developed.

By modern-day standards, the nineteenth-century system of diagnosing insanity in the mania, melancholia, and dementia matrix was, to say the least, imprecise. Its application was complicated by the primitive state of the medical specialty of neurology, which meant that a wide variety of behaviors actually attributable to neurological conditions such as brain tumors, degenerative neurological diseases, and the effects of communicable diseases such as syphilis (leading eventually to the much-dreaded tertiary stage neurosyphilis with locomotor ataxia, severe mental deterioration, and eventual general paralysis) were not always readily diagnosed and recognized for what they were—somatic illnesses. Symptoms of abnormal behavior in such cases were often analyzed in accordance with the mania, melancholia, and dementia construct, and viewed as general psychological problems, even though there was an underlying (but at that time unknown) physical basis for the behavior.[6]

How did the military understand and apply the concept of insanity in enrolling men into or discharging soldiers from the service? At the time of the Civil War, the Union Army did recognize insanity as grounds for exclusion or discharge from the service, but there was little reference in military manuals to contemporary theoretical tracts on insanity or medicine, and no great effort was expended to provide precise or definitive explanations for physicians entrusted with administering the system. Hence standards were somewhat imprecise on paper, but tended—to the extent that they were articulated—to be exacting, with the key word being "manifest." For instance, Union regulations established to guide physicians in their examination of men called in the draft during the Civil War provided that exemptions could be granted to exclude men from the service in cases involving "manifest imbecility or insanity" or "acute or organic diseases of the brain or spinal chord [which leave] no reasonable doubt of the man's incapacity for military service." Head injuries which left a man with epilepsy, impaired intellectual faculties, or other manifest nervous or spasmodic symptoms could also exempt him from service. Subsequent amendments to these regulations indicated that men should be rejected for "manifest imbecility" and "insanity," and that this was to include "well-established recent insanity, with liability to a recurrence." "Manifest," "well-established," and "no reasonable doubt" were the key phrases. According to data provided in the *Official Record of the War of the Rebellion*, these exemptions were rarely employed to reject men for service. A report of November 1863 indicated that of 38,414 men examined by one point, only 256 had been rejected for manifest imbecility or insanity (6.6 per thousand); this was a low rejection rate compared with the 94 men per thousand rejected for mental or moral defects by the American military in World War II.[7]

Regarding discharges from the army once men had been inducted into the service and had joined units, the official Union Army policy was, again, focused on maintaining and maximizing manpower, particularly in the latter stages of the war. Discharges of soldiers for insanity or imbecility could only be made if the condition was "manifest" and, as was the case for discharges for physical ills, the unit's commanding officer as well as medical officer had to jointly approve. Moreover, official regulations required that insane men be sent to the Government Hospital for the Insane in Washington, D.C., so that decisions regarding discharge from the army for insanity would ideally be entrusted to government asylum doctors expert in the matter of insanity. As an additional safeguard, the entire process of sending men to Washington was under the control of the Adjutant-General's Office (rather than that of the Medical Department), which had the authority to screen all men submitted for commitment to the government insane asylum. Last of all, an army circular of 1863 brought an end—at least in theory—to medical officers in the field discharging men from the army on the basis of insanity; from 1863 on, the exclusive method of discharge from the army for insanity was to be through the Government Hospital for the Insane in Washington.[8]

How did this system of discharging insane soldiers from the army work in practice? In most respects, it was as exacting and unsympathetic as one might imagine from examining the official guidelines and policies on paper. Contrary to the policy of the United States Army in World War II of maximizing efficiency by cutting loose the "ineffectives," and to the post-Vietnam emphasis on sympathy for the plight of the psychologically troubled soldier and veteran, the U.S. Army in the Civil War era was determined to keep men in the ranks if at all possible, and seemed to be convinced that any man seeking a discharge on the basis of a mental or physical disability was probably a malingerer. It thus became official army policy to presume that all soldiers presenting themselves in a deranged or overwrought state and seeking discharge from the army were shirkers, who should be returned to duty if at all possible. The thought was that if a man were really ill or hopelessly insane, he would show up at sick call again anyway, and could eventually be granted a medical discharge if need be.

As an indication of how extreme this attitude could be, when men presented themselves with hysterical paralysis of an arm or leg, they were anesthetized to see if they really were suffering from paralyzed limbs as they claimed; if the limb was found to have no organic or objective deficit, the man was considered to be a malingerer and returned to duty. One Union Army circular stated: "When a march is likely to be made the Surgeon is . . . called upon to make a careful and rigid examination to avoid imposition; for the terrifying effect of a prospective battle will cause men to limp who never limped before, and many hitherto good soldiers will make an effort to escape it." This general outlook and treatment recalls some of the more ruthless and brutal methods employed in World War I by both British and German doctors, who would use techniques such as isolation, electrical current, and outright physical pain in an attempt to intimidate and coerce stuttering, trembling, and mute men back to "health" or, more to the point, to continued military service.[9]

Union rank-and-file doctors thus generally seemed to consider it their duty to return "shirkers" to the front lines, and the letters, diaries, and memoirs of these medical men generally reflect almost a zeal to implement the official policy of detecting cases of feigned insanity in soldiers seeking to escape combat or to secure a discharge from the service. One Union medical man recalled that a surgeon had to be a detective, devising a range of tests to spot the frauds that soldiers would perpetrate to escape hazardous duty, and another doctor wrote of the ingenuity of the "deadbeats." A U.S. Army medical circular proposed that all subjective symptoms and accounts of soldiers seeking discharges be ignored, and that separation from the military only be granted based on "objective" assessments of disease. Seemingly, regimental surgeons only felt comfortable granting discharges (or sending men to the government asylum) on the basis of insanity if the man involved had nothing to gain by being declared insane and if his behavior was so utterly and completely mad as to rule out all possibility of artifice. This fixation on the detection of malingering was even present in the attitude of the era's preeminent neurologists, William W. Keen and S. Weir Mitchell, who got their start and established the foundation for their postwar discoveries in neurology when they served as Union Army surgeons during the Civil War. Keen, Mitchell, and their colleague George R. Morehouse wrote: "Every means should be adopted to ascertain positively the reality of the deception."[10]

Were these Civil War soldiers actually malingering, or were some of them suffering from what would have been diagnosed in the twentieth century as shell shock, combat fatigue, or PTSD? It seems quite likely that many if not most of these men would have been regarded as psychiatric casualties from the modern point of view, and indeed, Mitchell himself seemed to recognize this when he wrote in 1914: "[In the Civil War it] became the custom to turn over to us the cases suspected of malingering. These were the scamps or cowards, and in some cases the victims of a strange form of psychic disorder. . . . I regret that no careful study was made of what was in some instances an interesting psychic malady, making men hysteric and incurable except by discharge."[11] Despite, however, the differences in theory between the twentieth century's approach of establishing front-line psychiatric treatment stations and the nineteenth century's tendency to view terrified infantrymen flocking to the rear as despicable shirkers, it is interesting to note that the primary emphasis in both systems was on returning men to combat to preserve military manpower levels.

Not surprisingly, then, given the Union Army's rigorous standards regarding discharge from the army for insanity along with the highly skeptical outlook of those doctors entrusted with administering the system, only about 1,231 Union soldiers were sent to the Government Hospital for the Insane (later known as "St. Elizabeth's") during the Civil War. While evidence is thus limited, and while nineteenth-century asylum records from the Government Hospital for the Insane are woefully inadequate (records on individual cases—aside from an admissions ledger—were not kept until about 1910), details on some of these 1,231 cases can be retrieved by cross-referencing names from the asylum admissions ledger with extant federal pension files. Many of these cases of insane soldiers sent to the asylum during the Civil War involved men who had broken down in battle and had either gone berserk on the spot or had deserted, were captured and confined, and were eventually sent to the asylum from prison. For instance, Darius Bateman of the 25th New Jersey Regiment broke down during the Battle of Fredericksburg; his unit had huddled behind an embankment for hours listening to the terrifying thunder of artillery fire on the battlefield before being sent on a frontal assault against Rebel cannons. Running into "death-dealing artillery," a "sheet of fire and flame," and "leaden rain and iron hail," the ranks were shredded as men were cut down in their tracks; survivors of this debacle were quickly forced to fall back. The next day Bateman was "talking funny" and appeared to be light-headed, and was eventually transported to the asylum.[12]

Other men were sent to the asylum after suffering from breakdown at engagements such as the battles of Weldon Railroad, Vicksburg, and Gettysburg. David Harper participated in the Valley Campaign in the Shenandoah Valley during the summer of 1862 when Union forces attempted to trap Stonewall Jackson's Rebel "foot cavalry"; there was doubtless great anxiety as to where Jackson would next emerge, and subjected to this kind of uncertainty and stress, Harper wandered off from his unit. After subsequently being found acting strangely, he was sent to the hospital and diagnosed as having "acute melancholia." Xavier Hinderlet of the 1st N.Y. Artillery was knocked down by the windage of a shell at the Battle of Chancellorsville; fellow soldiers found him wandering around afterward in a deranged state with glassy eyes, expressing a fear of being captured and killed. Hinderlet was confined, but went completely mad and scalped a guard before finally being sent to the asylum. David Kells, who fought at Chancellorsville and Gettysburg, "was worn out, sick and exhausted and deserted"; he was eventually arrested and sent to the hospital because of his condition. Francis Steck, who had apparently been in some kind of hospital ever since the Battle of Chancellorsville, was eventually sent to the Government Hospital for the Insane, and committed suicide there by drowning himself on October 21, 1863.[13]

A number of men were also sent to the asylum after they experienced psychological repercussions from gunshot wounds. Albert S. Green of the 7th Maine Infantry was fighting at the Battle of the Wilderness when he was hit by a spent ball: "I remember that he grabbed both hands over his bowels and hollowed and screamed and was about frightened to death." He subsequently deserted, but was recaptured and cleared of all charges on grounds of insanity. However, the officers in his unit had apparently not looked kindly on the incident and subsequently tied him up to a tree while a battle was in progress. If Green had not already been on the verge of a complete mental collapse, "that nearly scared him to death." He was eventually sent to the Government Hospital for the Insane in 1865 with acute mania. After being discharged, his condition continued to deteriorate, and his mother recalled that one day he was standing, looking out the window, when he suddenly exclaimed: "[T]hey are after me, They are after me." Green later got up in the middle of the night and ran out screaming, "They are after me." He seemed beyond help from that time on, and was committed to an insane asylum in Maine in 1876. Another striking case is that of John G. Hildt of the 1st Michigan Infantry. His unit was on the front line at the beginning of the Seven Days' Battles in June and July of 1862, and his regiment absorbed very high casualties at the Battle of Gaines Mill: twenty-seven killed and eighty-one wounded. Hildt himself received a catastrophic gunshot wound to the right arm, which required amputation of the entire arm at the shoulder. He became insane in the hospital while recovering from these wounds, and was transferred in December of 1862 to the Government Hospital for the Insane, where he spent the remainder of his life in a profoundly psychotic state. A board of physicians which examined him in 1890 noted: "He is now the victim of chronic dementia. Is completely irrational. Does not know what day it is or what time of day. Does not know the physician who has had charge of him for seven years."[14]

The capacity of the Government Hospital for the Insane was expanded from 117 in 1859 to almost 300 near the end of the Civil War,[15] but, although over 1,000 soldiers were treated at this hospital during the war, most mentally troubled soldiers probably never got anywhere near Washington, D.C., but, rather, remained in the field and were dealt with in an ad hoc fashion. Despite the official policy (after 1863) of sending all soldiers deemed insane to the asylum in Washington, D.C., some men were either committed to local asylums or released to relatives, and essentially discharged from the army. Several Indiana volunteers were dealt with in this manner and committed to asylums in Virginia, Tennessee, or Indiana. For instance, Uriah Slagle was called from his home in northern Indiana to come get his son, Francis, who was being held in a military hospital in New Albany, Indiana, on the Ohio River. Francis, a member of the 17th Indiana Regiment, was in poor mental and physical shape: "[H]e was insane, and would take all of his clothes off and try to walk about stark naked; . . . continually spitting up bloody matter and running off from the bowels." Slagle took his son home, but his condition failed to improve and he was subsequently sent to the Indiana Hospital for the Insane, where he died six months later. Confederate policy did not focus on the use of a central insane asylum like the one in Washington, D.C., but, rather, provided that an insane soldier should be committed to any available asylum in the district in which he fell ill; hence, official Confederate policy resembled the ad hoc way in which Union veterans were actually handled.[16]

Consistent with the Union Army practice (sometimes in spite of official policy) of utilizing local insane asylums when convenient, many Northern soldiers were committed to the Indiana Hospital for the Insane in Indianapolis during the Civil War. Its capacity stood at about three hundred during the war years, and from 1861 to 1865, thirty-five soldiers were admitted to the hospital, along with a similar number of civilians suffering explicitly from "war excitement." Some of these soldiers were sent directly to the asylum from camp after they had failed to adjust to military life; others were sent back to Indiana from points in the South, as was the case with Anthony Bihler, who broke down at the Battle of Pea Ridge in Arkansas in the spring of 1862. The most common cause of insanity in soldiers was listed as "exposure in the army," but other causes included fright before a battle, war excitement, the "shock of battle," "shell explosions," or "The War." Dozens of females were committed to the asylum for war-related concerns, the following descriptions being typical: "Death of son who died in the Army"; "has a son in Army that she grieves very much about"; "death of brother in army." These commitments of females in incidents related to the war continued into the postwar years as indicated by two cases from 1867 and 1868: "Husband died in the army"; "has talked much of loss of son in the army."[17]

One notices similar patterns in other Northern state insane asylums. Soldiers were committed to the Illinois State Insane Asylum at Jacksonville both from camp and from the field, sometimes from "exposure" and at other times on account of "war excitement," "fatigue," "sunstroke," "overexertion," or directly after breakdown at a battle. For instance, the commitment report of one soldier read: "Was in battle at Perryville Ky. Oct 1862. & has not been well since. Has had chronic diarrhoea. Is homicidal Threatens to burn buildings." These commitments sometimes extended into the postwar years, dealing with either lingering psychological problems or cases of war-related stress with a delayed onset: "Has not been well since his return from the army." As in Indiana, women in Illinois were adversely affected by the war and as a result were committed to the asylum on occasion, often for general "fright" or sometimes for more specific concerns: "Has been anxious about her brothers, two of whom are in the army"; "[c]aused by anxiety of mind about a son in army"; "Her husband entered the Army about one and a half years since and was killed at Mission Ridge. She has not been right since he enlisted but was not violent until after he was killed." The same tragic anguish, suffering, and grief emerge from the asylum records at the Columbus Hospital for the Insane and the Longview Hospital in Cincinnati, Ohio. For men, the story is one of illness, exposure, and fright; for women, there is concern over loved ones in the army, grief over menfolk killed in action, and fear of the Confederate raider, General Morgan. In Longview Hospital, one also notes the commitment of at least two political prisoners, who were imprisoned for opposition to the war, which resulted in extreme and intractable depression: "He was arrested for *Opinion's sake* and put in prison at Camp Chase Ohio, but as no evidence of disloyalty were found, he was released. The mental excitement incident to his arrest brought upon him the sad calamity of a deranged mind . . . sometimes he screams out in his sleep and wakes up frightened."[18]

In the Vietnam era, advocates of Vietnam veterans argued that many discipline problems actually involved men suffering from stress disorders, who were simply acting out; a major effort was made in the post-Vietnam years to remove dishonorable discharges from the records of veterans disciplined during the war itself. One suspects that many cases of men behaving in a disorderly manner or refusing to obey orders during the Civil War also involved soldiers who had reached the limits of their endurance, and could easily have been considered psychiatric casualties of war; in most cases, however, these men were punished severely. One soldier who refused to go on duty was dishonorably dismissed from the service and sent to a military prison in Norfolk, and made to sweep the streets in a convict's dress. In another case, an officer reacted to an enlisted man who refused to obey orders by punching the man in the mouth with a bayonet, and then tying him up and eventually putting him at hard labor for a month. Other men were "bucked and gagged," a form of punishment in which a man's hands were tied over his knees, a stick was inserted between his arms and legs, and a bayonet would then be tied in his mouth—which frequently left the man a bloody mess.[19]

The case of Daniel McElfresh probably involved an instance of an insane or severely disturbed man being treated as a discipline problem by military authorities. After participating in the Battle of Stones River, a fellow soldier noted of McElfresh: "I saw him shortly after the Battle and he was very much [exhausted?] and seemed to be suffering mentally." Thereafter, McElfresh could not do his duty properly, and would wander off or lose his accoutrements. His commanders disciplined him by both restraining him and physically punishing him; although the exact methods employed are not known, his fellow soldiers were shocked at the treatment, and tried to cover for him. In postwar years several expressed the opinion that the severity of this punishment had contributed to pushing McElfresh further and further toward insanity. Observers noted that his eyes indicated "wildness and fear"; he couldn't hold a job, and had persistent delusions of fighting off Rebel charges: "On one ocasion he came into the Road just at dark marching back and forth giveing command as if he was adressing soldiers . . . giveing command to immaginary soldiers to charge the Rebels this kept up for some Three or more hours it was moon light."[20] Other accounts from Civil War soldiers reveal that in at least one instance, at the Battle of Spotsylvania Courthouse, a court-martial was conducted on the battlefield *during* the battle, and, on another occasion when men were noticed roaming around in a disoriented condition, the situation was dealt with by means of courts-martial. These occurrences recall the Western Front early in World War I when British soldiers found to be wandering around aimlessly away from their units were court-martialed for desertion and shot; it turned out on closer examination that many of these men were disoriented because of shell shock, and the practice of rapid executions following summary process was generally halted.[21]

Some clearly insane soldiers who were initially treated as discipline problems eventually ended up in asylums, as is demonstrated by the cases of Cornwell Meek and G. H. E. Bailey. Meek was on a skirmish line at the Battle of New Market, Tennessee, on December 23, 1863, when an enemy shell exploded nearby and knocked him to the ground. He subsequently became irrational and melancholy, and tried to blow up a magazine of ammunition. A board of surgeons which examined him initially determined that he was feigning insanity, so Meek was confined by being locked up in an old outhouse. One of his acquaintances was notified and came to Chattanooga, and found Meek entirely naked, smeared with his own excrement, and with bruises and infections on his arms, face, and thighs; in the friend's opinion Meek was absolutely and desperately insane. The medical board reconvened, issued an order that Cornwell Meek was insane, and allowed his friend to take him back to Indiana where he was eventually committed, "weary, ill, and exhausted," to the asylum in Indianapolis. The case of G. H. E. Bailey is somewhat more mysterious. In June of 1862, Bailey refused to go on guard duty when ordered, and inexplicably flew into a rage, yelling at the sergeant: "I will be God damned if I will go on duty. I want to know by whose authority I am detailed for Guard duty." When arrested and ordered to quarters by the major, Bailey responded with threats: "Don't you take hold of me, just wait until we are out of the service and I will kick more damned Lager Beer out of you than you have drank for the last two years." Bailey was court-martialed, found guilty, reduced to the ranks, and sentenced to a year at hard labor. Apparently in lieu of actual imprisonment, however, the man was sent to the Government Hospital for the Insane.[22]

At the other end of the spectrum, some men who were unable to perform their duties as a result of stress disorders were kept in camp but given light duty and excused from participating in combat. One man who experienced ringing in his ears after the Battle of Shiloh was excused from duty when he felt he needed to rest; another shell-shocked man was excused from his responsibilities for weeks at a time. A third such case is that of James D. Campbell, who had been on a Union skirmish line at Missionary Ridge when a Rebel shell exploded overhead and killed the unit's sergeant and possibly several other men as well. This shell either knocked Campbell down or rendered him insensible, and he was thereafter regarded as nervous and of unsound mind: "[H]e was so crazy that I could not get anything out of him in regard to the matter." He was assigned to detached service as a teamster, and finished out his term with his unit in this capacity.[23]

Related to the issues of discipline and the detection of supposed malingering is the matter of desertion. During the Civil War, over 300,000 Union and Confederate soldiers deserted from the ranks. One suspects that many of these cases involved men who, suffering from post-traumatic stress, realized that they would not be granted a respite or discharge from the army, and simply took the matter into their own hands by fleeing an intolerable situation. The attitude of those who remained behind toward these "skulkers," "shirkers", "beats," or deserters could be quite ambivalent. On the one hand, most accounts mirrored the official attitude of the army and the medical department by condemning men who avoided or attempted to evade hazardous duty: "[C]owardly skulkers who would not stay on the firing line except a bayonet was at their back"; "[stragglers] can always be found in the rear when the action is fought"; "contemptible shirkers"; "the artful skulker." On the other hand, Civil War soldiers could also understand better than anyone else what drove men to desert; accounts in diaries, letters, or memoirs of Civil War soldiers actually approving of the execution of deserters are almost unknown, and soldiers who remained in the ranks could even sympathize with those who left: "Several of the boys in our Regiment said 'no use going any further,' and they started East. I saw them leave, and never thought hard of them for leaving. Oh war, war!"[24]

Were deserters actually suffering from stress disorders? By definition, these men tended to disappear and keep a low profile, speaking very little of what they had done, but the case of William Morris is suggestive of an answer. Morris had been in the 68th Indiana Infantry, but deserted from his unit at about the time of the Battle of Perryville in 1862; the motivation for his decision to desert may have been a combination of fear of combat and the need to support his family at

home. In applying for a pension after the war, Morris submitted a
rambling letter which began, "It is imposible for Neighbors to testify
to the amount of Suffering I have indured since being in the service."
He was disqualified from receiving a pension because of his desertion. After his death, his widow also applied for a pension on his
account, and a letter submitted to the Pension Bureau on her behalf
by John S. Benham, superintendent of the Ripley County Schools, in
1929 after the experience of World War I is most revealing:

> I am writing you in the interest of a pension for Mrs. Mary Morris,
> widow of the late William Morris. I am one of the few now living who
> was personally acquainted with this couple since their marriage about
> 1874. Mr. Morris was regarded as queer from the time of his return from
> the Civil War, and was rated as a Deserter. Spent some time as a patient
> in the State Insane Hospital, and for the past thirty years of his life was
> regarded as an "Incurable" and as such spent his time at the County
> Farm. A victim of "Shell Shock" would doubtless have been the verdict
> of similar cases of the World War Veterans.

And, to complicate matters for deserters, their original psychological
problems were sometimes compounded by the fear that they would
be caught and executed for having deserted, as is indicated by asylum records: "[F]ear of being shot for desertion . . . inability to sleep
with mental depression. . . . Leaves his home and stays in the woods
without food for a week at a time." Of the 291 men in the Indiana
Sample, 21 deserted from their units during the Civil War.[25]

After insanity, the second major diagnostic category used in the
Civil War era to describe what we would think of today as a stress
disorder was what was known as "homesickness," or "nostalgia," a
medical term based on the French diagnostic category *nostalgie,*
which had been in the medical lexicon since the seventeenth century
to explain the mental deterioration suffered by soldiers who were
stationed far from home. Incidents of nostalgia were observed as
early as 1634–1644 in the Spanish Army of Flanders, and the term
first appeared in the medical literature in a dissertation by Johannes
Hofer in 1678. By the nineteenth century, nostalgia was prominent in
French psychiatric literature, was increasingly thought of as a vari-
ation of melancholia, and was deemed particularly evident in armies
during periods of boredom, defeat, or catastrophe. Toward the mid-
nineteenth century, nostalgia was in decline as a diagnostic category,
but experienced a revival in the American Civil War. The Union
Army recognized nostalgia as an accepted category of disease, and

included it in *A Manual of Instructions for Enlisting and Discharging Soldiers* which was issued to army medical officers:

> Nostalgia is a form of mental disease which comes more frequently under the observation of the military surgeon. . . . Considered as a mental disease,—and there can be no doubt that the primary phenomena of this state are mental,—it belongs to the class Melancholia. The extreme mental depression and the unconquerable longing for home soon produce a state of cachexy, loss of appetite, derangement of the assimilative functions, and, finally, disease of the abdominal viscera,—in fact, the objective phenomena of the typhoid state. . . . As Nostalgia is not unfrequently fatal, it is a ground for discharge if sufficiently decided and pronounced.[26]

"Nostalgia" or "homesickness" is no longer considered a valid psychiatric diagnostic category, but Civil War accounts are peppered with the term; for the most part such references seemed to describe a general disorientation and depression: "I was not sick after reading your letters from June, but did feel very lonely & had symptoms of the disease called 'homesickness' "; "All those who return from furloughs are unhappy. They were sad, leaving their families, and they suffer from having again attacks of homesickness." When viewed as a psychiatric disease, it was often used to describe the mental deterioration of POWs, who would decline mentally and physically as they slowly lost all hope: "They became homesick and disheartened. They lost all interest in everything, and would sit in the same attitude hour after hour and day after day, with their backs against the wall and their gaze fixed on the floor at my feet . . . they were dying of nostalgia." Or, as another account described: "No amount of pluck will stand forever the putting off of hope . . . if the mind had only been at ease. Thousands more would have lived. Homesickness, the most pitiless monster that ever hung about a human heart, killed them. It killed as many in our army as did the bullets of the enemy."[27]

However, during the Civil War era, "nostalgia" was also engaged on occasion to describe a post-combat syndrome similar to PTSD, as when Henry H. Bellamy wrote in the aftermath of the Battle of Shiloh in April 1862:

> I wish I was out of this Regt. I would be Thankfull it is the most Damnable Institution Ever . . . all I wish is that I was out of this you would not ketch me in such a fix again very soon . . . there was very Poor Generaliship it was the Cause of a good many lives being lost . . . the

Battle Field is some 4 or 5 miles square the trees are all cut up it looks as though there had been a very heavy haile storm . . . I am not home Sick but sick of the hum bugd Connditions . . . thar is some of the Boy that is so Home Sick that thay Do not know what to do with them selves.[28]

Also at the Battle of Shiloh, thousands of Union soldiers, who were swept from their camp sites by a surprise Confederate attack on the first day of the battle, huddled in stark terror on the banks of the Tennessee River. Many of them, claiming the condition of "nostalgia," eventually sought evacuation. An observer at Shiloh noted: "Such looks of terror, such confusion, I never saw before, and do not wish to see again." After 11,000 soldiers were evacuated by boat, the authorities, noting that "it was found impossible to prevent the flocking on board of many whose only complaint was nostalgia" thought better of allowing such evacuations in the future. Although reports of nostalgia went up in the second year of the war (in the Army of the Potomac, which saw a great deal of combat, rates tripled), the incidence subsequently declined. This could indicate that recruits predisposed to suffer this ailment had been screened out, that active campaigning minimized the condition, or, more likely, that claims of nostalgia after battles came to be viewed as malingering or weakness, a possibility that is suggested by one letter from a veteran: "These *new fellers* ARE GENERALLY a homesick set. The toughening process affects them rather severely and their sick list is proportionately large." The *Medical and Surgical History* reports the following numbers of casualties (per thousand troops) during the Civil War:[29]

Date	Nostalgia	Insanity	Sunstroke	Total nervous diseases
7/61–6/62	2.05	1.77	1.49	97.48
7/62–6/63	3.35	1.39	1.99	85.70
7/63–6/64	1.96	.81	3.85	65.89
7/64–6/65	1.93	.75	3.78	72.11

Some Civil War surgeons pioneered the study of what was then called "irritable heart" or "trotting heart," which was basically a manifestation of stress. Dr. Henry Hartshorne noted the "muscular exhaustion of the heart" caused by long-continued overexertion without sufficient rest. He examined many cases resulting from steady marching and fighting for a number of weeks in the Peninsula Campaign, and concluded that several months of rest and treatment in the hospital improved but failed to cure these cases. He recommended discharge from the military as "cheaper and wiser." J. M. DaCosta also investigated this phenomenon, noting that the same syndrome had been observed by British doctors in the Crimean War. One of DaCosta's case studies noted a man with severe cardiac problems but with no ascertainable physical pathology. Although DaCosta noticed the onset of this condition in some men following involvement in a battle, he attributed this phenomenon more to hard marching or general overexertion than to exposure to combat. In postwar pension cases, veterans occasionally presented claims based on "smothering spells," which call to mind DaCosta's syndrome; one such file revealed: "Complains of dizziness during the summer. complains of palpitation of the heart and smothering spells. attacks of vertigo and falling to the ground. nervousness and sleepless at nights."[30]

After insanity, nostalgia, and irritable heart, the fourth diagnostic category one suspects was frequently used to identify stress disorders in the Civil War era was "sunstroke." In fact, it seems that "sunstroke," though a broad and complicated concept, was at times employed as the Civil War equivalent of modern-day "combat fatigue." On numerous occasions, men who broke down in battle were described as having fallen victim to sunstroke. Sunstroke was frequently equated with insanity, as in the cases of David Callaghan, who broke down during the Battle of Weldon Railroad in 1864 ("during that charge said Callaghan received a severe sunstroke and was sent to hospital"), and Thomas Farrell, who was stricken at Vicksburg ("whilst on Picket duty by being sun struck on account of excessive exposure to the sun"). Both of these men were sent to the Government Hospital for the Insane, where the diagnoses were, respectively, "acute febrile mania" and "acute mania." Also germane to the issue is the case of John Kiely:

> Serg't John Kiely . . . had been much fatigued and exhausted Sept. 17, 1862, at the battle of Antietam; a few days afterward, while on duty, he became insensible and fell from his horse. He was sent to Mount Vernon hospital, where he remained a month, when he was returned to his regiment. After a few days, being unfit for duty, he was sent to a New York hospital, where he remained six weeks, and was again forwarded

to his regiment; but his former symptoms returning while en route, he was sent to this hospital. Diagnosis—Sunstroke: Some emaciation; nervous excitability; dizziness on exertion. . .[31]

Last of all, one needs to consider the relationship between stress and physical illness in two respects: to what extent did stress produce physical ills such as chronic diarrhea? And to what extent did the diagnosis of a physical ailment mask an underlying or concurrent psychological ill? In respect to the first issue, the case of Charles Adams is intriguing: Adams served with the 44th Indiana Infantry, and was discharged from the service shortly after the Battle of Shiloh because he had contracted chronic diarrhea and general debility as a result of that battle. As Adams himself put the matter in his subsequent claim for a pension: "He states that while in the service aforesaid and in line of duty at the battle of Shiloh . . . incident to hardship and overexertion at said battle, he contracted Chronic diarrhoea and incident thereto general debility, which has permanently disabled him from performing military duty from that time, and now he is totally unable to perform manual labor." His commitment report at the Indiana Hospital for the Insane in 1871 listed "army diarrhea" under "physical disease" on the ledger, although the predisposing cause for the insanity was listed as "unknown." One wonders if Adams's chronic diarrhea was not in some measure stress-induced or stress-related.[32]

Other cases are equally suggestive. A friend recalled of Elijah Boswell: "[A] short time after the Stone River fight. I remember him complaining there of this chronic diarrhoea." Joel H. Miller took sick with chronic diarrhea after the Battle of Franklin in December of 1864, and in the years after the war alleged "chronic derangement of the system caused by disease in the army." Another soldier developed chronic diarrhea just before the Battle of Kennesaw Mountain. It could be that references to these battles were simply a convenient way of placing the onset of the disease in a familiar time framework, although, as with the case of Charles Adams, one wonders if the physical condition was not induced or caused by the fear, anxiety, and depression associated with combat.[33]

For the men in the Indiana Sample eventually committed to the Indiana Hospital for the Insane, many presented a wide array of physical ills from ever-present chronic diarrhea to rheumatism, neuralgia, malarial poisoning, typhoid fever, other fevers or epidemic disease, and diseases of the stomach, lungs, and heart. To the extent these men were discharged from the army for these physical conditions, their cases may have been instances of what has come to be known as "occult psychiatric casualties," that is to say, men who would have broken down and been dealt with as a psychiatric case were it not for the fact that they first were wounded or fell victim to a somatic illness or condition that removed them from the ranks before the psychological condition became full-blown and was officially diagnosed. Indeed, conditions during the Civil War were so wretched—and this is an important point to keep in mind concerning any comparison of Civil War and Vietnam veterans—that it is often impossible to tell if the men were suffering from a specific somatic illness, overall exhaustion, express psychological breakdown, or a mixture of all of these conditions. When a Confederate surgeon noted that his "poor emaciated men" were "suffering such mental anxiety" and were "completely exhausted," it is open to question exactly how to diagnose such cases. The same issue arises when a Union doctor writes that the men were without shelter or food in pouring rain for an entire day of combat and "a large number of men were thrown on my hands; some of them sick; most of them tired and exhausted." There were also the cases of nervousness and outright shock associated with gunshot wounds and the chronic cases of dysentery.[34]

Short of actual discharge from the military for a specific mental or physical infirmity, some soldiers who were no longer able to perform their duties were organized into the Invalid Corps (later called the Veteran Reserve Corps, or VRC), and it seems possible that its ranks might have included numbers of stress reaction cases. The Invalid Corps was first formally organized in the spring of 1863, and was intended as an alternative to outright discharge from the military; it took men who were unable to perform frontline military duty, but not completely incapacitated, and put them to work (in the "First Batallion") at tasks such as garrison and guard duty, and, for the more severely disabled (the "Second Batallion"), work in hospitals as cooks, nurses, ward masters, clerks, and orderlies. Men who were suffering from "manifest" insanity and other severe disabilities could not join the VRC, and this list of exclusionary conditions was, interestingly, expanded in July of 1863 to include "nervous debility, or excitability of the heart." In the latter stages of the war, any army surgeon contemplating discharging a man for disability was first required to assess his suitability for service in the VRC; from 1863 through the end of the war in early 1865, over 60,000 men served in the VRC, and, in the Indiana Sample, nine men saw duty in this corps.[35]

In the Civil War era, then, the U.S. Army specifically recognized psychiatric casualties by means of various categories (primarily insanity, nostalgia, irritable heart, and, in some instances, sunstroke), but generally demanded that the condition, in the absence of physical collapse, be "manifest," "decided," or "pronounced" before discharge from the army would be granted. The emphasis was on maintaining high levels of manpower, and many efforts of disturbed or frightened soldiers to avoid further exposure to combat were regarded as malingering or shirking. This attitude probably convinced many soldiers that desertion was the only escape valve, and it seems likely that many of the 300,000 men who deserted from the Union and Confederate armies were suffering from some form of what we would regard today as a stress disorder. There seemed to be a general understanding that military life could wear down the soldier mentally and physically, but the emphasis was on deterioration of one's physical health before disability discharges would be granted. No doubt many of the thousands of men granted such discharges from the army after their health had been completely shattered by military service were also suffering from symptoms of psychological distress; it is just that their physical problems—spitting up blood, emaciation due to typhoid fever or malaria, the aftereffects of painful gunshot wounds—overshadowed the usually more subtle and secondary psychological issues. In a sense, perhaps the post-Vietnam (or for that matter the twentieth century's) emphasis on recognizing the psychological wounds of war has required, as a prerequisite and a foundation, a certain level of physical health and well-being in the troops.[36]

"This Must End Sometime":
The Fate of the Civil War Veteran

In view of the fact that the psychological problems of many Civil War veterans extended well into the postwar era, how were these men treated and how were their problems understood? Were they viewed with understanding and sympathy, or were they dismissed as cowardly misfits? When these veterans claimed that they had lost their will power or had difficulty concentrating on any subject, or when they raved about fearing that they were being pursued or that they would be killed thirty and forty years after Lee's surrender at Appomattox Courthouse, were their problems attributed to the war? Did the medical and psychological theory of their day recognize the concept of post-traumatic stress, or if the exact concept of PTSD itself did not yet exist, were there comparable or surrogate diagnostic categories such as "nostalgia" or "sunstroke" by which the problems of disabled or distressed Civil War veterans could be recognized and treated? What specific medical treatment was available for these disturbed veterans, and was this treatment effective? Were pensions or financial support extended to Civil War veterans who were disabled by delayed stress reactions that developed years after the war, even when these men had displayed no evidence of overt psychological problems or breakdown during the war itself?

Any assessment of the medical treatment available for psychologically disturbed Civil War veterans must begin with an understanding of the role played by the insane asylum in the nineteenth century. Prior to the 1800s, the "insane" were not rigidly classified as such or regarded as a distinct deviant group in society, but were usually

lumped together with other socially dependent people, such as paupers, widows, or the physically disabled, and supported in the local
community. These "dependent poor" were first and foremost kept,
if at all possible, at home or with relatives; if without kin able to
provide for their needs (and if they met residency requirements), the
insane in colonial America would have been placed with local families who were reimbursed out of government funds for their keep,
or they might have been kept in the equivalent of local almshouses
or workhouses. Although insane asylums were constructed in the
mid- to late-eighteenth century in Pennsylvania, Virginia, and New
York, they were few and far between, and, compared with later developments in the nineteenth and twentieth centuries, very small. In
this era, mental disease was viewed as more an economic and social
problem than a medical one.[1]

In the early nineteenth century, however, the situation in the
United States, as well as in England and France, changed radically
as physicians and magistrates increasingly employed medical criteria
to identify and diagnose the mentally disturbed as a separate deviant
population, whereupon they were sent to asylums for short and,
eventually (by the 1890s), long-term care. Although there had been
no more than half a dozen insane asylums or hospitals that took
mentally ill patients in the eighteenth century, by the eve of the Civil
War twenty-eight of thirty-three states had central state insane asylums, and there were at least another dozen private "corporate" insane hospitals. By 1880 there were 140 insane asylums in the United
States, and the original optimum accommodation of 100 patients in
the ideal insane asylum had grown, in the Kirkbride plan, to 250
patients or more per facility; diverse pressures would lead to patient
populations per asylum of 1,000 or more by 1900.[2]

Most of these Civil War–era asylums refrained whenever possible
from using restraints (chains, manacles, "cribs," and the like) on their
patients and opted instead for a regimen of "moral therapy," which
involved creating a friendly and supportive environment, including
moderate work, recreation, adequate rest, and periodical social and
intellectual exercises such as dances, plays, or lectures. Perhaps influenced by the Enlightenment's belief in the powers of rationality,
the idea was that the patient's reason could be restored in the proper
therapeutic environment. This faith in the expansive possibilities of
social reform produced extreme optimism in which asylum superintendents routinely claimed cure rates of as high as 90 percent,

producing what has been described as the "cult of curability." The nineteenth-century insane asylum tended to be located in a rural setting with substantial grounds and adjoining farmland, which the patients could work for the support of the asylum and their own individual welfare. In this era there was not yet any "outpatient care," "community mental health," or local "therapists" purveying a wide variety of "talking cures"; patients were either kept at home under an ad hoc regimen or sent to the asylum, usually for a short stay.

Despite the increasing availability of asylum confinement when needed, most psychologically disturbed Civil War veterans were cared for, at least initially, in the traditional manner at home by their families, even though their mental torment was frequently a terrible burden on all concerned. William R. Durland, for instance, resided with his unmarried brother and sister, and these siblings seemed to accommodate themselves to William's mental problems, the main feature of which was a fear of strangers and a dread of leaving the house. A bit more problematic was William H. Guile, who lived with his mother and niece, worrying them with his talk about killing people, and how he would "do it quick." Less menacing was James B. Farr, who suffered from the psychological aftereffects of being shot by a Rebel sniper in the war. He was nervous, melancholy, forgetful, and sleepless; bothered by the heat, he also had to avoid anything that excited or upset him, and hence he could not work. As a result, his wife was responsible for running the household: "My life is one of constant watchfullness and care over him day and night, never leaving him or permitting him to go out of my sight without being with him or having someone else with him. . . . We are constantly on the alert to prevent any noise or exciting causes from troubling him." In a similar situation, Wesley Lynch suffered from debilitating rheumatism that sometimes drove him to temporary spells of insanity owing to the intense pain; Lynch's family had to treat him like a child, taking care of his needs and being available twenty-four hours a day. He would rise at all hours during the night suffering from insomnia and pain, prompting his wife to also get up and calm him down or tend to his needs. A neighbor commented: "[T]here is no better wife and children."[3]

Despite the best efforts of family members to care for psychologically disturbed Civil War veterans at home, when the situation reached crisis proportions with fits of violence or uncontrollable mania, some sort of restraint or institutional care became necessary—

and families would often first turn to the local jail. Eliza Foster remembered that when her brother came back from the army he was "out of his head" most of the time and had to be watched: "He gradually grew worse, until we had to keep him Shut-up. Sometimes in Jail." Thomas G. Conaty came home to Plainfield, Indiana, after the war, and opened up a grocery store, but his behavior increasingly frightened and worried the townfolk: "It was generally understood that it was not safe to go in there. . . . He had a wild look in his eyes, very nervous and irritable; would talk, make threats, usually wanting to hurt some body or kill somebody." The locals eventually had Conaty tied up and taken to jail "for safe keeping because they were afraid he might hurt some one." Men would sometimes be "committed to the jail," apparently consequent to some sort of judicial process or community consensus and held there until the crisis had passed, or until room was available at the asylum in Indianapolis (see Appendix C). At least nineteen members of the Indiana Sample were held in jail because of violent behavior at some point during their postwar lives.[4]

The flexibility of this policy of placing insane veterans in local jails is most clearly demonstrated by the case of Clinton Anderson. After returning from the army, Anderson's behavior became increasingly erratic as he tried to poison two local children, threatened to kill members of his own family, and on other occasions insulted local women. Alarmed by this antisocial and dangerous behavior, the people of Delphi, Indiana, had Anderson sent to the insane asylum in Indianapolis, but after returning, he still posed a threat to the good order and peace of mind of the community. He was therefore incarcerated at the local jail and made that place his home for over twenty years. For the first fifteen of these years, he was actually locked up and could not leave, but he apparently earned the trust of the jailer, and was eventually allowed to go out during the day, returning at night. He received room and board at the jail; in fact the jailer, Joseph A. Bridge, eventually became Anderson's legal guardian. Anderson would do odd jobs in the town while out during the day and, on occasion, bought liquor and got drunk—which prompted the sheriff to lock the cell door and deny him his liberty until he had sobered up. After visiting Delphi and thoroughly investigating the case, the Pension Bureau's special examiner concluded with some insight: "[Clinton Anderson] is a character around the town of Delphi that every one knows and knows well and yet as a matter of fact knows nothing about except what they see."[5]

When psychologically disturbed Civil War veterans were finally sent to the insane asylum, it was often as a result of violent behavior that could no longer be controlled at home. Of 411 commitments for the Indiana Sample for which diagnosis at the time of admission is available, mania was listed in 267 cases. The inquest papers for one man read, "He is visious . . . he is verry distructive brakes out the windows tears up clothing & beding," and, for another, the commitment ledger reported, "Many in the community from which he comes are afraid of him and vigorous effort has been made to secure his detention in the hospital." David Leaming similarly terrorized the residents of Cicero, Indiana. He had suffered from some sort of mental breakdown following the Battle of Shiloh in 1862, and from the time he returned home from the army in 1864, his mind was disturbed; his behavior eventually became frightening. On one occasion, he entered a church during a prayer meeting and smashed the piano (or, by another account, an organ), indicating that God had told him to do this. At other times, he would have "flighty spells" and get easily excited and nervous and appeared to be entirely wild. He alarmed neighbors by violently whipping his horses, and, in general, the people in the district had a dread of him: "I did not care to cross him, and never did." Leaming was declared insane in 1877 and sent to the Indiana Hospital for the Insane, but the hospital rejected his admission on the grounds that he was a chronic case and incurable. The Hamilton county clerk responded that he understood asylum policy, but "we have no means of taking care of him or treating him at all, and with this explanation hope to secure his admission." In fact, the clerk simultaneously sent patient, sheriff, and this letter back to the insane asylum, where the hospital staff finally relented and admitted Leaming.[6]

From 1861 to 1919, the 291 men in the Indiana Sample were admitted to the Indiana Hospital for the Insane a total of 465 times; available data indicate that each man was admitted an average of 1.64 times. The peak period for commitments for this group seemed to be from 1876 to 1890, a period eleven to twenty-five years after the end of the Civil War. The hospital staff assessed a wide variety of causes for the insanity observed in these men, from alcoholism ($N = 64$) to religious excitement ($N = 38$) and exposure in the army ($N = 22$). As is usual in the pragmatic nineteenth-century approach to mental illness, it is unclear if many of these "causes" were actual causes or merely manifestations of psychological problems. Complete information on the length of stay is available in only 291 cases, revealing an average length of residence at the hospital of 31 months, but this figure is skewed by several cases in which men were kept at the asylum for ten- or twenty-year periods, contrary to the general practice of that time against warehousing chronic cases. Hence the median period of commitment was only 8 months, with the most frequently occurring length being 1.5 months.

During the nineteenth century the insane asylum slowly evolved from a facility for short-term treatment of patients who were expected to rapidly recover into a long-term custodial facility for chronic cases. Initial optimism that 80 to 90 percent of cases of insanity could be cured with early intervention evolved by the end of the century into extreme pessimism. This view was influenced in equal measures by theoretical ideas of "degeneration" (based in part on Charles Darwin's discoveries and theories) that stressed the supposedly hereditary and intractable nature of insanity and by certain institutional factors, which funnelled increasingly large numbers of people with severe mental retardation, neurological cases, and cases of senile dementia as well as other hopelessly and permanently insane people into the asylums. What was the trend for Civil War veterans—toward the end of the century, were they held for longer periods of time, and were assessments regarding curability tempered by experience?

Data on length of stay at the asylum for members of the Indiana Sample are available in only 291 cases, and these do not show a strong correlation between date of commitment and length of stay (Pearson correlation = -0.03297). Throughout the sixty-year period observed, most commitments seem to be for a short period of time, and those commitments resulting in residence at the hospital for periods in excess of ten years were interspersed somewhat evenly over this time period. In 280 cases, asylum records indicate a definite resolution to the case, and these data paint, at least on the surface, a rather optimistic picture, indicating that 65 percent of these veterans either recovered or were cured, restored, or improved, as opposed to the almost 10 percent who were deemed unimproved or incurable. If one examines the situation more closely, however, these assessments of "cured" are somewhat suspect, for many men released as cured were readmitted to the asylum a second or even a third and fourth time. In such cases, a note of realism sometimes crept into the picture as subsequent releases tended to be characterized as "improved" rather than "cured."

For instance, Jacob Defferen was committed to the asylum in August of 1881 with acute mania and was held for about a month and a half before being released as "cured"; within six months, he was again committed at the asylum, this time with "recurrent mania." When he was released seven months later in October of 1882, the assessment was "improved" rather than "cured." In other cases, however, repeated commitments were concluded again and again with releases listed as "cures," as is evident in the case of John J. Cameron. In January of 1884, Cameron was committed to the asylum with acute mania and released about one month later as "cured." In May of 1884 he was readmitted with "recurrent mania," held for about six months and released again as "cured." Then four years later, in late 1888, he was admitted a third time, held for about five months, and released yet again as "cured." Cameron's case may have involved a situation in which an alcoholic was being periodically admitted to the asylum to dry out, but a more important factor driving these rapid releases and a high rate of turnover at the asylum was the fact that space was limited and each county in the state of Indiana was granted a quota. If a space were occupied for too long by one veteran, this would mean that one less person from that man's home county would be eligible for admission, and the waiting list, from the 1850s on, was always long. This attention to quotas could be quite explicit, as in the case of Daniel B. Kivett, who was admitted to the asylum in 1871 with insanity resulting from "Fever and Army Exposures": "He is now admitted because there is deficient quota from his county & it is understood by his friends that in course of a year he will probably give room for recent cases." It is not always easy to determine how admission and discharge decisions were made: many patients were turned away for being "chronic," and yet Joseph McCann was held at the asylum for thirty-nine years, certainly making him a "chronic case"; it could be that his family paid for his keep, which would have removed him from the county quota system. Then there was Ephraim Maple, with six admissions, only one of which lasted over two years. One suspects that politics, influence, and chance played a greater role than scientific or medical factors in determining which men would be admitted to the asylum and how long they would be held.[7]

Once at the asylum, what kind of treatment was provided for these Civil War veterans? As was the norm for "moral therapy," veterans participated in recreation and dances and engaged in work, which could entail kitchen duty, farm labor, or chores on the ward; if they could be trusted, they were given liberty to roam the three-hundred-acre grounds of the asylum in Indianapolis. In other cases, however, violence could break out as when one veteran attacked his attendants, or when Cornelius Luther became involved in a fight with another patient in which kicks were exchanged and Luther was struck with a chair. In such instances restraints such as straightjackets might be employed, although the preference seemed to be for the use of medications to sedate unruly or violent patients.[8] Both at the asylum and out in the community, a wide array of drugs were administered to disturbed veterans, and these seemed to fall into three general categories: (a) purgatives, which were thought to free the body of noxious agents or restore the ideal balance among the body's vital forces, fluids, humors, or juices (depending on one's theoretical orientation); (b) "tonics" such as iron or whiskey, which were used to build up strength; and (c) sedatives, from morphine to chloral hydrate and potassium bromide, which were generally effective in calming down agitated or maniacal patients. As late as 1882, some doctors were still bleeding (or "cupping") patients as a method to induce calm, but this practice had been falling out of favor since the 1840s and was somewhat rare by the late nineteenth century.[9]

Although the insane asylum offered one avenue for treatment for psychologically disturbed Civil War veterans, this alternative was somewhat limited in that it provided—in most cases—only short-term treatment for men deemed to be "curable." A great many psychologically disturbed veterans, particularly those cases regarded as "chronic" or "incurable," had to find support in other quarters; confinement at home, residence at the poorhouse or soldiers' homes, and poor relief administered in the community, though not desirable choices, were generally available when needed. In cases of violent veterans who could not secure admission at the asylum, families would often resort to the use of restraints at home, which generally consisted of locking the man in a secure room, a "strong room" with barred windows and a reinforced, locked door. In other cases, families—often with the aid of the sheriff or men from the community—would tie up a maniacal veteran until the "spell" passed away or until more permanent arrangements for confinement or restraint could be made.[10] For men not inclined toward violence, but still suffering from the disabling effects of a mental condition or disorder, state or federal soldiers' homes or the local poorhouse were alternatives. Twenty-six men from the Indiana Sample were admitted at one time or another to soldiers' homes, and sixteen men were housed at some point at the poorhouse, generally regarded as the last resort. Men customarily dreaded the latter institution to the point that they would sometimes contemplate suicide to avoid such a fate. Others lived on the fringes of the poorhouse, collecting poor relief from the township trustee or relying on the kindness of neighbors and old friends, or the local Grand Army of the Republic (G.A.R.) relief committee.[11]

While many Civil War veterans languished in poverty and obscurity, others benefited from a generous federal pension system first established during the war itself for disabled soldiers and dependent relatives of those men who had died in the war. The system was expanded periodically thereafter so that pensions were granted not only to those veterans who had incurred service-related disabilities but to veterans who were disabled for any reason (whether related to the service or not) and, eventually, to all surviving veterans simply as a matter of right; widows and children were also provided for, even if the death of the veteran was not service-related. The number of invalid pensioners from the Civil War increased from 4,337 in 1861 to 55,652 in 1866 and 343,701 in 1888. Although there were approximately 1.9 million Union veterans of the Civil War, by 1893 there were 935,084 active pension awards and 60,000 pension attorneys (Confederate veterans were not eligible for federal pensions). The pensioner list (including surviving veterans and dependent claims) reached a peak of 999,446 in 1902, and by one estimate, more than $8 billion was eventually spent on pensions for Civil War veterans and their families, an amount of money which exceeded that expended on the prosecution of the war itself.[12]

How did psychologically disturbed Civil War veterans fare in this pension system? Were their claims for disability based on mental distress as a result of their war experience recognized and compensated? Two hundred and twenty-six veterans (or their families) from the Indiana Sample applied for federal military pensions after the Civil War, and in 199 cases, an award of some type was granted, either to the veteran, his widow, or his children. In addition to claims for conditions such as chronic diarrhea ($N = 127$), disease of the heart ($N = 83$), rheumatism ($N = 81$), gunshot wounds ($N = 74$), and sunstroke ($N = 32$), these veterans also advanced a wide array of claims alleging mental problems, including insanity ($N = 93$), unsound mind ($N = 4$), affection of mind (mental affection) ($N = 2$), brain trouble ($N = 1$), disease of the head ($N = 4$), affection of the brain ($N = 5$), affection of the head ($N = 4$), neuralgia of the head ($N = 2$), mental impairment or mental trouble ($N = 8$), mental derangement (mind deranged) ($N = 6$), mental disability ($N = 1$), head trouble ($N = 1$), nervous debility ($N = 26$), nervous prostration ($N = 20$), nervous derangement ($N = 2$), nervousness (nerves)($N = 3$), hysteria (hystero-epilepsy) ($N = 1$), smothering sensation ($N = 3$), nervous affection ($N = 2$), nervous trouble ($N = 3$), neurasthenia ($N = 1$), partial dementia ($N = 1$), headache ($N = 4$), palpitation of heart ($N = 4$), irritable heart ($N = 1$), vertigo ($N = 8$), dizziness ($N = 8$), loss of memory ($N = 1$), and insomnia ($N = 1$).

In the analysis of these cases, three general points emerge: (a) in the absence of some physical wound or disease, and in the absence of a clear record of breakdown in the army, claims based on post-traumatic stress alone were disfavored; (b) prevailing concepts in medicine and science in the late nineteenth century preferred physical, somatic, and materialist explanations of the pathological process, including insanity, and therefore to the extent that mental disease could be understood as resulting from some physical trauma (especially to the head and brain) or as an internal process of "sympathy" within the nervous system, claims for mental disorders based on military experience had a better chance of being accepted; and (c) psychiatry in the late nineteenth century was influenced by Victorian notions of self-reliance and virtue, so that if a veteran exhibited certain "vicious habits" such as alcohol and drug abuse, masturbation, or the excessive use of tobacco, his insanity might be attributed to these vices and his claim for a pension accordingly disallowed. Deserters were also disqualified from receiving federal pensions, unless they somehow managed to have the charge removed from their service record.

In order to understand the way in which the Pension Bureau approached adjudication of disability claims filed by Civil War veterans, one must appreciate the fact that the theory and practice of medicine was in transition in the late nineteenth century, and combined certain antique and modern elements. Modern medical theory, with its sophisticated understanding of cell biology, physiology, pathology, disease localization, and the role of bacteria and viruses in causing disease, emerged in its present form during the late nineteenth and early twentieth centuries, found a stronghold in the new research universities of Germany, and eventually influenced American universities (especially Johns Hopkins and Harvard) and institutions (particularly the modern hospital). This modern form of scientific medicine did not fully control the Pension Bureau's regulations, medical examinations, and deliberations until the first decade of the twentieth century, however, and prior to that time, more old-fashioned and peculiar ideas of disease controlled. Inspired by the outlook of the Enlightenment, medical theory in the nineteenth century still largely adhered to eighteenth-century unified rational systems that posited a single pathogenic process and attempted to explain all disease as the result of imbalances in the human system; these ideas were the legacy in some measure of the ancient Greek theory that the body contained four humors (blood, phlegm, yellow bile, and black bile), and that all disease resulted from a morbid predominance of one or more of these humors. According to this view, an imbalance of forces within the human body would lead to "derangement" of the internal organs and the system as a whole.[13]

However, the mid- to late-nineteenth century also witnessed a period of rapid discovery and change in the field of psychiatry—one of psychiatry's many "paradigm shifts"—which would lead eventually to the abandonment of monistic theories based on the idea of humors, balance, and derangement. The thrust of these reforms led in a materialist direction, which was shaped by German "university psychiatry." Exemplified by Wilhelm Griesinger, of the University of Berlin, German university psychiatry rejected earlier romantic or pragmatic ideas and focused on the brain, which it regarded as the seat of mental disease. Griesinger and his contemporaries believed that psychiatry had to become an independent discipline and that its attitude had to be a rigidly medical one and not poetic or moralistic; although they recognized psychological causes for mental diseases, they warned against overrating such "psychogenic" causation. As a result, psychiatry came to focus somewhat obsessively on physical causation and an internal pathological process informed by neurology. In accordance with this orientation, alienists the world over began a quest to discover through autopsies performed on deceased mental patients the "lesions" on the brain that they believed accounted for mental pathology. Despite hundreds and hundreds of such autopsies and advances in neurology that began to classify and understand phenomena such as brain tumors and degenerative neurological disease, no "lesions" were ever discovered to explain mental illness not directly related to neurological disorders. This materialist orientation would eventually prove to be a dead end, and around the turn of the century Sigmund Freud would initiate yet another paradigm shift in psychiatry by deciding that strictly scientific, neurological explanations were inadequate to explain neurotic behavior; he thus launched his psychoanalytic movement that proved to be so influential in the twentieth century.[14]

In sum, these nineteenth-century theoretical ideas and reforms—notions of the importance of systemic balance with an emphasis on physical trauma as a causative factor in insanity and on the mechanical process of "reflex action of the nerves" in deranging the system—influenced the way that the problems of Civil War veterans were conceptualized. In the Pension Bureau's somewhat vague and (to the modern way of thinking) strange conception of pathology, the key concepts were *balance* and *restraint*, and the major threats to one's health were seen as coming from a "depletion of resources" that allowed powerful external stimuli to "derange" the system, often by means of "reflex action of the nerves." Lack of sleep and proper nutrition could render a person vulnerable, and if an internal organ of the body—the brain, heart, liver, spleen, or digestive system—were irritated in some respect by external physical or psychological forces and began to malfunction, this local derangement could lead to "morbid sensibility" and produce "perverted action of the nerves," which in turn deranged other organs in that vicinity or for that matter, throughout the entire body. Hence, in evaluating pension claims by Civil War veterans, nineteenth-century physicians constantly discussed disordered or deranged internal organs or systems ("disease of the heart," "disease of the head," "disease of the liver," "disease of the lungs") and the way in which they acted on one another. In this view, insanity was a complex and protean phenomenon, going well beyond a single, exact disease process; as treatises concluded, one may as well try to paint a voice or define poetry as to explain insanity with a simple definition: "It is thought no definition yet given will embrace all forms of mental diseases."[15]

As an example of this outlook, physicians (and veterans themselves when presenting claims to the Pension Bureau) routinely attributed insanity to the disordered functioning of internal organs, which eventually led to "irritation" of the brain: "The insanity is due in my opinion to the long continued invalid condition and to the morbid conditions of rectum and bladder"; "the affection of the oesophagus with the attendant symptoms was caused by dispepsia disturbing the pneumo-gastric nerve and as debility increased from inability to take food the spinal nerves became involved and were excited to perverted action especially [sic] the medulla oblongata"; "his rheumatism has been of a metastic character moving from one part of system to another and about 6 weeks ago it seemed to attack his head and neck"; "the walls of the Rectum were thickened & formed a pocket or [covety?] which became impacted with fecal matter pressing upon nerves given off from the spine this producing sympathetic nervous trouble & general debility which resulted in loss of mind." In one representative case, the Pension Bureau determined that physical disease, resulting mental infirmity, and consequent suicide could all be attributed to service in the army:

> I came to the conclusion that he became depressed, owing, first to his physical condition, and this preyed upon his mind to such an extent that he took his own life. His mind sympathized with his body and the case assumed the form of melancholia. . . . In other words the affection of his lungs and his physical condition resulted in and produced insanity.[16]

Civil War veterans whose mental problems coexisted with any sort of substantial physical disease—whether the disease produced the stress reaction in some measure or not—would thus generally have had a strong claim based on the underlying physical condition, and could additionally have maintained that this somatic illness had produced psychological effects. This same concept of pathological process by reflex action of the nerves sometimes influenced the way that gunshot wound cases were conceptualized. For instance, Er Julian had been shot in the hip during the Civil War, and the wound never entirely healed; according to a report from the insane asylum in Kansas to which he was committed in 1878, if the wound was open and running, Julian's mental health was fine. If the wound was closed, however, he was moody and melancholy and eventually became maniacal and violent—the idea being that the state of his wound affected his other internal organs and his system as a whole. Of course, the irony is that while these theories of "unbalanced humors" or "perverted action of the nerves" might have been speculative, or even in some respects ludicrous, the basic underlying premise of a relationship between physical disease and mental health ties in with current systems theory employed by behavioral medicine or "health psychology," which maintains that there is a link between stress and physical illness.[17]

Aside from cases in which physical disease and trauma (hard marching, sunstroke, exposure) or gunshot wounds were involved, how did Civil War veterans fare when their pension claims were based exclusively on insanity or some variety of nervous or mental disorder? Compared with post-Vietnam America's general presumption that almost any psychological problem experienced by a Vietnam veteran originated in the war, the Civil War generation generally demanded proof that a veteran's psychological problems developed during the war itself and continued thereafter before compensation would be forthcoming. There was also a definite preference for physical trauma as a causative factor. If a man was able to point to an exact incident in the service—preferably something to do with a shell explosion or concussion—that had an immediate effect on behavior, after which the man returned home and was immediately thought to be acting oddly and having changed from his prewar personality, such a claim would have had an excellent chance of being accepted by the Pension Bureau. In cases where the veteran's ills did not develop until after the war, or where there were gaps or intervals between episodes of the disease, the case might be more problematic.[18]

In accordance with these principles and outlook, veterans who advanced claims for what we would think of today as PTSD usually met with rejection. A doctor who examined Squire Ridgeway noted that insanity had not appeared until fifteen years after the war: "I do not believe his insanity was caused by his army service. I don't know the cause." In the case of Henry Sloan, a five-year lapse was regarded as fatal to his claim: "Rejection, upon the ground of no record of insanity or medical testimony showing treatment for same, nor satisfactory testimony of any description, showing existence of said insanity in service, at discharge, or until 1870." After John M. Smith committed suicide in 1875, his children filed a pension claim, alleging their father's death to be service-related, in that Smith had never been completely sane since returning from the army. His mental problems had contributed to his getting a divorce in 1872, and the neighbors agreed that he had become entirely insane and dangerous, before he finally killed himself. The Pension Bureau remained unconvinced: "Rejection on the ground that soldier's death from suicide in 1875 can in no way be attributed to his military service from which he was discharged in 1865. The alleged insanity is not shown by record, medical, or other competent evidence to have originated in the service." As a result of the Pension Bureau's skeptical attitude, only 42 percent of claims for service-related pensions based on allegations of insanity were accepted, compared with an acceptance rate of 77 percent for non-service-related pensions in like cases.[19]

Another factor that complicated stress-related disability pension claims for Civil War veterans was the Victorian emphasis on self-control and moral behavior and the related belief that intemperance, including "vicious habits" such as indulgence in alcohol or drugs or self-gratification through masturbation, could upset and derange the system and thereby produce insanity. If a veteran used drugs or alcohol, or if there was evidence of masturbation, it was thought that his disability claim should be rejected—either on the grounds that he had produced his own insanity or, in the alternative, that he was simply morally unworthy, regardless of whether he was literally responsible for his own disability. In addition, if a man had deserted from his unit during the Civil War, he would be entirely disqualified from receiving a federal pension, because he was deemed not morally deserving.

How did these principles operate in practice? On occasion the Pension Bureau would divide a case into separate parts and recognize the claim of an inebriated veteran for an illness such as chronic diarrhea which had nothing to do with his excessive drinking, while in the same case denying claims of insanity—based on the theory that the excessive drinking had in fact caused the mental illness (and not that the drinking was the *product* of mental stress, anxiety, and depression). Jerome Asbury's claim for a pension based on a service-related hernia was not jeopardized by his drinking ("Asbury is a profligate and drunkard"). But while John C. Britton was pensioned for chronic diarrhea, that part of his claim founded on service-related insanity was rejected because of his drinking. Interestingly, one witness testified that Britton's drinking "sprees" were triggered by mental problems: "He drinks to excess sometimes, but the peculiar actions and restlessness I speak of comes on and is manifest for three or four days before he goes to drinking. . . . I have attributed his drinking wholly to the disordered condition his mind would get into." The Pension Bureau remained unmoved.[20]

In other cases, however, alcoholism could result in rejection of the veteran's pension claim lock, stock, and barrel. William R. Durland experienced mental problems from the time he returned from the army ("he talked rather wild & looked wild out of his eyes"); acquaintances noticed that he became excited whenever he talked about the army, and he would go on periodic sprees, and this drinking was seemingly intended to numb feelings of anger and anxiety. His binges led to several bar fights, including one in which Durland suffered a substantial head wound when someone struck him with a lantern. After reviewing all of this evidence, the Pension Bureau denied Durland both a service-related pension and even a non-service-related disability pension for insanity—on the grounds that he was responsible for this "vicious habit" that had brought on or aggravated the insanity: "Rejection on the ground that the claimant's mental condition is the result of and due to his intemperate habits as shown by record of Central Ind. Hospl. for insane at Indianapolis, Ind." The Pension Bureau was also capable of looking the other way, however, as in the case of Spencer Goldsberry. He was described in two different sets of inquest papers as a chronic alcoholic: "His conduct is more like a beast than that of a human being. . . . He is addicted to drink, and to secure liquor will resort to any measure or means—will take anything in the house, and sell it to procure the means to get it." Yet his claim, based in part on nervous prostration, was accepted by the Pension Bureau, which seemed to overlook his lack of self-control, perhaps in deference to his long-suffering wife and children, who would benefit from this monetary award.[21]

From a modern-day perspective, the Pension Bureau's obsession with the supposedly unwholesome and pernicious effects of masturbation appears to be patently ridiculous—but nonetheless a number of claims for pensions filed by psychologically disturbed Civil War veterans were rejected on this ground. According to the medical theory of the day, low-level restlessness, nervousness, melancholy, and excitement as well as full-blown insanity and violence could all result from masturbation, sometimes termed "self-pollution" or "nocturnal pollution" ("he is a Chronic Masturbater by reason of which he has wholly lost control of his mind"). It was seen as a dangerous habit, a "withering incubus," for which those who indulged should be severely censured and punished: "The solitary vice of Self-pollution spreads desolation through the land." Joseph Batson was committed to the Indiana Hospital for the Insane in 1875 with acute mania, which in the inquest papers was attributed to masturbation: "His appearance is that of a self polutionest. He has sever spells of sick headache and complains of his head and shoulders hurting him." His subsequent application for a federal pension based on neuralgia and mental problems was initially denied on the basis of masturbation, although the bureau eventually ruled this out as a cause and granted Batson his pension. Less fortunate was Lewis Y. Crum, whose claim based on insanity was rejected owing to this habit: "His disability originated from Onanism."[22]

Although many Civil War veterans received financial compensation from the federal government, as well as what medical treatment was available at that time, for some men neither of these alternatives could relieve the intense mental suffering that had resulted from their war experience. In many cases, these men turned to suicide to deal with an intolerable situation. A review of the Indiana Sample reveals that at least 149 of these men (51 percent) either attempted or completed suicide, or were regarded in some measure as "suicidal" at the time of their commitment. These cases seem to break down into three general categories: (a) those suffering from purely psychological problems, often with PTSD symptomatology (depression, anxiety, flashbacks to wartime experiences, startle reactions); (b) those who received gunshot wounds during the Civil War, which continued to either cause intense physical pain or prompt remembrance of disturbing wartime incidents; and (c) those suffering from diseases incurred in the service, usually gastrointestinal distress or the aftereffects of typhoid fever or malaria, which continued to cause acute discomfort (if not physical emaciation) in the years after the war, leading eventually to psychological repercussions.

Illustrative of the first category of Civil War veteran, who suffered from the psychological consequences of service during the war, is the case of Newell Gleason. A successful civil engineer in private life, Gleason was commissioned lieutenant colonel with the 87th Indiana Regiment in August of 1862, and served with the Union Army until the end of the war. His unit was in the thick of battle at Chickamauga, Chattanooga, and Sherman's Atlanta Campaign of 1864. At the Battle of Chickamauga, Gleason's unit suffered casualties of 40 killed and 142 wounded (a casualty rate of over 49 percent out of a total strength of 366), and his own official report of the fighting referred to "furious" battle, "heavy fire," and bayonet charges on enemy positions. Gleason's commanding officer described him as having performed with "coolness and great promptness," and concluded that his energy and gallantry had contributed to local successes in what was otherwise an overall Union defeat: "Such officers are a credit to the service and our country." Having distinguished himself with bravery, Newell Gleason was promoted to brevet brigadier general, but a fellow officer noticed after the battle that Gleason seemed to be "nervous and excitable."[23]

After his promotion to command of the Second Brigade of the Third Division, Gleason participated in the Atlanta Campaign during the summer and fall of 1864. His psychological condition worsened, however, and one of his staff officers noticed that he seemed to be "rattled." By the time the Union Army reached South Carolina, some of Gleason's men felt that he had become mentally deranged, and pointed in retrospect to a peculiar incident: "The col. was at all times a strict disciplinarian but on this march he gave his men orders to shoot some hogs that crossed the road in front of them and further said to not leave a live thing in south Carolina. This was so opposed to his usual line of conduct that I noticed it at once." By the time the Union Army reached Washington, D.C., in April of 1865 to participate in the Grand Review, Gleason had become completely unhinged. At times he would cry like a child and become melancholy, and at others times he seemed to be jubilant and would laugh without any cause or reason. He took a fellow officer aside, and whispering to him with great urgency and fear stated that he was worried about being over-heard, and told him there was a conspiracy in the brigade to ruin him (Gleason), a matter which his fellow officer regarded as complete paranoia.[24]

A friend from his unit, Captain Milo Ellis, who was a physician, brought Newell Gleason home to Indiana separately from his unit, and in transit Gleason became frantic and had to be treated with opiates to quiet him down. Those who observed him during this time noted that his health had been shattered by his experience in the army, and concluded that he was suffering from complete mental prostration. When Gleason finally arrived at his home in Laporte, Indiana, his wife, Nancy, noticed that he was despondent and seemed to be entirely lacking in concentration or will power. He would set resolutions to do things, but would be unable to finish his work. At different times, he attempted to resume his career as a civil engineer and Nancy would accompany him on business trips to lend him emo-tional sustenance, but his condition worsened, and in 1874 after a three-day episode of violent mania in which he was raving and had to be restrained, he was taken to the Indiana State Hospital for the Insane. The admitting staff at the asylum noted in the commitment record: "Becomes much excited. supposes he is in battle gives com-mands &c." His condition improved sufficiently to merit his release from the asylum, but his mental torment continued. A physician who treated Gleason at this time noted that he was in a state of great depression, that his sleep was "laborious" and "filled with dreams that seemed to make sleep exhaustive rather than refreshing." Gleason would invariably wake up in the middle of the night and walk about the house in great mental distress, and then could not get back to sleep.[25]

Newell Gleason's mental anguish finally came to an end in 1886. He and his wife had visited another couple socially on the evening of July 4, where a friend observed: "[I] found him very despondent and showing more than usual weariness and agitation. [He said he] had lost his will power and was unable to decide upon anything." After returning home that evening, Gleason suffered throughout the night and slept very little; his wife stayed up with him most of the night applying cold applications to his head and spine to soothe and quiet him, but she finally fell asleep herself. At about 4 A.M. she awoke, went to look for him, and found him in an agitated condition at the head of the cellar stairs; he yelled or screamed at her to leave, and plunged headlong down the cellar stairs, where he died of a fractured skull. The circumstances of his death were somewhat ambiguous, and the family initially attempted to present his death as an accident, but in 1888 the Pension Bureau, in considering his widow's claim for a pension, reviewed the entire record and determined that the death had been a suicide. The coroner testified: "I am satisfied that his death was by suicide resulting from insanity. . . . Some years ago he was violently insane for a time and was sent to the Indiana State Hospital for the Insane at Indianapolis. It is my belief now that he had another attack and in his frenzy threw himself headlong down the cellar stairs." Another physician concluded that Newell Gleason's condition had been "induced by disorders and hardships incurred in the U.S. Military Service."[26]

During the Civil War there were over 236,000 cases of gunshot wounds in Union troops, and the suffering of these men by no means necessarily ended with the amputation of a limb or discharge from the service on account of the wound. Veterans suffering from gunshot or shell wounds constitute a second large group of men exhibiting symptoms of post-traumatic stress, which often resulted in suicidal behavior. In the Indiana Sample, about 15 percent had been victims of gunshot or shell wounds, and many of these men suffered terribly from physical and psychological aftereffects, as was the case with

John Agnew. He had served with Company C of the 50th Indiana Regiment, and received a gunshot wound to the right forearm at the Battle of Jenkin's Ferry in Arkansas in April of 1864. The ball lodged in his arm and resulted in paralysis of the hand and forearm, and caused increasing distress in the years after the war. An examining board of physicians noted in 1880 that the condition of his arm prevented him from sleeping after exercise, and acquaintances noticed spells of despondency. One friend recounted that Agnew had frequently talked of his disabilities, and stated that if he did not get better, he intended to take his life. On June 14, 1898, John Agnew committed suicide by hanging himself with a rope to a cross-beam in his barn.[27]

A similarly tragic case is that of Logan P. Herod, who served with Company H of the 12th Indiana Regiment. He was shot in the left thigh and testicle at the Battle of Richmond, Kentucky, on August 30, 1862. Herod apparently continued to serve with his regiment, and was not mustered out of the service until June of 1865, but in the years after the war, this gunshot wound caused increasing physical discomfort and mental distress. Owing to swelling and pain, he was frequently unable to walk about or engage in labor, and a friend noted that each year his mind seemed to grow worse until he became violent and threatened suicide. For about a year before he was confined in the insane asylum in 1873, he would frequently say that it would be better for him if he were dead. He was subject to fits of depression and crying spells, which would be worse according to the severity of pain in the wound, and he would often say that he wished he had been shot in the head instead of in the privates.

One evening while at dinner with his family, he was evidently overcome by the hopelessness of his situation, and attempted to cut his throat with his knife. The knife was not sharp enough to cut the skin, but Herod, even when seized by family members who attempted to restrain him, continued to grasp the knife with great force and persisted in making cuts. Although Herod was successfully restrained on this occasion, his mind was shattered as a result of unbearable physical pain. He eventually succeeded in killing himself on September 5, 1873, apparently by again cutting his throat—this time, unfortunately, with a sharper knife.[28]

The last major category of Civil War veteran that seemed to be at risk of suicide included those men who suffered from chronic or debilitating diseases as a result of exposure during the Civil War. The

Civil War, in which several hundred thousand men died of disease, has been characterized as a form of "biological warfare." Nor were those who survived the war years immune from continuing repercussions from earlier exposure to smallpox, typhoid, malaria, measles, mumps, and a wide variety of fevers and digestive and gastrointestinal ailments. Although some men recovered their health and went on to lead normal and productive lives, others suffered from physical ills related to their service in the war until they finally died—often prematurely at their own hand.[29]

During his time with the 149th Indiana Regiment, Joshua Jordan contracted malaria and also developed a severe case of rheumatism, which affected his whole body but especially his knees and ankles. In the service, he had experienced heart spasms that were so bad he had to fall out of the ranks and rest. Upon any hard march or hard duty, he would feel the pain in his heart, and the rheumatism continued until he was discharged. A medical board which examined Jordan in 1896 noted heart problems, including hypertrophy, dyspnea, and cyanosis; the doctors of the board also diagnosed severe vertigo and dizziness, which they attributed to "a disturbed nervous condition a result of malarial poison & heart trouble." Unable to bear the physical pain and discomfort resulting from his chronic diseases, in early 1902 Joshua Jordan attempted to cut his throat and was committed to the insane asylum, but his physical agony continued after his release from the hospital. One can only begin to imagine the panic and despair experienced by Mary Jordan on May 14, 1903, when she found her husband, Joshua, hanging by the neck from a rope tied to a tree in their orchard. Mrs. Jordan rushed to the house to frantically ring the farm bell to call for aid and assistance from their neighbors, but by the time George M. Beaman and others arrived, it was too late. Beaman later testified: "I found Mr. Joshua Jordan Hanging to an apple tree in his orchard. He was dead when I got there. I cut the Rope by which he hung himself and let him down and helped to carry him to the house."[30]

Another common physical ailment for Civil War veterans was gastrointestinal distress, which was often described as "chronic diarrhea," "disease of the stomach," "dyspepsia," "indigestion," or "disease of the bowels." John W. Robinson of the 66th Indiana Regiment was typical in suffering from such problems, both during army service and afterward. His bunkmate from the army recalled: "I have seen him spit up his victuals many times. verry bad, and we never thought he would get through the war." When he was committed to the insane asylum in 1897, the inquest papers described Robinson as follows:

> [W]alking the floor, crying & talking incoherently . . . has complained of his stomach and heart. . . . Very restless at nights—will get up and walk the floor. . . . All sharp instruments, such as his razor knives, forks, &c have to be kept away from him. He thinks the Poor House is staring him in the face and he talks of not being with his family long. Wants to kill himself. . . . He will either commit suicide or kill some of his family if he is permitted to be at large . . . very much depressed.

In a similar case, Benjamin Welch suffered from intense pain in the region of the liver, stomach, and bowels; as his doctor noted: "At the last visit he was very much emaciated. could eat but little food. his digestion very bad . . . he was melancholy, nervous, and very irritable." He talked incessantly of his physical discomfort, and, on September 9, 1884, having reached the end of his rope, Benjamin Welch committed suicide by shooting himself in the head.[31]

Given the fact that many Civil War veterans resorted to suicide as a means of dealing with intolerable mental and physical pain, what was the reaction of family, friends, neighbors, and the state to these desperate and violent acts? Historians such as George Rosen and Michael MacDonald have documented the shifting attitudes toward suicide from a general acceptance in the classical world to Christian condemnation in A.D. 563 at the Council of Braga; in order to punish and deter suicide (regarded as a form of murder) sanctions employed in the years from 1500 to about 1660 were particularly drastic, and included forfeiture of the decedent's estate, degradation of the corpse (through public desecration or by driving a stake through the heart), and denial of burial in consecrated ground. By the late seventeenth century in England, however, a process of secularization began to transform views on the matter of suicide. By 1800 forfeiture of the estate of the decedent practically never occurred, and in almost all cases, coroner's inquests returned a verdict that the decedent had been "non compos mentis" at the time of death, and was therefore not morally culpable for the act.[32]

By the years following the Civil War, suicide was thus no longer generally regarded as a heinous crime, and yet one notices a tendency in the families of Civil War veterans who committed suicide to disguise or deny the act. A friend who attended the funeral of Newell

Gleason remarked that the family attempted to make his death look like an accident. In another case, Daniel Shearer, a Civil War veteran who had served with the 59th Indiana Regiment, attempted suicide by drowning, and eventually killed himself by taking poison in 1874. His family, however, tried to deny this suicidal behavior: "We found him once in the field near a corn shock, he had been in the creek and whether he had tried to drown himself or not I dont know, nor what his idea was." Even after he drank a bottle of horse medicine, which by one account "cooked his insides," and led to death within a week, his wife still attempted to present this behavior as an accident or as a matter of little consequence. A doctor caring for Logan Herod (who had made a vigorous effort to cut his throat until physically overpowered and restrained) claimed that the act was an "epileptic form paroxysm . . . induced by reflex irritation, arising from a wound" while Herod was unconscious and, by implication, free of moral blame. Here one sees both denial and an extreme attempt at medicalization of the act to the point of denying not just intent, but consciousness as well.[33]

Probably the most fascinating case of presenting a suicide attempt as an accident was that of Lineas Risley. Serving with the 18th Indiana Regiment, Risley was sent home from the front in early 1863 to recruit for his regiment, and during that time suffered from two accidents: he shot himself in the foot with a shotgun, and he fell out of a third-story window in a military hospital. What makes this case intriguing is a report from a Dr. Harding that Risley was suffering from vertigo during this recruiting trip and "that whilst suffering from this disease of vertigo he shot himself in his left foot *laboring under the hallucination that he was in the presence of the enemy. . . .*" (emphasis added). Risley was subsequently sent to a military hospital where he "fell" from a third-story window, and then to the insane asylum, where the immediate cause of his insanity (diagnosed as "mania") was deemed to be "Home Sickness and War Excitement and an attack of fever." One suspects that this was a case of self-mutilation while experiencing a combat flashback, followed by a suicide attempt, but Risley presented his ailments (the gunshot wound and the injury to his head from the fall) to the Pension Bureau as the result of accidents, and was granted a pension.[34]

It could be that Risley feared that if his injuries were presented as the result of willful self-injury that the Pension Bureau would have rejected any claims of insanity and disqualified him from receiving benefits, but, in other cases, the Pension Bureau did not view suicide as a sin or a disgrace, or as disqualifying survivors from receiving pension benefits. It viewed suicide as the result of insanity, rather than a voluntary and morally culpable act. For instance, in the case of *Hannah McClellan (Dependent Mother)*, the relevant appellate authorities in the Department of the Interior (which oversaw Pension Bureau cases) concluded: "The act of suicide is strong, if not conclusive, evidence of mental disease." Such cases often seemed to give dependent widows the benefit of the doubt when causation of the insanity that led to suicide was an issue: "But who can say whence or by what process or for what reason the human mind becomes deranged in every instance?"[35]

There are ten documented cases of completed suicide in the Indiana Sample. In three of five cases, the Pension Bureau granted the claims of widows who alleged that the deaths of their husbands by suicide in the years after the war were "service-related," either the result of disease, wound, or psychological distress that had its origin in military service. In the case of Logan Herod, the Pension Bureau officials who reviewed his widow's claim for a pension concluded: "Soldier's death from suicidal mania can be accepted as a probable result of [the gunshot wound he received eleven years earlier in the service] . . . Testimony shows that soldier suffered great pain . . . that his mind was shattered about 1870 & he committed suicide Sept. 5 1873." In the case of Benjamin Welch, who was suffering from excruciating pain from physical ills at the time of his death, the Pension Bureau granted his widow's claim on the grounds that his death resulted from mental impairment terminating in suicide.

Although it may be clear that many Civil War veterans were driven to suicide by a variety of problems, a number of questions remain to be answered: How typical were these veterans? Can one form some sort of idea as to the suicide rate in all Civil War veterans from this sample? How did the suicide rate of veterans compare with that for civilians in the years after the Civil War? Unfortunately, determination of suicide rates for all veterans, or comparative suicide rates for veterans and civilians in the nineteenth century probably cannot be derived because uniform death certificates were not introduced in Indiana (or elsewhere in the United States) until the 1880s, and even then, these documents would not always have reliably reflected whether the death was a suicide or not. Particularly in cases of drowning and jumping, but in poison and gunshot cases as well, death would doubtless often have been presented as an accident.

One does note that the Indiana veterans in this sample demonstrating suicidal behavior seemed by most criteria to be "average" or "unremarkable"; for instance, the average age at enlistment in the army was 24 years. Over 80 percent of these veterans married, and on average had over four children. The average age at death was over 63, although the average age at death for those who completed suicide was 51.3 years of age. Looking at other criteria such as occupation or religion, it does not seem that statistically significant differences between the "suicidal" veterans and either nonsuicidal veterans in the Indiana Sample or Civil War veterans from the general veteran population emerge. In the final analysis, one must accept the fact that the exact number of Civil War veterans who resorted to suicide in the years after the war will most likely remain a mystery.

Psychologically disturbed Civil War veterans were thus not entirely ignored in the years after the war, but their problems were probably understated and inadequately understood and/or treated and compensated for a number of reasons: first of all, thousands of these veterans, including the approximately 200,000 Union army deserters (many of whom most likely suffered from PTSD) and those involved in alcohol or drug abuse, were viewed not as psychiatric victims, but as lacking in manly courage or virtue; with a few exceptions, these men were excluded from the pension system and blamed for their own problems. Second, while medical treatment was available, it was mainly of a stopgap variety, intended through short commitments to insane asylums or through the use of sleep-inducing agents to weather dangerous spells of mania in agitated and exhausted veterans. Despite the continuing "cult of curability" in psychiatry in the middle and even late nineteenth century, repeated asylum commitments of veterans demonstrate the intractability of their mental problems. Finally, the purely psychological problems of Civil War veterans took a backseat because, as was the case during the war itself, their physical problems, such as chronic diarrhea, rheumatism, complications resulting from communicable diseases such as typhoid and malaria, and the aftereffects of hard marching, exposure to the elements, and gunshot and shell wounds, tended to be overwhelming. Although these physical problems might produce stress disorders, and although some physical and psychological problems doubtless coexisted, a veteran who suffered no physical wounds or diseases and was anything short of stark raving mad and yet complained of mental problems originating in the war probably would have been regarded as a malingerer in this era. An emphasis on physical trauma in psychiatric theory also probably tended to downplay the purely "psychogenic" foundations of stress reactions in Civil War veterans, thus leaving the impression that these problems were secondary, derivative of physical ills, or insignificant. As if this were not enough, the Pension Bureau's insistence on proof that any disability must have originated in the service and continued thereafter would have mediated against the recognition and compensation of post-traumatic stress disorders, which by definition often have a delayed onset.

"Tramping by Night and Day":
Indiana Veterans

Although it is clear that a number of Civil War veterans suffered from terrible psychological problems in the years after the war, several critical questions remain to be answered: To what extent can the problems of these men be attributed to the Civil War itself? Is the Indiana Sample of 291 men representative of Civil War veterans in Indiana or elsewhere? Can the problems of the men in this sample be generalized to a significant proportion of the approximately 180,000 Indiana veterans or the 1.9 million Union veterans of the Civil War? Could it be that the evidence adduced thus far in this book pertains to a group of men who were not typical Civil War veterans, and that for the most part—congruent with claims of Vietnam Veteran advocates—Civil War veterans readjusted well after they came home from the war and suffered no substantial psychological aftereffects of their experience in the military?

Statistical analysis offers one way of addressing these questions, and one needs to consider the possibilities of engaging the techniques of both descriptive and inferential statistics to cast additional light on the matter of the psychological problems of veterans of the American Civil War. Descriptive statistical methods organize, simplify, summarize, and present data in a more manageable and comprehensible form than one would see with raw scores alone. These statistical methods can be used to describe the Indiana Sample in a detailed and useful way, but they would not indicate per se whether the group was typical or atypical. On the other hand, inferential statistical methods *can* be used to make general statements about a population; the basic approach is to derive a random sample from a general population, and then, on the basis of one's findings regarding the sample, make generalizations about the population from which the sample was selected. In short, inferential statistical methods are the more useful in addressing the key questions posed above.

This chapter will employ statistical analysis in four phases: first, descriptive statistics will be used to illustrate features of the Indiana Sample such as physical characteristics, social status, marriage patterns, and exposure to combat and death in the Civil War; second, using what information is known about general populations of Civil War veterans in Indiana and throughout the North, an assessment will be made regarding the typicality of the Indiana Sample; third, casualty statistics will be presented on Indiana regiments that fought in the Civil War to demonstrate typical patterns of exposure to death and disease; and, last of all, casualty indices for the Indiana Sample will be compared with general data from all Indiana regiments to determine whether the Indiana Sample was exposed excessively to combat, disease, or death in the Civil War, and whether these factors might have accounted for resulting psychopathology. As promising as statistical analysis might appear, one must always remember that nineteenth-century records are fragmentary, that true random sampling cannot be conducted among populations long dead, and that any conclusions reached will be, at best, suggestive rather than definitive.

The Indiana Sample contains 291 Civil War veterans (see Appendix A). This sample was derived by compiling a list of men committed to the Indiana Hospital for the Insane from 1861 to 1919, and then cross-checking this list against military and pension records to determine which men had fought in the Civil War. On each member of the sample, definite information is available regarding dates of service in at least one Indiana unit in the Civil War and at least one commitment to the insane asylum thereafter, but beyond these basic facts, the information can be quite uneven: on many men, next to nothing is known; on others, particularly those who received federal pensions, a great deal of information can emerge. In reviewing basic descriptive statistics on this group, therefore, one must note the unevenness of data throughout, and keep in mind the fact that substantial numbers of missing values in many categories make assessments and conclusions tentative at best.

The majority of men in the sample were born in Indiana (58.4 percent), with the only other significant groups with American nativity coming from Ohio (11.7 percent) and Kentucky (5.5 percent); reflecting immigration patterns of the mid-nineteenth century, men of German (5.8 percent) and Irish (2.8 percent) nativity also appear in the sample (see Table 8.1). Religious affiliation was widely scattered, with Protestant denominations representing about 36 percent of the sample, while a greater percentage either claimed to have no religious affiliation (38.1 percent) or simply presented no information regarding such beliefs (19.2 percent = "unknown" or no information provided) (see Table 8.2). The majority (54.3 percent) of the men were farmers, with the remainder holding occupations ranging from carpenters, laborers, and boilermakers to lawyers, doctors, and teachers (see Table 8.3).

Information on wealth can primarily be determined by whether members of the sample were supported by their own estates or by their local county at the time of their commitment to the insane asylum. Information is available on 206 men and indicates that only 82 were clothed and supported by their own funds; this does not, however, indicate that the remainder of the sample were paupers. The size of the average estate of men supported and clothed at the asylum by their own funds reveals a mean value of $2,564.63. Information on marriage and children is somewhat fragmentary, but what data

Table 8.1 Nativity of members of the Indiana Sample

Nativity	Frequency	Percentage
Indiana	170	58.4
Ohio	34	11.7
Germany	17	5.8
Kentucky	16	5.5
Pennsylvania	10	3.4
Ireland	8	2.8
North Carolina	4	1.4
New York	4	1.4
England	3	1.0
Scotland	2	0.7
Tennessee	2	0.7
Other	10	3.4
Unknown	11	3.8

Note: If frequency = 1, entries are consolidated under "Other."

Table 8.2   Religious affiliation of members of the Indiana Sample

Religion	Frequency	Percentage
None	111	38.1
Unknown	56	19.2
Methodist	41	14.1
Christian	17	5.8
Catholic	16	5.5
Baptist	14	4.8
Presbyterian	13	4.5
United Brethren	10	3.4
Lutheran	2	0.7
Quaker	2	0.7
Other	9	3.1

Note: If frequency = 1, entries are consolidated under "Other."

are available indicate that at least 78 percent of the men in the sample married, and that they were married an average of 1.3 times, this figure being elevated somewhat due to a mean of 1.71 for widowed men (the mean for nonwidowers was 1.02 marriages). Of men on whom data is available, 35.3 percent were already married at the time of their service in the Civil War, and for the unmarried members of the sample, there appeared to be a sharp increase in the number of first marriages in the years from 1865 to 1869 as single men returned from the war and married; second marriages did not tend to cluster in this fashion.

Men who had been disabled (73.4 percent versus 80.2 percent for the nondisabled), suffered from gunshot wounds (83.3 percent versus 77.2 percent for non–gunshot wound victims), or who were taken prisoner of war (79.5 percent versus 78.2 percent for non-POWs) during the Civil War seemed to marry at about the same rate for veterans who did not fall into these categories. Of the men in the sample 88.4 percent had children, and the average number of children per family was just over 4. Again, men who had been disabled, suffered from gunshot wounds, or who were taken prisoner of war during the Civil War seemed to have children at about the same rate as men who escaped these conditions. Of the sample, 18.5 percent were divorced at some time, and 38.2 percent were widowed. Although measurements could often be quite unreliable, the average height of men in the sample was 68.6 inches and the average weight 150.7 pounds.

Table 8.3 Occupations of members of the Indiana Sample

Occupation	Frequency	Percentage
Farmer	158	54.3
Skilled labor	58	19.9
Unskilled labor	32	11.0
Professional	29	10.0
Commerce	12	4.1
None	2	0.7

Note: "Skilled labor" includes carpenter, blacksmith, baker, shoemaker, stonemason, machinist, miller, and wheelwright. "Unskilled labor" includes laborer, miner, painter, and gardener. "Professional" includes lawyer, doctor, teacher, minister, and clerk. "Commerce" includes merchant, salesman, banker, business, and grain dealer.

Average age at death was 63.7 years, with the mean being 66, and the mode 76.

The majority of men (77.7 percent) in the Indiana Sample served with only one unit during the Civil War, and the average length of service during the war was 21.5 months (infantry = 21.03; cavalry = 26.16; artillery = 25.37). The overwhelming majority (74.8 percent) served as privates, with 7.9 percent serving as officers and 15.1 percent as non-coms. Most of these men served in the infantry (85.9 percent) as opposed to the cavalry (9.6 percent) or artillery (3.4 percent); 81.3 percent of the men were volunteers, as compared with recruits (13.4 percent), drafted men (4.1 percent), and substitutes (1.0 percent). Most (85.1 percent) served in the western theater (west of the Alleghenies with the exception of Sherman's campaigns in the last two years of the war). Of the total sample, 17.5 percent became insane during their service in the army, which indicates that the postwar psychological problems of the remaining 82.5 percent—to the extent that these developments can be attributed to service in the war —were delayed in onset and of a post-traumatic variety. In the sample 18.6 percent suffered from gunshot wounds, 13.4 percent were taken prisoner of war at some point, 27.1 percent were discharged from the military for a disability, and 3.1 percent served in the Veteran Reserve Corps. Deserters or those going AWOL made up 7.6 percent, and 5.2 percent reenlisted as a veteran in the latter stages of the war. The average age at first enlistment was 24.2 years.

In the years after the war, violence and antisocial behavior were problems for over half of the men in the sample: 118 men (40.5 percent) attempted or committed acts of violence; another 63 (21.6 percent) threatened violence, often triggering commitment to the insane asylum. Such violence was often directed toward members of the veteran's family (in 26.8 percent of the Indiana Sample), as story after horrific story from inquest and pension records reveals. John W. Blake, who had been court-martialed during the Civil War for becoming drunk while commanding his troops at the Battle of Stones River, continued to struggle with alcoholism after the war; an examining Pension Bureau medical board noted that he was seriously affected after ingesting even small quantities of alcohol, and that his alcoholism seemed to be a form of insanity. Blake's inquest papers from 1887 indicated that he had been out in the yard running around without his clothes on, that he imagined that people were conspiring to harm him, and that he had threatened to kill his family. Other incidents were documented in which he broke up the furniture in the house, threatened to burn the entire house down, and also threatened to kill his wife and daughter.[1]

In other cases, threats against wives and family members developed into actual violence, as when one veteran choked his wife, and another tried to choke his wife and threatened to kill his children as well. The inquest papers of other veterans reveal similar situations: "Assaults his wife frequently, striking and choking her"; "[he] grabs her throat and tries to choke her and destroy furniture in the room." John J. Cameron frequently beat his wife, and on several occasions attempted to shoot her: "since his discharge has beaten his wife." Captain Frank Knorr had become deranged at the Battle of Chickamauga, and was discharged from the service shortly thereafter; after returning home, he continued to be nervous, excitable, seclusive, and cross, and in any conversation regarding the war, he entirely lost control of himself and became wild. He directed much of his frustration and anger at his wife: at one time shortly after his discharge from the army, he took his revolver and fired at her; when questioned about his actions, he said he wanted to show her how he used to make the Rebels run. A neighbor recalled a time when he visited the Knorr household at 7 A.M. and discovered that the door was locked and Captain Knorr was inside whipping his wife; Knorr emerged briefly and threatened to shoot this visitor. John Kirk was known as a hard drinker, and one of his friends recalled the following conversation: "[H]e told me he was going home and cut off his wife's head and use it for a ball in a bowling alley . . . my wife got so she was afraid to have said Kirk come around." Owing to actual and threatened violence of this sort, Martha Russell obtained a peace bond against her former husband, Manville, but this did not seem to deter him in the slightest, as the local marshal testified: "[W]hile I had the warrant for him he stated that he had a right from heaven to stay in Greenwood and no power could remove him Except from the Power above . . . he told me . . . that his divorced wife must not live with any other man or he would kill her."[2]

This domestic violence could also be directed against a veteran's children, and the methods employed often seemed to have been learned in the army. When Frank Knorr wanted to punish his children, he would tie them up by the thumbs in regular military style, and Arthur Brenton threatened to tie up his fifteen-year-old son with ropes, until his wife intervened to protect the boy. Jacob Fink drove his sixteen-year-old son away from home, and took his wife away from home about three miles and left her at a stranger's house saying he would leave her there until she learned to behave herself; he would regularly strike, kick, and abuse members of his family. Samuel Martin, an opium addict, threw a hatchet at his daughter, and another troubled veteran assaulted his fifteen-year-old son with a knife and, even more disturbingly, confessed that he had a compulsion to stomp his new-born baby to death.[3]

Exploding in rage and frustration, many veterans drove their families away from home and often accompanied such acts with threats of violence and murder; in other cases, frightened and terrified wives reacted to the threat of mayhem and murder by fleeing at the first signs of incipient violence. Recognizing oncoming attacks of insanity, Nancy Hoover would take her children and go and stay with neighbors until her husband, William, had returned to normal. In a similar situation, each night at dusk Ellen McKinney would take her children and leave, and only return at daylight. Another psychologically disturbed veteran, John C. Britton, seemed to be seized with a homicidal compulsion, and his wife, Anna, would sometimes accompany him in long walks in the woods at night to prevent him from carrying out an insane belief that he was compelled to take the life of one of his children; on other occasions, she simply removed the entire family from their home and would sleep elsewhere until the situation seemed to improve. This kind of menacing violence with which the wives of many veterans had to contend day in and day out was epitomized by the behavior of Ephraim Maple, who attempted to kill his niece with a knife until restrained, and who was subsequently committed to the insane asylum. His inquest papers reported: "[H]e has threatened to kill anyone that crosses him in any way." One can see that in many of these cases, the insane asylum was less a means of "social control" than a last-gasp measure to protect people in the community: "[I]f not soon admitted to the assylum [Robert M. Higgins] will murder some of his family. The case is very urgent, and if you can possibly make room for him do so."[4]

Aside from domestic violence, some veterans actually attacked and killed or were killed by strangers. Martin V. Toney murdered another inmate at the poorhouse by bludgeoning the man with a hoe: "[H]e is at present wild refuses to talk and shows signs of violence. he eats or sleeps but little . . . he is dangerous and it takes two or three men to control him." William H. Hobson had an uncontrollable temper and would periodically get into fights, including one that ended his life when another man, in self-defense, shot and killed Hobson in 1896. In the Indiana Sample, 6.2 percent ($N = 18$) of the men engaged in other criminal acts, from arson and burglary to horse theft and battery. Of the total, 5.8 percent were deemed at one time or another to have engaged in rude or insulting behavior, from foul language to indecent exposure or, in an extreme case, attempted rape.[5]

Sleepless and disturbed by memories of the war, some veterans simply left home and went off "tramping," walking or riding on railroad cars to wander the countryside; 28 veterans (9.7 percent) of the Indiana Sample exhibited this type of behavior, which took many forms. On the one hand, some psychologically disturbed veterans became the "street people" of their day and wandered about aimlessly in close proximity to home, if they still had one. The commitment papers of Joseph Valentine reported: "He recently left home and could not be induced to return. Has been living on the streets. Preaching and praying." John A. M. Cox would wander the streets all day long, talking incoherently and annoying passersby; his condition was probably the result of alcoholism. Intemperate, violent toward his family, anxious, and with a dread of being killed, Leonard C. Griffith also wandered about the city in an aimless way until he was finally committed to the insane asylum. Another veteran's inquest papers stated: "He is tramping by night and day and taking things that do not belong to him."[6]

In other cases, this wandering seemed to be related to "sprees" that involved episodes of hard drinking and carousing. Maggie Glover testified to the Pension Bureau concerning her husband: "We lived together at Mulhall, from our marriage until he deserted me and his family about five years after our marriage. He was a hard drinking man and would get on a spree and leave and come back when he got sober and then when he got drunk again he would leave and finally he got drunk and left and never came back." The infamous Frank Knorr, who whipped his wife and strung up his son by the thumbs, was constantly afraid the Rebels were after him, and during these unsettled spells would go off "tramping" for weeks at a time, usually down to Cincinnati where he would get drunk and get into fights; then, just as unexpectedly as he had left, he would show up at home again, frequently in a disheveled state. After being committed to the asylum he escaped and went wandering over the countryside, and eventually died of exposure and exhaustion.[7]

For other men, however, wandering and tramping seemed to be related more to wanderlust than to alcoholism. After the Civil War, Robert Walsh lived in Colorado, Kansas, Missouri, and Wyoming: "I was a wanderer in the wild west at That time. Roaming over Colorado New Mexico, Arizona, Texas, Indian Territory and Kansas." Robert D. Commons went tramping off to Chicago, and then down to St. Louis, where he was apparently arrested under a vagrancy law and put to work on a chain gang, before his family finally discovered where he was and rescued him. Jacob Mann would periodically go off on long journeys without any reasonable object in view, and Joel J. Porter would regularly disappear, on one occasion attempting to sell his belongings to get train fare. Another veteran was described as a "worthless, trifling vagabond," who hung out with prostitutes and gamblers, and had never been right in his mind since his return from the army; one observer noted: "Some said that the poor boy had been sinned against more than sinning."[8]

In addition to the 22.4 percent ($N = 65$) of veterans in the Indiana Sample who abused alcohol, another 5.2 percent ($N = 15$) abused drugs, usually chloral hydrate, cocaine, morphine, or opium. Perry B. Bowser had used morphine during his service in the army, and continued to be seriously addicted to this drug for the remainder of his life. He took up to 60 grains a day and suffered from serious psychological problems such as paranoia, leading to two suicide attempts. He testified to the Pension Bureau: "[I] can not live without its use unless with the most terrible suffering, . . . I first used morphine at the Marine hospital in Vicksburg and coming home in Nov. 1865.

It is impossible to do without it and remain sane." Such drug abuse usually developed after men had first been treated with these narcotics for physical pain, either in the army or after release. For instance, Lewis Chowning was given morphine for stomach pain, and then became an addict; it was unclear whether his subsequent nervous problems related to his physical ills or to his drug addiction. George A. C. Gooch was given opium for a cough, related to his tuberculosis, and Samuel M. Martin apparently developed his drug habit after being treated with opiates for a gunshot wound incurred at the Battle of Pea Ridge in 1862. For William H. Bradley, the opium habit clouded his mind, and resulted in death by accidental overdose:

> I have found him at times and at one time especially very delirious and at night when I was with him he was sleepless and was up & walking around all night & with some delusions. . . . He is the servant of his appetite for narcotics, and is controlled by the desire to satisfy the appetite. At times he shuns his friends and acquaintances. His business matters are unattended to . . . When not under the influence of Morphia he is wild and kicks and swears, and prays and screams and wanders, and is sleepless of nights. imagines himself on fire and suspicious of friends and relatives & when he is under the influence of Morphia, he is much the same only not so wild but is feared by his family.[9]

To what extent were the problems of the men in the Indiana Sample typical for Civil War veterans? In inferential statistics, the key is random sampling; if one could derive a random sample (numbers in the range of several hundred would suffice) of Civil War veterans and nonveterans from the late nineteenth century, then one could estimate the total number of psychologically disturbed Civil War veterans and begin to compare veteran and nonveteran behaviors, in order to determine whether veterans experienced mental problems in greater numbers than civilians, and whether these veterans demonstrated a different profile of psychopathology. The key questions are whether the Indiana Sample can be used to make assumptions about Civil War veterans in general, and whether veteran and nonveteran samples can be derived to determine whether the psychological problems of the Indiana Sample were similar to what one might encounter in a group of civilian asylum patients. Unfortunately, the Indiana Sample does not constitute a random sample, and, in addition, it is impossible to derive veteran and nonveteran samples for comparative purposes.

Why isn't the Indiana Sample a random sample, either of all Indiana Civil War veterans or, more specifically, of all insane Indiana Civil War veterans? It was not randomly selected from a known population. There are two basic problems: first, the Indiana Sample was derived from the records of the Indiana Hospital for the Insane, but not all insane people or insane veterans in Indiana were sent to this hospital, in that "chronic cases" (not a clinical description) were excluded from this asylum until about 1900, and, moreover, most insane people were cared for at home in the nineteenth century. Patient slots in insane asylums in Indiana (and elsewhere) were limited from 1861 until about 1900, and, as noted earlier, each county was granted a quota; only "curable" cases of insanity were accepted until a custodial function was developed for the insane asylum around the turn of the century. Hence, the majority of the mental ill in the nineteenth century were treated in local poorhouses and jails or at home, and data on such cases cannot be retrieved. Second, the Indiana Hospital for the Insane in Indianapolis did not serve one consistent geographical area over time. This hospital (from whence the Indiana Sample is derived) was the only state-supported insane asylum in Indiana from the 1850s until about 1890, when satellite or regional insane asylums were built in Logansport, Richmond, and Evansville; at that point, the Indianapolis asylum became known as Central State Hospital and served only the population of central Indiana. Patient records for the regional asylums have been almost completely destroyed; hence, only the data from the Central State Hospital is available for quantitative analysis, and this is skewed in the years after 1890 to represent the counties of central Indiana. As a result of these problems, patients who were formally committed to the Indiana Hospital for the Insane will represent only an unknown portion of the overall insane population of all of Indiana or of central Indiana, and are not necessarily representative of the overall population of psychologically disturbed Civil War veterans for any given district. Thus one cannot simply calculate that the Indiana Sample is x percent of the total asylum population, which was y percent of the total insane population of Indiana, and thereby derive total numbers of insane Civil War veterans in the State of Indiana.[10]

In addition, veteran and nonveteran samples (either for asylum or nonasylum populations) cannot be derived for analytical purposes, for the simple reason that it is impossible to establish a nonveteran sample with any degree of confidence. Asylum records generally do not identify patients as being veterans or nonveterans, and in an age before the Social Security number and before dates of birth were commonly employed in vital statistics, it proves exceedingly difficult to determine who was or was not a veteran by reviewing and comparing surviving nineteenth-century insane asylum and military records. To prove a negative (the lack of military service), one would have to compare each patient's name against the muster roll records of all Union and Confederate states that organized and fielded military units during the Civil War, and this would be an utter impossibility, not only because of the huge amount of muster roll material that is available, but also because of incomplete and missing records in many states. Hence, with what asylum data survives, it is not feasible to determine who was or was not a veteran with complete confidence, and comparative statistics between veterans and civilians cannot be derived, other than from local or opportunity samples. Of course, female asylum patients could be used as a control group and one could be reasonably certain that these women had not served in the Civil War, but the issue of gender would cloud any direct comparisons in behavior and psychopathology between male veteran and female nonveteran groups.

Given all of these difficulties, is it possible to determine whether the Indiana Sample was a "typical" group of Civil War veterans or not? To some extent, yes, for information survives on the characteristics of all (or most) Indiana and Union veterans—mainly pertaining to age, nativity, occupation, and casualty statistics. One can therefore determine (allowing for a number of problems) how different the Indiana Sample was from the greater population of all Civil War soldiers. First of all, the percentage of men in the Indiana Sample discharged from the military for disabilities was 27.1 percent, well above the overall disability rate of 8.9 percent for Indiana soldiers, the general range from 5.8 percent to 9.7 percent given by the *Official Record* for Civil War soldiers in various districts, or the range of from 8.1 percent to 9.7 percent for all Union soldiers suggested in authoritative medical histories of the war. As illustrated in earlier chapters, this would indicate that for Civil War soldiers, chronic disease, gunshot wounds (leading to discharge), and mental breakdown in the service might have predicted post-service psychological problems. Likewise, the desertion rate of 7.6 percent in the Indiana Sample was well above the overall rate of 3.7 percent (per the Adjutant General's Report) or 5.3 percent (from an independent analysis of the Adjutant General's data) for all Indiana soldiers, although similar to the rate of 6.3 percent for all Union soldiers listed in the war's *Official Record,* and below the desertion rates of over 10 percent for New Jersey, Connecticut, and New Hampshire troops. Again, one suspects that many of the more than 300,000 men who deserted during the Civil War were suffering from undiagnosed stress disorders of some type.[11]

Chi-square analysis for goodness of fit suggests that the Indiana Sample was younger, or younger in critical ranges than typical Union volunteers. Based on numbers for all Indiana volunteers, one would expect in a sample of 291 men to find 1 member who was in the thirteen- to sixteen-year age bracket; in the Indiana Sample, there were 12 men in this bracket; over 10 percent of the Indiana Sample was seventeen years of age or younger at the time of first enlistment in the military, and this proves to be significantly different than was the case for all Indiana volunteers [χ^2 (7, $n = 291$) = 133.606, $p < .005$; the age bracket of thirteen to sixteen years accounts for 127.836 of the chi-square statistic]. This difference is also noted when one compares only the volunteers in the Indiana Sample ($N = 236$) with all Indiana volunteers [χ^2 (7, $n = 236$) = 52.875, $p < .005$; almost the entire chi-square statistic (49.866) is accounted for by the thirteen-to-sixteen-year age bracket]. One is reminded immediately of the claims that Vietnam veterans suffered from proportionately more psychological problems than World War II veterans because of their comparative youth, which is to say that adolescents are less resilient to the stresses of military life in wartime. However, this significant difference does not persist across all age brackets, and while the overall mean age for members of the Indiana Sample (24.26) was almost one year younger than that for all Union volunteers (25.29), it was actually *higher* than the mean for all Indiana volunteers (24.17); at the same time, the mean age of volunteers in the Indiana Sample (24.19) was almost identical to the mean for all Indiana volunteers. The fact that complete data is not available for all Indiana or Union soldiers obscures any clear-cut conclusions regarding the matter of age.

Information on nativity for all Indiana volunteers indicates that the Indiana Sample came from Indiana in greater numbers than one might expect. Employing chi-square analysis for goodness of fit, one can see that 170 of the 291 members of the Indiana Sample hailed from Indiana, whereas, based on population parameters for all Indiana veterans, one would expect a number of only 135; accordingly, numbers of Indiana Sample members from other states such as Ohio, New York, Pennsylvania, and elsewhere were lower than one might have expected. The differences in this analysis easily reach "significant" levels [χ^2 (6, $n = 291$) $= 23.343$, $p < .005$].[12]

Likewise, information on occupation indicates significant differences between the men in the Indiana Sample and all Indiana volunteers, in that the sample had fewer farmers and markedly increased numbers of men in the skilled labor, professional, and commercial classes [χ^2 (4, $n = 291$) $= 165.452$, $p < .005$]. These results could be interpreted in at least two ways: on the one hand, because information on occupation can often only be derived from asylum records, and because many of these men were committed to the asylum ten and twenty years after the war ended, it would stand to reason that their occupation level had increased accordingly over time—this is to say that the occupation level of the Indiana Sample reflected the acquisition of skills after the war, whereas general data on Civil War soldiers reflect the occupation-level of young men who have not yet embarked on careers in civilian life. On the other hand, many men in the Indiana Sample were dysfunctional, were being repeatedly committed to the insane asylum or were collecting federal disability pensions, and were not necessarily acquiring job skills over time—hence, there is the possibility that this significant difference in occupations is explained by other factors, either that those with more job skills had more political influence and were able to gain admittance to the asylum or, perhaps, that there was something about this profile that made these men better able to claim or articulate mental problems or that put them at risk of developing psychological problems in the first place.

In sum, statistical analysis suggests that the postwar psychological problems of the men in the Indiana Sample may have been associated with (or resulted from) incurring more physical and mental disabilities in the service, having entered the service at a younger age than the norm, and having been subjected to pressures that led to elevated rates of desertion. Differences pertaining to nativity and occupation are less easy to interpret. And, last of all, there is the matter of exposure to combat—was this also a factor in causing postwar mental breakdown?

Studies of Vietnam veterans have usually concluded that men exposed to combat are more likely to develop PTSD symptomatology than is the case for noncombat military personnel or civilians. The data differ significantly from study to study, but one researcher concluded that in one sample 27 percent of Vietnam veterans who experienced heavy combat could be diagnosed as having PTSD—compared with 19 percent of all Vietnam veterans and 12 percent of non-Vietnam veterans and nonveterans.[13] Building on the conclusions of such studies, one wonders whether elevated levels of exposure to combat might have contributed to producing the psychological problems experienced by members of the Indiana Sample; in short, can one conclude that exposure to combat accounted for the many resulting mental problems of Civil War veterans as was the case for Vietnam veterans? How can one retrospectively measure such combat exposure?

Those conducting post-Vietnam studies investigating the relationship of combat to psychopathology inevitably begin each inquiry by presenting the veterans under scrutiny with extensive and detailed questionnaires in order to determine their past exposure to combat. For Civil War veterans long dead, the only way to systematically investigate exposure to combat and death for the Indiana Sample would seem to be through examination of surviving regimental and company casualty statistics. Two sets of data exist for overall regiments and individual companies, and are discussed in more detail in Appendix B. First, regimental casualty statistics ("Regimental Data") for the 174 Indiana regiments that served in the Civil War are available in the eight-volume Terrell's Adjutant General's Report for the State of Indiana and reveal overall death rates for all men in each regiment (see Table 8.4). Second, company-level data are also contained in the eight-volume Adjutant General's Report from Indiana; these records do not include data on officers, but do offer information on death rates, disability discharges, and battle casualties for enlisted men; in addition, these data distinguish between volunteers and recruits. Where the categories between the Regimental Data and the Company Sample address the same populations, one can see that the data are highly similar: for instance, the overall death rate from Regimental Data for enlisted men and non-coms in Indiana units was 12.5 percent, whereas the overall death rate from the Company Sample (which excludes officers) was 12.9 percent.

What was the overall casualty profile for Indiana regiments in the Civil War? Table 8.4 provides information on three indices—the battle casualty rate [(killed in action + died of wounds + discharged for wounds)/total men in unit], the death rate, and the total casualty index [(killed as result of battle + died of disease + discharged for disability)/total men in unit]—per branch of service (infantry, cav-

Table 8.4   Average casualty rates for Indiana Civil War units (in percent)

	Battle casualties	Death rate	Total casualties
Rank			
Officers	N/A	9.94 (RD)	N/A
Enlisted men	3.98 (CS)	12.52 (RD)	24.05 (CS)
Total	N/A	12.41 (RD)	N/A
Volunteers (enlisted men)	5.48 (CS)	14.23 (CS)	27.53 (CS)
Recruits (enlisted men)	2.28 (CS)	8.17 (CS)	13.53 (CS)
Total (enlisted men)	3.98 (CS)	12.94 (CS)	24.05 (CS)
Branch of service (enlisted men)			
Infantry	4.28 (CS)	13.14 (RD)	24.53 (CS)
Calvary	2.5 (CS)	11.68 (RD)	21.82 (CS)
Heavy Artillery	3.33 (CS)	14.61 (RD)	22.63 (CS)
Light Artillery	1.62 (CS)	10.01 (RD)	20.14 (CS)
Term of service (enlisted men)			
3 months	0.21 (CS)	0.99 (RD)	1.50 (CS)
6 months	0.19 (CS)	8.00 (RD)	4.19 (CS)
12 months	0.34 (CS)	5.53 (RD)	5.74 (CS)
36 months	5.63 (CS)	16.21 (RD)	32.94 (CS)
Theater (enlisted men)			
East	4.02 (CS)	7.87 (RD)	15.69 (CS)
West	3.87 (CS)	13.00 (RD)	25.61 (CS)

Source: W. H. H. Terrell, *Report of the Adjutant General of the State of Indiana,* 8 vols. (Indianapolis: W. R. Holloway, 1865). "CS" signifies information derived from the Company Sample; "RD" signifies information on total casualties for all Indiana Regiments in the Civil War (see Appendix B).

Note: "Battle casualties" are defined as killed in action + died of wounds + discharged from the army on account of wounds incurred in battle; "death rate" equals the number of men who died of disease or from wounds, divided by the total number of men in the unit; "total casualties" equals number died + number discharged for disabilities, divided by the total number of men in the unit. N/A = Not available.

alry, artillery), per service term (from 1 to 36 months), per theater served (East versus West), for recruits versus original volunteers, and overall totals. As is clear, casualty rates were far from uniform for all regiments or companies: enlisted men suffered from a higher rate of casualties than officers,[14] infantry units had higher rates on average than cavalry units,[15] units enlisting for 36 months incurred substantially higher rates than units in the service for only 3, 6, or 12 months, volunteers had higher rates than recruits,[16] and casualty rates were higher for Indiana units fighting in the western than in the eastern theater.[17] Although certain districts of Indiana seem to have higher casualty rates, glm tests (because of unbalanced classes) reveal that elevated rates for some districts do not reach the point of being statistically significant.[18]

The last question with which we are concerned is whether this casualty data can be employed to discover if members of the Indiana Sample were exposed to greater than normal levels of combat, death, and disability during their service in the Civil War; if so, could this help explain the cause of their postwar psychological problems? Could it suggest that other Civil War veterans in a similar situation might also have been at risk of developing post-traumatic stress?

Because it is impossible to obtain details of personal experience directly, one has to rely on two other ways of making a general assessment regarding the exposure of the men in the Indiana Sample to combat and death during the war: (a) by comparing the general experience of the units in which members of the Indiana Sample served against an "average control group"; and (b) by determining a more individualized rate of exposure to battle, death, and disability for members of the Indiana Sample, and, again, comparing this with some sort of control or "average" group or making internal comparisons between significant subgroups.

First of all, general casualty statistics can be compared among the 243 Indiana units in the Company Sample (used as a kind of control group) and the 292 units in which members of the Indiana Sample served. There are two major problems with this approach: (a) there is some overlap between companies in the two groups ($N = 40$); and (b) members of the Indiana Sample did not always stay with one individual unit throughout the war—a number of men transferred to different units, and a good number of the men were discharged from the service with disabilities before the war had ended. Hence one should not necessarily attribute the exposure of the unit for the entire course of the war to men who were not there the whole time.

Nonetheless, with these complications in mind, comparisons can be made: a series of t-tests were run on ten different casualty indices[19] between the two groups (the Company Sample and the Indiana Sample) as a whole and between a series of subgroups (all volunteers, all recruits, all infantry units, volunteers in infantry units, recruits in infantry units, all cavalry units, volunteers in cavalry units, recruits in cavalry units, all light artillery units, volunteers in light artillery units, recruits in light artillery units, and all heavy artillery units) derived from each of the two groups. For the Indiana Sample, battle (percentage killed, died of wounds, discharged due to wounds), disability (percentage disabled), and overall casualty rates (percentage died plus disabled) were higher, although none of the differences was statistically significant; only the disability index t-test approached significance levels,[20] which does tend to bear out earlier observations that disabilities resulting in discharge from the service may have been related in a critical way to postwar psychological problems: 27.1 percent of the members of the Indiana Sample were discharged from the military for a disability, compared with an overall rate of 8.9 percent for all Indiana units per the Adjutant General's final report.

For volunteers in Indiana units (those generally enlisting at the beginning of the war and serving the longest), all major casualty indices were higher for the Indiana Sample than for the Company Sample, and again the greatest difference, achieving levels of statistical significance, appeared in the area of the disability index [t (533) = $-1.971, p = 0.0492$, two tails]. For cavalry units as a whole, all major casualty indices were higher for the Indiana Sample, and the indices for total casualties [t (57) = $-2.4327, p = 0.0182$, two tails) and percentage disabled [t (57) = $-2.169, p = 0.0343$, two tails) were higher for the Indiana Sample by statistically significant margins. For artillery units, the same pattern was repeated as the disability index was higher for the Indiana Sample than for the Company Sample "control group."

A second method of comparing and analyzing casualty rates for the Indiana Sample is possible: in this instance, the monthly casualty indices were taken for each unit in which members of the Indiana Sample served, and these indices were multiplied by the number of months the soldier served in that unit. If the man served in more than one unit, the totals for the two or three total units were added together to produce four general casualty indices—for battle, death, disability, and total (death plus disability). This approach has the advantage of "individualizing" the indices to reflect the time that members of the Indiana Sample actually spent in a company—the idea is to establish a monthly exposure index for the unit with which the man served, and then weight the index per the months that the man was actually in the unit.[21] A series of t-tests and glm tests were run on the output, and, in the realm of the significant, reveal the following: (a) of the 67 men rendered disabled during the Civil War, those incurring gunshot wounds suffered the highest exposure to battle, death, and disability—for instance, their adjusted battle index was 5.0 percent compared with 3.2 percent for all disabled men, and 3.2 percent for the nondisabled; (b) POWs suffered from higher indices across the board compared with non-POWs;[22] (c) those experiencing problems with alcoholism in the years after the war had higher indices, but not by statistically significant margins. One must keep in mind, however, that any such internal comparisons between subgroups are rendered tentative and highly conditional by the fact that nineteenth-century data are fragmentary, meaning that it is difficult if not impossible to establish mutually exclusive categories; to assert that x percent of the men were alcoholics simply means that we know that x percent of men had problems with alcohol, and the situation regarding the balance of the sample is unknown.

In the final analysis, because of a number of problems with nineteenth-century records, including fragmentary data, indifferent and inconsistent record keeping, the difficulty of matching record groups, the impossibility of assembling nonveteran control groups, and the impossibility of ascertaining individual experience, it is difficult to make clear-cut and dramatic conclusions concerning the experience of the psychologically disturbed members of the Indiana Sample, and to generalize their experience to other populations of Civil War veterans. Nonetheless, one does notice a consistent pattern throughout that the members of the Indiana Sample seemed to have incurred disabilities at an above-average rate in the Civil War, and to have been associated with units that had higher than expected exposure to disabilities—whether from communicable diseases, chronic diseases, gunshot wounds, or mental breakdown. On balance, however, perhaps the most salient point about the Indiana Sample is how close to average it seems to be in so many other respects—its exposure to battle, disease, disability, and death in the Civil War was for the most part remarkably similar to the experience of all Indiana regiments, and of the Company Sample. One is tempted therefore to think that the problems of the Indiana Sample could not have been atypical, and at the minimum, this sample is significant for revealing a wide range of psychological and social problems that have not heretofore been associated with the Civil War veteran.

"I Am Glad I Served My Country":
Vietnam Reconsidered

The Civil War was devastating in its impact. Over 600,000 soldiers died in a four-year period at a time when the total population of the United States was 35 million; by comparison, the Vietnam War claimed 58,000 American lives over a ten-year period when the population of the United States exceeded 200 million. For Indiana regiments enlisting for three-year terms in the Civil War, it was not at all unusual for 40 percent, 50 percent, or even 60 percent of the original volunteers either to die (of disease or in battle) or to succumb to disabilities before their terms of service had expired; the overall casualty rate (death plus disability) was 24 percent for Indiana troops, and in the vicinity of 25 percent for Union soldiers as a whole. For American troops in Vietnam, exposure in the war zone was limited to one year (thirteen months for Marines) unless individual soldiers chose to reenlist, and the overall death and disability rates were in the range of 5.5 percent. American soldiers in Vietnam had all sorts of "luxuries" such as regular R&R, advanced medical care and medivac helicopters, USO entertainment, and almost instantaneous air support at the touch of a button; Civil War troops were lucky if they were fed regularly and if on such occasions their hardtack was not worm-infested. Troops in Vietnam who suffered psychological breakdown could expect to be examined by psychiatrists and sent home, whereas Civil War soldiers—North and South—who cracked under the pressure and sought to escape an intolerable situation were almost universally regarded with contempt as malingerers and shirkers. Hundreds of deserters in that war were captured, brought back to their regiments, and shot to death by military authorities.

For those who would distinguish the Vietnam War from earlier American wars on the grounds that America lost a war for the first time in its history, that there was a lack of public support for the war effort, and that because of this indifference returning troops did not have their psychological distress washed away by exuberant homecoming celebrations as had been the practice in past wars, it would be well to take a closer look at the Civil War. There were deep divisions in both the North and the South over the wisdom of fighting the Civil War, and fervent and sometimes treasonous antiwar and peace movements—including the notorious "Copperheads" and those involved in the New York City Draft Riot of 1863—flourished in both sections. Regarding the contention that Vietnam was the first war America lost, one should keep in mind the Confederate veteran, who served a lost cause and at war's end sometimes came home to find his house burned to the ground, his possessions and farming implements ruined or stolen, and his family scattered to places unknown—a world turned upside down that few Vietnam veterans experienced in quite the same way. And regarding the assertion that homecoming parades dispel memories of violence and killing, one should not forget that many of the Union men in the Indiana Sample continued for the rest of their lives to suffer mental anguish, torment, and guilt relating to memories of the war, despite having received exuberant welcomes from appreciative civilians.

Unlike American veterans in the nineteenth century who largely had to fend for themselves or rely on their families, returning Vietnam veterans were entitled to a comprehensive package of G.I. Bill benefits, including the right to reclaim their old job (or a similar one with like seniority, status, and pay), the right to educational benefits, the right to federally insured home loans at below-market rates, the right to preferences in hiring for federal employment, many preferences in state and local government hiring, the right to unemployment compensation and disability benefits when appropriate, the right to loans from the U.S. Small Business Administration, an array of benefits and special consideration from other governmental offices and entities, and even their own health care system (the VA hospital and nursing home system). Vietnam veterans have used the G.I. Bill to pursue their education, especially at the college and university level, in unprecedented numbers, and as a result they are the best-educated veterans in American history. As of 1979, something like two million guaranteed or insured home loans worth over $56 billion had been granted to Vietnam-era veterans to purchase residential property. American veterans, including Vietnam-era veterans, have a higher median income than nonveteran civilians. The list goes on.[1]

For those who would argue that the detriment incurred by Vietnam veterans had more to do with wounded feelings than with objective economic harm, a comprehensive study conducted by Lou Harris for the Veterans Administration in 1980 demonstrated that the civilian population of the United States rejected the Vietnam War, but did not blame the Vietnam veteran: "The public clearly discriminates between its negative attitudes toward the war in Vietnam and its feelings for the warriors who fought there." This study indicated that civilians had a high regard for Vietnam veterans, and further noted that pride rather than shame was the most common characteristic of the Vietnam era veteran, with 71 percent responding that the statement "Looking back, I am glad I served my country," matched their feelings very closely. Seventy-seven percent of Vietnam era veterans felt they received a "very friendly" reception from family and close friends upon their return from the service (an additional 15 percent described the reception as "somewhat friendly"). Various surveys have indicated that by a considerable margin (2–1 or higher), Vietnam vets themselves feel that their wartime experience "benefitted" them rather than "set them back," and some veterans view their tour in the war zone as a time when they were part of a "team" or a "family," and as the most exciting and meaningful experience of their lives. Regarding readjustment, one survey demonstrated that 78 percent of Vietnam vets were homeowners, 80 percent were married, and of those married, 90 percent had children; many Vietnam vets have reported that their experience in the military improved them as human beings by giving them increased self-confidence, inner strength, and compassion.[2]

Although one would not want to minimize the misfortune of many American soldiers in Vietnam, perhaps it is time to at least entertain the notion that contrary to the rhetoric of the past thirty years and contrary to what has become conventional wisdom in the United States, the Vietnam veteran—in the larger scheme of things—may not have fared so badly. It would seem that the rhetoric about Vietnam vets having received "shameful" and "disgraceful" treatment at the hands of the American people and the U.S. government has, at a minimum, been exaggerated; the image of the Vietnam veteran as a uniquely troubled and scorned individual in American history may have more to do with political manipulation and a variety of social and cultural factors than with underlying objective reality. This chapter will suggest that six factors during the 1970s and 1980s helped to produce the enduring image of the Vietnam veteran as unique for his or her travails.

First of all, the Vietnam veteran has been a powerful tool for those who have wished to shape American society or influence the course of American politics. The original negative image of the Vietnam veteran was born in the days of the anti-Vietnam War movement from 1969 to 1973, when critics attempted to show that America should withdraw from Vietnam—sometimes regardless of the consequences—in part because the war was doing psychological damage to the American troops; according to this view, American soldiers and veterans were supposedly haunted by guilt from war experiences (from seeing friends die or from having committed atrocities) and, as a consequence, were experiencing psychological problems in unprecedented numbers. In order to pursue this antiwar agenda, critics such as Robert Jay Lifton, a self-described "antiwar psychiatric investigator," placed the Vietnam veteran at the center of the debate, and seem to have grossly exaggerated the problems of these returning veterans in order to achieve a political agenda. In the words of Lifton: "[T]he Vietnam veteran serves as a psychological crucible of the entire country's doubts and misgivings about the war." The portrayal of the Vietnam vet as well-adjusted and untroubled by the war would have undermined this antiwar agenda, and hence evidence that Vietnam veterans were readjusting or had readjusted well to American society tended to be drowned out by excited and strident recriminations leveled against the U.S. government.[3]

The image of the Vietnam veteran as nearly demented and drenched in blood and gore from the victims of his atrocities could also be used as a way of demonizing those in favor of further prosecution of the war, in that antiwar demonstrators would, at least on occasion, fling the epithet of "baby-killer" at uniformed service personnel. From the outset, the representation of the Vietnam veteran as psychologically disturbed because of alleged widespread participation in atrocities has thus had a peculiar double-edged quality, involving elements of sympathy and contempt. In either case, however, the salient point is that from the late 1960s on, the Vietnam veteran has stood at the center of any debate concerning the wisdom and meaning of the Vietnam War, and such debates have tended to be extraordinarily politicized and to involve the use of hyperbole and exaggeration. In such a highly charged atmosphere, calm, considered, and dispassionate study and reflection regarding the actual welfare of the Vietnam veteran have been difficult to come by.

The Vietnam soldier and veteran have also served as a kind of barometer for measuring the morality of the Vietnam War as reflected in the concern whether minorities and the poor constituted a disproportionate percentage of service personnel (or combat service personnel) in the U.S. armed forces in Vietnam. From the late 1960s on, critics argued that African-Americans and men from lower socioeconomic groups constituted a disproportionate number of American soldiers killed in Vietnam, and that the war was "fought for us by our servants," or that it was a "class war." Although statistical studies have revealed that blacks did not die in disproportionate numbers in Vietnam, and that the characterization of a "class war" was grossly overstated, the idea persists that no American war can be entirely moral unless the composition of the armed forces closely reflects percentages of various racial, ethnic, and economic groups in the general population. Again the arguments have been emotional. In attempting to judge the morality of the Vietnam War according to the perceived fate and welfare of the American soldiers engaged in that conflict, critics have sometimes overstated their case.[4]

Although the political left initially seemed to be most responsible for exploiting the image of the Vietnam veteran as having been badly used by his government, in the 1980s those on the right of the political spectrum helped solidify this dogma when they began to interpret the Vietnam veteran not as a victim of war's madness but as a frustrated patriot, betrayed by his own country that had not "let him win." The words of President Ronald Reagan typified this revisionist outlook: "Several years [ago], we brought home a group of American fighting men who obeyed their country's call and fought as bravely and well as any Americans in our history. They came home without a victory not because they had been defeated but because they had been denied permission to win." In accordance with this new view of the matter, "payback" and "revenge" movies such as *Missing in Action, Uncommon Valor,* and *Rambo* fantasized about "getting even" and refighting the Vietnam War, this time with "no holds barred" (neglecting, however, to consider the matter of possible Chinese intervention).[5]

The general conservative appropriation to its own uses of the image of an aggrieved Vietnam veteran, along with the intimation that such a feckless limited war strategy would not be tolerated on its watch, appealed to Americans who were hungry for reconciliation and eager to dispel the self-doubt of the 1960s. Pursuant to this revisionism, the image of the Vietnam vet was modified from that of a victim of war's madness (the paraplegic and POW) to that of the "survivor-hero" in the 1980s, a gritty, capable, can-do American hero, along the lines of a Sylvester Stallone or a Chuck Norris. Some critics of this trend questioned the meaning of the emotional parades of the 1980s in which up to 200,000 veterans marched in front of audiences that contained as many as one million people, and charged that the vets were "being used a second time around" as part of an effort to make war fashionable again.[6]

The remarkable product of all of the image management and manipulation that has gone on between the left and right for the past thirty years concerning the Vietnam veteran is the resultant illusion of a consensus concerning the "lessons of Vietnam": the left's abhorrence of war is fused with the right's fantasies of decisive action and then merged again with a new-found faith in the power of high-tech weapons (notwithstanding the fact that massive technological advantage proved to be nondecisive in Vietnam) to produce the idea that "next time" a war will be fought only under circumstances in which there is unquestioned public support and the conflict can be won quickly and decisively, employing high-tech weapons and incurring a minimum of casualties. One wonders if this is, in fact, not simply a formula for either abstinence, when a tenacious foe such as the Vietcong is encountered, or for obvious victory, when a woefully outgunned and undercommitted adversary, with no protecting patron saint such as the Soviet Union or China, is blown out of the water quickly in a post–Cold War skirmish. If the United States were again faced with a situation like that in Korea in June of 1950 when vital interests were at stake, but all-out war would trigger Chinese intervention and practical stalemate, it is doubtful that the "lessons of Vietnam" would in fact point to a painless and quick solution or would enable us to avoid the frustrations of limited war.[7]

Second, beyond proponents of specific political points of view, Vietnam veterans themselves have used their image as having been badly treated to entrench and extend their already extensive benefit package from the federal government. Statements frequently made by Vietnam veterans to the effect that "billions are spent on defense but only pennies, by comparison, for providing fully staffed hospitals" belie the fact that veterans in the United States have become a privileged class, and that it is difficult for any politician to say "no" to the veterans' lobby. The sociologist Willard Waller, writing in 1944, captured the power of the veteran and the veterans' lobby: "The veteran is always a powerful political force, for good or evil, because others cannot protect themselves from him. He has fought for the flag and has absorbed some of its *mana*. He is sacred. He is covered with pathos and immune from criticism." Hence, as *The Viet Vet Survival Guide* rather crassly put it: "The most important thing to realize about your benefits is that the VA Regional Office is essentially a bank."[8]

The Veterans Administration is one of the largest federal agencies and has a budget of over $28 billion (FY1989), a work force of 240,000, and a hospital system that includes 172 hospitals, 226 outpatient clinics, and 106 nursing home centers. For every American war through World War I, at least as much, and usually much more money has been spent on the veterans than on the conduct of the war itself, and before all the veterans of World War II, Korea, and Vietnam have died, these wars will follow the same pattern. It has been projected that veterans' benefits to Vietnam vets and their dependents will be paid through the year 2100. Because of civil service preferences in hiring, 50 percent of the federal government's work force in 1978 consisted of veterans, while veterans constituted only 25 percent of the general work force in the United States. Nevertheless, in the congressional fights over funding for the vet centers, increases in the G.I. Bill, increases in disability pensions, inclusion of cost-of-living allowances (COLAs), and provision of maternity and day-care benefits for veterans and their families, it has been useful for the veterans' lobby to perpetuate and use to its continued benefit the image of the "neglected" Vietnam veteran.[9]

An irony of much of the Vietnam veterans' movement is that it has called for special treatment for the Vietnam veteran. When President Carter's call in 1978 for the elimination of civil service preferences for all veterans except Vietnam-era veterans and disabled veterans was defeated, Vietnam veterans charged "favoritism" for older vets. In fact, the Vietnam vets were asking for and expecting a preference for themselves over all others (civilians and even other veterans), and when it was not delivered, claimed "yet another betrayal." Vietnam vets have accused the VA of bureaucratic insensitivity and bungling and of being a bloated welfare state, but have often failed to recognize that they themselves are its beneficiaries. Much of the reemergence of the Vietnam veterans' movement in the late 1970s related to a conscious effort at lobbying for more government benefits.[10] Although veterans resist the characterization, the public policy expert Sar Levitan wrote that there were, in effect, two welfare systems in the United States, one for veterans, and the other for civilians: "The welfare standards in effect for veterans are much more liberal than for nonveterans, and the rules of the game are also different. Though the means test controls both veterans' and nonveterans' programs, the veterans' program operates with due regard for the dignity of the individual, while the recipients of welfare aid are held in opprobrium."[11]

Some would justify this difference on the basis of the assertion that veterans "fought" for their country and deserve a special status for their efforts and risks, but one wonders if such a distinction can be sustained in an era in which 85 percent to 90 percent of personnel in the American armed forces function in a noncombat support role of some kind. One insightful critic noted:

> A typical response to someone who has served in Vietnam is that he has undergone a surreal ordeal which is difficult for a civilian to comprehend. However, in reality, although some endured extreme hardships under inhuman conditions and risked their lives daily, a large majority of the servicemen in Vietnam lived and worked in relative safety in stabilized, established areas. One out of ten soldiers and one out of seven Marines are the commonly accepted figures for those who were in the field with a combat unit.[12]

In the 1980s and 1990s, television programs in the United States have routinely revealed that the conditions at various VA hospitals are sometimes "scandalous" and need to be improved; the questions rarely asked are "why is there a separate medical system for veterans in the United States," and "why are civilians in geographical areas that are badly underserved by hospitals and doctors denied access to veterans' medical facilities?"[13]

Third, the Vietnam War marked the predominance of a new type of military history that tends to emphasize the experience of the common soldier. John Keegan in *The Face of Battle* noted that military history has primarily consisted in the past of the study of generals and generalship, and advocated a new approach to investigate the experience of the common soldier. Unfortunately, there are dangers to this type of military history, for in the small unit, the greater purpose and flow of the war is rarely evident; to the common soldier in all eras, war has seemed a chaotic and terrifying business. S. L. A. Marshall has demonstrated that even in a war such as World War II with a clearly defined enemy and a seemingly clear ideological struggle between democracy and totalitarianism, the infantryman was still motivated primarily by loyalty to his immediate unit, and sought mainly to survive. Overemphasis on the common soldier in one's study of war may thus produce not clarity and greater understanding, but a sense of meaninglessness and futility.[14]

In the portrayal of American participation in the Vietnam War, the primary focus in both literature and motion pictures has been on the experience of the individual soldier. Accordingly, the public has been bombarded with images of chaos, destruction, and meaningless death, and the larger questions of military and political strategy are essentially ignored. Was the Vietnam War in fact necessary to contain communism in the early 1960s? Did the war only become absurd after detente? What were the alternatives to military intervention in South Vietnam in the early 1960s? Would disengagement by the Kennedy administration have led to the collapse of South Vietnam and another round of recriminations on the order of "Who Lost China," and what would have been the domestic political repercussions? Contrary to the rhetoric of America's having "lost the war," was the United States not in fact in the process of sustaining a fragile but hard-won military advantage in the early 1970s, had it only been willing to continue to support the Thieu regime after the withdrawal of U.S. troops from Vietnam? In light of the fact that after their "victory," doctrinaire Communist economic planners in Vietnam were shunted aside and Western investment—which will no doubt eventually include Coca-Cola and McDonald's restaurants—was welcomed with open arms, could not one argue that the real veterans who were "betrayed" and who "lost the war" were the Vietcong and NVA regulars, who made astonishing sacrifices for several decades, only to see the Americans and western values triumph in the end? In a climate in the United States where the overwhelming emphasis is on lamenting American loss of life in the Vietnam War, and where war in general is condemned as wasteful and immoral, these questions have not been seriously debated or even considered. This skewed presentation of the Vietnam War has revealed the Vietnam vet, even under the best of circumstances, as a victim and survivor, and not as an advocate, pro-

ponent, or defender of anything worthwhile, decent, or construc-
tive.[15]

Fourth, the role of the media must be considered. The conventional
wisdom on the Vietnam War is that the media, particularly television,
was instrumental in the loss of American will to fight—that "negative coverage" of the war by the media turned the American public
against the war. Daniel C. Hallin, however, has refuted this view and
argues that the media, employing "objective journalism," did not
shape, but primarily reacted to events. It was only when divisions
over the war emerged within the government, when the antiwar
movement penetrated large segments of the American population,
and when the morale of American troops in Vietnam began to plum-
met after the Tet offensive that the media portrayed the war in negative terms.[16]

In a similar way, although in a different context,[17] one could argue
that the media reacted to rather than shaped the emerging image of
the Vietnam veteran. Particularly in the case of television, the image
of a "troubled and scorned" Vietnam vet did not supersede issue
coverage and become dominant until the late 1970s, well after this
image had become familiar in the print media. For instance, despite
extensive coverage in the print media of the "Post-Vietnam Syndrome" in the late 1960s and early 1970s (articles by Robert Lifton
appeared in a variety of newspapers and magazines), television news
had very few references to the possible psychological problems Vietnam veterans at this time. What coverage there was concerning troubled readjustment in the late 1960s focused on widows, a population
almost completely ignored after the emergence of the image of the
problem-filled Vietnam vet in the 1980s; the atrocity issue was also
first presented by the print media in the wake of revelations of the
massacre at Mylai.[18]

Once the Vietnam veteran had become a national concern, however, television coverage in particular may have been critical in reinforcing and embellishing emerging stereotypes on two counts:
(1) television news carried very few dissenting views on the Vietnam
veteran issue, as opposed to the print media, which contained numerous articles that questioned whether the Vietnam veteran was
actually violent or in worse shape than veterans of past American
wars;[19] (2) television news tended to dramatize and simplify the issues, and fastened onto the Vietnam veteran as an interesting "victim," just as it would with the survivors of a hurricane, earthquake,

or any other catastrophe. In the 1980s television seemed to portray the problems of Vietnam veterans as bigger and worse than ever, even as views began to emerge in the print media at that time questioning the "Vietnam vet myth." By the late 1970s and early 1980s, the usual coverage on television showed Vietnam veterans in extreme agony: "I started flashing back; I was in the Nam . . . ; I burned a village to the ground and everyone in it . . . I need help"; "[i]t's like we've been pushed under the rug. They don't want to have anything to do with us"; "[i]t's too late for me"; "[w]e were made into weapons of war and then discarded"; "I feel betrayed, let down"; "I was 19; it was all women and children . . ."; "I'm living the war just like I was there yesterday. I can't shake it"; "[t]hey fought and struggled and came home to a public that didn't care."[20] Such a tendency to present the news as dramatic, without alternative viewpoints or historical analysis, may be the result of what Neil Postman has described as the descent of television into triviality as it becomes entertainment and little more. Television cannot be singled out for blame, however, as the print media also promoted the stereotype, churning out obligatory articles on the tenth anniversary of the American withdrawal from Vietnam, the tenth anniversary of the fall of South Vietnam, and so on—repeating the same assertions again and again.[21]

This tendency of the media to latch onto and to embellish a simplistic dramatic image is particularly troublesome because the Vietnam veterans' movement has actually become a mass of contradictions that require careful analysis and criticism. Although the Vietnam War is widely denounced by Vietnam vets as pointless and almost a crime against the American men and women who were sent there to fight, politicians who served in the National Guard in that era (Dan Quayle) or who protested against the war (Bill Clinton) are condemned by the veterans' lobby as lacking in patriotism or moral backbone for not having, apparently, had the guts to go over to Vietnam and fight the Communists in this meaningless war. Although post-Vietnam rhetoric has centered on "reconciliation," "closure," and "healing," the Vietnam veterans' lobby protested vigorously throughout the 1970s that the country was trying to ignore them (even while they were fully eligible for G.I. Bill benefits), and that the war and the fate of the veterans should not be forgotten. The continuing anger and bitterness emanating from some Vietnam veterans suggests, essentially, an inability to ever forget or put the war into any sort of realistic perspective. In the realm of treatment for PTSD, it is unclear whether the solution for troubled vets is to "uncover and deal with" a repressed and troubling memory, or to try to banish an obsession from consciousness. In much of the rhetoric concerning the Vietnam War, the war is presented as meaningless and the veterans as pathetic victims, yet one can also detect a theme (particularly in rituals related to the Vietnam Veterans Memorial) that considers the Vietnam veteran as heroic for having fought for and defended his nation's freedom and honor.

Although the original point of the Vietnam veterans' movement in the 1970s was to "come to terms with the war as a whole," in effect the movement has become highly self-centered: hundreds of newspaper and magazine stories agonize about the 2,000–3,000 Americans missing in action from the war, but almost nothing is mentioned in American newspapers concerning the more than 300,000 Vietcong and North Vietnamese soldiers similarly unaccounted for. Compared with 58,000 American dead, something like 600,000 North Vietnamese and 300,000 ARVN (Army of the Republic of Vietnam, U.S.-allied) soldiers died in the conflict, but they are rarely, if ever, mentioned in media accounts of the tragedy of the war. The ARVN soldiers must be the truly "betrayed" or "lost" veterans of the Vietnam War: they fought for a country that was defeated and, in fact, no longer exists, and these men have nowhere to turn for assistance in dealing with disabilities or health problems resulting from their service.[22]

Although a great deal has been written about the deleterious effects of temporary exposure of American troops to Agent Orange, little to no discussion can be detected in the American media concerning the Vietnamese civilians who had to survive in "free-fire zones" during the war, and, after the war, actually live and farm day in and day out in areas that were heavily sprayed with Agent Orange or that are still saturated with mines and unexploded antipersonnel bombs. In the peculiar universe of post-Vietnam America, more attention is paid to the mental anguish of American soldiers who committed atrocities in Vietnam than to the Vietnamese civilians who were slaughtered and crippled in the cross-fire.[23]

Fifth, a particularly important factor contributing to the regnant image of the Vietnam veteran has been the "rights revolution" in the United States since the early 1960s, which has produced widespread change in attitudes regarding risk and responsibility. Across the board, American law has seen sweeping reform in which rights have been redefined in order to "empower" the individual, and to hold governmental entities to higher and higher standards of conduct in respecting or protecting these individual rights. In voting rights cases, the Supreme Court intervened to establish the principle of "one man, one vote" as traditional state autonomy in determining voting districts and voting rights has fallen by the wayside; in the realm of gender and family law, the U.S. Supreme Court established and expanded abortion rights, thereby sweeping away or severely limiting the traditional rights of states to prohibit or restrict such procedures, and displacing the concept of decision making within the family with an emphasis on individual gender rights as recognized and enforced by courts; in obscenity cases, the Supreme Court placed severe limitations on the traditional right of communities to restrict and seize from individuals literature, art, or other materials that the larger citizenry previously might have viewed as "obscene"; in criminal cases, the Supreme Court granted defendants new "Miranda rights," and, in search and seizure cases, the right to have evidence excluded from consideration by judge or jury if the state violated the individual's privacy rights by failing to obtain a proper search warrant.

And perhaps most important, in the area of tort law, courts and legislatures have expanded the rights of individuals to sue corporations and governmental entities for negligent behavior, on the theory that extending such rights would produce a barrage of lawsuits that would ultimately result in more socially responsible corporate or governmental behavior. The cost of settling such lawsuits would not only force governments and corporations to compensate individual victims but, because of the expense of such payouts, would ultimately encourage governments and corporations to change their behavior and practices in order to avoid repetition of such litigation in the future. The cost of such settlements could be spread across the board to other consumers of products or services through incremental increases in prices. Consequent to this wide-ranging revolution in American law there has been a wave of rising expectations, along with cultural fallout—what some social critics have described as an obsession with risk (the "fear of living"), "survival chic" (the celebration of the survival of various social ills—broken marriages and drug addiction seeming to be the leading afflictions), or, in perhaps its most extreme form, the codependency movement of the 1980s and 1990s, in which every American could view himself or herself as a victim who has suffered some kind of abuse or wrong, and who is "in recovery" but seemingly never fully recovered. Wendy Kaminer has characterized this celebration of triumph over addiction and abuse as the new log cabin story in American culture.[24]

The Vietnam veterans' movement can be seen as a manifestation of this growing trend of blaming available governmental entities or corporations for harm and incurred risk. The risk at issue here has been the risk associated with war, most notably exposure to Agent Orange, but through PTSD, exposure to all facets of life in the war zone that would tend to affect a person adversely. Although individual soldiers and veterans generally do not have the legal right to sue the federal government, this has seemed almost irrelevant in an environment over the past twenty years in which the American government has been lambasted for a series of perceived wrongs against the Vietnam veteran: the government should not have gotten into the war to begin with, it placed an undue burden in fighting the war on the poor and on minorities, it poisoned its own troops with Agent Orange, it committed genocide against the Vietnamese people, it failed to repatriate its troops in a way so that they could adjust to civilian life, it tried to sweep the problems of the Vietnam veterans under the rug, it refused to establish G.I. Bill educational benefits at adequate levels, it abandoned the MIAs, it resisted establishing vet centers to counsel disturbed Vietnam vets, and it wouldn't allow the army to win in Vietnam. These are among the charges that have been leveled against the U.S. government in an atmosphere of extreme anger and bitterness.[25]

In the same way that a woman assaulted in a parking garage will ignore the actual perpetrator (who, if apprehended, is usually penniless) and launch a substantial, often multimillion-dollar lawsuit against the parking garage or municipality involved for neglecting to provide adequate security, the Vietnam veterans' movement has focused its rage and indignation against the U.S. government for allowing the war to be fought or to be fought badly, rather than against the NVA or Vietcong soldiers who actually killed over 40,000 Americans during the Vietnam War. Consistent with the spirit of tort reform, the Vietnam veterans' movement has been highly reform-oriented: the message or implication has constantly been that if the U.S. government had only done this or that differently, the soldiers and veterans would not have been subjected to harm (or harm could have been minimized).

The salient and rarely asked question, however, is whether one can reasonably expect the government to wage such a "casualty-free," "perfect" war in the same way that one can expect a corporation to manufacture a toaster that will not spontaneously catch on fire in the kitchen and burn down the house. In the United States, where million-dollar verdicts are routinely returned by juries for such civil wrongs as sexual harassment or for having hot coffee spilled in one's lap, it seems inconceivable that the population would ever tolerate a situation—with resultant body bags, flag-draped caskets, and weeping relatives on television every evening—in which thousands of young men and women were killed or mutilated in a war, without the assurance of immediate victory to justify the losses and put an end to the carnage. One wonders whether the recriminations of Vietnam veterans against the United States government have led essentially to a situation in which the prosecution of any large-scale war has become an impossibility—even with an all-volunteer army. Taking these developments into account, it could be that the Vietnam veteran has not been singular in American history for having been treated badly by his government, but, rather, that the Vietnam War was fought at a time and in a cultural context when a protracted war in which thousands of young Americans were being killed or coming home with serious physical or mental wounds became—and will remain—intolerable and absurd. It may be that in a society which is unwilling to accept pain, suffering, and death, and in which great effort is expended to expose and correct a wide variety of injustices which impede the ability of individuals to achieve (or attempt to achieve) happiness, that death in battle has simply become unspeakably obscene. Perhaps this is a good thing; perhaps it has created serious handicaps for American foreign policy. At a minimum, one would hope that the phenomenon could be fully recognized and understood for what it is.[26]

Last of all, a particularly critical factor in the creation of the image of the "troubled and scorned Vietnam veteran" has been the movement for psychiatric reform during the 1970s that culminated in 1980 when the American Psychiatric Association recognized Post-Traumatic Stress Disorder as a distinct mental illness or "disorder." Accounts of the psychological problems of Vietnam veterans inevitably present statistical data to the effect that, for instance, up to 50 percent of Vietnam veterans have suffered from PTSD, or that 15 percent currently have "full-blown" PTSD, or that 60 percent of combat veterans have PTSD symptomatology—and one tends on such occasions not only to be alarmed and saddened, but to equate PTSD

with any other distinct disease such as measles or
led to believe by the certainty of statistics that PTSL
inite disease process, that this process is at work wi
of afflicted Vietnam veterans, and that doctors, psychi.
chologists, employing scientific principles and methods,
how the disorder is caused, how it is manifested, what its
be, and how to treat it. The nature of PTSD is much more cc
than this, however, and casts doubt on much that has bee.   ..ten
about how unique Vietnam veterans are for having suffered from
high levels of this disorder.

The fact is that psychologists and psychiatrists disagree strenu-
ously among themselves on whether PTSD is a free-standing or even
a valid psychiatric disorder. Studies have indicated that PTSD almost
always coexists with other psychiatric diagnoses such as depression,
anxiety disorders, or at times, character and personality disorders;
for instance, a survey of clinical reports demonstrates that where
PTSD is diagnosed, investigators have also noted alcohol abuse in 39
percent to 84 percent of those examined, depression in 36.5 percent
to 50 percent of the subjects, anxiety disorders in as many as 47 percent of those studied, and antisocial personality in up to 14 percent
of the sample involved. One study noted PTSD as a free-standing
psychiatric disorder in only 1.6 percent of the patients examined. This
phenomenon of multiple diagnoses, described in the psychiatric literature as "co-morbidity," raises the question of whether PTSD is a
distinct psychiatric disorder or rather a grab-bag of symptoms, which
simply lumps together patients suffering from other problems,
thereby creating the illusion of conceptual and clinical unity.[27]

What does unify PTSD as a psychiatric diagnosis is the requirement that the patient have experienced some "extraordinary" stress
"outside the range of usual human experience" that would be "markedly distressing to almost anyone." Critics have questioned why "extraordinary" stress should be differentiated from "ordinary" stress in
heavy doses (for instance, getting divorced, losing one's job, mis-
placing the car keys, experiencing a death in the family, and gaining
10 pounds—all within a short period of time), whether stress can be
objectively defined and measured (certainly subjective impressions
along with social context and the individual characteristics of the
patient are as, if not more, important), or why one psychiatric illness
would revolve, by definition, around one kind of cause, since most
psychiatric disorders are not etiologic-specific. Given all of the dis-

...es on definitions and methodology, different studies have produced wildly divergent figures on the exact incidence of PTSD in the Vietnam veteran population, varying from 3.5 percent to 25 percent to 50 percent—the point being that there can be little scientific certitude when the numbers are that far apart. One set of researchers concluded: "Although conceptual paradigms and treatment approaches have been developed for individuals manifesting PTSD, debates have continued over the past 30 years, culminating in an empirical vacuum that indicates little consensus with respect to conceptualization or treatment strategies."[28]

Even more disturbing is the fact that researchers—psychologists, psychiatrists, and physicians—cannot, even after hundreds of studies over the past several decades, explain exactly what "disease process" is at work within the body, brain, or mind to account for the way that impressions of traumatic experience convert into traumatic memory, and then continue to disturb or haunt the person affected —sometimes intermittently, sometimes for the first time years after the fact. Is it that psychic trauma literally causes physical changes in neural pathways within the brain, imbalances in neurotransmitters, physical changes in brain structures, or disordered functioning that makes it impossible for the mind to process information properly? Researchers are still uncertain.

The current controlling paradigm in psychiatry is the biological one, which generally repudiates the Freudian attention to internal mental thought (analysis of dreams and so on) and stresses instead physical structures and processes, such as the pituitary-adrenal-cortical axis, the possibility of cortical neuronal changes in the nervous system, thalamo-amygdala subcortical connections, and levels of epinephrine and norepinephrine. The emphasis is on using MRI and PET scans to localize brain function and to observe brain activity in those who have been diagnosed as suffering from clinical psychopathology. However, although researchers know that chronic stress in animals can lead to certain physical changes in brain structures or brain chemistry, such consistent changes have not been uniformly observed in human patients diagnosed as having PTSD. A great deal remains a mystery—even those psychologists who insist that PTSD is a valid diagnostic category are uncertain whether it causes other disorders, results from other disorders, is a transitional or a chronic state (or both), and why one observes seeming spontaneous remission or delayed onset years after the trauma was experienced. In defense of the diagnostic category, some psychiatrists have claimed that PTSD is similar as a medical condition to the somatic disease of syphilis, which is to say that it does have underlying conceptual unity, but simply manifests itself in a multitude of ways that tend to perplex and confound scientific investigators. Unfortunately, such conceptual unity for PTSD has yet to be proved or demonstrated, and the most that can be said is that PTSD is a "work in progress." Psychologists may yet conclude that PTSD is not a free-standing, unitary psychological syndrome, but, rather, that the concept should be radically redefined or even abandoned. The words of a psychiatrist written in 1907 concerning problems in categorizing mental pathology are still apt in describing the overall uncertainty of PTSD research:

> I still believe . . . that we physicians connected with insanity resemble gardeners rather than botanists, that the fact must be recognised that we classify for convenience rather than upon a scientific basis, because in point of fact no such basis, or finality of mode, has as yet been discovered. And perhaps little wonder, since many have to be treated as lunatics in whose brains and nervous systems no change whatever can be found.[29]

Another serious problem that undermines or taints clinical studies by psychologists on PTSD in Vietnam veterans is the overwhelming reliance in such studies on self-reporting. When researchers investigate the experience of Vietnam veterans to determine what percentage currently suffers from PTSD, what percentage has ever suffered from PTSD in the past, and what might have caused these mental problems, they invariably rely on self-reporting, that is, explanations and accounts from individual Vietnam veterans themselves concerning their experience in the war, the range and intensity of resultant symptoms, and the date of onset for these symptoms. Usually the only objective checking done by researchers is to review VA or military records to make sure that the subject was indeed in the military and in a combat zone; beyond that, nothing is done (and perhaps nothing can be done) to objectively check the veteran's self-report of his experiences to see if the person actually (as reported) committed atrocities, shot and killed enemy soldiers, saw a friend killed by a land mine, was depressed and anxious, and, if so, when these symptoms occurred.

The problem in relying on self-reporting is that accounts from veterans, particularly when the inquiry pertains to something that happened twenty years ago, are subject to "retrospective bias," including memory decay, augmentation, and misspecification—in essence, forgetting or the willful reconstruction of the past for self-serving purposes. In a highly charged atmosphere like that in the United States following the Vietnam War, in which the image of the Vietnam vet was manipulated by a variety of interests and in which the conventional wisdom was and remains that Vietnam veterans were treated in a disgraceful and shameful manner, it seems quite likely that many Vietnam veterans who participated in these psychological studies have exaggerated or embellished their experiences, or have overstated their readjustment or postwar mental problems. One clinical report from 1983 revealed cases of five supposed PTSD patients who had fabricated stories of having been in Vietnam or of having been POWs in Vietnam. In reality none had been POWs, four had not been stationed in Vietnam, and two had never even been in the military. These researchers concluded: "Because the war events are now distant and the condition's symptoms are mostly subjective, posttraumatic stress disorder can be easily simulated." And consistent with the emphasis in the 1980s and 1990s on psychological explanations for all human behavior, psychiatrists tend to view these dissemblers as suffering from yet another syndrome, "factitious PTSD."[30]

For some Vietnam veterans who have engaged in such exaggeration, the tendency might have been to displace personal problems or failures onto the war experience, which would serve to lend dignity to personal failure; for others, the motivation might have been more complex. Guenter Lewy in *America in Vietnam* noted that Vietnam veterans in the 1970s often claimed to have participated in atrocities when the evidence suggested that no such thing had occurred. Lewy concluded that some Vietnam vets achieved a feeling of importance and solidarity with the antiwar movement by calling attention to themselves in this way. Charles Moskos has suggested that the atrocity stories that came out of Vietnam were the functional equivalent of the heroic war stories that came out of World War II. Both gave the soldiers' participation in these wars a meaning that could resonate with certain elements of the public back home. The work of George Rosen raises the possibility that PTSD and other abnormal behavior was embraced by certain Vietnam veterans for a variety of reasons.[31]

Beyond all of these problems of measuring the exact incidence of PTSD, there is the question of what it really means to have PTSD. As critics have pointed out, one could be diagnosed as having PTSD and still be entirely functional—married, with children, owning a home, pursuing a successful career. One study of World War II–era POWs noted that 50 percent of the men had experienced symptoms of PTSD after their release, but the study concluded: "Nevertheless, after their liberation these individuals typically maintained successful careers and stable family lives. Many of them are now retired after many years of steady employment." PTSD is defined in such an amorphous way (a long list of symptoms, several of which the subject must have experienced at some time to qualify as having the disorder) that any veteran, especially a combat veteran, who had an occasional nightmare or squeamish feelings regarding his experiences in the military could well fit into the category. This raises a key point: isn't it normal to experience such feelings of dread, guilt, or sadness when one remembers scenes of violence and killing from one's years in the service? Is psychology attempting to pathologize memory by classifying it as a psychological syndrome? One recalls the case of the Ohio Civil War veteran William Henry Younts, who, in the middle of an exuberant homecoming, could not help remembering his fallen comrades, whose bodies lay in graves or unburied on battlefields in the South. Younts wrote: "I felt glad in entertaining [thoughts of mourning] on such occasions. I had no desire to separate myself permanently from them." If a person could experience and participate in extreme violence—killing others or watching friends die—and not feel discomfort in remembering the experience, it would seem that such a person could be classified as a sociopath. Hence it should not be surprising that studies routinely indicate that of all veterans, those who experienced combat have the highest incidence of PTSD.[32]

Given all of the problems—disagreements over how PTSD should be defined, disputes over whether PTSD is even a legitimate category of mental pathology, arguments over whether the incidence in Vietnam vets is 3.5 percent or 25 percent or 50 percent, the inability to describe an underlying disease process, the very real danger that the subjects of these studies have exaggerated their experience, the fact that PTSD may be less a mental illness than the normal manifestation of human emotion on remembering fallen comrades and scenes of chaotic violence—it is remarkable that the firm impression has been registered in the mind of the American public that PTSD is a meaningful concept, that Vietnam veterans experienced the syndrome in unprecedented numbers (of course, comparative data on earlier

American veterans have been largely absent), and that on this account Vietnam veterans are, or have been, in a continuing crisis. This impression of scientific certitude in the midst of substantial and potentially crippling problems is a tribute to the ability of psychologists and the psychiatric profession to acquire and wield power.

In considering the role that politics and professional self-interest have played in the emergence of the prevailing paradigm of the Vietnam veteran as a psychiatric victim, one should examine three factors: the circumstances surrounding the genesis of this diagnostic category in the 1970s, the relationship of psychiatry and psychology to the military in the twentieth century, and the historical role of diagnostic categories in expanding the influence of the psychiatric profession. First of all, PTSD was not accepted by the American Psychiatric Association as a legitimate psychiatric disorder until 1980, and the syndrome was not simply discovered at that time in some scientist's petri dish in a laboratory; rather, the entire concept of PTSD and its close association with the Vietnam veteran were very much the products of antiwar fervor in the early 1970s and the determined agitation of a number of antiwar psychiatrists and psychologists.

In the late 1960s and early 1970s Robert Jay Lifton brought together groups of antiwar Vietnam vets in "rap groups" to discuss their experiences and feelings. Taking an antiwar stance in which the Vietnam War was viewed as an "atrocity-producing situation," these rap groups created the impression that atrocities committed by American soldiers in Vietnam had been widespread, that the Vietnam War was singular in American history in this respect, and that, as a result, large numbers of Vietnam veterans were suffering from a unique form of psychopathology and were in need of special treatment. One neutral psychiatrist observed at that time: "[I]t seems to me that some mental health professionals have . . . overstepped their data to support their politics," and another suggested that these rap group sessions actually functioned to foster feelings of rage and helplessness in the participants. The probable overall effect of the determined efforts of Lifton, Chaim Shatan, Charles Figley, John Wilson, and others was to exaggerate the problems of Vietnam vets and to ignore the well-adjusted Vietnam veteran who was not paralyzed by guilt.[33]

Moreover, this most recent episode in the history of psychiatry and psychology demonstrates yet again the dynamic relationship that has emerged in the twentieth century between military psychiatry and the mental health professions. As we saw in Chapter 2, psychiatry and psychology have used war to expand their influence, and in turn have been changed by their discoveries and experiences in warfare. Up until the 1960s, the professions of psychology and psychiatry tended to serve the interests of the military, often to the detriment of the individual's welfare. With the Vietnam War, a new generation of antiwar psychiatrists and psychologists emerged, and the mental health professions have consequently reoriented themselves: the emphasis is no longer on preserving military manpower levels at the expense of the individual's welfare, but in serving the interests of the individual—often at the expense of the military's or the nation's ability to fight a war. The important point is that the approach of the mental health professions to war has rarely been entirely "neutral," but has usually been biased or shaded by a political agenda; in the case of Vietnam, an antiwar agenda predominated, and there has been a consequent tendency to exaggerate and overstate the psychological and readjustment problems of the American veterans of that war.[34]

In addition, psychiatry as a profession has long used diagnostic categories such as PTSD to advance its standing and influence. Historians such as Andrew Scull, Jan Goldstein, Ian Dowbiggin, David Rothman, and Barbara Sicherman have argued that "mental illness" is not a neutral term, but rather that innovations in psychiatric theory and practice are frequently driven by politics and culture rather than by scientific discoveries or principles. Accordingly, a variety of medical men, alienists, and psychiatrists ("moral entrepreneurs" in the words of Scull) used nineteenth-century diagnoses such as "monomania," "hysteria," "neuropathic degeneration," and "neurasthenia" to extend and consolidate their professional power. These diagnostic categories were usually shaped by the scientific orthodoxy of the day, resonated with prevailing cultural beliefs (such as late nineteenth-century ideas concerning the dependency and fragility of females in the case of "hysteria"), frequently mimicked changes in allopathic medicine, but, most important, were presented to the public as "scientific" and as based on knowledge and principles known only to and mastered only by members of the profession. While diagnoses such as "hysteria" or "neurasthenia" are regarded as meaningless today, what has endured has been the acquisition of power and influence by the psychiatric profession. This is not to say that many of the people diagnosed as having PTSD are not in distress; rather, the salient point is that the mental health professions have a track record of advancing diagnostic categories that lack clear underlying unity based on scientific evidence, but that, nonetheless, have the effect of responding to popular needs and aggrandizing the power and authority of mental health professionals.[35]

PTSD, born in an era of vehement antiwar sentiment, cast its net widely over many aspects of human behavior that had never before been considered a "mental illness." Dreams, flashbacks, and low-level feelings of depression, anxiety, and guilt, even when not disabling, were now considered to be a mental illness or "syndrome." Mental health reformers (advocates of both the recognition of PTSD and the establishment of vet centers) thus created the impression that Vietnam was unique because large numbers of veterans from that war suddenly seemed to be mentally ill. The truth of the matter was that expanding categories of disease were including more and more people who would have been considered "normal" in the past.[36]

If cultural, legal, and medical factors account for the way in which the problems of Vietnam veterans have been exaggerated and manipulated, what was the case for the Civil War veteran? Did no such excesses exist in the late nineteenth and early twentieth centuries? As indicated in Chapter 7, the Civil War veteran tended not to be viewed as a psychiatric victim for a number of reasons: psychological problems were frequently overshadowed or subsumed within the perimeter of more serious or more obvious physical conditions (and hence became "occult" psychiatric disorders); medical theory in the late nineteenth century tended to focus on somatic explanations for disease, and mistrusted the idea of psychogenic causation (such as terror or fear resulting from combat) for abnormal psychological behavior; the influence of Darwin and "neuropathic degeneration" resulted in theoretical views of mental illness and insanity which emphasized genetic and hereditary factors, rather than nurture or environmental determinants (such as experience on a battlefield); and Victorian values stressed the fragility of females but the resiliency of males, who were supposed to be able to endure combat and warfare.[37]

Indeed, the issue of gender is critical: men in the Civil War era who expressed fear and dread and wanted to escape from duty were generally regarded with contempt as unmanly and as despicable shirkers. One sees these attitudes reflected most clearly in exhortations in Southern newspapers after the Confederate defeat, which counseled application of the fortitude that Southern men had demonstrated in Civil War battles to the "battle of life":

Poverty and defeat are apt to bring despondency. *Never despond!* The young men of the South must bear with a manly fortitude the evils that have resulted from an unsuccessful revolution. They must be brave and cheerful, energetic and hopeful. They bore themselves during the unequal contest with a manliness and courage, which have excited the admiration of friends and foes. Now they must not despond. . . . No self reliant, virtuous young man was ever known to fail . . . let them on to the great battle of life. They must be cheerful in poverty, hopeful in adversity, patient under defeat, and firm and self-reliant in all circumstances.[38]

Another Southern newspaper account lamented the poverty facing Confederate veterans: "But the commiseration felt for these unfortunate individuals is modified by the fact that they are men—men with strong hands, high hearts and hardened nerves—men, consequently, who will know how to battle successfully with the difficulties of their lot." Despondency was characterized as "unmanly": "It is he only who meets what fate has in store for him, with manly fortitude, who is truly great." Union soldiers also regarded the tendency to complain as being "unmanly," as demonstrated by the account in one Northerner's diary, which recounted the continual complaining of a tent-mate and concluded: "He is more like a woman than a man . . . [he] puts me in mind of some old woman fretting around and sticking his lips out about a foot when he gets displeased which is pretty often." As in the South, advice columns in Northern newspapers counseled the necessity of manly virtue, fortitude, and endurance; one such piece noted how a disability could "unman" one's energy, but another counseled:

> The battle of life, in by far the greater number of cases, must necessarily be fought UP HILL; and to win it, without a struggle, is perhaps to win it without honor. If there were NO DIFFICULTIES, there would be no SUCCESS; if there were nothing to struggle for, there would be nothing to be achieved. Difficulties may intimidate the weak, but they act only as a stimulus to a man of pluck and resolution. . . . stand up manfully against misfortune.[39]

In addition, the Civil War era did not share post-Vietnam America's antiwar sentiments. Accounts of Civil War battles written both during and after the war could be unrelentingly realistic in their depiction of dead bodies strewn on battlefields, but did not demonstrate a conviction that war is absurd or obscene. Rather, in the Civil War era, the focus was on irony (a man is shot for spying, and it turns out he was just looking for his brother; a spy is hanged, and it turns out the person was a female) and sentimental portrayals of death and suffering. The overall message seemed to be that war was a complex, awful, mysterious, and sometimes grand experience, as indicated by the title of one tome: *Camp-Fire Chats of the Civil War; Being the Incident, Adventure and Wayside Exploit of the Bivouac and Battle Field, as related by Veteran Soldiers Themselves. Embracing the Tragedy, Romance, Comedy, Humor and Pathos in the Varied Experiences of Army Life.* Victorian sentiment was also important, as reflected in a deathbed scene recounted by Louisa May Alcott, which displays a style and outlook typical of literature and personal accounts from the Civil War era:

> I felt a tender sort of pride in my lost patient; for he looked a most heroic figure, lying there stately and still as the statue of some young knight asleep upon his tomb. The lovely expression which so often beautifies dead faces, soon replaced the marks of pain, and I longed for those who loved him best to see him when half an hour's acquaintance with Death had made them friends.

It is inconceivable that such a passage could have been written concerning the death of an American soldier in Vietnam.[40]

The most famous novel about the Civil War, Stephen Crane's *The Red Badge of Courage,* contains many striking descriptions of the experience and terror of the common soldier and his view of battle as violent and chaotic. For instance, Crane depicts war as the "red animal," the "blood-swollen god," as a "composite monster," a fierce and cruel god (with slaves toiling in its temple), a death struggle in a dark pit, a frightful debauch, or as a horrible machine: "The battle was like the grinding of an immense and terrible machine to him. Its complexities and powers, its grim processes, fascinated him. He must go close and see it produce corpses." Yet Crane's overall structure seems to be that of a "coming of age" tale, in which his protagonist ultimately experiences personal growth and acquires confidence and wisdom as a result of his experiences and trials. One would probably have to consult the works of Ambrose Bierce, who was something of an anomaly in his own time, to find anything remotely resembling the Vietnam era's negative and nihilistic view of war.[41]

Hence, Civil War veterans were generally not viewed as psychiatric victims, and war was not generally dismissed as a negative phenomenon in the late nineteenth century. Nonetheless, did political factions and the veterans themselves engage in exaggeration or demagoguery centering around the idea of the veteran as victim to promote various agendas in the post–Civil War era? Certainly, as is evident from the Republican Party's continual efforts from 1865 on to wave the "bloody shirt," the Union veterans' drive for a pension system that ultimately seemed to award a pension to any Union veteran alive, and the construction of an image of a suffering and sanctified Confederate veteran by the "Lost Cause" in the South. These efforts centering on the image of the Civil War veteran as suffering or sanctified, however, generally seemed to portray such men as heroic or praiseworthy, rather than as pathetic victims. The Lost Cause is of particular interest, because some historians have suggested that it celebrated and deified the Southern fighting man even in defeat, and thereby served to prevent the development of psychological and social problems.[42]

The Lost Cause emerged in the years directly after the Civil War as Southern women congregated to tend the graves of fallen Confederate soldiers. Eventually, efforts in the Lost Cause centered on bringing the bodies of Confederate soldiers back to the South for reinterment, building statues and monuments to the memory of the Confederate soldier and to Confederate generals such as Robert E. Lee and Thomas J. "Stonewall" Jackson, and on parades, conventions, and quasi-religious ceremonies to honor the Confederate veteran and the families and descendants of Confederate veterans.[43] These ceremonies began as early as 1866:

> Yesterday week [October 1866] there was a celebration here, for the Confederate dead within a radius of five miles from this place, gotten up by Miss Sallie Lynch. Some fifty names were collected. Some young lady bore a banner for each of the martyrs draped with black with the name, date, & place of death on one side & an appropriate motto on the other. First, early in the morning, those interested visited the old Stone Church yard, & wreathed the graves there, then we all met at the Baptist church, & formed into a procession.... She was followed by a pack of children strewing flowers in the way of the returned soldiers.... We marched through the three grave yards; the Baptist, Methodist, & Episcopal, wreathing each soldiers grave as we came to it, with wreaths we wore over our shoulders. Then we mounted Mrs. Van Wyck's porch, & ranged ourselves on either side, (all dressed in half mourning) while Gens. Hampton, & Early delivered addresses. Father introduced them, & Mr. Mullaly began with prayer.[44]

The activities of organizations such as the United Daughters of the Confederacy eventually included not only tending graveyards but encouraging schools to teach the "correct" version of the war, buying gray uniforms for those veterans who couldn't afford such purchases, helping to support soldiers' homes, and the general advancement of the cause of "Americanism." By the end of the century, Lost Cause ceremonies had become fantastic conventions that brought young and old from throughout the region to various Southern cities to participate in these rituals, which usually centered on honoring the Christ-like Confederate soldier and veteran:

> It is my one ardent wish to-day, speaking as the unworthy representative of the generation that has grown up since the great war, to give expression to the deathless gratitude that every true-hearted man, woman and child in the South feels to the Confederate soldier. . . . The Confederate soldier served with might and valor. Pluck, courage, and undying devotion to his cause, from the very beginning marked his incessant footsteps. Nothing did he consider as detentive to the achievements and fulfillment of his illustrious Chief's wishes. To him obstacles were obligatory and necessary instruments of war and should be overcome regardless of hazards. . . . Pure patriotism, resolution and devotion to that noble cause bore his genuine interest. The rare and insatiable ardor of these wearers of the gray bespeaks of them in inexpressible fervor.[45]

This extreme idolization of the Confederate veteran certainly paid attention to the tribulations of those who had fought in the Civil War, but what historians of the South have tended to overlook is the extent to which all of this adulation might also have functioned as a kind of straightjacket: if one had deserted during the war, or expressed bitterness about losses incurred, or was in fact a psychiatric victim suffering from anxiety, depression, and alienation from one's society and social surroundings, it seems unlikely that such a Confederate veteran would have fit into and have been easily honored by the Lost Cause. The Lost Cause had such an inflated and grandiose view of the virtue of the Confederate veteran and the meaning of the Civil War for the South as a region that it seemingly had no ability to understand and absorb victims of that war who, as a result of their experience, might have detested and repudiated war. The unanswered question is whether a forced consensus between the veteran and the civilian regarding the meaning of war will invariably exclude (or force into silence) many veterans who do not accept or participate in rosy reconstructions of the past.

Thomas C. Leonard has argued that the Civil War generation had a simplistic view of the war, as heroic, as a test of character, and as basically sanitized; he finds to some extent that the veterans were to blame for this, because they knew the reality, but nonetheless encouraged or by their silence allowed a new generation to think that the battlefield was the crucible that tested character. Whether one would ultimately think it appropriate to assess blame, and whether the veterans or various social and political groups would be thought to be most culpable, it does seem clear that the Civil War generation—even those who had experienced defeat—generally tended to derive positive meanings and lessons from the Civil War.[46]

To argue that the Vietnam veterans' movement has become solipsistic and mired in contradiction, and to assert that the problems of Vietnam veterans were overstated and exaggerated during the 1970s and 1980s is not the same as denying that serious problems existed for some returning Vietnam vets, and that all Vietnam veterans had to go through a sometimes awkward period of readjustment to civilian life. In these respects, Vietnam veterans have much in common with veterans throughout history, both in the United States and elsewhere. A number of points concerning the commonalities among all veterans should be noted. It would appear that all soldiers subjected to combat suffer some incidence of psychiatric breakdown (categorized as PTSD, shell shock, psychoneurosis, or outright insanity), both of an acute variety on the battlefield and in delayed form after the end of hostilities; although a lack of the use of consistent diagnostic categories over time makes direct comparisons impossible, exposure in concentrated doses to indirect artillery fire of the kind experienced particularly in World War I would seem to be the most devastating type of trauma. Second, the first five years after repatriation tend to be the most difficult time for the veteran, who usually finds it hard to "settle down," either because of disturbing wartime experiences or simply because he has "seen the world" and is dissatisfied with narrow horizons; slightly elevated (compared with civilian peers) mortality rates, caused by suicide or violent death, for this "five-year window" were noted in both World War II and Korean War veteran populations.[47]

Third, by definition, by the very nature of the experience, the veteran comes home somewhat bitter and angry. As evidence from the Civil War indicates, soldiers in the field in most wars seem to become alienated from the civilian population at home, and sometimes even begin to view the enemy in sympathetic terms as a fellow sufferer. Upon returning home after the war is concluded, the veteran will frequently shun parades, feeling that they are irrelevant to his readjustment; he can feel that the civilians who are making such a fuss do not have the slightest idea what war is actually about, and in a sense, he may feel that they are attempting to idealize something he has grown to hate. The veteran often feels that civilians have profited from the war at his expense and now fear and distrust him—after the Civil War, some soldiers felt that they had to hide their service record, for fear that employers would actively discriminate against them for the supposedly bad moral habits of ex-soldiers.[48]

Davis R. B. Ross maintains that the World War II veteran (to which the Vietnam veteran is most frequently compared) was the exception, not the rule, in the history of American veterans. With the World War II veteran, for the first time, broad readjustment benefits were made available to all returning veterans, not just those who could prove a disability. Prior to World War II, the usual pattern for American veterans was a period of neglect after the conclusion of a war until a veterans' organization such as the Society of the Cincinnati (Revolutionary War), the Grand Army of the Republic (Civil War), or the American Legion (World War I) emerged to advocate benefits and pensions for ex-soldiers. Veterans often felt spurned and frustrated, and from these feelings emerged a separate veteran identity and often hostility or bitterness toward the civilian population.[49]

To the extent that some Vietnam veterans experienced readjustment problems and felt rejection and bitterness toward civilian society, they were typical of veterans throughout American history, and far from unique. What *is* unusual about the Vietnam veteran is the development of this actual or imagined hostility and bitterness in veterans even in the face of World War II–type readjustment benefits. To attribute uniqueness to the "loss" of the Vietnam war would overlook the bitter frustration of Korea as well as the Confederate experience and the disillusionment following World War I.[50]

The fact that the Vietnam veteran could readjust to civilian life so well in objective terms and yet either feel or be portrayed as feeling bitter and betrayed indicates, first, that the image of the veteran is potent and will always be subject to use by different factions in society to achieve their agenda; this has been true from Reconstruction to Weimar Germany. Second, expectations have increased to the point where all veterans have a claim for governmental assistance of some kind, not only the traditional categories of disability or readjustment benefits, but new benefits and sympathy relating to issues such as

PTSD or Agent Orange. The presumption has perhaps been established in the mind of the veteran and the public that the veteran, whether in combat or not (approximately 85 percent of Vietnam veterans were not attached to combat arms), is inevitably adversely affected by war and must now be compensated.[51]

Last of all, the idea of military service now appears to be in jeopardy. The President's Commission on Veterans' Pensions, chaired by Omar N. Bradley, suggested in 1956 that military service be viewed essentially as just that, service to the country due from its citizens; Franklin D. Roosevelt, in addressing the American Legion in 1933, also maintained that able-bodied veterans, simply because they had worn the uniform, should not be viewed as a privileged class entitled to benefits to which civilians were not entitled. The Vietnam veteran has perhaps marked the end of, or certainly has raised an additional challenge to, the concept of military service in the United States.[52]

CONCLUSION

"A Spectacle Grand and Awful to Contemplate"

As Robert Jay Lifton asserted in the early 1970s, the Vietnam veteran has come to serve in the United States as a psychological crucible for the entire country's doubts and misgivings about the Vietnam War, and about war in general. Consequently, America's continuing agony, grief, and obsession with Vietnam is largely explained by the perception that Vietnam veterans incurred harm that was catastrophic, tragic, persistent, and completely out of proportion to any good that the war accomplished or might have accomplished. Post-Vietnam thinking concerning the American veteran has revolved around two specific propositions: first, that the Vietnam veteran was singular in American history for having suffered in substantial numbers from a new and insidious psychological syndrome, Post-Traumatic Stress Disorder, which was caused by the unique and surreal circumstances of the war in Vietnam, and frequently manifested itself for the first time years after the war had ended. In essence, the Vietnam veteran has acquired a primary identity as a psychiatric victim, or in its more dramatic manifestations, a "stressed-out baby-killer" or a "walking time bomb," whose government put him in an impossible situation, poisoned him with Agent Orange, and then abandoned him. Second, influenced by the Vietnam generation's antiwar convictions, observers have tended to reinterpret the experience of veterans of earlier American wars to discover that they, too, suffered from widespread psychological problems. In essence, it is possible that the American veteran in general will also acquire, retrospectively, a primary identity as a victim, one who is generally (with a few exceptions) badly used by his government. Needless to say, these two propositions are somewhat contradictory, but do cohere around a post-Vietnam anti-war outlook, which tends to see war as tragic and absurd.

As this book has attempted to demonstrate, however, a careful consideration of the experience of Civil War veterans calls into question these post-Vietnam images and beliefs in several respects: first of all, although the absence of modern diagnostic categories and the presence of a different set of cultural ideas in the nineteenth century concerning disease and suffering make it difficult to quantify the exact incidence of post-traumatic stress disorders in the Civil War veteran population, such problems—frequently severe in magnitude—existed and do not appear to have been isolated. The continued explicit or implicit claims of some that Vietnam veterans' post-traumatic stress made them unique in American history should thus be regarded with some skepticism. More important, a careful investigation of the hardships endured by Civil War veterans raises questions concerning the great emphasis that has recently been placed on PTSD. In the wake of Vietnam, psychologists have researched in great depth the phenomena of flashbacks, nightmares, survivor guilt, cognitive dysfunction, startle reactions, and the like. With all of the emphasis on the psychological repercussions of warfare, PTSD has subtly been transformed into a kind of "definitive misery index," that is to say, the greater the incidence of PTSD in a veteran population, the more one tends to conclude that the relevant group of veterans has suffered. This research has logically been extended backward in time, and studies increasingly focus on Korean War or World War II veterans, with the objective of establishing what percentage of these veterans experienced PTSD symptoms and when.

What all of this emphasis on PTSD and the psychological repercussions of war tends to overlook is the fact that soldiers and veterans before the twentieth century encountered death and suffering from physical disease on a scale that has been practically unknown to veterans after 1900, who have benefited from the late nineteenth-century revolution in medicine. In the Civil War, two men died of disease for every man who died in battle; for earlier wars such as the Mexican War or the Napoleonic Wars, as many as ten men died of disease for every battle death. Those who came home alive had to struggle with the consequences of exposure to disease during wartime. Thousands and thousands of Civil War veterans were wracked with pain for the rest of their lives from the consequences of malaria, typhoid, rheumatism, camp fevers and epidemic diseases, unrelenting gastrointestinal pain and discomfort, and agonizing pain from poorly performed operations on gunshot wounds, from which bone fragments would work their way out ten and twenty years after the war—all of this in addition to the psychological complications of warfare, such as flashbacks, nightmares, survivor guilt, and the like.[1]

By contrast, from World War I on, the percentage of soldiers dying from disease has been, by historical standards, surprisingly low; for instance, while the death rate from disease for Union troops in the Civil War was in the neighborhood of 100 such deaths per thousand men, this rate had fallen to 0.6 deaths per thousand men by World War II, and continues to decline. Even given the Agent Orange controversy, what marks Vietnam veterans in contrast to Civil War veterans is their relatively good physical health upon return from the war zone. One should also keep in mind that while over 90 percent of soldiers in the Civil War era were in the "combat arms" branches of the military, only about 30 percent of American soldiers in World War II experienced combat, and this ratio dropped to 15 percent in Vietnam. To the extent that historical analysis and comparison between veteran populations is desirable and possible, it should by no means be limited to the narrowly psychological repercussions of warfare.[2]

Regarding the second proposition that all American veterans can be understood primarily as victims, the evidence of psychological torment and physical suffering in Civil War veterans should not necessarily lead to the conclusion that this was the sum total of their existence. In understanding the experience of the veteran, Civil War veterans included, one must avoid the tendency to see these men (and women) as victims, or to philosophize about the salutary effects of homecoming parades in producing reconciliation, healing, and closure. In understanding the phenomenon of the veteran, one must deal with a number of difficult problems, centering around paradox, illogical consequences, structural problems in communication, and the danger of willful manipulation. Simply stated, the veteran is a complicated phenomenon: studies have indicated again and again that the soldier fights mainly for personal survival and out of loyalty to immediate comrades, yet as a veteran he becomes a symbol of civic virtue and sacrifice for the nation; the soldier/veteran protects the nation, yet can threaten (through military coup d'état) its existence, or, at a minimum, redefine its values. Although the veteran may on one level crave recognition and understanding, he frequently has an ambivalent attitude toward civilians, and many veterans either do not wish to discuss what they went through or seem to firmly believe that no civilian is capable of understanding combat. Suspicion and resentment can make frank and open discussion and complete reconciliation between veteran and civilian difficult if not impossible, even under the best of circumstances.[3]

One sees this complex and paradoxical nature of war at work in the experience of Civil War soldiers and veterans: young men were often anxious to prove themselves and feared that hostilities would end before they had a chance to participate in the glory, but these same young men could react with fear and horror to their first actual experience with battle. Compared with the boredom and death from disease typical of camp life, morale usually improved at the start of a campaign; however, extended exposure to fire and combat during such campaigns could lead to psychological breakdown and desertion. During breaks from battle, Union and Confederate troops would chat amiably and exchange coffee for tobacco, but when fighting resumed, snipers would shoot and kill without warning any enemy soldier who exposed his head above the parapet. Men were anxious to hear from home, but at the same time, the longer they were in the service, the more they seemed to develop a distrust of and contempt for most civilians (aside from immediate family), whom they viewed as shirkers or professional patriots. And most important, many if not most soldiers in the Civil War era had an intense love-hate relationship with the service. On the one hand, they frequently deplored the hardships and danger; on the other hand, perhaps because of their ability to withstand these tribulations, they considered the experience to be riveting, the most meaningful time of their lives, something that could never—for better or worse—be forgotten or trivialized. As one Civil War soldier wrote after a battle: "On every living face was seen the impress of an excitement which has no equal here on earth."[4]

Does this mean, then, that war is at best meaningless or at worst absurd, productive of a kind of addiction to the exhilaration associated with encountering violence in a life-and-death situation? No, at least not to the men and women who go through the experience. An underappreciated fact concerning Vietnam veterans is the extent to which these people, including those who suffered terribly, believe that they have been strengthened by the experience. Senator John McCain, who was held as a POW in Vietnam for five years and brutally tortured by his captors, commented: "I don't recommend the treatment, but I know that I'm a better person for having experienced it." To be subjected to a severe ordeal of this nature and magnitude, and to come through the trial alive, can give a person a sense of inner strength, self-reliance, and compassion for others. Senator McCain's feelings are reflected again and again in studies of other Vietnam POWs, who have testified that they benefited from their experience in that they were now more patient and optimistic, had more insight into themselves, got along better with others, and were better able to differentiate the important from the trivial. Overall, these former POWs have testified that they experienced personal growth and felt that they had acquired wisdom as a result of their wartime experience. Remarkably, these attitudes were positively related to the harshness of the treatment these men endured in captivity.[5]

In addition to these paradoxes and seeming anomalies, one must also understand that image manipulation has been part and parcel of the phenomenon of the veteran throughout American history. Civil War historians have long understood that for the first twenty years after the end of the war, the veterans were a largely dormant force; then, in the mid-1880s, there was renewed interest in the war and a flurry of activity centering on the Civil War veteran: monuments and statues dedicated to those who fought in the war were built at an unprecedented pace, veterans' organizations—the Grand Army of the Republic (GAR) in the North and the United Confederate Veterans (UCV) in the South—experienced sudden and marked growth in membership, the federal government expanded its generous pension system and Union veterans flocked to register their claims, and, in the South, activities in the Lost Cause, which tended to sanctify and idealize the Confederate veteran, reached an apex. Historians have interpreted this sudden activity in different ways: Gaines Foster has argued that the Lost Cause emerged in the late 1880s in response to economic and political transformation in the New South; it was middle class, forward looking, and a tool for coping with economic change and development. In contrast, Charles Reagan Wilson has argued that the Lost Cause was a means of interpreting and coping with defeat; it became a civil religion in the South, emphasized religious virtue and the Confederate veteran's sacrifices, and sought to convert the old Southern nationalism of the Confederacy into a vehicle that produced cultural unity and revealed a redemptive destiny for the South as a region.[6]

On the manipulation of the image of the Union veteran, historians such as Mary Dearing have long noted that Republican politicians in the years after the war waved the "bloody shirt" to demonize their Democratic opponents for having supposedly been either traitorous or less than fully loyal to the Union during the Civil War—the goal was to identify the Republican party as the more patriotic alternative, and to attract the veteran vote at election time. More recently, David Montgomery has argued that the celebration of the Civil War hero in the 1880s and the Republicans' campaign commitment of 1888 to the veterans and their families was an attempt to solidify a conservative political base in the midst of social change and upheaval, a conscious response to the class conflict of the 1880s and the flip side of blaming foreigners for strikes and other violence. Regardless of which of these arguments one finds to be most persuasive (perhaps all have merit), the salient point is that various political or social factions in the United States, including the veterans themselves, have repeatedly used the image of the suffering, heroic, or sanctified veteran to advance a particular agenda. This is not to say that there has been no underlying objective reality of suffering or heroism; it is simply to point out that the very real problems of veterans, which are difficult to quantify, understand, and discuss in the first place, are frequently if not routinely manipulated and exaggerated for a variety of purposes.[7]

The ability to understand the complexities of the veteran and to sort out emotional excess from proof of objective harm is not strictly a theoretical or academic exercise, but becomes particularly important in the formation of public policy in veterans' affairs. As critics of tort reform have noted regarding litigation on issues such as Agent Orange, one must be aware that highly emotional appeals can conflict with scientific judgment or what one would ordinarily think of as objective reality. The key is to refine the court system so that victims can be reasonably compensated, but in a manner so that the entire structure does not come crashing down due to excess. In the realm of veterans' affairs, the challenge is to bridge the gap between the public's traditional apathy and willingness to abandon the veteran and the veteran's peculiar internal world of anger and resentment, in which he imagines a universe in which he can trust only his buddies next to him in the foxhole, and in which all other "outsiders," including the enemy, his superior officers, his own government, and civilians in general seem to be intent on killing him, getting him killed, or would greet news of his death with utter indifference. One would hope to avoid extremes, where either the rightful claims of veterans are ignored, or where veterans are granted special programs and privileges completely out of proportion to actual detriment incurred in the service.[8]

Last of all, one cannot avoid the irony that different paradigms have been applied when discussing Vietnam and Civil War veterans. For the Vietnam veteran, the emphasis has been on tragic loss and waste of life, and the centerpiece of public discussion and memory has been the Vietnam Veterans Memorial in Washington, D.C., a black marble wall on which are inscribed the names of all of the servicemen and women who died in Vietnam.[9] Over 57,000 names were initially etched into the wall, and over the years additional names are added to the wall when it has been discovered that some deceased soldier was overlooked. On occasion, an argument is made to add the names of veterans who died ten and twenty years after the war, on the grounds that they were delayed casualties. In all of this, the theme emerges of war as unnecessary and as a tragic mistake. In this climate of brooding anger, resentment, and sorrow, it would be practically impossible to argue that the Vietnam War was necessary for whatever reason: that the alternative of withdrawing and allowing the collapse of the Diem regime in 1962 would have been catastrophic to the political viability of the Democratic party, that a stand against communism was necessary in the 1960s, that the Vietnam War only became an absurdity after detente in the early 1970s. The continued anger and indignation over the fate of America's Vietnam soldiers and veterans has not only tended to shut off debate over the necessity of the war, but has also produced a climate of opinion in the United States in which, even with a professional army, excessive (defined as anything over several hundred) American casualties in any future war will probably not be tolerated.[10]

By contrast, historical scholarship over the past forty years—even during and after the Vietnam War—has tended to celebrate the American Civil War as a crusade against slavery and as a necessary struggle to establish equal rights for all Americans.[11] In light of the fact that the nineteenth century ended with southern states in the process of writing and implementing Jim Crow segregation laws, however, can one so convincingly argue that the Civil War was all about antislavery and equal rights, or, if indeed the establishment of civil rights became an objective of the war, could not one argue that over 300,000 Union soldiers died in vain? In addition, although there are hundreds of Civil War monuments throughout the land, one wonders what a Vietnam Veterans Memorial–style black marble wall in Washington, D.C., with the names of all 600,000 men who died in the Civil War would look like. Taking into account the suffering of Union veterans such as Newell Gleason, Raney Johns, Allen Wiley, James B. Farr, and Joshua Jordan, should one be so quick to declare the Civil War as entirely justified? At the minimum, one would hope that the radical discontinuity between the way Civil War and Vietnam War casualties have been viewed would be addressed: perhaps we should be neither so keen to justify the Civil War as necessary and glorious, nor so quick to dismiss the Vietnam War as unnecessary and tragic. A more complete and nuanced understanding of the American veteran would seem central to such a reassessment.

APPENDIX

The Indiana Sample

Central to much of the analysis in this book is the "Indiana Sample," a group of 291 Civil War veterans who served with Indiana units and who experienced psychological problems in the years during or after the end of that war. The state of Indiana offered a unique opportunity for the study of such veterans in that insane asylum records maintained at the Indiana State Archives are completely open for review without restriction, if the relevant records were created more than seventy-five years ago; in most other states, such records are either severely restricted, reviewable only with a court order, or nonexistent (having been discarded long ago). This Indiana Sample was obtained by reviewing Central State Hospital (an insane asylum) admissions ledgers at the Indiana State Archives for the years from 1861 to 1919, and listing the names of all men of an age (thirteen to forty-five years old in 1861) to have served in the Civil War. This completed list contained 6,925 names, and the next step was to determine which of these men had fought in the Civil War. Insane asylum records almost never identified a man as a veteran, or, if there was some indication that the man had served in the Civil War, the ledgers almost never specified the unit with which that particular patient had served. The following information is typical of that available in Central State Hospital asylum records:

Admission No.: 6926
Name of Patient: Andrew J. Hopper
Clinical Record:
County: Scott
Addr. of next friend: Melvina Hubbard
Scottsburgh, Indiana

Age: 46
Civil Condition: married
Occupation: laborer
Education: unknown
Religion: unknown
Nativity: Indiana
Diagnosis (confirm): Melancholia with delirium
No. of Attacks: 1
Admitted: Jan. 15, 1886
Duration before: 2 weeks
Discharged: Feb. 24, 1886
Result: cured
Clothed by: county
Removed by: sheriff
Remarks: Imagines he is to be shot or poisoned—made several attempts
    at suicide neck was cut on admission

It was therefore necessary to consult enlistment ("muster roll records") records for Civil War military units to determine which of the original list of 6,925 men had actually served with Indiana units in the Civil War; these records are maintained at the Indiana State Archives. The following information is typical of that available in muster roll records:

Name: John Miles
Pvt. Co.: H 29
Regt Time: 3 years
Enrolled: Sept. 12, 1861
at: Laporte, Indiana
by: Capt. Shuler
Mustered in: Sept. 12, 1861
at: Laporte, Indiana
by: Col. Miller
Age: 23
Eyes: blue
Hair: light
Height: 5–4
Complexion: light
Nativity: Billington, England
Occupation: farmer
Discharged/Mustered out at: transferred to Co. I

I alphabetized the asylum list of names and then compared it against these Indiana muster roll cards to determine which men from the asylum list had served with Indiana Civil War units; only the names of those indicating a strong probability of a match were retained when this procedure had been completed [$N = 1,125$; these were rated as "certain match" ($N = 404$), "probable match" ($N = 300$), and "in need of verification" (N = 421)]. The great difficulty in matching insane asylum patient records against military service records is that in the nineteenth century, no social security numbers existed, and other distinguishing data such as date of birth were rarely recorded in either insane asylum records or military service records. Hence, important "markers" used to match records were usually middle initial, place of birth, age, occupation (if it was other than "farmer") and hometown (particularly if this was an out-of-the-way village). This method of matching records is, by its nature, an inexact and almost intuitive process.

To demonstrate how extraordinarily difficult it could be to match asylum and military records, a few examples will suffice: (a) The original asylum list of men who were of an age to have fought in the Civil War included three "John Martins" along with a "John C. Martin" and a "John S. Martin." There were thirty-seven muster roll cards for "John Martin," twenty of which had no data aside from age, regiment, and muster-in data, and sometimes no data at all other than regiment; because the majority of men enlisting in Civil War regiments were young (eighteen, nineteen, or twenty years of age), age alone was often next to useless in declaring a match. There were an additional fifty-six cards for "John Martin" with varying middle initials, and varying amounts of data; (b) the asylum list included one "Charles Miller," but there were forty-two muster roll cards for a variety of "Charles Millers," making it impossible to declare a certain match; (c) the asylum list contained a "William Adams Miller," a "William F. Miller" and "William H. Miller," two commitments for a "William J. Miller," and five commitments from 1866 to 1884 for a "William Miller," who appeared to be one and the same person. In the muster roll records, there were sixty cards for "William Miller," which listed no middle initial, and varying amounts of data; and (d) the asylum list included a "John C. Smith," a "John H. S. Smith," a "John M. Smith," a "John Smith, Jr.," and ten other commitments for "John Smith," two of which seemed to relate to one person, and the other eight possibly to eight other John Smiths. In the muster roll records, there were 123 cards for "John Smith," 43 of which listed no middle initial and presented basically only regimental information and age. If one were trying to match a "John Martin," "Charles Miller," "William Miller," or "John Smith" against muster roll cards, it would thus be practically impossible to narrow the search down to one record; again and again, one is left juggling a dozen (or more) different muster roll records, any one of which could match the patient record. This frustration extended well beyond the "John Smith" example, and was, in fact, a constant problem.

To further complicate matters, there were numerous instances in which a patient had served with two different Civil War units, and the information between these two different muster roll cards did not match, or the information between patient and military records was an imperfect match. The hometown might be listed differently, or a man might be described as 5'4" in one record and 5'7" in another record—and this when the two records actually were describing one and the same person. This is all to say that nineteenth-century records are fragmentary, inexact, and frequently contain errors.

Muster roll cards exist for all Indiana Civil War regiments—infantry, cavalry, and artillery—but I excluded the cards for the "minute men" infantry regiments, from the 102nd Indiana Regiment to the 114th Indiana Regiment, because these units were raised to respond to Confederate General John Morgan's invasion of Indiana in 1863, and were only in existence for periods of time varying from three to ten days to respond to this crisis, and then were sent back home. As a result, muster roll cards for these units generally contained only the name, age, and mustering-in site, and no other critical or defining data.

After the review of muster roll records was complete, I then matched the list of 1,125 names against federal pension records at the National Archives in Washington, D.C., to gather additional information and to continue the process of determining which asylum and military records actually matched and which names should be discarded as false matches. Federal pension records are a magnificent but sometimes overwhelming source of information. For instance, the mere index to these files is contained on hundreds and hundreds of rolls of microfilm, and it took three weeks of solid work to go through the index to see which names on the muster roll list (of 1,125 names) might correspond to a federal pension file. The federal pension file index basically lists name and regiment, so, again, one is faced with the prospect of frequently reviewing two, three, or four federal pension files which might match a name on the list. Usually the only way to determine a match among asylum, muster roll, and pension files was to meticulously review the entire pension file, searching for some mention of an asylum commitment or other such data that would demonstrate a clear match among all the record groups involved. This was a painstaking, time-consuming, and often mind-numbing process, which in the final analysis required three months at the National Archives. One benefit of working with federal pension records, however, is the depth of information available, and the fact that these files identify all units with which a man served in the Civil War: if service with one unit led me to the pension file, I would then have discovered all other units with which the Indiana veteran had served. Federal pension records could thereby also help clear up confusion when it appeared that one asylum patient had served with two different Civil War regiments.

Once the federal pension review was complete, cases that had proved not to be a match were discarded, along with all cases (even if a clear match) deemed to be "neurological," that is to say the result of neurological rather than psychogenic or purely psychological conditions. In the late nineteenth century, the medical subspecialty of neurology was making rapid advances but was still in its infancy, so asylum doctors were not very skilled at sorting out cases of mental pathology clearly resulting from conditions such as brain tumors or degenerative neurological diseases. Owing to inadequate clinical observation and description, it is difficult to make retrospective diagnoses, but an attempt was made in this study to exclude four classes of neurological cases pertaining to organic brain disorder and physical trauma: (a) cases of senile dementia (usually pertaining to veterans committed to the asylum in the early twentieth century); (b) cases of epilepsy; (c) cases of men who at some point in their lives had contracted syphilis, thus putting them at risk of developing tertiary neurosyphilis, with its attendant severe mental deterioration; and (d) all cases indicating severe physical trauma to the head (from falls, accidents, fights, gunshot or shell wounds), which often accounted for subsequent erratic behavior. In addition, any case involving unexplained paralysis, seizures, locomotor ataxia, or gross abnormalities in sensation or movement were excluded from the sample. In some cases, it was extremely difficult to tell whether abnormal psychological behavior was caused by purely psychological factors or some underlying neurological condition—in such cases, I reviewed all the available data (usually quite limited) and made the best judgment possible under the circumstances, freely consulting my Merck Manual and asking questions of physician friends.

With the Indiana Sample pared to approximately 350, I culled additional information from two last sources: inquest papers at the Indiana State Archives and military service records at the National Archives. When men were committed to the insane asylum in the nineteenth century, the process began with a medical and judicial inquest in the man's home county, and the resulting affidavits, medical opinions, and judicial orders were preserved in inquest records—which were fairly meager until the 1880s, when they developed into extensive detailed descriptions of behavior. These records were preserved over the years in the basement of the Central State Hospital in Indianapolis, and have recently been added to the collection of the Indiana State Archives. When I was working on this project, the records had not yet been alphabetized and catalogued, and in return for my alphabetizing the entire run of inquest records from the 1850s through the 1960s, Bob Horton of the Indiana State Archives was kind enough to personally copy all records pertaining to the men in the Indiana Sample.

Last of all, I reviewed military service records at the National Archives in Washington, D.C., for each unit served by each soldier in the Indiana Sample: these records appear in the form of one packet for each man in a regiment, and present the date of enlistment and discharge from a specific unit, the amount of bounty collected, deductions for lost or purchased equipment, roll call records noting sicknesses or absences, notations of gunshot wounds or serious injury, and, on occasion, records of courts-martial, requests for leave, prisoner of war records, and notations of desertion or reenlistment. To collect additional information on dates of marriage and death, I reviewed genealogical information in the WPA-era bound volumes (running from about 1880 to the 1930s) maintained at the Indiana State Library in Indianapolis. For pension records not available at the National Archives, I put in requests to the Veterans Administration (which still controls a small number of Civil War vintage pension files) and reviewed what files were available at the VA's Hartford, Connecticut, branch office.

Once the final number of men in the Indiana Sample had been established at 291, I developed a set of codes and entered information on the sample into a QuattroPro 5.0 spreadsheet, utilizing 230 fields for data pertaining to a wide variety of information, from name, county, occupation, marital status, and children, to military service, details on commitments to the insane asylum, descriptions of behavior, other confinements, information on pension claims, and the like. I used database functions to complete basic queries and graphing, but also translated the data into a SAS data set for more sophisticated and comprehensive statistical analysis (including t-tests, ANOVA, correlations, regression analysis, and glm procedures) with the SAS statistical package at Yale University's Statistics Laboratory. After completing SAS data analysis, I entered the output back into QuattroPro.

In addition to the Indiana Sample, a second sample of psychologically disturbed Civil War soldiers ($N = 84$) from all states of the Union was derived from the records of the Government Hospital for the Insane ("St. Elizabeth's") in Washington, D.C. I began this process by reviewing the adjutant general's ledger listing approvals for commitment of all of the soldiers admitted at that asylum from 1861 to 1866 ($N = 1,380$). I then searched for pension records for a sample of 25 percent ($N = 345$) of this entire list, but, surprisingly, particularly in light of the fact that these men were committed to an insane asylum during the war and would presumably have had abundant evidence to support a postwar medical claim for disability based on insanity, I located pension records for only about 30 percent of the men. Most of the pension claims for these men seemed to have been filed between 1865 and 1875 when the pension system was still in its infancy, and when sophisticated systems of adjudication and bureaucratic notation had not yet evolved—hence the data in these files tended to be sparse, and the exact resolution of several cases and the fate of the men involved remained a mystery. Despite these limitations, data derived from these cases have been used, primarily in Chapter 6.

APPENDIX

Casualty Statistics: The Company Sample and Regimental Data

In order to determine if members of the Indiana Sample were exposed to abnormally high levels of combat during the Civil War, it was necessary to establish a baseline against which to compare the experience of these men. Average or typical casualty statistics for Indiana troops in the Civil War can be derived in two ways: first of all, regimental casualty statistics ("Regimental Data") for the 174 Indiana regiments (this figure includes all major infantry, cavalry, and artillery units) that served in the Civil War are available on a mere three pages in the eight-volume Terrell's Adjutant General's Report. From this source, one can derive overall death rates (from battle and disease) for officers and enlisted men as well as desertion and reenlistment data for all regiments; however, the Regimental Data do not specify whether men died as a result of battle or of disease, it includes no statistics on numbers of men disabled by their military service, and its casualty data do not make a distinction between volunteers and recruits. In addition, no information is presented for the "minute men" units (the 102nd Indiana Regiment through the 114th Indiana Regiments) raised in 1863 to respond to the invasion of Indiana by the Confederate raider, General John Morgan.

In sum, casualty indices can be developed from the Regimental Data for the overall death rate for officers, the overall death rate for enlisted men and noncoms, and the total death rate for the entire regiment. These three numbers in turn can be divided by the actual number of months the unit was in service to derive death rates per month; of course, in considering the monthly casualty rates, one must keep in mind that while death by disease might have been a fact of life for a Civil War regiment, and hence somewhat regular, most units were not constantly in the thick of battle. If a unit was badly chopped up in a particular fight, it might be held back from exposure to heavy fighting until it had been rested or replenished.

Second, another set of casualty indices can be derived by examining company-level data (a company contained a hundred men, and there were basically ten to twelve companies per regiment depending on the branch of the service), which occupies several complete volumes of the eight-volume Adjutant General's Report from Indiana. This data devotes one line to each enlisted man in the company, indicating date of enlistment and outcome (killed in battle, discharged with a disability, deserted, reenlisted, mustered out at war's end, and so on). For our analytical purposes, company data were collected and analyzed on every sixth company ($N = 243$) for all Indiana Regiments from the first three-month units to the last hundred-day outfits; this sample has been referred to throughout as the "Company Sample."

Unlike the Regimental Data, the Company Sample contains no data on officer casualties, but it does offer additional information in three respects: (a) it provides data on the number of men killed in battle or discharged from the military for wounds received in battle; (b) it provides data on the number of men discharged from each company for disabilities (denoted as "discharged, disability" in the early years of the war, and evolving into a simple "discharged" in the last two years of the war); and (c) it distinguishes between volunteers and recruits (those men brought in later to shore up regiments which had sustained substantial casualties early in the war). Where the categories between the Regimental Data and the Company Sample address the same populations, one can see that the data is highly similar: for instance, the overall death rate from Regimental Data for enlisted men and non-coms in Indiana units was 12.8 percent, whereas the overall death rate from the Company Sample (which excludes officers) was 12.9 percent.

One problem with collecting information at the company level pertains to incomplete reporting. For most companies, complete data were available, but for some companies, the final accounting would note "no information provided," and, for others, information was spotty and obviously incomplete, and one has to consult volume 8 of Terrell on supplemental reports to find out what happened to the men in the unit. In some instances, the supplemental data volume actually did account for most or all of the men, but, in other instances, information was available on less than half of the men in the unit. Overall, about 4 percent of men serving in Indiana regiments during the Civil War were unaccounted for in the final report; this does not mean that they were missing in action

—the problem was simply one of accurate record keeping. Because of incomplete reporting, data on fifteen companies (six from the Company Sample, and nine for men from the Indiana Sample) was excluded from the Company Sample ($N = 243$) and companies in which men of the Indiana Sample served ($N = 292$).

If one had the time and resources, probably the most definitive casualty data could be derived by reviewing the individual service record packets on each man in each company of a regiment; these records are maintained at the National Archives. The advantage in using National Archives service records is that they tend to contain the most detailed information on men, including all instances of a soldier being taken POW (even if only for short periods), accounts of gunshot wounds and illnesses, records of absences and detached duty, and, on occasion, transcripts of courts-martial or other information such as requests for home leave. Unfortunately, it would take a small army of researchers, with years at their disposal, to accumulate enough data on a broad enough sample of companies to present data representative of all Indiana regiments.

In Chapter 8 the casualty indices for Regimental Data, the Company Sample, and the Indiana Sample are examined. As indicated by the discussion in that chapter, interesting comparisons and trends emerge, although the differences do not always reach the level of statistical significance.

Nineteenth-Century
Indiana Insane Asylums and
Involuntary Commitment Procedures

Before statehood was granted to Indiana in 1816, there were no insane asylums in the district. Territorial law provided that whenever a county court "received satisfactory information" that a person had become insane, it was to convene a jury of twelve, to include at least one physician, which would then determine whether the person was truly insane. In such an eventuality, three guardians were to be appointed to manage the person's property, and to use said property for the support of their ward. If the insane person had no property, then he was to be treated and supported like any other pauper.[1]

How were paupers supported? After statehood, poor law provided that overseers in each township would be responsible for the support of the poor; this presumably meant that the overseer could take whatever means deemed reasonable to support such people in the local district. However, if the poor person became "a permanent charge," or, for that matter, at the discretion of the local board of justices, paupers could be removed to local "asylums," essentially workhouses or almshouses, where they could be required to work and had to "submit to such discipline, as shall be proper and reasonable." Through the 1840s, the only "asylums" mentioned in Indiana statutes were these local poorhouses.[2]

In 1844 the Indiana State Legislature first approved funding for the "Indiana Hospital for the Insane," to be constructed in Indianapolis, and the first patients were accepted in 1848. The asylum held 196 patients in 1855, which was expanded to about 300 during the Civil War. From the 1850s, space was a problem, and asylum records from 1855 indicated a backlog of 600 applications. Most patients designated as "chronic" were either refused admission or discharged fairly quickly. Indiana created a board of state charities in 1889, and regional insane asylums (designated Eastern, Southern, and Northern) were constructed around 1890 in Richmond, Evansville, and Logansport. Even with these expanded facilities, one notes a report from Eastern Hospital in 1896 that mentioned overcrowding,[3] and asserted that many insane were still held in local poor houses or in local homes. Institutionalization would appear to have been *demand*-driven, and not a policy imposed from above.[4]

With the state insane asylum in Indianapolis "open for business" in 1848, a new state law provided the exact procedure by which patients would be declared insane and sent to the hospital. Unlike earlier territorial and state law, the new procedures provided that after "some respectable citizen" had filed appropriate papers alleging insanity, an associate judge of the county, with the assistance of "some respectable physician," would visit the allegedly insane person, examine the person, and make a declaration as to the person's sanity. Following a declaration of insanity, the attending physician was required to provide certain information to asylum officials preceding admission to the state insane asylum; the information provided (as to age of patient, history of case, duration of condition, exciting cause of insanity, whether the person had attempted violence on himself or others, etc.) was retained as a set of "inquest papers." These papers have been preserved over the years, and are presently available for review at the Indiana State Archives in Indianapolis.

After preparation of the inquest papers, the county clerk was to contact the asylum superintendent to request admission; in the interim, the patient was to be housed in an appropriate place, such as a local jail. Available beds at the asylum were limited, and each county in Indiana was granted a quota based on population. The asylum commissioners had the final say on patients admitted and in some instances would temporarily bypass the quota system in an emergency, but generally seemed to follow the county allotment system. "Idiots" were not eligible for admission, and recent cases of insanity were favored over "chronic" (that is, duration of more than one year) cases. For insane people not having a legal settlement in a county of Indiana, admission to the asylum was possible, but only after the prospective patient or his guardians had filed the requisite documents indicating ability to pay.[5]

This 1848 statute providing for declaration of insanity and admission to the state insane asylum continued to coexist with the traditional alternative of allowing local juries to declare a person to be of unsound mind and, if the person had adequate resources, appoint guardians to provide for the support of the person in the local community. Also as had always been the case, if the person were a pauper, he could be housed at the poorhouse, and, if dangerous, presumably held in the local jail—"the court shall make such order for his safekeeping as may be necessary."[6]

The fact that the insane asylum never had adequate room for all people declared insane according to the law of 1848 is demonstrated by a law of 1855, which provided judicial process for the apprehension and disposition of people who were insane and dangerous and at large in the community: "[A]n emergency is hereby declared to exist for the immediate taking effect of this act . . ." This procedure allowed for commitment of the insane in the state hospital, but seemed to recognize that adequate space might not be available; hence, an alternative disposition for such cases was provided: "If the jury find that such person is insane and dangerous to community if suffered to remain at large, such justice shall appoint some resident of the county to take charge of and confine such person, for which he shall receive a reasonable compensation by the board of commissioners." Presumably, this statute resulted in many insane people, who were deemed dangerous, being confined in local jails—either until space became available at the state asylum, or indefinitely if the asylum was unwilling to accept such a case.[7]

Public policy favored admission of only "curable" cases to the state insane asylum, and there was always a long waiting list for both recent and long-standing cases of insanity. As early as 1866, the state legislature recognized that additional space was needed for these "chronic" or "incurable" cases, but additional insane asylums were not built and opened in Indiana until 1890.[8] As with the law dealing with immediate disposition of insane people deemed to be dangerous and at large in the community, this statute also declared: "It is hereby declared that an emergency exists for the immediate taking effect of this act, therefor it shall be in force from and after its passage."

The 1848 and 1852 laws regulating commitment of the insane to the state insane asylum were updated in 1881 by a law that provided, basically, for the same procedures, but required much more comprehensive statements from the person seeking the commitment and from the medical personnel involved. From this point forward, the inquest papers generated by these commitments tended to be detailed descriptions of behavior, a boon to historians investigating issues pertaining to nineteenth-century insanity.[9]

Confederate Veterans

Information on Confederate veterans is presented throughout this book, but such data can be abundant in some chapters and almost absent in others: for instance, in Chapters 3 and 4 on the wartime experience of Civil War soldiers, equal amounts of information are presented on Confederate men as on Union soldiers. In Chapters 6 and 7 concerning official military policy on the treatment of psychiatric casualties and postwar medical theory, however, mention of the Confederate veteran is almost absent. Some readers might be inclined to demand that the Confederate veteran either be granted more attention—equal space—or be dropped altogether. The first alternative is impossible, and the second unwise.

Information on the psychological problems of *any* Civil War veteran is generally hard to come by, but it is definitely easier to accumulate data on Northern veterans for a number of reasons: (a) Union Army records on service, casualties, and medical treatment survived the war, whereas many Confederate records were lost or destroyed, particularly when much of the Confederate capitol at Richmond, Virginia, was burned at the end of the war; (b) the United States Government made a concerted effort to collect and publish information on the Civil War through a number of postwar publications, from the seventy-volume (in 128 parts) *Official Record of the War* to the multivolume (depending on its exact incarnation) *Medical and Surgical History* of the Civil War; (c) a generous system of disability and old-age pensions were made available to Union veterans (see Chapter 7), and over time this system generated an enormous amount of data on individual veterans—information that is now maintained in thousands of case files available for review without restriction at the National Archives; (d) in Northern states, postwar record keeping of all kinds seemed to be more systematic and exhaustive than was the case in the South; for instance, when it comes to insane asylum records, more detailed and extensive information is available in the Indiana State Archives than in the archives of Southern states (such as South Carolina or Georgia) that make this information available for review.

For Confederate veterans, sources such as the periodical *The Confederate Veteran* would seem to offer promise, because this publication served for several decades as a forum in which Southern veterans reminisced, discussed, and debated the meaning of their war experience. There is only one entry in the index regarding "insanity," however, and this pertains to the story of a Confederate soldier who was visiting home behind Union lines and feigned insanity so as not to be apprehended or detained by Union soldiers who came across him.[1] I also scanned at random actual issues of the *Confederate Veteran* for stories of shell-shocked or troubled veterans, and found nothing of substance. The *Southern Historical Society Papers* would also seem to be a useful source, but, upon close review, yielded nothing on the topic—other than long and repetitive speeches regarding the Lost Cause and its heroes. Indeed, the emphasis in Southern materials (and this evidence is abundant in all Southern state archives) was on the Lost Cause—the celebration of the noble, Christ-like, but ultimately doomed Confederate veteran, who fought in vain for high-minded goals. Some historians have suggested that the Lost Cause functioned as a kind of therapeutic device to help reintegrate the Confederate veteran into Southern society, but such assertions—while intriguing—remain speculative and unproved.

Several Southern states make their mental health records available for review, and I visited state archives in South Carolina, Georgia, Florida, and Tennessee to see what I could find. Unfortunately, the records in Florida did not begin until the 1890s, well after the war ended, and the records in Tennessee were limited (as far as I could discern) to patient lists from various asylums, with no patient records or descriptions of commitments or behaviors and symptoms. The records in South Carolina, from antebellum times, were quite systematic and continued into the war years, but were at no time very deep. Then, in Reconstruction years, the system seemed to break down altogether, and for the critical decades after the war, little information was available. The best records I came across in the South were at the Georgia State Archives, in which I discovered information (usually about a paragraph per case) not only on Confederate soldiers, but psychologically troubled veterans as well.

I have included this information pertaining to insane asylum records from South Carolina and Georgia in Chapter 5.

It is important to note, however, that insane asylum records from the nineteenth century, even under the best of circumstances, can serve mainly as a finding aid, which is to say that they identify men who had psychological problems, but do not in and of themselves provide much detail on specific cases. The key is to connect these records with information from other, more substantial, sources. For Union veterans, federal pension records serve this function (see above), but Confederate veterans were not eligible for federal pensions. In the late nineteenth century, Southern states developed their own state pension systems (or systems of soldiers' homes) for Confederate veterans (for instance, such a system was established in South Carolina in 1887) in which these veterans became eligible for assistance in the state where they resided; however, Confederate pensions (or eligibility to reside in the state soldiers' home) were always meager when compared with those of the generous federal system. The Southern system was essentially one of old-age (rather than disability) pensions, and if a veteran was able to work, had independent means, or had relatives who could support him, he normally was not eligible for state assistance.[2]

For instance, the application for admission to the South Carolina soldiers' home (initially called "the Confederate Infirmary"), which opened in 1909, stated that each county of the state would be entitled to place two veterans at the home, and that these men would have to be destitute and infirm because of disability and age before they would be eligible for admission. Almost all applications seemed to be for men in their seventies, who were totally disabled on account of their age and were without family members who could support them. The following application from P. A. McDavid, Pension Commissioner for Greenville County, for Mayberry Alberson, a man sixty-three years of age, is atypical in seeking admission for such a "youthful" veteran, but in other respects is quite typical in tone and emphasis:

> I know it is a little irregular—but it is a case of dire necessity that I send poor old Maberry Alberson to the home at once. No home—no place to stay and he is in bad shape generally. Hope you will try to make the poor old man comfortable. This fills our number for Greenville County—but still there are others who want to go. He will hand you all the papers.

A detailed and systematic study of the psychologically disturbed Confederate veteran is thus hampered by a lack of surviving military records and by the lack of a pension system centering on the recognition and compensation of service-related mental problems for veterans who were not aged. This does not mean, however, that the sparse information that is available on Confederate veterans should be omitted altogether. From it we learn that the Confederate soldier's experience was often similar to that of his Union counterpart, and that occasionally his travails offer an interesting comparison to the Union perspective.

Notes

Introduction

1. See affidavits of Alexander Pollock, July 1, 1889, William A. Payton, February 2, 1889, Buford Peak, May 14, 1889, and Philip B. O'Riley, June 21, 1886, federal pension file of Owen Flaherty [C 125 Ill. Inf.], National Archives, Washington, D.C. The locations of archives cited in the notes are given in the Acknowledgments.

2. See affidavits of James G. Peyton, February 1, 1889, George Winning, February 4, 1889, federal pension file of Owen Flaherty [C 125 Ill. Inf.], National Archives.

3. Affidavit of John McVey, February 5, 1889, federal pension file of Owen Flaherty [C 125 Ill. Inf.], National Archives.

4. Affidavit of Peter O'Toole, February 6, 1889 [regarding Resaca], Thomas A. Mathews, February 5, 1889 [Flaherty sleeping alone], Matthew Gray, April 4, 1889 [regarding Flaherty's threat to kill John McVey], federal pension file of Owen Flaherty [C 125 Ill. Inf.], National Archives.

5. Affidavit of Matthew Gray, April 4, 1889, federal pension file of Owen Flaherty [C 125 Ill. Inf.], National Archives.

6. See affidavits of Thomas Maloy, June 21, 1886 [noticing something wrong with Flaherty's mind after the war], Jacob Bennet, June 21, 1886 [Flaherty's employer], Charles Flaherty (guardian), June 21, 1886 [episode of wandering off in the night], Mary Flaherty, June 22, 1886 [wife's testimony], Daniel Crowe, June 21, 1886 [policeman's testimony regarding violence], Nicholas Dailey, June 22, 1886 [supt. of poor farm; regarding Flaherty's anger at mention of the army], Philip B. O'Riley, June 21, 1886 [regarding laughing about condition], federal pension file of Owen Flaherty [C 125 Ill. Inf.], National Archives.

7. See medical board report, n.d., the claim advanced by Flaherty's guardian, August 18, 1884, and the decision of the Pension Bureau, June 10, 1889, federal pension file of Owen Flaherty [C 125 Ill. Inf.], National Archives. For the

insane asylum commitment of Owen Flaherty, see commitment no. 3431, August 30, 1876, Indiana Hospital for the Insane (later known as Central State Hospital), Indiana State Archives, Indianapolis.

8. W. H. H. Terrell, *Report of the Adjutant General of the State of Indiana,* 8 vols., vol. II, *1861–1865* (Indianapolis: W.R. Holloway, State Printer, 1865), pp. 637–639.

9. For Green's commitment record, see commitment no. 3798, Indiana Hospital for the Insane, Indiana State Archives. See also medical board report, October 13, 1891, federal pension file of James P. Green [A 69 Ind. Inf.], National Archives.

10. For emphasis on the experience of the common soldier in the Civil War, see Bell Irvin Wiley, *The Life of Johnny Reb: The Common Soldier of the Confederacy* (Baton Rouge: Louisiana State University Press, 1943); idem, *The Life of Billy Yank: The Common Soldier of the Union* (Baton Rouge: Louisiana State University Press, 1952); Pete Maslowski, "A Study of Morale in Civil War Soldiers," *Military Affairs,* 24 (1970): 122–126; Michael Barton, *Goodmen: The Character of Civil War Soldiers* (University Park: Pennsylvania State University Press, 1981); Marvin R. Cain, "A 'Face of Battle' Needed: An Assessment of the Motives and Men in Civil War Historiography," *Civil War History,* 28 (1982): 5–27; H. David Williams, " 'On the Fringes of Hell': Billy Yank and Johnny Reb at the Siege of Kennesaw Mountain," *Georgia Historical Quarterly,* 70 (4) (Winter 1986): 703–716; Conrad C. Crane, "Mad Elephants, Slow Deer, and Baseball on the Brain: The Writings and Character of Civil War Soldiers," *Mid-America,* 68 (3) (October 1986): 121–140; Gerald F. Linderman, *Embattled Courage: The Experience of Combat in the American Civil War* (New York: Free Press, 1987); William L. Burton, *Melting Pot Soldiers: The Union's Ethnic Regiments* (Ames: Iowa State University Press, 1988); Earl Hess, *Liberty, Virtue, and Progress; Northerners and Their War for the Union* (New York: New York University Press, 1988); Reid Mitchell, *Civil War Soldiers: Their Expectations and Their Experiences* (New York: Viking, 1988); James I. Robertson, Jr., *Soldiers Blue and Gray* (Columbia: University of South Carolina Press, 1988); Joseph Allan Frank and George A. Reaves, *"Seeing the Elephant": Raw Recruits at the Battle of Shiloh* (Westport, Conn.: Greenwood, 1989); Maris A. Vinovskis, "Have Social Historians Lost the Civil War? Some Preliminary Demographic Speculations," *Journal of American History,* 76 (1) (June 1989): 34–58; idem, ed., *Toward a Social History of the American Civil War: Exploratory Essays* (Cambridge: Cambridge University Press, 1990); Daniel E. Sutherland, "Getting the 'Real War' into the Books," *Virginia Magazine of History and Biography,* 98 (2) (April 1990): 193–220; Gerald F. Linderman, "The Burden of Civil War Combat," *Northwest Ohio Quarterly,* 62 (1–2) (Winter-Spring 1990): 3–10; Larry J. Daniel, *Soldiering in the Army in Tennessee: A Portrait of Life in a Confederate Army* (Chapel Hill: University of North Carolina Press, 1991); Joseph Allan Frank, "Profile of a Citizen Army: Shiloh's Soldiers," *Armed Forces and Society,* (18) (1) (Fall 1991): 97–110; Larry M. Logue, "Union Veterans and Their Government: The Effects of Public Policies on Private Lives," *Journal of Interdisciplinary History,* 22 (3) (Winter 1992): 411–434; Reid Mitchell, *The Vacant Chair: The Northern Soldier Leaves Home* (New York: Oxford University

Press, 1993); and Larry M. Logue, *To Appomattox and Beyond: The Civil War Soldier in War and Peace* (Chicago: Dee, 1996).

Historians focusing on the African-American experience in the Civil War have also recently centered their attention on the common man. See Ira Berlin, Barbara J. Fields, Thavolia Glymph, Joseph P. Reidy, and Leslie S. Rowland, eds., *Freedom: A Documentary History of Emancipation, 1861–1867, Selected from the Holdings of the National Archives of the United States,* vol. I, *The Destruction of Slavery* (Cambridge: Cambridge University Press, 1985); Ira Berlin, Joseph P. Reidy, and Leslie S. Rowland, eds., *Freedom: A Documentary History of Emancipation, 1861–1867, Selected from the Holdings of the National Archives of the United States,* series II, *The Black Military Experience* (Cambridge: Cambridge University Press, 1982); and Joseph T. Glatthaar, *Forged in Battle: The Civil War Alliance of Black Soldiers and White Officers* (New York: Free Press, 1990).

I have characterized the recent emphasis on the Civil War as a crusade to abolish slavery and institute civil rights for the freedman (and all Americans) as the "total war/antislavery synthesis." See Eric T. Dean, Jr., "Rethinking the Civil War: Beyond 'Revolutions,' 'Reconstructions,' and the 'New Social History,' " *Southern Historian,* 15 (Spring 1994): 28–50. One should keep in mind, however, that Civil War scholarship has not always taken such a sanguine view of things; in the wake of the carnage of World War I, James G. Randall and Avery Craven reinterpreted the Civil War as unnecessary, and as having involved a tragic loss of life—hence their appellation the "needless war." Randall and Craven viewed the politicians and leaders who led the sections into bloodletting as the "Blundering Generation," and much of the scholarship inspired by this outlook focused on political leaders, such as the "fire-eaters" in the South or the abolitionists in the North, concluding that these men had been irresponsible and that their agitation had resulted in an unnecessary war. However, this "Blundering Generation" school of thought did not result in any significant studies of the common soldier in the Civil War.

For early attempts to examine the psychological repercussions of the Civil War, see Eric T. Dean, Jr., " 'We Will All Be Lost and Destroyed': Post-Traumatic Stress Disorder and the Civil War," *Civil War History,* 37 (2) (June 1991): 138–153; idem, " 'A Scene of Surpassing Terror and Awful Grandeur': The Paradoxes of Military Service in the American Civil War," *Michigan Historical Review,* 21 (2) (Fall 1995): 37–61; John E. Talbott, "Combat Trauma in the American Civil War," *History Today,* 46 (3) (March 1996): 41–47; and idem, "Soldiers, Psychiatrists, and Combat Trauma," *Journal of Interdisciplinary History,* 27 (3) (Winter 1997): 437–454.

11. In general, see Eric T. Dean, Jr., "The Myth of the Troubled and Scorned Vietnam Veteran," *Journal of American Studies,* 26 (1) (April 1992): 59–74.

1. "Unwelcome Heroes"

1. The media programs or articles analyzed in this chapter are as follows: (a) all articles on Vietnam veterans appearing in the *Reader's Guide to Periodical Lit-*

erature from 1963 through 1993; (b) all articles from the *New York Times* relating to Vietnam veterans from 1963 to August of 1988 (156 + articles); (c) selected articles on Vietnam veterans appearing in the *Washington Post,* the *Chicago Tribune,* and the *Los Angeles Times* from 1965 to 1988; (d) all articles concerning Vietnam veterans and Post-Traumatic Stress Disorder from major American newspapers (including the newspapers listed above) on NEXIS from October of 1987 through April of 1995; (e) all programs on Vietnam veterans in the Vanderbilt Television News Abstracts from the beginning of this series (which covers the television news on ABC, CBS, and NBC) in August 1968 through November 1993. In addition, I viewed approximately 75 television news programs at the Vanderbilt Television News Archives in Nashville, Tennessee, to check the accuracy of the abstracts (which I found to be quite accurate).

2. See "When Johnnie Comes Marching Home," *America,* March 24, 1973, p. 255; "Heroes without Honor Face the Battle at Home," *Time,* April 23, 1979, p. 31; NBC, February 7, 1979; Matthew J. Friedman, "Post-Vietnam Syndrome: Recognition and Management," *Psychosomatics,* 22 (11) (November 1981): 942.

3. For assertions that veterans of prior American wars received enthusiastic parades which washed away psychological problems, and that Vietnam veterans were unique in receiving no such parades, see "The Vets: Heroes as Orphans," *Newsweek,* March 5, 1973, p. 22; "Second-Class Heroes," *Nation,* July 9, 1977, p. 36; and James Reston, Jr., *Sherman's March and Vietnam* (New York: Macmillan, 1984), p. 193. Regarding the role of the Lost Cause, see Gaines M. Foster, "Coming to Terms with Defeat: Post-Vietnam America and the Post-Civil War South," *Virginia Quarterly Review,* 66 (1) (1990): 17–35.

4. "The War and the Arts: There Has Been a Cultural Turnaround on the Subject of Vietnam," *New York Times Magazine,* March 31, 1985, pp. 51, 54.

5. "Veterans Find Jobs Faster," *New York Times,* May 3, 1968, p. 35:7; "Ford Fund May Help Police to Recruit Minority Members," *New York Times,* February 22, 1968, p. 28:5 [Ford Foundation efforts to assist veterans]; letter from W. J. Driver, Administrator, Veterans Administration, *New York Times,* April 21, 1968, section VI, p. 12 [regarding VA establishing 20 one-stop vet centers intended to give advice to vets]; "Preference for Veterans," *New York Times,* March 13, 1968, p. 18:4 [Post Office jobs]; "The Re-Entry Problem of the Vietvets," *New York Times,* May 7, 1967, VI, p. 23 [concern over underutilization of the G.I. Bill]; "Veterans' Lobby Outdoes Itself," *New York Times,* April 23, 1968, p. 46:1 [regarding danger of creating a mercenary class].

6. "A Marine Comes Home from Vietnam," *Look,* March 8, 1966, pp. 30–32+, and *New York Times,* May 7, 1967, section VI, p. 118 [kindness from strangers]; "Joy in Seattle; Troops Withdrawn from Viet Nam," *Time,* July 18, 1969, p. 15 A [first parade for Vietnam vets]; "Invisible Veterans," *Nation,* June 3, 1968, pp. 723–726 [comparing Vietnam with Korean veterans]. Daniel C. Hallin, in *The "Uncensored War": The Media and Vietnam* (New York: Oxford University Press, 1986), p. 130, contrasts the "visceral grimness and a sense of psychological damage done by the war" which appears in veterans' memoirs of the 1970s with television coverage in the 1960s which rarely reflected this view.

7. For views of the Vietnam War as unique, see "Never Before a War Like This," *Look*, December 13, 1966, pp. 27–35, and "What It's Like for the Fighting Man," *Readers Digest*, November 1966, pp. 68–73; for articles expressing the opinion that the Vietnam veteran was accordingly experiencing unique problems, see "The Re-Entry Problem of the Vietvets," *New York Times*, May 7, 1967, section VI, p. 23, and Murray Polner, "Vietnam War Stories," *Trans-Action*, 6 (November 1968): 8–16+.

8. For a discussion of the problems of demobilization in American wars through World War I, see Willard Waller, *The Veteran Comes Back* (New York: Dryden Press, 1944). Regarding public shock over atrocities, see Phillip Knightley, *The First Casualty* (New York: Harcourt, Brace, and Jovanovich, 1975), p. 393. Following extensive coverage of atrocities, a "Heart of Darkness" theme became quite popular in Vietnam literature; see Peter C. Rollins, "The Vietnam War: Perceptions through Literature, Film, and Television," *American Quarterly*, 36 (3) (1984): 419–432. Regarding use of disillusionment of the Vietnam veteran to drive a reform agenda, see "Society and the Vietnam Veteran," *Catholic World*, January 1971, p. 188.

9. "Returning Heroes Get the Cold Shoulder," *Business Week*, July 31, 1971, pp. 46–48. Regarding disproportionate unemployment rates for Vietnam veterans, see "Home from the War," *New Republic*, January 30, 1971, p. 11; and "Why Vietnam Veterans Feel Like Forgotten Men," *U.S. News and World Report*, March 29, 1971, pp. 42–44. For television programs, see NBC, November 6, 1970 [noting 80,000 jobless blacks in Chicago]; CBS, November 16, 1970 [noting that 6.5 percent of Vietnam veterans were unemployed in the summer of 1970, compared with 5 percent of the general labor force].

10. "Jobless Problem for Ex-GI's Eases," *New York Times*, January 15, 1973, p. 61:4 [citing comparable unemployment rates for vets and nonvets in 1971]; "Second-class Heroes: Vietnam Veterans," *Nation*, July 9, 1977, pp. 35–36 [presents inflated veteran unemployment rates]. For allegations of continuing employment problems and blatant bias against Vietnam veterans, see "The War That Has No Ending," *Discover*, June 1985, pp. 44–47+, "The War Came Home," *Time*, April 6, 1981, p. 17, and "Lifting the Vietnam Stigma: Mary Stout on the Veterans' Self-Image," *U.S. News and World Report*, November 16, 1987, p. 10. For television reports on unemployed Vietnam veterans, see NBC, January 27, 1977 [noting a high percentage of Vietnam veterans on the unemployment rolls]; CBS, January 11, 1984 [a supposedly representative veteran stated that he couldn't hold a job or stay married]; and ABC, September 29, 1987 [that the problems of Vietnam vets included unemployment].

11. Regarding the heroin epidemic, see "Veterans Still Fight Vietnam Drug Habits; Heroin Use, Stressed by U.S., Is Only Part of the Problem Plaguing Ex-G.I.'s," *New York Times*, June 2, 1974, section 1:4, p. 46. Regarding the fact that drug use was not regarded as the *product* of military service, see CBS, October 6, 1969 [reporting on Operation Intercept, focusing on the Mexican border], and CBS, January 14, 1969 [that Pentagon figures showed that 90 percent of soldiers aged 18–24 court-martialed had smoked marijuana before entering the service]. For reports on use of drugs by the American soldiers

responsible for the atrocities at Mylai, see ABC and NBC, March 24, 1970. See also NBC, April 19, 1971 [drug problem in military as an "epidemic"]; NBC, January 25, 1971 [drug problem as "out of hand"]; CBS, March 2, 1972 [Vietnam veterans thought to be bringing drugs back into the U.S.]; NBC, March 2, 1972 [David Brinkley view]; *Legacies of Vietnam: Comparative Adjustment of Veterans and Their Peers,* a study prepared for the Veterans' Administration submitted to the Committee on Veterans' Affairs, U.S. House of Representatives, Washington, D.C., 1981, p. 371 [noting similar drug use by Vietnam veterans and nonveterans]; Special Action Office for Drug Abuse Prevention, *The Vietnam Drug User Returns* (Washington, D.C.: U.S. Government Printing Office, 1973), p. viii [that only 2 percent of returning Vietnam vets were using narcotics]; and Lee N. Robins, John E. Helzer, and Darlene H. Davis, "Narcotic Use in Southeast Asia and Afterward," *Archives of General Psychiatry,* 32 (August 1975): 955–961.

12. James Reston, "The Forgotten Veterans," *New York Times,* June 2, 1974, section IV, p. 21:1.

13. "The Vietnam-Veteran Blues," *New York Times,* March 29, 1974, p. 35:2; "Will Somebody Please Welcome This Hero Home?" *Today's Health,* June 1971, pp. 54–56+; "The Vietnam Vet: 'No One Gives a Damn,'" *Newsweek,* March 29, 1971, pp. 27–28+; "Vietnam Veterans: A Shocking Report on Their Damaged Lives," *Redbook,* May 1973, pp. 94–95+; "As Johnny Comes Marching Home," *Time,* January 11, 1971, pp. 58–59 ["unheralded, even unwanted"]; "When Johnnie Comes Marching Home," *America,* March 24, 1973, pp. 255–256 ["trained killers"].

14. "Addiction in Vietnam Spurs Nixon and Congress to Take Drastic New Steps," *New York Times,* June 16, 1971, p. 21:1; NBC, April 22, 1974 [Donald Johnson sacked]; NBC, February 26, 1974 [President Nixon's "Vietnam Veterans Day"]; CBS, October 28, 1974 [President Ford]; "Nixon Seeks 8% Increase in School Aid to Veterans; Congress Leaders Say Proposed Rise Is Too Small—President Also Calls for Higher Pensions for Ex-G.I.'s," *New York Times,* January 29, 1974, p. 14:1 [veteran rate of unemployment returns to civilian level].

15. *Legacies of Vietnam,* pp. 122ff. Studies have consistently demonstrated—and the point is not really in doubt—that American veterans in general, and Vietnam-era veterans specifically, have higher median incomes than nonveterans. Some studies have argued that Vietnam-era veterans stationed in the war zone itself or specific subgroups of Vietnam veterans such as combat veterans have lower median incomes, less education, or lower-status jobs than their civilian peers. However, even the worst-case scenario presented by these studies could not support the traditional extreme contentions that Vietnam vets were afforded "shameful" or "disgraceful" treatment. In general, see Dennis N. De Tray, *Veteran Status and Civilian Earnings* (Santa Monica, Calif.: Rand Corp., 1980), Richard V. L. Cooper, *Military Retirees' Post-Service Earnings and Employment* (Santa Monica, Calif.: Rand Corp., 1981), Eva M. Norrblom, *The Returns to Military and Civilian Training* (Santa Monica, Calif.: Rand Corp. report prepared for the Defense Advanced Research Projects Agency, 1976), Eva Norrblom, *An Assessment of the Available Evidence on*

the Returns to Military Training (Santa Monica, Calif.; Rand Corp. report prepared for the Defense Advanced Research Projects Agency, 1977), Dennis De Tray, *Veteran Status as a Screening Device* (Santa Monica, Calif.: Rand Corp., 1980), Paul A. Weinstein, *Labor Market Activity of Veterans: Some Aspects of Military Spillover* (Final Report of the Military Training Study, University of Maryland Department of Economics, 1969), and Adele P. Massell and Gary R. Nelson, *The Estimation of Training Premiums for U.S. Military Personnel* (Santa Monica, Calif.: Rand Corp., 1974); Jere Cohen, David R. Segal, and Lloyd V. Temme, "Military Service Was an Educational Disadvantage to Vietnam-Era Personnel," *Sociology and Social Research,* 70 (3) (April 1986): 206–208; idem, "The Educational Cost of Military Service in the 1960s," *Journal of Political and Military Sociology,* 14 (2) (Fall 1986): 303–319; Sharon R. Cohany, "Employment and Unemployment among Vietnam-Era Veterans," *Monthly Labor Review,* 113 (4) (April 1990): 22–29; Yu Xie, "The Socioeconomic Status of Young Male Veterans, 1964–1984," *Social Science Quarterly,* 73 (2) (June 1992): 379–396.

16. "GI Bill Improvement Act of 1977," hearings before the Subcommittee on Health and Readjustment of the Committee on Veterans' Affairs, United States Senate (Washington, D.C.: U.S. Government Printing Office, 1977); "Vietnam Veterans' Readjustment," hearings before the Committee on Veterans' Affairs, United States Senate, 96th Congress, 2nd Sess., February 21, March 4, and May 21, 1980 (Washington: U.S. Government Printing Office, 1980), pt. 2, pp. 828 [median years of schooling: 12.5 for Vietnam vets, compared with 12.3 for Korean War vets and 11.5 for World War II veterans], 849 [same], 868 [utilization of G.I. Bill]; "Hearings on Employment Programs for Veterans," hearings before the Subcommittee on Education, Training and Employment of the Committee on Veterans' Affairs, House of Representatives, 96th Congress, 1st sess., May 8 and May 15, 1979 (Washington: U.S. Government Printing Office, 1979), p. 19 [percentage of G.I. Bill use for college]; "Home from Vietnam—For 2.3 Million U.S. Veterans: A New Way of Life," *U.S. News and World Report,* February 12, 1973, pp. 21–23 [more Vietnam vets using G.I. Bill benefits for higher education than ever before]; "Use of GI Bill Is Found Greatest in West," *New York Times,* December 29, 1976, p. 23:4.

17. The March issue of the *Atlantic* in 1978 was entitled "Soldiers of Misfortune; The Treatment of Vietnam Veterans Is a National Disgrace." See Jack Anderson, "Carter and U.S. Forget Vietnam Vets," *Washington Post,* May 29, 1978, p. D-12–2C ["leech-infested rice paddies"]; Loren Baritz, *Backfire: A History of How American Culture Led Us into Vietnam and Made Us Fight the Way We Did* (New York: Ballantine Books, 1985), p. 297 [14 percent assigned to combat as of 1967; see also below, Conclusion, note 2]; "Vietnam Veterans in an Iowa Town Begin Organizing to Reach Their Goals," *New York Times,* July 16, 1981, p. 13:1 ["volunteer corn"]; "Vietnam Veterans—Peace at Last?" *U.S. News and World Report,* January 29, 1979, pp. 36–37 [reports of extreme abuse of Vietnam veterans]; "A Vietnam Veteran Stills Audience with a Rebuke," *New York Times,* May 30, 1979, p. 1:4.

18. These topics, however, rarely escape mention in a discussion of Vietnam

veterans. As late as 1985, some still raised the problem of underutilization of the G.I. Bill. See "The War That Has No Ending," *Discover,* June 1985, pp. 44–47 + .

19. For the Vietnam syndrome, see " 'Syndrome' Found in Returned G.I.'s," *New York Times,* June 7, 1971, p. 7:1; "The Post-Vietnam Syndrome," letter from Henry L. Rosett, M.D., *New York Times,* June 12, 1971, p. 28:3, and "Now That He's Home Again," *McCalls,* January 1969, pp. 44–45 + . For stories of crime, see "Vietnam Veteran Releases Hostages and Gives Up in Ohio after 9 Hours," *New York Times,* August 27, 1976, section I, p. 17:5; "Vietnam Vets Seize Statue of Liberty," *Washington Post,* June 9, 1976, p. A-11–1; "Vietnam Veteran Held in Boston after Firing on Imaginary Enemy," *New York Times,* March 5, 1979, section II, p. 10:6; "Death Provides Final Escape for Tormented Vet," *Chicago Tribune,* May 24, 1981, p. 1-5-1-P [James Hopkins].

20. "Wounded Vietnam Vet on Hostage Adulation: 'It's Damned Unfair,' " *Washington Post,* January 31, 1981, p. A-6–6, and "Viet Vets Smarting over Reception for Returning 52," *Chicago Tribune,* February 1, 1981, p. 1-2-1-P; "The Vet Offensive," *New Republic,* August 1–8, 1981, pp. 23–25; Michael Herr, *Dispatches* (New York: Alfred A. Knopf, 1977); "Apocalypse Now," United Artists, 1979 (directed by Francis Ford Coppola); "Taxi Driver," Columbia, 1976 (directed by Martin Scorsese).

21. "The War and the Arts: There Has Been a Cultural Turnaround on the Subject of Vietnam," *New York Times Magazine,* March 31, 1985, p. 54; Herr, *Dispatches;* "The Literature Born of Vietnam," *Humanist,* March/April 1986, pp. 30–31; "Vietnam as Fable," *New Republic,* March 25, 1978, pp. 21–24; "A Veteran Writes," *Harpers,* December 1980, pp. 41–56 ["The press loves a victim"]; Tom Wicker, "The Vietnam Disease," *New York Times,* May 27, 1975, p. 29:1.

22. American Psychiatric Association, *Diagnostic and Statistical Manual of Mental Disorders,* 3rd ed. (Washington, D.C.: American Psychiatric Association, 1980), pp. 236–238; "V.A. Target: Vietnam Veterans Who Cannot Readjust," *New York Times,* March 30, 1978, p. 13:1 [high estimates of incidence of PTSD]; "Vietnam Veterans—Peace at Last?," *U.S. News and World Report,* January 29, 1979, pp. 36–37 [Wilson estimate]; "Postwar Wounds," *Time,* September 2, 1974, p. 63 [Cedarleaf estimate]. Regarding common estimates, see "War Echoes in the Courts," *Newsweek,* November 23, 1981, p. 103 [cites 700,000], "Veterans of Vietnam Gaining New Aid to Fight Addiction," *New York Times,* December 26, 1985, section I, p. 1:5 [cites 800,000], and " 'Just Don't Fit'; Stalking the Elusive 'Tripwire' Veteran," *Harpers,* April 1985, pp. 55–63 [estimates between 750,000 and 900,000]. For statistics on the number of Vietnam and World War II veterans rated as disabled because of psychiatric or neurological conditions, see Administrator of Veterans Affairs, *Annual Report 1978* (Washington, D.C.: U.S. Government Printing Office, 1978), p. 189, and Administrator of Veterans Affairs, *Annual Report 1946* (Washington, D.C.: U.S. Government Printing Office, 1947), p. 109.

23. Regarding a missed rite de passage, see Christopher Buckley, "Viet Guilt: Were the Real Prisoners of War the Young Americans Who Never Left Home?" *Esquire,* September 1983, pp. 68–72; and "Apocalypse Continued," *New York Times Magazine,* January 13, 1985, p. 60. Regarding early articles on

the neglected female Vietnam veteran, see "Women Speaking Out on Effects of Duty in Vietnam; Like Men Who Fought, They Tell of Anxiety and Painful Recall," *New York Times*, March 23, 1981, p. 1:1; "Aid for Women Who Served in War Zones," *New York Times*, January 8, 1983, section 23, p. 1:1; "Lifting the Vietnam Stigma," *U.S. News and World Report*, November 16, 1987; and June A. Willenz, *Women Veterans: America's Forgotten Heroines* (New York: Continuum Publishing Company, 1983).

24. Regarding the vet centers, see Arthur S. Blank, Jr., "Apocalypse Terminable and Interminable: Operation Outreach for Vietnam Veterans," *Hospital and Community Psychiatry*, 33 (11) (November 1982): 913–918; "Vietnam's Sad Legacy: Vets Living in the Wild," *U.S. News and World Report*, March 12, 1984; and "V.A. Is Ordered to Drop Plans to Close 9 Counseling Centers," *New York Times*, June 30, 1987, section I, p. 20:4; "Veterans Call Cutbacks 'Another Betrayal,'" *New York Times*, May 4, 1981, section II, p. 11:1. For the politics of PTSD, see Wilbur Scott, "PTSD in DSM-III: A Case in the Politics of Diagnosis and Disease," *Social Problems*, 37 (3) (August 1990): 294–310.

25. For what is apparently the first major television report on Agent Orange, see CBS, March, 23, 1978; in general, see *Newsday*, September 19, 1988, pt. 2, p. 4; Michael Gough, *Dioxin, Agent Orange: The Facts* (New York: Plenum Press, 1986); Caroline D. Harnly, *Agent Orange and the Vietnam Veteran: An Annotated Bibliography* (Monticello, Ill.: Vance Bibliographies, 1985); Peter H. Schuck, *Agent Orange on Trial: Mass Toxic Disasters in the Courts* (Cambridge, Mass.: Harvard University Press, 1986); J. D. Erickson, J. Mulinare, P. W. McClain et al., "Vietnam Veterans' Risks for Fathering Babies with Birth Defects," *Journal of the American Medical Association*, 252 (1984): 903–912; USAF School of Aerospace Medicine, *Project Ranch Hand II: An Epidemiologic Investigation of Health Effects in Air Force Personnel Following Exposure to Herbicides: Baseline Mortality Study Results* (June 1983); ibid., *Project Ranch Hand II: Mortality Update—1984*, United States Air Force, Brooks Air Force Base, Texas (February 1985), pp. 69–76; ibid., *Air Force Health Study: An Epidemiologic Investigation of Health Effects in Air Force Personnel Following Exposure to Herbicides*, USAF, Brooks Air Force Base, Texas (1987); Veterans Administration, Department of Medicine and Surgery, *Synopsis of Scientific Literature on Phenoxy Herbicides and Associated Dioxins, No. 1, 2, 4, and 5* (Washington, D.C.: Veterans Administration, 1985, 1985, 1987, 1988).

26. CBS, May 7, 1980 [that the U.S. government poisoned its own army in Vietnam]; see also "Anatomy of a Cover-up," *The Nation*, November 30, 1992, pp. 658–662+; "A Cover-up on Agent Orange?" *Time*, July 23, 1990, pp. 27–28; "Agent Orange: Congress Impatient for Answers" *Science*, July 21, 1989, pp. 249–250 [CDC study vs. American Legion–funded study]; "Case Closed," *Newsday*, September 19, 1988, pt. 2, p. 4 [Vietnam vets stalked by Agent Orange]; "Agent Orange Study Blasted," *Nature*, 340 (July 20, 1989): 179 [veterans' organizations condemn CDC study]; "Activist Calls Agent Orange Bill Inadequate," *Los Angeles Times*, February 1, 1991, pt. B, p. 3; ABC, November 11, 1988 [Stellman/American Legion–funded study]; "Agent Orange Furor Continues to Build: For Vietnam Veterans, the Herbicide Has Become a Symbol for Everything That Was Wrong about the War," *Science*, 205 (August 1979): 770–772.

27. For analysis and the CDC study, see Michael Gough, *Dioxin, Agent Orange: The Facts* (New York: Plenum Press, 1986), pp. 108–110; and Erickson, Mulinare, McClain et al., "Vietnam Veterans' Risks for Fathering," [CDC study]. Gough points out that on the basis of current morbidity rates about 700,000 Vietnam veterans would be expected to develop cancer during their lifetimes, and 560,000 will probably die from the disease; these would be the probable figures entirely aside from exposure to Agent Orange in Vietnam. Gough also notes that only 1,269 men actually served in Operation Ranch Hand in which Agent Orange was sprayed from airplanes in Vietnam, and that Air Force studies of these men revealed lower cancer rates than in a control group (pp. 64, 68). See the government studies on Operation "Ranch Hand" cited in note 26. See also "Agent Orange Study Hits Brick Wall," *Science,* 237 (September 1987): 1285, 1287 [CDC concludes data inadequate to conduct retrospective study].

28. "Horror Festers in Viet Nam Vets," *Chicago Tribune,* April 18, 1981, p. N1-9-3-P; "Coming Home," *Progressive,* April 1981, 45:10; "The War That Has No Ending," *Discover,* June 1985, 6:44–47; CBS Evening News, March 5, 1986; Daniel A. Pollock et al., "Estimating the Number of Suicides among Vietnam Veterans," *American Journal of Psychiatry,* 147 (6) (June 1990): 772–776, 774 [6.6 times].

29. For studies on the incidence of suicide in Vietnam veterans, see Norman L. Farberow et al., "Combat Experience and Postservice Psychosocial Status as Predictors of Suicide in Vietnam Veterans," *Journal of Nervous and Mental Disease,* 178 (1) (1980): 32–37; Charles E. Lawrence et al., "Mortality Patterns of New York State Vietnam Veterans," *American Journal of Public Health,* 75 (3) (March 1985): 277–279; Norman Hearts et al., "Delayed Effects of the Military Draft on Mortality," *New England Journal of Medicine,* 314 (10) (March 6, 1986): 620–624; CDC, "Postservice Mortality among Vietnam Veterans," *Journal of the American Medical Association,* 257 (6) (February 13, 1987): 790–795; Colleen A. Boyle and Pierre Decoufle, "Postdischarge Mortality from Suicide and Motor-Vehicle Injuries among Vietnam-Era Veterans," *New England Journal of Medicine,* 317 (8) (August 20, 1987): 506–507; Pollock et al., "Estimating the Number of Suicides among Vietnam Veterans," pp. 772–776, 774; Lee Hyer et al., "Suicidal Behavior among Chronic Vietnam Theatre Veterans with PTSD," *Journal of Clinical Psychology,* 46 (6) (November 1990): 713–721; Herbert Hendin and Ann Pollinger Haas, "Suicide and Guilt as Manifestations of PTSD in Vietnam Combat Veterans," *American Journal of Psychiatry,* 148 (5) (May 1991): 586–591; Daniel A. Pollock, "PTSD and Risk of Suicide," *American Journal of Psychiatry,* 149 (1) (January 1992): 142–143 (letter). Studies of World War II and Korean War veterans had also discovered such a "five-year window" of increased mortality for veterans directly after the relevant wars.

30. For assertions of elevated mortality or suicide rates in Vietnam veterans, see "Suicide Risk Double for Viet Veterans," *Chicago Tribune,* March 6, 1986, section 1, p. 14:2; "Some Thoughts on Veterans Day," *Chicago Tribune,* November 13, 1994, Tempo Southwest, p. 3 ["high" suicide rate]; "Maine Veterans Place Support Behind Olympia Snowe," *Bangor Daily News,* October 4, 1994 [more

than 130,000 Vietnam veterans have committed suicide]; "'The Iliad' as Illustration of Epic Struggle with Post-Vietnam Stress," *Baltimore Sun*, September 4, 1994, p. D6 [72 percent higher suicide rate for Vietnam veterans]; "'Gettysburg' Makes a Muddle of Meditation," *Washington Times*, March 19, 1994, p. B3 (book review) [159,000 Vietnam vets committed suicide]. For anecdotal accounts of Vietnam veterans committing suicide, see "Veteran, 44, Kills Himself at VA Hospital," *Roanoke Times & World News*, December 30, 1994, p. B4; "Viet Vet Kills Self in Clinton Protest," *Newsday*, June 9, 1994, p. A19; and "Vietnam Vet Dies—Self-Immolation," *UPI*, September 24, 1987. Most stories recounting the psychological difficulties of Vietnam vets mention suicide as one of the problems for this group; see "Survivor of Unpopular War Pursues a Sad, Solitary Crusade," *Denver Post*, December 13, 1994, p. B1. For Tom Wicker story on 500,000 suicide attempts, see note 31.

31. Tom Wicker, "The Vietnam Disease," *New York Times*, May 27, 1975, p. 29:1 [500,000 suicide attempts by Vietnam veterans], and correction, *New York Times*, August 1, 1975, p. 27:1 ["Its publication in this space is regretted"].

32. "Black Vietnam Vets: No Peace Yet," *Essence*, December 1981, pp. 76–77 + [125,000; citing figures from Amnesty International]; "Coming Home," *Progressive*, April 1981, p. 10; "Mentally Wounded Are Rare, But Not Nearly Rare Enough; In Some Minds Vietnam Goes Marching On," *New York Times*, April 15, 1979, section IV, p. 18:3 [58,000 veterans in prison; majority of them Vietnam vets]; "Jailed Vets Fight Scars of Vietnam," *Chicago Tribune*, September 23, 1993, p. 8 [Vietnam veteran post organized in a prison]; "From Voices Free or Fettered Comes a Call to Remember; In a Maryland Prison, Inmate-Veterans Come Together for Comfort, Support," *Washington Post*, November 12, 1989, p. C3 [strong belief]. Regarding television coverage, see "Vietnam Requiem," a special aired by ABC on July 15, 1982 [assertion that 100,000 Vietnam veterans who experienced heavy combat were in prison, and that their arrest rate was twice that of civilians].

33. NBC, May 28, 1979; ABC, November 11, 1979; CBS, April 26, 1981.

34. "New Yorkers Roar Thanks to Veterans," *New York Times*, May 8, 1985, section I, p. 1:1; Colman McCarthy, "Veterans Owed Apologies, Not Parades," *Washington Post*, June 29, 1986, p. G-10-d [Chicago parade]; "Vietnam Veterans March in Houston," *Washington Post*, May 24, 1987, p. A-18-e; CBS, June 3, 1979 [Modesto, California]; NBC, March 28, 1981 [Anderson, Indiana]; CBS, October 23, 1982 [Northfield, Vermont]; NBC, April 28, 1985 [Kalamazoo, Michigan].

35. "Diverse Crowd Is Unanimous in Homage to Vietnam Veterans," *Washington Post*, November 14, 1982, p. A 18 a; ABC, November 10, 1982.

36. Bob Greene, "A Heroic Vision That Transforms Villainy," *Chicago Tribune*, April 21, 1982, section 3, p. 1:4.

37. See "Viet Vets Fight Back," *Newsweek*, November 12, 1979, p. 44 +; "After Vietnam: Voices of a Wounded Generation," *Washington Post*, May 25, 1980, section B, p. 5; "Bringing the Viet Nam Vets Home," *Time*, June 1, 1981, p. 40 +; "The War-Scarred Assemble at Vietnam Memorial," *New York Times*, November 11, 1984, section I, p. 28:2.

38. See "'Just Don't Fit,'" pp. 55–63, which indicates that these men were re-

peatedly lied to, used by arrogant and selfish men, wasted like pieces of meat on a slab, and then discarded. See also "Still Shuddering at 'Distant Thunder'; Vietnam 'Bush Vets' Helped Shape Film about Soldiers' Trauma," *Los Angeles Times*, November 11, 1988, pt. 6, p. 1:2; and "Lost in America," *Time*, February 11, 1991, pp. 76–77, 76, which discusses "clusters" of such veterans, and notes: "An accurate count is tough to come by."

39. See "Nation's Homeless Veterans Battle a New Foe: Defeatism," *New York Times*, December 30, 1987, section A, p. 1, col. 1 [citing estimates from 230,000 to more than 750,000 homeless veterans, about two-thirds of whom served since the beginning of the Vietnam era]; "Veterans of Failure; For Many Homeless, the Despair Was Born in a War Called Vietnam," *Los Angeles Times*, November 11, 1988, pt. 5, p. 1, col. 3 [cites figure of between 50,000 and 100,000]; "On Their Day, Many Veterans Homeless," *St. Petersburg Times*, November 11, 1988, p. 1A [that veterans constitute 30 percent of America's homeless population]; "Served by Their Country?" *St. Petersburg Times*, January 5, 1988, p. 16A [that treatment of homeless veterans is shameful]; "About New York," *New York Times*, June 8, 1991, section 1, p. 27 [allegations of "broken promises" to the homeless veterans].

40. See "Exiles on Main Street," *Rolling Stone*, June 24, 1993, pp. 62–66+ [that 900,000 Vietnam vets have had full-blown PTSD, and another 350,000 have suffered from a milder form of that syndrome]; "Rather Goes to the Wall for 'Wall Within,'" *Los Angeles Times*, June 2, 1988, pt. 6, p. 10 [about 1 million Vietnam veterans have suffered from delayed-stress disorder or the mental scars of the war]; "Inmate Aid Proposed," *Newsday*, September 1, 1989, p. 34 ["hundreds of thousands" affected; at least one-third of total]; "A Memorial of Growing Concern; Vietnam Vet's Forest Is a Symbol of Peace," *St. Petersburg Times*, May 29, 1989, p. 1D [over 100,000 suicides].

41. "The Angels of Vietnam; For Two Navy Nurses, a Memorial to a Time They Won't Forget," *Washington Post*, November 11, 1993, p. C1; "Vietnam Defused: It's OK to Say You Went; Women Served and Suffered," *Chicago Tribune*, November 7, 1993, p. D3.

42. "It's a Risky Business; Football's Violence Often Takes a Late Toll on Players in the Form of Long-Term Disability and—According to Some Studies—Premature Death," *Newsday*, September 4, 1988, p. 4 [football players]; "In Iowa, Mental Anguish Still Racks Families," *Wall Street Journal*, May 18, 1988, section 1, p. 70 [farmers in rural Iowa]; "Terror in the Air; For Many Survivors, the Fear Has Just Begun," *Los Angeles Times*, July 27, 1989, pt. 5, p. 1 [airplane crashes]; "Survey Likens Homeless to Combat Vets," *San Francisco Chronicle*, August 3, 1990, p. B7 [homeless]; "Pristine Past Just an Echo in Prince William Sound," *Orlando Sentinel Tribune*, March 25, 1990, p. A1 [oil spills]; "'I Don't Know How I Will Get By'; Phillips Blast Still Taking Toll; Post-traumatic Stress Puts Workers and Company at Odds," *Houston Chronicle*, September 25, 1991, p. A1 [industrial accidents]; "Slaves to the Sale; Many Former Workers Left with Vivid Nightmares, Expert Says," *Houston Chronicle*, August 19, 1992, p. A11 [traveling salesmen]; "'If I Only Could Have, I Would Have'; Shock, Guilt Consume Faultless Drivers Who Kill Pedestrians," *Phoenix Gazette*, April 12, 1993, p. A1 [auto accidents]; "Coping;

When Incest Haunts Love; Partners of Its Victims Face Leftover Traumas," *Washington Post*, August 27, 1990, p. D5 [incest and rape]; "After Seeing Horrors, Emergency Crews Need Emotional First Aid," *Los Angeles Times*, April 25, 1993, p. B5 [rescue personnel]; "Survey Seeks Reactions to Earthquake," *Los Angeles Times*, May 1, 1988, pt. 9, p. 1 [earthquake victims]; "The Mind Is the Key to Survival; Mentally Active Hostages Cope," *Newsday*, March 16, 1990, p. 4 [hostages]; "On Streets Ruled by Crack, Families Die," *New York Times*, August 11, 1989, p. A 1 [teen drug abusers]; "U.S. Parents Push 'Supertots' to be Sporting Champs," *The Sunday Times*, June 24, 1990, Overseas news [young adults pushed too hard]; "The Other America; Reporter Documents Story of Young Brothers Growing Up in Poverty, Living with Violence," *Houston Chronicle*, February 24, 1992, p. 1 [children exposed to violence]; "The Final Self-Defense," *New York Times*, December 31, 1989, section 7, p. 17 [battered women]; "How Many More?" *St. Petersburg Times*, July 21, 1989, p. 1D [African-Americans].

43. William K. Lane, Jr., "Vietnam Vets: Ambushed in Hollywood," *Reader's Digest*, December 1988, pp. 118–120; "Dead of 'Forgotten War' Get Belated Honors with Memorials," *Chicago Tribune*, December 27, 1989, p. C30; "Another Vietnam Vet Goes Haywire," *Los Angeles Times*, November 7, 1988, pt. 6, p. 3; "Same Story, Different Actors," *Newsday*, March 10, 1989, Weekend, p. 3; "Disorder du Jour: A Rundown of the 'In' Syndromes," *Orlando Sentinel Tribune*, April 14, 1990, p. D3. See also CBS, November 11, 1988 [concern over commercialization at Vietnam Veterans Memorial].

2. "Every Man Has His Breaking Point"

1. See, for instance, "Beginning to Remember Korea," *Christian Science Monitor*, August 8, 1995; and "Remembering Heroes of the Forgotten War: Belatedly, the Nation Honors Those Who Stopped Aggression in Korea Four Decades Ago," *San Diego Union-Tribune*, July 30, 1995, editorial, p. G-4. One even sees Vietnam Memorial–style monuments being built for World War II veterans: "Submarine Veterans Remember Their Own," *New York Times*, August 27, 1995, section 13, p. 1. See also "War without End," *Life*, April 1991, pp. 55–63, with its theme that all American veterans have lived "under a shadow."

2. To freely speak of "psychiatry" or "psychiatrists" in the nineteenth century is misleading. The term "psychiatry" was apparently coined or first used by Reil in 1803, but before the early twentieth century, medical men who treated the mentally disturbed or who were in charge of insane asylums were usually referred to in the English language as "mad-doctors," "alienists," or, literally, "asylum superintendents." The first professional organizations of these men emerged in the United States in 1844, in England in 1841, and in France in 1852. The professional association of asylum superintendents in the U.S. was called the Association of Medical Superintendents of American Institutions for the Insane (AMSAII); it was renamed the American Medico-Psychological Association in 1892, and the American Psychiatric Association in 1921. The American Board of Psychiatry and Neurology was formed in 1934.

3. Michael R. Trimble, *Post-Traumatic Neurosis: From Railway Spine to the Whiplash* (New York: John Wiley and Sons, 1981), pp. 7–17, 24–28; Bessel A. van der Kolk, Nan Herron, and Ann Hostetler, "The History of Trauma in Psychiatry," *Psychiatric Clinics of North America*, 17 (3) (September 1994): 583–600; Carl Weidner, "Traumatic Neurasthenia," *American Practitioner and News*, (Louisville), 39 (1905): 410–420, 410–411 [shock], 412–413 [symptoms].

4. In general, see Erwin H. Ackerknecht, *A Short History of Psychiatry* (New York: Hafner, 1968); Norman Dain, *Concepts of Insanity in the United States, 1789–1865* (New Brunswick, N.J.: Rutgers University Press, 1963); Albert Deutsch, *The Mentally Ill in America: A History of Their Care and Treatment from Colonial Times* (New York: Columbia University Press, 1937); Gerald N. Grob, *Mental Institutions in America: Social Policy to 1875* (New York: The Free Press, 1973); idem, *Mental Illness and American Society, 1875–1940* (Princeton, N.J.: Princeton University Press, 1983); J. Hall, G. Zilboorg, and H. Bunker, eds., *One Hundred Years of American Psychiatry* (New York: Columbia University Press, 1944).

5. Theodore Diller, "Traumatic Nervous Affections," *American Journal of the Medical Sciences* (Philadelphia), 116 (1898): 291–306, 306 [actual]; Carl Weidner, M.D., "Traumatic Neurasthenia," *American Practitioner and News* (Louisville), 39 (1905): 410–420 [jarring, granular]; H. G. Brainerd, "Traumatic Neuroses," *California State Journal of Medicine* (San Francisco), 2 (1904): 43–45, 43 [nutrition]; Sanger Brown, "Etiology of Neurasthenia," *Chicago Medical Recorder*, 20 (1901): 311–316 [vital fluids]; W. B. Outten, "Injuries to the Nervous System without Evident Gross Lesions: A Study of Their History and Treatment," *Medical Mirror* (St. Louis), 4 (1893): 461–469, 461.

6. Michael Howard, "Men against Fire: The Doctrine of the Offensive in 1914," in Peter Paret, ed., *Makers of Modern Strategy: From Machiavelli to the Nuclear Age* (Princeton, N.J.: Princeton University Press, 1986), pp. 512–525; and John Keegan, *The Face of Battle* (New York: Dorset Press, 1986), p. 255 [Kee].

7. Howard, "Men against Fire," pp. 512–525; Keegan, *The Face of Battle*, p. 232 [aerial torpedoes], 204–284 [Battle of the Somme]; Alistair Horne, *The Price of Glory: Verdun, 1916* (New York: Harper and Row, 1962), p. 327.

8. According to P. S. Ellis ["The Origins of the War Neuroses" (pt. II), *Journal of the Royal Naval Medical Services*, 71 (1985): 32–44, 33], Dr. Charles S. Myers, a Cambridge University laboratory psychologist serving with the Royal Army Military Corps, coined the term "shell shock" in 1915, thinking it to be related to commotional impact of shells. Trimble, *Post-Traumatic Neurosis*, p. 98 [commotional]; Emanuel Miller, *The Neuroses in War* (New York: Macmillan, 1940) [symptoms]; Report of the War Office Committee of Inquiry into "Shell-Shock," Cmd 1734 (1922), p. 35 [hunted animal].

9. Elaine Showalter, *The Female Malady: Women, Madness, and English Culture, 1830–1980* (New York: Pantheon Books, 1985), pp. 168 [40 percent], and 178 [Rivers]; Martin Stone, "Shellshock and the Psychologists," in W. F. Bynum, Roy Porter, and Michael Shepherd, eds., *The Anatomy of Madness: Essays in the History of Psychiatry*, vol. II, *Institutions and Society* (New York: Tavistock Publications, 1985), pp. 242–271 [200,000]; Ted Bogacz, "War Neurosis and Cultural Change in England, 1914–22: The Work of the War Office Committee

of Enquiry into 'Shell-Shock,'" *Journal of Contemporary History*, 24 (1989): 227–256; Anthony Babington, *For the Sake of Example: Capital Courts-Martial, 1914–1920* (New York: St. Martin's Press, 1983) [executions]; Pat Barker, *Regeneration* (New York: Viking, 1991) [Rivers and Siegfried Sassoon]; Siegfried Sassoon, *Memoirs of an Infantry Officer* (Boston: Faber and Faber, 1978); Charles S. Myers, *Shell-Shock in France* (Cambridge: Cambridge University Press, 1940).

10. For the Russian system in the Russo-Japanese War, see R. L. Richards, "Mental and Nervous Disease in the Russo-Japanese War," *Military Surgeon*, 26 (1910): 177–193; Albert J. Glass, "The Role of Military Psychiatry in the Development of Community Mental Health Centers," *Military Medicine*, 135 (5) (May 1970): 345–355, 346; Meyer Maskin, "Psychodynamic Aspects of the War Neuroses: A Survey of the Literature," *Psychiatry*, 4 (1941): 97–115, 99; and P. S. Ellis, "The Origins of the War Neuroses" (pt. I), *Journal of the Royal Naval Medical Services*, 70 (1984): 168–177, 174. For precedents of "shell-shock" or psychiatric breakdown antedating the twentieth century, see Richard A. Gabriel, *No More Heroes: Madness and Psychiatry in War* (New York: Hill and Wang, 1987), pp. 45–57; Charles J. Hudson, "The First Case of Battle Hysteria?" *British Journal of Psychiatry*, 157 (July 1990): 150 [case from Greece; 490 B.C. at Battle of Marathon].

11. David K. Kentsmith, "Principles of Battlefield Psychiatry," *Military Medicine*, 151 (February 1986): 89–96, 94 [unable to function]; Edward A. Strecker, "II. Military Psychiatry: World War I, 1917–1918," in Hall, Zilboorg, and Bunker, eds., *One Hundred Years of American Psychiatry*, pp. 385–416, 388 [preparations], 389 [order to preserve manpower levels], 390–394 [methods of treatment], and 398 [cure rate]; Samuel Futterman and Eugene Pumpian-Mindlin, "Traumatic War Neuroses Five Years Later," *American Journal of Psychiatry*, 108 (1951–1952): 403 [idea that evacuation promoted neurosis owing to loss of group morale]; Eric J. Leed, *No Man's Land: Combat and Identity in World War I* (New York: Cambridge University Press, 1979); Thomas W. Salmon, *The Care and Treatment of Mental Diseases and War Neuroses ("Shell Shock") in the British Army* (New York: War Work Committee of the National Committee for Mental Hygiene, 1917); Charles S. Myers, "Contributions to the Study of Shell Shock," *Lancet*, 1 (March 18, 1916): 608–613; Thomas W. Salmon, "The War Neuroses and Their Lessons," *New York Journal of Medicine*, 109 (1919): 933–994; Pearce Bailey et al. (Surgeon General), *The Medical Department of the United States Army in the World War*, vol. X, *Neuropsychiatry* (Washington, D.C.: U.S. Government Printing Office, 1929); vol. XV, *Statistics*, pt. 2 (Washington, D.C.: U.S. Government Printing Office, 1925).

12. Martin Stone, "Shellshock and the Psychologists," pp. 242–271, 251, 243, 245, 246. See also Showalter, *The Female Malady*, esp. chap. 7. For pre-Freudian "talking cures," as well as Freud's U.S. influence, see Barbara Sicherman, "The Uses of a Diagnosis: Doctors, Patients, and Neurasthenia," *Journal of the History of Medicine and Allied Sciences*, 32 (1) (January 1977); idem, "The Quest for Mental Health in America, 1880–1917" (diss., Columbia University, 1967), pp. 412–418 [mental hygiene teams].

13. F. G. Gosling, *Before Freud: Neurasthenia and the American Medical Community*,

1870–1910 (Urbana: University of Illinois Press, 1987); Nathan G. Hale, Jr., *Freud and the Americans: The Beginnings of Psychoanalysis in the United States, 1876–1917* (New York: Oxford University Press, 1971); Sicherman, "The Quest for Mental Health in America, 1880–1917"; Jacques M. Quen and Eric T. Carlson, eds., *America Psychoanalysis: Origins and Development,* Adolf Meyer Seminars (New York: Brunner/Mazel, 1978); and Grob, *Mental Illness and American Society, 1875–1940.*

14. Herbert Hendin and Ann Pollinger Haas, *Wounds of War: The Psychological Aftermath of Combat in Vietnam* (New York: Basic Books, 1984), pp. 22–23; Trimble, *Post-Traumatic Neurosis,* pp. 101–103; Sandor Ferenczi, ed., *Psychoanalysis and the War Neuroses* (London: International Psycho-Analytical Press, 1921); Abram Kardiner and H. Spiegel, *War Stress and Neurotic Illness* (London: Paul B. Hoeber, 1941); Andre Leri, *Shell-Shock, Commotional and Emotional Aspects* (London: University of London Press, 1919); Frederick W. Mott, *War Neuroses and Shell Shock* (London: Hodder & Stoughton, 1919); E. C. Southard, *Shell-Shock and Other Neuro-Psychiatric Problems* (Boston: W. M. Leonard, 1919); War Office Committee on Shell-Shock, *Report of the War Office Committee of Enquiry into Shell Shock* (London: HMSO, 1922); Lawrence C. Kolb, "The Post-Traumatic Stress Disorders of Combat: A Subgroup with a Conditioned Emotional Response," *Military Medicine,* 149 (3) (May 1984): 237–243 [Kardiner's "conditioned behavior"]; Bessel A. van der Kolk, "The Drug Treatment of Post-Traumatic Stress Disorder," *Journal of Affective Disorders,* 13 (1987): 203–213 [Kardiner's "physioneurosis"]; Ghislaine Boulanger, "Post-Traumatic Stress Disorder: An Old Problem with a New Name," in Stephen M. Sonnenberg et al., eds., *The Trauma of War: Stress and Recovery in Viet Nam Veterans* (Washington, D.C.: American Psychiatric Press, 1985), p. 16 [Kardiner quote].

15. For background information on the topic, see Avram H. Mack et al., "A Brief History of Psychiatric Classification: From the Ancients to DSM-IV," *Psychiatric Clinics of North America,* 17 (3) (September 1994): 515–528; Erwin H. Ackerknecht, *A Short History of Psychiatry* (New York: Hafner, 1968), pp. 76–79 [Kraepelin]; Richard Harrison Shryock, *The Development of Modern Medicine: An Interpretation of the Social and Scientific Factors Involved* (Philadelphia: University of Pennsylvania Press, 1936), p. 354 [Kraepelin]; Sicherman, "The Quest for Mental Health in America, 1880–1917," pp. 207–222 [Kraepelin textbooks in U.S.]; Gerald N. Grob, *From Asylum to Community: Mental Health Policy in Modern America* (Princeton, N.J.: Princeton University Press, 1991), pp. 95–98 [first statistical manuals in U.S.].

16. David R. Jones, "The Macy Reports: Combat Fatigue in World War II Fliers," *Aviation, Space, and Environmental Medicine,* 58 (8) (August 1987): 807–811, 808. Eli Ginzberg, James K. Anderson, Sol W. Ginsburg, John L. Herma, *The Ineffective Soldier,* vol. 1, *The Lost Divisions* (New York: Columbia University Press, 1959), pp. 142 [rejection rate], 145 [separation rate]; Glass, "The Role of Military Psychiatry," p. 350 [high rate]; Kelly L. Cozza and Robert E. Hales, "Psychiatry in the Army: A Brief Historical Perspective and Current Developments," *Hospital and Community Psychiatry,* 42 (4) (April 1991): 413–418, 414; A. J. Glass and M. S. Mullins, eds., *Neuropsychiatry in World War II,*

vol. II, *Overseas Theatres* (Washington, D.C.: U.S. Government Printing Office, 1973), p. 27 [even in 1943, some American commanders demanded that psychiatric casualties be examined by the Judge Advocate as well as the Medical Corps—to detect malingering].

17. William Hausman and David McK. Rioch, "Military Psychiatry: A Prototype of Social and Preventive Psychiatry in the United States," *Archives of General Psychiatry*, 16 (June 1967): 727–739; Albert J. Glass, "Psychotherapy in the Combat Zone," *American Journal of Psychiatry*, 110 (April 1954): 725–731, 727–728; and Glass and Mullins, eds., *Neuropsychiatry in World War II*, vol. II, *Overseas Theatres*, pp. 9–17 [North Africa and Italy], 135 [catastrophe], and 64 [shellfire].

18. Glass and Mullins, eds., *Neuropsychiatry in World War II*, vol. II, *Overseas Theatres*, pp. 16–17 [Pentothal abreaction]; and Roy R. Grinker, "Brief Psychotherapy in War Neuroses," in *War Psychiatry*, proceedings of the Second Brief Psychotherapy Council, Chicago, Ill., January 1944 (Chicago: Institute for Psychoanalysis), p. 11 [electrifying].

19. Ackerknecht, *A Short History of Psychiatry*, pp. 91–93 [Freud, Breuer, and hypnosis]; Henri F. Ellenberger, *The Discovery of the Unconscious: The History and Evolution of Dynamic Psychiatry* (New York: Basic Books, 1970), p. 331 [Janet and cathartic theory]; Peter Gay, *Freud: A Life for Our Time* (New York: Doubleday, 1989), pp. 51, 71 [Freud at Nancy in 1889]; Glass, "Psychotherapy in the Combat Zone," p. 727 [15 percent]; Hausman and Rioch, "Military Psychiatry," p. 731 [over 50 percent].

20. Eli Ginzberg et al., *The Ineffective Soldier*, vol. 2, *Breakdown and Recovery* (New York: Columbia University Press, 1959), p. 126 ["Only fools enter battle unafraid"]; Kolb, "The Post-Traumatic Stress Disorders of Combat," p. 239 [100 days as the limit of effective action]; Francis C. Steckel, "Morale and Men: A Study of the American Soldier in World War II" (diss., Temple University, 1990), pp. 288 [shell shock occurred primarily in two groups: those in combat less than five days, and those kept in combat four months or longer without relief], and 324 [200 days]; Ellis, "The Origins of the War Neuroses" (pt. I), p. 172, quotes Lord Byng as reporting that 80 to 90 days under fire was regarded as the limit for British troops in the Crimean War; Roger J. Spiller, "Isen's Run: Human Dimensions of Warfare in the 20th Century," *Military Review*, 68 (5) (May 1988): 16–31, 29 [250 days of combat as soldier's maximum in World War II]; Glass and Mullins, eds., *Neuropsychiatry in World War II*, vol. II, *Overseas Theatres*, p. 50 [old sergeant's syndrome]; Eli Ginzberg et al., *The Ineffective Soldier*, vol. 1: *The Lost Divisions* (New York: Columbia University Press, 1959), pp. 107–112 [age group effectiveness].

21. Grob, *From Asylum to Community*, pp. 110–111; Carol Cina, "Social Science for Whom? A Structural History of Social Psychology" (diss., State University of New York–Stony Brook, 1981) [social psychology emerged after World War II; military experience central in origins].

22. Gerald N. Grob, "World War II and American Psychiatry," *Psychohistory Review*, 19 (Fall 1990): 41–69, 59 [numbers trained in military]; idem, *From Asylum to Community*, pp. 29–41, 71–92, and 182–238. See also Albert J. Glass et al., "The Current Status of Army Psychiatry," *American Journal of Psychiatry*,

117 (February 1961): 673–683; Joseph Dubey, "The Military Psychiatrist as Social Engineer," *American Journal of Psychiatry* 124 (1) (July 1967): 90–96; Hausman and Rioch, "Military Psychiatry," pp. 727–739; Jack R. Ewalt and Patricia L. Ewalt, "History of the Community Psychiatry Movement," *American Journal of Psychiatry*, 126 (1) (July 1969): 43–52; Glass, "The Role of Military Psychiatry in the Development of Community Mental Health Centers," pp. 345–355; idem, "Military Psychiatry and Changing Systems of Mental Health Care," *Journal of Psychiatric Research*, 8 (1971): 499–512; William Hausman, "Applications of the Military Medical Model to Civilian Psychiatry," *Journal of Psychiatric Research*, 8 (1971): 513–520; and Henry J. Friedman, "Military Psychiatry: Limitations of the Current Preventive Approach," *Archives of General Psychiatry*, 26 (February 1972): 118–123.

23. "Friends of the Shell-Shocked," *London Times*, March 1, 1920, p. 11.

24. "A Victim of Base Ingratitude; Unemployed Ex-Soldier's Suicide," *London Times*, April 3, 1920, p. 7; "An Officer's Suicide: Pitiful Last Letter to Daughter," *Pall Mall Gazette*, April 8, 1919, p. 2 [a veteran of the Somme]; "Unhinged by War: Ex-soldier's Determined Suicide at Brookwood," *Pall Mall Gazette*, June 4, 1919, p. 7 [a veteran of Gallipoli].

25. U.S. Department of Commerce, Bureau of the Census, *Historical Statistics of the United States: Colonial Times to 1970*, pt. 2 (Washington, D.C.: Department of Commerce, 1970), p. 1151 [Series Y 1010–1027]; Gustavus A. Weber and Laurence F. Schmeckebier, *The Veterans' Administration: Its History, Activities, and Organization* (Washington, D.C.: Brookings Institution, 1934), p. 459; Willard Waller, *The Veteran Comes Back* (New York: Dryden Press, 1944), p. 166 [one half]; William Pyrle Dillingham, *Federal Aid to Veterans, 1917–1941* (Gainesville: University of Florida Press, 1952), p. 235 [presumption of perfect condition]; Davis R. B. Ross, *Preparing for Ulysses: Politics and Veterans during World War II* (New York: Columbia University Press, 1969), pp. 20–21 [neuropsychiatric disease].

26. Samuel Futterman, and Eugene Pumpian-Mindlin, "Traumatic War Neuroses Five Years Later," *American Journal of Psychiatry*, 108 (December 1951): 401–408 [fresh cases of war-related stress still encountered]; Herbert C. Archibald et al., "Gross Stress Reaction in Combat—A 15-Year Follow-Up," *American Journal of Psychiatry*, 119 (1962): 317–322; Herbert C. Archibald and Read D. Tuddenham, "Persistent Stress Reaction after Combat: A 20-Year Follow-Up," *Archives of General Psychiatry*, 12 (May 1965): 475–481 ["veterans' chronic stress syndrome"]; Norman Q. Brill, and Gilbert W. Beebe, "Follow-Up Study of Psychoneuroses: Preliminary Report," *American Journal of Psychiatry*, 108 (December 1951): 417–425 [955 veterans]; D. Dobbs and W. P. Wilson, "Observations on Persistence of War Neurosis," *Diseases of the Nervous System*, 21 (December 1960): 686–691 [combat sounds].

27. For military psychiatry in Vietnam, see Franklin Del Jones, "Experiences of a Division Psychiatrist in Vietnam," *Military Medicine*, 132 (12) (December 1967): 1003–1008; William J. Tiffany, Jr., and William S. Allerton, "Army Psychiatry in the Mid-'60s," *American Journal of Psychiatry*, 123 (7) (January 1967): 810–821; Edward M. Colbach and Matthew D. Parrish, "Army Mental Health Activities in Vietnam, 1965–1970," *Bulletin of the Menninger Clinic*, 34 (6) (No-

vember 1970): 333–342; Peter G. Bourne, "Military Psychiatry and the Viet Nam Experience," *American Journal of Psychiatry*, 127 (4) (October 1970): 481–488; and Robert E. Huffman, "Which Soldiers Break Down: A Survey of 610 Psychiatric Patients in Vietnam," *Bulletin of the Menninger Clinic*, 34 (6) (November 1970): 343–351.

28. For these Vietnam rates, see Edward M. Colbach and Matthew D. Parrish, "Army Mental Health Activities in Vietnam, 1965–1970," *Bulletin of the Menninger Clinic*, 34 (6) (November 1970): 333–342, 338. Rates of psychiatric breakdown for military personnel are usually expressed in one of five ways: (a) as a percentage of casualties evacuated from any specific battle (note that a higher percentage may simply indicate that there were fewer physically wounded in that engagement); in modern warfare, this percentage is usually from 10 percent to 25 percent [see Steven Hazen, "Battle Fatigue Identification and Management for Military Medical Students," *Military Medicine*, 156 (6) (June 1991): 263–267]; (b) as a percentage of casualties evacuated from any specific theater (note that this figure might include large numbers of support troops who were never in battle); (c) as a rate per 1000 (or 10,000) troops/year; (d) as a rate of discharges from the military; for instance, 20 percent of British soldiers discharged for a disability in World War I had had psychiatric disorders such as "shell shock," "war neurosis," or "neurasthenia" [see Ransom J. Arthur, "Reflections on Military Psychiatry," *American Journal of Psychiatry* (Supplement), 135 (July 1978): 2–7, 3]; (e) as a rate of pensions granted to veterans. The issue of comparative rates is further clouded by the fact that diagnostic categories have shifted over time, from "shell shock" to "combat exhaustion," "psychoneurosis," "combat fatigue," and "PTSD." In addition, the entire point of front-line treatment methods is to avoid a formal psychiatric diagnosis, based on the theory that symptoms will become "fixed." Hence, one must approach all comparative statistics in this matter with caution.

29. David K. Kentsmith, "Principles of Battlefield Psychiatry," *Military Medicine*, 151 (February 1986): 89–96 [in World War II psychiatric cases constituted from 15 to 31 percent of all medical evacuations]; Peter G. Bourne, "Military Psychiatry and the Viet Nam Experience," *American Journal of Psychiatry*, 127 (4) (October 1970): 481–488, 487 [optimistic].

30. Theodore Van Putten and Warden H. Emory, "Traumatic Neuroses in Vietnam Returnees: A Forgotten Diagnosis?" *Archives of General Psychiatry*, 29 (November 1973): 695–698; "Postwar Shock Besets Ex-GI's," *New York Times*, August 21, 1972, p. 1:2; Peter H. Schuck, *Agent Orange on Trial: Mass Toxic Disasters in the Courts* (Cambridge, Mass.: Harvard University Press, 1986), p. 21 [1-year tour of duty]; Robert J. Lifton, "Vietnam: Betrayal and Self-Betrayal," *Trans-Action*, 6 (October 1969): 6–7; and Chaim F. Shatan, "The Grief of Soldiers: Vietnam Combat Veterans' Self-Help Movement," *American Journal of Orthopsychiatry*, 43 (4) (July 1973): 640–653.

31. Regarding assertions of Vietnam being unique, see Richard A. Kulka et al., *Trauma and the Vietnam War Generation: Report of Findings from the National Vietnam Veterans Readjustment Study* (New York: Brunner/Mazel, 1990), p. v; Sonnenberg et al., eds., *The Trauma of War*, p. xiii; Robert S. Laufer et al., "War

Stress and Trauma: The Vietnam Veteran Experience," *Journal of Health and Social Behavior*, 25 (March 1984): 65–85, 67; Arthur S. Blank, Jr., "Apocalypse Terminable and Interminable: Operation Outreach for Vietnam Veterans," *Hospital and Community Psychiatry*, 33 (11) (November 1982): 913–918, 914; and Erika H. Marchesini, "Vietnam Veterans Are Different," *American Journal of Nursing*, 73 (January 1973): 74–76, 74. Various reasons have been posited for this uniqueness: (1) guerrilla war—leading to atrocities; (2) language barriers; (3) lack of sense of glory, honor, and purpose in soldiers; (4) vague, limited military objectives; (5) unrest at home; (6) no heroes' welcomes for returning troops; (7) returning vets not encouraged to discuss war experiences; (8) lack of time for returning vets to decompress; (9) failure of the military to debrief vets; (10) lack of cohesive bonds in units; (11) government ignored Vietnam vet problems; (12) difficulties for Vietnam vets in obtaining treatment, because they were suspicious of the VA and felt a generational and cultural gap with older therapists; and (13) negative images of the war and its warriors in the media.

32. See "Armed Forces' Unsuitability Discharges Scored," *New York Times*, March 21, 1974, p. 46:2; John A. Renner, Jr., "The Changing Patterns of Psychiatric Problems in Vietnam," *Comprehensive Psychiatry*, 14 (March-April 1973): 169–181, 171; and George F. Solomon et al., "Three Psychiatric Casualties from Vietnam," *Archives of General Psychiatry*, 25 (December 1971): 522–524, 522.

33. For criticism of "single-dimension" war zone measures, see David A. Grady, Robert L. Woolfolk, and Alan J. Budney, "Dimensions of War Zone Stress: An Empirical Analysis," *Journal of Nervous and Mental Disease*, 177 (6) (1989): 347–350. For early descriptions of PTSD, see " 'Syndrome' Found in Returned GIs," *New York Times*, June 7, 1971, p. 7:1 ["Vietnam Syndrome"]; "The Post-Vietnam Syndrome," *New York Times*, June 12, 1971, p. 28:3; Shatan, "The Grief of Soldiers," pp. 640–653 ["Post-Vietnam Syndrome"]; "Invisible Army," *Harpers*, August, 1972, p. 18 ["Vietnam-Veteran Syndrome"]; M. Straker, "The Vietnam Veteran: The Task Is Re-Integration," *Disease of the Nervous System*, 37 (2) (February 1976): 75–79 ["Re-Entry Syndrome"]; and "Post-War Wounds: Psychiatric Problems of Vietnam Veterans," *Time*, September 2, 1974, p. 63 ["Post-Viet Nam Psychiatric Syndrome (PVNPS)"].

34. Arthur Egendorf, "The Postwar Healing of Vietnam Veterans: Recent Research," *Hospital and Community Psychiatry*, 33 (11) (November 1982): 901–908 [account of origins]; Arthur L. Arnold, "Diagnosis of Post-Traumatic Stress Disorder in Viet Nam Veterans," in Sonnenberg et al., eds., *The Trauma of War*, pp. 101–123 [elements]; Thomas Choy and Farideh De Bosset, "Post-Traumatic Stress Disorder: An Overview," *Canadian Journal of Psychiatry*, 37 (October 1992): 578–583; David A. Tomb, "The Phenomenology of Post-Traumatic Stress Disorder," *Psychiatric Clinics of North America*, 17 (2) (June 1994): 237–250 [overview]; Matthew J. Friedman et al., "Post-Traumatic Stress Disorder in the Military Veteran," *Psychiatric Clinics of North America*, 17 (2) (June 1994): 265–277; Shatan, "The Grief of Soldiers," pp. 650–651 [advocacy]. For an excellent analysis of the politics of PTSD, see Wilbur J. Scott, "PTSD in DSM-III: A Case in the Politics of Diagnosis and Disease," *Social Problems*, 37 (3) (August 1990): 294–310; and idem, *The Politics of Readjustment: Vietnam Veterans since the War* (New York: Aldine De Gruyter, 1993).

35. "Vietnam Veterans—Peace at Last?" *U.S. News and World Report,* January 29, 1979, pp. 36–37 [John Wilson estimate of at least 250,000 and possibly as many as 500,000]; J. P. Wilson, "Identity, Ideology, and Crisis: The Vietnam Veteran in Transition," pt. 1 (unpub. monograph, Cleveland State University, 1977) [50 percent]; Charles Figley, ed., *Stress Disorders among Vietnam Veterans: Theory, Research and Treatment* (New York: Brunner/Mazel, 1978), pp. xiii–xxvi [50 percent]; Egendorf, "The Postwar Healing of Vietnam Veterans," pp. 901–908 [the "subclinical malaise" affects 2 million]; Kulka et al., *Trauma and the Vietnam War Generation,* p. xvii [NVVRS (National Vietnam Veteran Readjustment Study) based on a total sample of 2,348 veterans estimated a current case rate in male theater veterans of 15.2 percent, additional symptomatology in another 11.1 percent males, and lifetime prevalence for male theater vets of 30.6 percent]; Josefina J. Card, "Epidemiology of PTSD in a National Cohort of Vietnam Veterans," *Journal of Clinical Psychology,* 43 (1) (January 1987): 6–17 [19 percent of Vietnam vets aged 36 have PTSD]; John E. Helzer et al., "Post-Traumatic Stress Disorder in the General Population," *New England Journal of Medicine,* 26 (December 24, 1987): 1630–1634 [study of 2,493 people; estimates rate of 1 percent in general U.S. population and rate of 3.5 percent for general Vietnam veteran population (similar to rate for civilians exposed to physical attack), but rate of 20 percent in Vietnam vets wounded in the war]; "Study Raises Estimate of Vietnam War Stress," *Science,* 241 (August 12, 1988): 788 [Vietnam Experience Study (conducted by CDC in Atlanta) found PTSD rates in Vietnam vets of 2 percent].

36. American Psychiatric Association, *Diagnostic and Statistical Manual,* 3rd ed., 1980), p. 7; Leon Eisenberg, "Mindlessness and Brainlessness in Psychiatry," *British Journal of Psychiatry,* 148 (1986): 497–508; Steven M. Southwick et al., "Psychobiologic Research in Post-Traumatic Stress Disorder," *Psychiatric Clinics of North America,* 17 (2) (June 1994): 251–264.

37. Meyer Maskin, "Psychodynamic Aspects of the War Neuroses; A Survey of the Literature," *Psychiatry,* 4 (1941): 97–115, 98 [W. H. R. Rivers's emphasis on the importance of motility]; Bourne, "Military Psychiatry and the Viet Nam Experience," pp. 481–488 [artillery fire as most devastating]; Peter Watson, *War on the Mind: The Military Uses and Abuses of Psychology* (New York: Basic Books, 1978), p. 216 [artillery]; H. H. Price, "The Falklands: Rate of British Psychiatric Combat Casualties Compared to Recent American Wars," *Journal of the Royal Army Medical Corps,* 130 (2) (June 1984): 109–113 [general discussion].

38. For the origins of psychology, and its claims to scientific certitude and efficiency, see Mitchell G. Ash and William R. Woodward, eds., *Psychology in Twentieth-Century Thought and Society* (Cambridge: Cambridge University Press, 1987); John M. O'Donnell, *The Origins of Behaviorism: American Psychology, 1870–1920* (New York: New York University Press, 1985); Michael M. Sokal, ed., *Psychological Testing and American Society, 1890–1930* (New Brunswick, N.J.: Rutgers University Press, 1987); and Richard T. M. Von Mayrhauser, "The Triumph of Utility: The Forgotten Clash of American Psychologies in World War I" (diss., University of Chicago, 1986). For a typical article around the turn of the century, advocating the application of psycho-

logical and psychiatric methods to the study of the military, see C. H. Hughes, "A plea for the extension of psychiatry in the American army; the brain break and nerve strain of the American soldier, his mind and nerve exhaustion and insanity," *Alienist and Neurology* (St. Louis), 21 (1900): 477–486. This article advocated viewing the soldier as a machine, and suggested that psychology could give expert advice to preserve and maintain this machine. See also Charles E. Woodruff, "Degenerates in the Army," *American Journal of Insanity*, 57 (July 1900): 137–142 [how to detect them]; Robert L. Richards, "A Study of Military Offences Committed by the Insane in the United States Army, for the Past Fifty Years," *American Journal of Insanity*, 68 (October 1911): 279–291; and R. L. Richards, "Military Psychiatry," *American Journal of Insanity*, 67 (July 1910): 91–108.

39. See Edward M. Colbach, "Ethical Issues in Combat Psychiatry," *Military Medicine*, 150 (5) (May 1985): 256–265; Norman M. Camp, "The Vietnam War and the Ethics of Combat Psychiatry," *American Journal of Psychiatry*, 150 (7) (July 1993): 1000–1010 [combat psychiatrists are influenced by powerful, potentially competing value systems]; and letters in response to Camp article, *American Journal of Psychiatry*, 151 (6) (June 1994): 948–952.

40. See Dennis H. Grant, "Psychological Damage of Combat," *American Journal of Psychiatry*, 148 (2) (February 1991): 271 [that men were not made to fight wars; shouldn't presume any can come through unscathed]; Jonathan Borus, "Incidence of Maladjustment in Vietnam Returnees," *Archives of General Psychiatry*, 30 (April 1974): 554–557 [criticism of political advocacy of antiwar psychiatrists].

41. Javier I. Escobar, "Posttraumatic Stress Disorder and the Perennial Stress-Diathesis Controversy," *Journal of Nervous and Mental Disease*, 175 (5) (1987): 265–266 [predisposition vs. environment]; Jack Goldberg et al., "A Twin Study of the Effects of the Vietnam War on Posttraumatic Stress Disorder," *Journal of the American Medical Association*, 263 (9) (March 2, 1990): 1227–1232 [role of genetics]; Ackerknecht, *A Short History of Psychiatry*, p. viii [complex].

3. "Dangled over Hell"

1. Francis Wayland Dunn, diary entry of October 30, 1862, Bentley Historical Library, University of Michigan, Ann Arbor ["destroying manner of living"]; W. H. H. Terrell, *Report of the Adjutant General of the State of Indiana*, vol. II (Indianapolis: W. R. Holloway, 1865), pp. 85 [11th Ind. Inf.], 439 [44th Ind. Inf.]; Dwight Fraser to his sister Lizzie, April 11, 1864, Fraser Papers, Indiana Historical Society ["walking"]; Rice C. Bull, *Soldiering: The Civil War Diary of Rice C. Bull, 123rd New York Volunteer Infantry*, ed. K. Jack Bauer (San Rafael, Calif.: Presidio Press, 1977), p. 38 [jettisoning items].

2. C. Macfarlane, *Reminiscences of an Army Surgeon* (Oswego, N.Y.: Lake City Print Shop, 1912), p. 55 [forced march]; Robert Watson memoirs, entry of July 4, 1863, Florida State Archives, Tallahassee [vomiting]; federal pension record of John C. Martin [F 42 Ind. Inf.], National Archives [epileptic fit]; David Ballenger to his mother, September 7, 1862, and May 8, 1863, South Caroliniana Library [continuous marches]; Thomas Clark to his wife, Martha Ann, September 7, 1862, Florida State Archives, Tallahassee [killed at Antietam].

3. Spencer Glasgow Welch, *A Confederate Surgeon's Letters to His Wife* (Marietta, Ga.: Continental Book Co., 1954; originally published in 1911), p. 31; John G. Perry, *Letters from a Surgeon of the Civil War*, ed. Martha Derby Perry (Boston: Little, Brown and Co., 1906), p. 144.

4. Edward G. Longacre, ed., *From Antietam to Fort Fisher: The Civil War Letters of Edward King Wightman, 1862–1865* (Cranbury, N.J.: Associated University Presses, 1985), p. 32.

5. Disability discharge papers, September 10, 1862, federal pension file of Wesley Lynch [A 35 Ind. Inf.], National Archives.

6. Aurelius Lyman Voorhis journal, entry for December 5, 1862, Indiana Historical Society [shivering]; Andrew Jackson Smith diary, entries for January 2, December 19, and December 25, 1864, Indiana Historical Society [blues]; David R. Trego to his brother, October 3, 1863, Bentley Historical Library [wet bed]; Wash Vosburgh to Ella, January 30, 1863, Nina L. Ness Collection, Bentley Historical Library [covered with snow]; John Johnston memoirs, p. 29, Confederate Collection, Tennessee State Archives [wretched feeling]; James N. Wright to his brother, Squire, November 17, 1864, John Johnson Papers, Indiana Historical Society [freight cars].

7. Henry W. Reddick, *Seventy-Seven Years in Dixie: The Boys in Gray of 61–65* (Santa Rosa, Fla.: H. W. Reddick, 1910), p. 21; Wash Vosburgh to Ella, May 13, 1864, Nina L. Ness Collection, Bentley Historical Library.

8. Carroll Henderson Clark memoirs, p. 9, Confederate Collection, Tennessee State Archives [equipment abandoned; breadth of mud]; Augustus M. Van Dyke to his parents, August 12, 1861, Indiana Historical Society [Cheat Mountain]; DeWitt C. Goodrich memoirs, p. 114, Indiana Historical Society [at Shiloh]; Bull, *Soldiering*, p. 123 [wet feet], 234 [Sherman's men].

9. Paul E. Steiner, *Disease in the Civil War: Natural Biological Warfare in 1861–1865* (Springfield, Ill.: Charles C. Thomas, 1968). The *Medical and Surgical History of the War of the Rebellion*, Medical History, pt. I, vol. I (Washington, D.C.: U.S. Government Printing Office, 1870), indicates that for Union troops (white and black), there were 6,454,834 cases of disease, with 195,627 deaths from disease. In general, see Courtney Robert Hall, "Confederate Medicine: Caring for the Confederate Soldier," *Medical Life*, 42 (1935): 445–508; William M. Straight, "Florida Medicine and the War between the States," *Journal of the Florida Medical Association*, 67 (8) (August 1980): 748–760; Alfred Jay Bollet, "To Care for Him That Has Borne the Battle: A Medical History of the Civil War," *Resident and Staff Physician*, 35 (November 1989): 121–129; James O. Breeden, "Confederate Medicine: The View from Virginia," *Virginia Medical Quarterly*, 118 (4) (Fall 1991): 222–231; and John Ochsner, "The Genuine Southern Surgeon," *Annals of Surgery*, 215 (5) (May 1992): 397–408.

10. In general, see George W. Adams, *Doctors in Blue: The Medical History of the Union Army in the Civil War* (Dayton, Ohio: Morningside Press, 1985), and Horace H. Cunningham, *Doctors in Gray: The Confederate Medical Service* (Gloucester, Mass.: Peter Smith, 1970). DeWitt C. Goodrich memoirs, pp. 9–10, Indiana Historical Society [primitive state of medicine]; Andrew Newton Buck to Myron and Susan, January 28, 1862, Buck Family Papers, Bentley Historical Library [executioner].

11. R. Maurice Hood, "Medicine in the Civil War," *Texas Medicine,* 63 (March 1967): 53–55, 53, 54; W. H. Taylor, "Some Experiences of a Confederate Assistant Surgeon," *Trans. Coll. Phys. Phila.,* 28 (1906): 104, 105 [standard practice]; James Houghton diary, entry from July 1863, Bentley Historical Library [canteen].

12. Roderick Gospero Shaw to his sister, October 8, 1863, Florida State Archives, Tallahassee [fangs of disease]; Henry G. Noble to Ruth, February 26, 1863, Bentley Historical Library [Rebel lead]; Chauncey H. Cooke, *Soldier Boy's Letters to His Father and Mother, 1861–5* (privately published, 1915), p. 23 [muffled drum]; Ben C. Johnson, *Soldier's Life: Civil War Experiences of Ben C. Johnson,* ed. Alan S. Brown, Faculty Contributions, ser. VI, no. 2 (Kalamazoo, Mich.: Western Michigan University Press, 1962), pp. 48–49.

13. James J. Nixon to his wife, May 11, 1864, P. K. Yonge Library of Florida History, University of Florida, Gainesville.

14. Col. James L. Cooper memoirs, p. 4, Confederate Collection, Tennessee State Archives; DeWitt Goodrich memoirs, p. 106, Indiana Historical Society; Rice C. Bull, *Soldiering,* p. 36.

15. Abner R. Small, *The Road to Richmond: The Civil War Memoirs of Major Abner R. Small of the Sixteenth Maine Volunteers, Together with the Diary Which He Kept When He Was a Prisoner of War,* ed. Harold Adams Small (Berkeley: University of California Press, 1939), p. 185 [real test]; Bull, *Soldiering,* p. 51; William Henry Younts memoirs, pp. 51–53, Indiana Historical Society [Ohio soldier].

16. Elbridge J. Copp, *Reminiscences of the War of the Rebellion, 1861–1865* (Nashua, N.H.: Telegraph Publishing Co., 1911), pp. 134–135 [horror and dread]; William Baird memoirs, p. 16, Bentley Historical Library [Michigan volunteer]; Perry, *Letters from a Surgeon,* p. 168 [screaming officers; singing soldier]; Small, *The Road to Richmond,* p. 71 [trembling soldier]; Major and Surgeon S. C. Gordon, "Reminiscences of the Civil War from a Surgeon's Point of View," in Military Order of the Loyal Legion of the United States, Maine Commandery, *War Papers* (Portland, Maine: Lefavor-Tower, 1898–1919), p. 143 [trembling soldiers]; George T. Ulmer, *Adventures and Reminiscences of a Volunteer, or a Drummer Boy from Maine* (1892), p. 28 [loss of control of bowels].

17. Charles A. Fuller, *Personal Recollections of the War of 1861* (Sherburne, N.Y.: News Job Printing House, 1906), p. 20 [first volley]; Major Rufus R. Dawes [*Service with the Sixth Wisconsin Volunteers*], quoted in Henry Steele Commager, ed., *The Blue and the Gray: The Story of the Civil War as Told by Participants* (New York: Bobbs-Merrill, 1950), p. 213 [demoniacal fury]; Robert S. Robertson, *Diary of the War,* ed. Charles N. Walker and Rosemary Walker (Fort Wayne, Ind.: Allen County–Fort Wayne Historical Society, 1965), pp. 181–182 [shouts which startle the dead]; Bull, *Soldiering,* p. 149 ; Copp, *Reminiscences of the War of the Rebellion,* p. 142 [hellish scene]; Washington Davis, *Camp-Fire Chats of the Civil War: Being the Incident, Adventure and Wayside Exploit of the Bivouac and Battle Field, as Related by Veteran Soldiers Themselves. Embracing the Tragedy, Romance, Comedy, Humor, and Pathos in the Varied Experiences of Army Life* (Lansing, Mich.: P. A. Stone, 1889), pp. 302–303 [revenge]; Franklin H. Bailey to his parents, April 8, 1862, Bentley Historical Library.

18. William Lewis McKay memoirs, p. 37, Confederate Collection, Tennessee State Archives.

19. William A. Ketcham memoirs, p. 4, Indiana Historical Society [forgot personal needs]; B.S.P., "Battle Impressions," in *The Soldier's Friend*, July 1867, p. 1 [sense of disembodiment]; Bull, *Soldiering*, p. 57 [sharp sting]; Copp, *Reminiscences of the War of the Rebellion*, p. 377 [blow from club]; Fuller, *Personal Recollections of the War of 1861*, p. 95 [arm ceased to function]; William E. Sloan diary, September 19, 1863, Confederate Collection, Tennessee State Archives [terror of the wounded]; Robertson, *Diary of the War*, p. 183 [legs knocked out]; James L. Cooper memoirs, p. 39 [felt like struck with board], Confederate Collection, Tennessee State Archives; S. Weir Mitchell, George R. Morehouse, and William W. Keen, *Gunshot Wounds and Other Injuries of Nerves* (Philadelphia: J. B. Lippincott & Co., 1864), p. 14 [by far].

20. Mitchell et al., *Gunshot Wounds*, p. 87 [case study of David Schively, E 114 Pa. Inf.; staggered]; James L. Cooper memoirs, p. 22 [excitement], Confederate Collection, Tennessee State Archives.

21. George E. Ranney, "Reminiscences of an Army Surgeon," in *War Papers Read before the Michigan Commandery of the Military Order of the Loyal Legion of the United States*, vol. 2 (Detroit: James H. Stone & Co., 1898), p. 189 [awful shock and rage of battle]; Small, *The Road to Richmond*, p. 133 [the Battle of the Wilderness as "that howling acre"]; Alfred A. Atkins to parents, February 11, 1864, Georgia State Archives [rumbling, grinding noise]; David Ballenger to his mother, May 8, 1863, South Caroliniana Library [Chancellorsville]; declaration of January 2, 1900 [blood gushing], federal pension file of Thomas B. Hornaday [E 70 Ind. Inf.], National Archives. For a typical pension claim for deafness induced by cannonading, see federal pension file of Elijah Wingert [D 118 Pa. Inf.], National Archives.

22. William B. Miller diary, entry for September 19, 1863 [Chickamauga]; Robertson, *Diary of the War*, p. 182 [Spotsylvania]; Gus F. Smith, "Battle of Franklin," in *War Papers Read before the Michigan Commandery of the Military Order of the Loyal Legion of the United States*, p. 262 [awful grandeur]; Copp, *Reminiscences of the War of the Rebellion*, p. 242 [the half].

23. *John Dooley War Journal* (Washington, D.C., 1945), p. 23, quoted in Horace H. Cunningham, *Field Medical Services at the Battles of Manassas (Bull Run)*, University of Georgia Monographs, no. 16 (Athens, Ga.: University of Georgia Press, 1968), p. 87.

24. Copp, *Reminiscences of the War of the Rebellion*, pp. 143, 447 [chill of horror]; George F. D. Paine, *How I Left Bull Run Battlefield*, p. 31, quoted in Cunningham, *Field Medical Services* [bullets chug]; Austin C. Stearns, *Three Years with Company K: Sergt. Austin C. Stearns, Company K, 13th Mass. Infantry (Deceased)*, ed. Arthur A. Kent (Rutherford, N.J.: Fairleigh Dickinson University Press, 1976), p. 109 [wounded man].

25. Robertson, *Diary of the War*, p. 182.

26. From Thomas L. Livermore, *Days and Events*, quoted in Commager, ed., *The Blue and the Gray*, p. 222; for a similar incident, see Fuller, *Personal Recollections of the War of 1861*, p. 60.

27. John Johnston memoirs, pp. 30, 74, 138, Confederate Collection, Tennessee

State Archives [running man shot down]; Joseph T. Glatthaar, *Forged in Battle: The Civil War Alliance of Black Soldiers and White Officers* (New York: Meridian Books, 1991), pp. 155–158 [racially motivated atrocities]; Robert Hale Strong, *A Yankee Private's Civil War* (Chicago: Henry Regnery Co., 1961), p. 16 [Fort Pillow]; Bull, *Soldiering,* pp. 155, 136 [deadly sniper fire]; Wladimir Krzyzanowski, *The Memoirs of Wladimir Krzyzanowski,* trans. by Stanley J. Pula, ed. James S. Pula (San Francisco: R & E Research Associates, 1978), p. 49.

28. Franklin H. Bailey to his mother, January 3, 1865, Bentley Historical Library; Victor E. Comte to wife Elise, May 12, 1863, Bentley Historical Library [sparrows]; Elvira J. Powers, *Hospital Pencillings: Being a Diary while in Jefferson General Hospital, Jeffersonville, Ind., and Others at Nashville Tennessee, as Matron and Visitor* (Boston: Edward L. Mitchell, 1866), p. 107 [Negro soldiers killed]; Elijah P. Burton, *Diary of E. P. Burton, Surgeon 7th Reg. Ill. 3rd Brig. 2nd Div. 16 A.C.* (Des Moines, Iowa: Historical Records Survey, 1939), p. 26 [forager killed]; David Wiltsee diary, February 28, 1862, Indiana Historical Society [dead animals]; Michael Fellman, *Inside War: The Guerrilla Conflict in Missouri during the American Civil War* (New York: Oxford University Press, 1989), p. 25 [Quantrill raid]. See also Stephen V. Ash, "Sharks in an Angry Sea: Civilian Resistance and Guerrilla Warfare in Occupied Middle Tennessee, 1862–1865," *Tennessee Historical Quarterly,* 45 (3) (Fall 1986): 217–229; and Gary L. Cheatham, " 'Desperate Characters': The Development and Impact of the Confederate Guerrillas in Kansas," *Kansas History,* 14 (3) (Autumn 1991): 144–161.

29. Horace Charles to unknown, October 23, 1862, Bentley Historical Library [burned houses]; Victor E. Comte to Elise, May 12, 1863, Bentley Historical Library [burning and plundering in retaliation]; William R. Stuckey to unknown, December 19, 1861 [could shoot guerrillas himself], April 27, 1863 [captured mail], Indiana Historical Society; Russell F. Weigley, *Quartermaster General of the Union Army: A Biography of M. C. Meigs* (New York: Columbia University Press, 1959), pp. 307–308 [retribution after Union soldier killed]; Judson L. Austin to wife, Sarah, July 11, 1863, Nina L. Ness Collection, Bentley Historical Library [summary execution]; Reddick, *Seventy-Seven Years in Dixie,* p. 35 [six bushwackers executed]; John Johnston memoirs, p. 39, Confederate Collection, Tennessee State Archives [Union ways].

30. Joseph Dill Alison diary, entry for May 19, 1861, P. K. Yonge Library of Florida History, University of Florida, Gainesville [pale]; John H. Sammons, *Personal Recollections of the Civil War* (Greensburg, Ind.: Montgomery & Son, n.d.), p. 13 [awful]; for the Cundiff case, see affidavits of Henry C. Coffin, May 8, 1893, Harrison Walters, May 8, 1893, Harvey R. Benshan (guardian), June 5, 1894, John A. Jordan, June 6, 1894, James H. Pebworth, June 6, 1894, and L. B. Ashby, June 6, 1894, federal pension file of John A. Cundiff [H 99 Ind. Inf.], National Archives.

31. George W. Campbell case records, Longview Hospital (Cincinnati), Ohio State Archives, Columbus, Ohio. For others adversely affected by Morgan's Raid, see cases 4125 (Lydia M. Shaw) and 4156 (James Johnson), from Case Records, Columbus Hospital for the Insane, Ohio State Archives, Columbus, Ohio. Case no. 1913, Emma D. Lawrence, Case Records, Illinois State Asylum

(Jacksonville State Hospital), Illinois State Archives, Springfield; A. T. Volwiler, "Letters from a Civil War Officer," *Mississippi Valley Historical Review,* 14 (4) (March 1928): 510–521, 512.

32. See Edward A. Strecker, "II. Military Psychiatry: World War I, 1917–1918," in J. Hall, G. Zilboorg, and H. Bunker, eds., *One Hundred Years of American Psychiatry* (New York: Columbia University Press, 1944), pp. 385–416, 385; Harold Wiltshire, "A Contribution to the Etiology of Shell Shock," *Lancet,* 1 (June 17, 1916): 1207–1212; and Eric J. Leed, *No Man's Land; Combat and Identity in World War I* (New York: Cambridge University Press, 1979), pp. 163–192; R. L. Richards, "Mental and Nervous Disease in the Russo-Japanese War," *Military Surgeon,* 26 (1910): 177–193, 179 [mysterious].

33. Bull, *Soldiering,* p. 41; Small, *The Road to Richmond,* pp. 105, 185 ["screaming metal"].

34. Robertson, *Diary of the War,* p. 73 [rabbits]; William B. Miller diary, September 19, 1863 [Chickamauga]; William Lewis McKay memoirs, p. 37, Confederate Collection, Tennessee State Archives ["hugging the ground"]; Calvin Ainsworth diary, p. 42, Bentley Historical Library [canister]. For an explanation of varieties of Civil War artillery, see Wayne Austerman, "Case Shot and Canister: Field Artillery in the Civil War," *Civil War Times Illustrated,* 26 (5) (September 1987): 16–48.

35. John Gibbon, *Personal Recollections of the Civil War* (New York: G. P. Putnam's Sons, 1928), pp. 147–149 [sense of time]; Charles B. Haydon, *For Country, Cause, and Leader: The Civil War Journal of Charles B. Haydon,* ed. Stephen W. Sears (New York: Ticknor & Fields, 1993), p. 306 [two seconds]; Cooke, *Soldier Boy's Letters to His Father and Mother,* p. 75 [bombardment in May, 1864]; Richard Harwell, ed., *A Confederate Marine: A Sketch of Henry Lea Graves with Excerpts from the Graves Family Correspondence, 1861–1865,* Confederate Centennial Studies (Tuscaloosa, Ala.: Confederate Publishing Company, 1963), p. 63 ["death dealing cannon"]; James Garvin Crawford, *"Dear Lizzie,"* ed. Elizabeth Ethel Parker Bascom (privately published, 1978), p. 75 ["belching cannons"]; James L. Cooper memoirs, p. 58, Confederate Collection, Tennessee State Archives ["villainous" artillery]; John Francis Lanneau, "Remembrances of the Civil War," p. 26, South Caroliniana Library ["messenger of death"]; Robert Richardson to his sister, July 7, 1863, Richardson Collection, Georgia State Archives [unprecedented]; Joseph Dill Alison Diary, June 10, 1863, P. K. Yonge Library, University of Florida, Gainesville [Vicksburg]; Abram Hayne Young to sister, May 13, 1862, South Caroliniana Library [can't describe].

36. Jane S. Woolsey, *Hospital Days* (New York: D. Van Nostrand, 1970), p. 112 [man buried at Petersburg]; William Meade Dame, *From the Rapidan to Richmond and the Spottsylvania Campaign* (Baltimore: Green-Lucas Co., 1920), p. 122 [demoralized man]; Ferdinand Davis memoirs, pp. 127–128, 141, Bentley Historical Library [man rendered speechless; terrified officer]; declaration of Albert Frank, June 7, 1884, and affidavit of Henry Moody, October 15, 1884, federal pension file of Albert Frank [B 8 Conn. Inf.], National Archives. For Frank's admission to the Government Hospital for the Insane, see admission number 1707, November 17, 1864, National Archives. For a case of

aphonia, see William W. Keen, S. Weir Mitchell, and George R. Morehouse, "On Malingering, Especially in Regard to Simulation of Diseases of the Nervous System," *American Journal of Medical Sciences* 48 (July-October 1864): 367–394, 383.

37. Affidavits of Allen M. Bridges, February 3, 1888, and Thomas McMahon, February 1, 1888, federal pension file of John Bumgardner [26 Ind. L.A.], National Archives.

38. P. L. Ledford, *Reminiscences of the Civil War, 1861–1865* (Thomasville, N.C.: News Printing House, 1909), p. 67 [grim monster death]; Washington Ives, *Civil War Journal and Letters of Serg. Washington Ives, 4th Florida C.S.A.* (Jim R. Cabanniss, privately published, 1987), p. 44; Ulmer, *Adventures and Reminiscences of a Volunteer*, pp. 40–41 [slumbering camp]; Samuel Elias Mays, *Genealogical Notes on the Family of Mays and Reminiscences of the War between the States* (Plant City, Fla.: Plant City Enterprise, 1927), p. 65 [drowning Yankees].

39. Gervis D. Grainger, *Four Years with the Boys in Gray* (Dayton, Ohio: Morningside Press, 1972; originally published in 1902), p. 21 [bayonets]; Jesse B. Connelly diary, p. 33, Indiana Historical Society [one family]; James L. Cooper, pp. 50–51, Confederate Collection, Tennessee State Archives [Franklin]; J. M. Coleman to Mrs. R. B. Hanna, April 29, 1862, Robert B. Hanna Papers, Indiana Historical Society [enough of war]; DeWitt C. Goodrich memoirs, pp. 113–115, Indiana Historical Society [Shiloh]; Stephen Lampman Lowing to sister, Mary, May 17, 1862, Bentley Historical Library [unwell].

40. Calvin Ainsworth diary, pp. 23–24, Bentley Historical Library.

41. Samuel Futterman and Eugene Pumpian-Mindlin, "Traumatic War Neuroses Five Years Later," *American Journal of Psychiatry*, 108 (1951–1952): 417 [soldiers in graves registration units at risk for traumatic war neuroses]; James E. McCarroll et al., "Symptoms of Posttraumatic Stress Disorder Following Recovery of War Dead," *American Journal of Psychiatry* 150 (12) (December 1993): 1875–1877; Patricia B. Sutker et al., "Psychopathology in War-Zone Deployed and Nondeployed Operation Desert Storm Troops Assigned Graves Registration Duties," *Journal of Abnormal Psychology*, 103 (2) (1994): 383–390 [psychological aftermath of war-zone participation involving the task of handling human remains was profound]; James H. Jones to his parents, January 9, 1863, Indiana Historical Society [pieces of bodies]; William G. Le Duc, *Recollections of a Civil War Quartermaster: The Autobiography of William G. Le Duc* (St. Paul, Minn.: North Central Publishing Company, 1963), p. 77 [unendurable stench]; John Johnston, p. 99, Confederate Collection, Tennessee State Archives [loathsome task].

42. Rufus W. Jacklin, Records of the Military Order of the Loyal Legion of the United States, Michigan Commandery, 1885–1937, p. 14 [valley of death]; Robertson, *Diary of the War*, pp. 23–24 [horrors]; Curtis Buck to unknown, May 23, 1864, Buck Family Papers, Bentley Historical Library [shocking sight]; Eli Augustus Griffin diary, entry of May 3, 1864, Bentley Historical Library [ghastly]; Franklin H. Bailey to parents, April 8, 1862, Bentley Historical Library [shudder]; Judson L. Austin to wife, September 12, 1863, Nina L. Ness Collection, Bentley Historical Library [you would not want to witness].

43. In *Desertion during the Civil War* (Gloucester, Mass.: Peter Smith, 1966), Ella Lonn estimates that there were 103,400 Confederate deserters and 278,644 Union deserters from 1863 to 1865. In *Stop the Evil: A Civil War History of Desertion and Murder* (San Rafael, Calif.: Presidio Press, 1978), p. 77, Robert I. Alotta concludes that nearly 60,000 Union deserters returned to duty, and that the actual number of deserters apprehended and brought to trial is unknown.

44. Joshua Hoyet Frier memoirs, Florida State Archives, Tallahassee [dark ages]; William B. Miller diary, p. 320–321, Indiana Historical Society [murder]; Ferdinand Davis memoirs, pp. 63–64, Bentley Historical Library [shock]; George M. Fredrickson, *The Inner Civil War: Northern Intellectuals and the Crisis of the Union* (New York: Harper and Row, 1965), p. 85.

4. "A Gizzard Full of Sand"

1. James Reston, Jr., *Sherman's March and Vietnam* (New York: Macmillan, 1984), p. 193 [parades]; Gaines M. Foster, "Coming to Terms with Defeat: Post-Vietnam America and the Post-Civil War South," *Virginia Quarterly Review*, 66 (1) (1990): 17–35 [effect of Lost Cause].

2. Francis Wayland Dunn diary, entry for November 20, 1862, Bentley Historical Library [quoits]; DeWitt C. Goodrich memoirs, p. 121, Indiana Historical Society [irreverent]; Charles B. Haydon, *For Country, Cause, and Leader: The Civil War Journal of Charles B. Haydon*, ed. Stephen W. Sears (New York: Ticknor & Fields, 1993), p. 144 [6 months].

3. William G. Le Duc, *Recollections of a Civil War Quartermaster: The Autobiography of William G. Le Duc* (St. Paul, Minn.: North Central Publishing Company, 1963), p. 77 [battle better than death by disease]; William Watson, *Letters of a Civil War Surgeon*, ed. Paul Fatout (West Lafayette, Ind.: Purdue University Studies Humanities Series, 1961), p. 27 [pleasant]; Victor E. Comte to wife, Elise, April 1, 1864, Bentley Historical Library [veterans]; C. Macfarlane, *Reminiscences of an Army Surgeon* (Oswego, N.Y.: Lake City Print Shop, 1912), p. 59 [Petersburg]; Washington Ives, *Civil War Journal and Letters of Serg. Washington Ives, 4th Florida C.S.A.* (Jim R. Cabanniss, privately published, 1987), p. 37 [brains]; Spencer Glasgow Welch, *A Confederate Surgeon's Letters to His Wife* (Marietta, Ga.: Continental Book Co., 1954; originally published in 1911), pp. 16–17 [unconcerned]; W. E. Yeatman memoirs, Confederate Collection, Tennessee State Archives [head rests]; Rice C. Bull, *Soldiering: The Civil War Diary of Rice C. Bull, 123rd New York Volunteer Infantry*, ed. K. Jack Bauer (San Rafael, Calif.: Presidio Press, 1977), p. 234 [Sherman].

4. Ives, *Civil War Journal*, p. 34 [prayer]; Alfred A. Atkins to his parents, June 1, 1864, Georgia State Archives [protected by God]; Melvin Jones, ed., *Give God the Glory: Memoirs of a Civil War Soldier* (privately published, 1979), p. 61 [fatalism]; Victor E. Comte to his wife, Elise, November 6, 1863, Bentley Historical Library [odds]; Abner R. Small, *The Road to Richmond: The Civil War Memoirs of Major Abner R. Small of the Sixteenth Maine Volunteers, Together with the Diary Which He Kept When He Was a Prisoner of War*, ed. Harold Adams Small (Berkeley: University of California Press, 1939), p. 186 [invulnerabil-

ity]; Henry W. Reddick, *Seventy-Seven Years in Dixie: The Boys in Gray of 61–65* (Santa Rosa, Fla.: H. W. Reddick, 1910).

5. Ives, *Civil War Journal*, pp. 35, 37, 40, 49 [sad]; John Johnston memoirs, p. 139, Confederate Collection, Tennessee State Archives [Hood's men]; F. P. Fleming to Aunt Tilly, July 28, 1862, P. K. Yonge Library of Florida History, University of Florida, Gainesville [Seven Days]; Wade Hampton to Mrs. M. R. Singleton, September 5, 1861, Hampton Family Papers, South Caroliniana Library; Carroll Henderson Clark memoirs, p. 26, Confederate Collection, Tennessee State Archives [Perryville].

6. William B. Miller journal, p. 36, Indiana Historical Society [feelings]; Judson L. Austin to wife, March 4, 1863, Nina Ness Collection, Bentley Historical Library [Dying Brother].

7. Thomas D. Duncan, *Recollections of Thomas D. Duncan, A Confederate Soldier* (Nashville, Tenn.: McQuiddy Printing Co., 1922), pp. 136–137 [younger brother]; Louis C. Duncan, *The Medical Department of the United States Army in the Civil War* (Department of Defense, 1917), p. 32 [trenches and individual graves]; William Baird memoirs, p. 18, Bentley Historical Library [pine boughs, handkerchiefs]; James Houghton memoirs, pp. 16–17, Bentley Historical Library [preparation of the dead]; John Johnston memoirs, p. 16, Confederate Collection, Tennessee State Archives [sadness]; John Beatty, *Memoirs of a Volunteer, 1861–1863*, ed. Harvey S. Ford (New York: W. W. Norton, 1946), p. 139 [convulsive sobs].

8. *Combat Exhaustion*, quoted in John Keegan, *The Face of Battle* (New York: Random House, 1976), p. 329.

9. James Richmond Boulware diary, entry for July 10, 1862, South Caroliniana Library [fatigue and exhaustion]; David Ballenger to Nancy, October 29, 1864, South Caroliniana Library ["extreme fatigues of a battle"].

10. Joseph Taylor Smith to Netti, October 19, 1863, Indiana Historical Society [Chickamauga]; Charles A. Fuller, *Personal Recollections of the War of 1861* (Sherburne, N.Y.: News Job Printing House, 1906), p. 20 [trembling]; Franklin H. Bailey to parents, April 8, 1862, Bentley Historical Library [shudder]; Erasmus C. Gilbreath Papers, p. 102, Indiana Historical Library [even the bravest].

11. Franklin H. Bailey to parents, April 8, 1862, Bentley Historical Library [shudder]; A. T. Volwiler, "Letters from a Civil War Officer," *Mississippi Valley Historical Review*, 14 (4) (March 1928): 515–517 [Samuel Merrill]; *War Letters of Aden G. Cavins*, p. 75, 91, 93, Indiana State Historical Library [strange that I am alive]; Milo M. Quaife, ed., *The Civil War Letters of General Alpheus S. Williams: From the Cannon's Mouth* (Detroit: Wayne State University Press and the Detroit Historical Society, 1959), pp. 307, 333, 309.

12. Quaife, ed., *The Civil War Letters of General Alpheus S. Williams*, p. 333. In general, see James Lee McDonough and James Pickett Jones, *War So Terrible: Sherman and Atlanta* (New York: Norton, 1987); Albert Castel, *Decision in the West: The Atlanta Campaign of 1864* (Lawrence: University of Kansas Press, 1992); and John F. Marszalek, *Sherman: A Soldier's Passion for Order* (New York: Free Press, 1993).

13. For the casualty estimate of 65,000, see James M. McPherson, *Battle Cry of*

Freedom (New York: Oxford University Press, 1988), 742; Thomas L. Livermore, *Numbers and Losses in the Civil War in America, 1861–65* (Bloomington: Indiana University Press, 1957; originally published in 1900), estimates casualties (killed and wounded) from the Wilderness, Spotsylvania, Cold Harbor, and Petersburg at about 44,553, but his numbers understate the true magnitude of loss in that they omit several engagements and do not count the missing as part of total casualties; Bruce Catton, *Never Call Retreat* (New York: Washington Square Books, 1965), p. 343 [Bloody Angle], 347 [Cold Harbor]; Surgeon General Joseph K. Barnes, U.S. Army, ed., *The Medical and Surgical History of the War of the Rebellion (1861–65)* (Washington, D.C.: U.S. Government Printing Office, 1870), pt. I, Medical Volume, Appendix, p. 150 [self-mutilation]; Spencer Glasgow Welch, *A Confederate Surgeon's Letters to His Wife* (Marietta, Ga.: Continental Book Co., 1954; originally published in 1911), p. 97 [impressions of Bloody Angle]. In general, see William D. Matter, *If It Takes All Summer: The Battle of Spotsylvania* (Chapel Hill: University of North Carolina Press, 1988).

14. John G. Perry, *Letters from a Surgeon of the Civil War*, ed. Martha Derby Perry (Boston: Little, Brown and Co., 1906), pp. 188–189 [sharpshooters]; Joseph C. Carter, *Magnolia Journey: A Union Veteran Revisits the Former Confederate States*, arranged from letters of correspondent Russell H. Conwell to the *Daily Evening Traveller* (Boston, 1869) (University: University of Alabama Press, 1974), p. 18 [death familiar]; Watson, *Letters of a Civil War Surgeon*, ed. Fatout, p. 84 [played out]; John Putnam diary, entry for October 16, 1864, South Caroliniana Library [gun proofs].

15. Claudia J. Dewane, "Posttraumatic Stress Disorder in Medical Personnel in Vietnam," *Hospital and Community Psychiatry*, 35 (12) (December 1984): 1232–1234; Barbara Rogers and Janet Nickolaus, "Vietnam Nurses," *Journal of Psychosocial Nursing*, 25 (4) (1987): 11–15; Rodney R. Baker, Shirley W. Menard, and Lois A. Johns, "The Military Nurse Experience in Vietnam: Stress and Impact," *Journal of Clinical Psychology*, 45 (5) (September 1989): 736–744; and Elizabeth M. Norman, "After the Casualties: Vietnam Nurses' Identities and Career Decisions," *Nursing Research*, 41 (2) (March/April 1992): 110–113. In the popular media, see "The Nurses of Vietnam, Still Wounded, Only Now Are They Healing Themselves," *New York Times Magazine*, November 7, 1993, pp. 36–43 +.

16. For general descriptions, see Horace H. Cunningham, *Field Medical Services at the Battles of Manassas (Bull Run)* (Athens: University of Georgia Press, 1968), p. 16; James O. Breeden, "The 'Forgotten Man' of the Civil War: the Southern Experience," *Bulletin of the New York Academy of Medicine*, 55 (7) (July-August 1979): 652–669; and W. W. Blackford, *War Years with Jeb Stuart* (New York: Scribner's, 1945), pp. 27–28; Philip A. Kalisch and Beatrice J. Kalisch, "Untrained but Undaunted: The Women Nurses of the Blue and the Gray," *Nursing Forum*, 15 (1) (1976): 4–33; Kate Cumming, *The Journal of Kate Cumming; A Confederate Nurse, 1862–1865*, ed. Richard Harwell (Savannah, Ga.: Beehive Press, 1975), pp. 5–6 [horrors]; William E. Boggs to Jane Ann Smyth, July 26, 1861, Adger-Smythe-Flynn Family Papers, South Caroliniana Library [saddest day].

17. Mary Boykin Chesnut, *A Diary from Dixie* (Gloucester, Mass.: Peter Smith, 1961; originally published in 1905), p. 108 [close eyes]; George T. Ulmer, *Adventures and Reminiscences of a Volunteer, or a Drummer Boy from Maine* (1892), p. 59 [arms and legs]; Bull, *Soldiering*, p. 25 [lasting impression]; Amanda Akin Stearns, *The Lady Nurse of Ward E* (New York: Baker and Taylor, 1909), p. 255.

18. Cumming, *The Journal of Kate Cumming*, pp. 6–8, 10, 15, 25, 30, 98, 116, 124, 246, 284.

19. James Houghton journal, pp. 15–16, Bentley Historical Library [steel nerve]; and Macfarlane, *Reminiscences of an Army Surgeon*, p. 16 [first patient].

20. Perry, *Letters from a Surgeon of the Civil War*, pp. 175 [exhausted], 184 [nervous], 187 [heartsick], 207–209 [maelstrom].

21. C. T. Quintard, *Doctor Quintard, Chaplain C.S.A. and Second Bishop of Tennessee: Being His Story of the War (1861–1865)*, ed. A. H. Noll (Sewanee, Tenn.: University Press of Sewanee, 1905), pp. 60–61; Welch, *A Confederate Surgeon's Letters to His Wife*, p. 52 [drinking].

22. Gilbert W. Beebe, "Follow-Up Studies of World War II and Korean War Prisoners: II. Morbidity, Disability, and Maladjustments," *American Journal of Epidemiology*, 101 (5) (May 1975): 400–422, 403 [numbers]; Raina E. Eberly and Brian E. Engdahl, "Prevalence of Somatic and Psychiatric Disorders among Former Prisoners of War," *Hospital and Community Psychiatry*, 42 (8) (August 1991): 807–813 [types of injuries]; M. Dean Nefzger, "Follow-Up Studies of World War II and Korean War Prisoners: I. Study Plan and Mortality Findings," *American Journal of Epidemiology*, 91 (2) (January 1970): 123–138; Alden V. Halloran, "Comparison of World War II, Korean, and Vietnamese Prisoners of War," *Minnesota Medicine*, 53 (8) (August 1970): 919–922.

23. Patricia B. Sutker et al., "Person and Situation Correlates of Post-Traumatic Stress Disorder Among POW Survivors," *Psychological Reports*, 66 (1990): 912–914 [46 percent to 90 percent]; John C. Kluznik et al., "Forty-Year Follow-Up of United States Prisoners of War," *American Journal of Psychiatry*, 143 (11) (November 1986): 1443–1446 [67 percent met PTSD criteria at some point since repatriation]; Robert A. Zeiss and Harold R. Dickman, "PTSD 40 Years Later: Incidence and Person-Situation Correlates in Former POWs," *Journal of Clinical Psychology*, 45 (1) (January 1989), 80–87 [55.7 percent]; Gerald Goldstein et al., "Survivors of Imprisonment in the Pacific Theater during World War II," *American Journal of Psychiatry*, 144 (9) (September 1987): 1210–1213, 1213 [50 percent for Japanese-held POWs]; Nancy Speed et al., "Posttraumatic Stress Disorder as a Consequence of the POW Experience," *Journal of Nervous and Mental Disease*, 177 (3) (1989): 147–153 [strongest predictors were proportion of body weight lost and torture]. In general, see William Frank Page, *The Health of Former Prisoners of War: Results from the Medical Examination Survey of Former POWs of World War II and the Korean Conflict* (Washington, D.C.: National Academy Press, 1992).

24. Beebe, "Follow-Up Studies of World War II and Korean War Prisoners," p. 404 [weight loss]; Eberly and Engdahl, "Prevalence of Somatic and Psychiatric Disorders among Former Prisoners of War," pp. 807–813 [higher rates of psychopathology].

25. Rice Bull, *Soldiering*, p. 63 [kind treatment]; Oliver C. Haskell diary, n.d. [August 1862?], Indiana Historical Society [kind treatment]; James Greacen, "Fourteen Months and Ten Days as a Prisoner of War during the Rebellion: 'Life in Southern Prisons' " (Kalkaska, Mich., n.d.) [lined up]; John H. Sammons, *Personal Recollections of the Civil War* (Greensburg, Ind.: Montgomery & Son, n.d.), p. 47 [taunted by southern citizens].

26. Greacen, "Fourteen Months and Ten Days" [dead line]; Luther S. Trowbridge, "Light and Shadows of the Civil War," *War Papers Read before the Michigan Commandery of the Military Order of the Loyal Legion of the United States*, vol. 2, from December 7, 1893, to May 5, 1898 (Detroit: James H. Stone & Co., 1898), p. 102 [deliberate suicide of some POWs]; Melvin Grigsby, *The Smoked Yank* (Chicago: Regan, 1891), p. 114 [dead line]; John L. Maile, *Prison Life in Andersonville* (Los Angeles, Calif.: Grafton Publishing Co., 1912), p. 31 [killing on the dead line]; John M. Porter memoirs, p. 130, Confederate Collection, Tennessee State Archives [dead line in Union POW camps].

27. Small, *The Road to Richmond*, p. 172 [fixed stare]; Macfarlane, *Reminiscences of an Army Surgeon*, p. 73 [pitiful mass]; *Opium Eating: An Autobiographical Sketch*, by An Habituate (Philadelphia: Claxton, Remsen & Haffelfinger, 1976), p. 55 [black midnight]; Sammons, *Personal Recollections of the Civil War*, pp. 44, 40 [insanity].

28. John M. Porter memoirs, pp. 127–128, Confederate Collection, Tennessee State Archives [Sandusky Bay]; James T. Wells, "Diary of a Confederate Soldier and Recollections of a Federal Prison during the War," no pagination, South Caroliniana Library [moon blindness, etc.; hostages]; Charles M. McGee, Jr., and Ernest M. Lander, Jr., eds., *A Rebel Came Home* (Columbia: University of South Carolina Press, 1961), pp. 89–90 [loss of hope for southern POWs]; William Spencer, "Seven Months in Libby Prison," pp. 27–29, Indiana Historical Society [retaliatory hanging threatened].

29. Oliver Lyman Spaulding, "Military Memoirs of Brigadier General Oliver L. Spaulding," p. 66, Bentley Historical Library [sorry spectacle]; declaration of Samuel M. Gordon, 1885 [scurvy]; affidavit of David I. Spencer, March 29, 1886 [leaden look]; affidavit of J. R. Glenis, M.D., March 23, 1886 ["horible wreck"], federal pension file of Samuel M. Gordon [G 82 Ind. Inf.], National Archives; affidavit of Patrick Harrington, March 11, 1884, federal pension file of John Dugan [B 35 Ind. Inf.], National Archives [didn't think he would live].

30. See declaration of Jason Roberts, January 6, 1887; affidavit of Maria F. Roberts, January 6, 1887, in the federal pension file for Jason Robert [B 5 Ind. Cav.], National Archives; for the commitment to the Indiana Hospital for the Insane, see commitment no. 6944 (February 1, 1886), Indiana State Archives.

31. For the inquest papers to Jason Roberts's commitment to the Indiana Hospital for the Insane in 1886, see the file at the Indiana State Archives. For testimony of neighbors and the special examiner on his condition, see affidavits of H. C. Leeson, January 7, 1887 ["wild looks"]; Silas H. Kersey, M.D., January 7, 1887 ["very eccentric"]; William F. King, M.D., January 7, 1887 ["monomaniac on religion"]; J. H. Gentry, January 7, 1887 ["wild & incoherent"]; Joseph A. Bowen, January 7, 1887 [talks of sufferings in prison]; John

W. Sullivan and Madison Sullivan, June 15, 1886 [Roberts was in wretched condition on return from service]; federal pension file of Jason Roberts [B 5 Ind. Cav.], National Archives.

32. Affidavit of James M. Carvin, M.D., February 14, 1887 [constitution]; Josephine Alexander, February 18, 1887 [sister]; federal pension file of Erastus Holmes [F 5 Ind. Cav.], National Archives.

33. Affidavits of Emma F. Berry, February 11, 1887 [daughter]; and Maurice J. Barry, March 15, 1887 [son-in-law]; federal pension file of Erastus Holmes [F 5 Ind. Cav.], National Archives.

34. Affidavits of Mrs. Lucy J. Patterson, April 16, 1887 [neighbor]; Emma F. Berry, February 11, 1887 [daughter]; pension medical board reports, July 24, 1891, and December 5, 1892; federal pension file of Erastus Holmes [F 5 Ind. Cav.], National Archives.

35. Elbridge J. Copp, *Reminiscences of the War of the Rebellion, 1861–1865* (Nashua, N.H.: Telegraph Publishing Co., 1911), p. 395 [puzzled].

36. DeWitt C. Goodrich memoirs, p. 138, Indiana Historical Society [home leave]; Charles Beneulyn Johnson, M.D., *Muskets and Medicine, or Army Life in the Sixties* (Philadelphia: F. A. Davis Co., 1917), p. 176 [burning desire]; Gervis D. Grainger, *Four Years with the Boys in Gray* (Dayton, Ohio: Morningside Press, 1972; originally published in 1902), p. 32 [monotonous quiet]; James W. Willett diary, entry for June 12, 1864, Bentley Historical Library [painful stillness]; Cumming, *The Journal of Kate Cumming*, p. 30 [sense of purpose].

37. In general, see James M. McPherson, *Ordeal by Fire: The Civil War and Reconstruction* (New York: McGraw-Hill, 1992), pp. 248–250 [paradox]. See muster roll records, Indiana State Archives, and federal pension records and federal service records, National Archives, for John O. Todd [A 53 Ind. Inf.; B 117 Ind. Inf.; C 148 Ind. Inf.] and William Stoneking [F 35 Ind. Inf.]. For the statement concerning Stoneking's insanity, see affidavit of Martin Stoneking, July 17, 1890 (brother and guardian), and army discharge papers, June 18, 1862, federal pension file of William Stoneking [F 35 Ind. Inf.]. Aurelius Lyman Voorhis diary, entry for September 30, 1862, Indiana Historical Society [surprised]; Haydon, *For Country, Cause, and Leader*, pp. 33–34 [attractions].

38. Perry, *Letters from a Surgeon of the Civil War*, pp. 100–101 [never better]; Elbridge Copp, *Reminiscences of the War of the Rebellion, 1861–1865*, p. 139 [magnificent]; Nelson Stauffer, "Civil War Diary" (California State University, Northridge, Libraries, 1976), pp. 140–141 [thrill]; Carter, *Magnolia Journey*, p. 7 [charm]. For a suggestion that veterans engaged in selective recall in romanticizing their war experience, see Gerald F. Linderman, *Embattled Courage: The Experience of Combat in the American Civil War* (New York: Free Press, 1987), pp. 266–297. For comparative statistics on desertion, reenlistment, and casualty rates, see W. H. H. Terrell, *Report of the Adjutant General of the State of Indiana* (Indianapolis: W. R. Holloway, State Printer, 1865).

5. "For God's Sake Please Help Me"

1. W. Claude Herndon to sister, December 10, 1861, Georgia State Archives [pleasant moments]; James Morris Bivings to mother, December 21, 1861,

South Caroliniana Library [waited]; Morris Stuart Hall memoirs, p. 23, Bentley Historical Library [deeper interest; weeping soldier]; Adolphus Origen Mitchell to parents, November 18, 1862, Indiana Historical Society [three times]; David Lane, *A Soldier's Diary: The Story of a Volunteer, 1862–1865* (privately published, 1905), p. 179 [hope]; John Franklin Reiger, "Anti-War and Pro-Union Sentiment in Confederate Florida" (M.A. thesis, University of Florida, 1966), p. 80 [wives' letters].

2. Ferdinand Davis memoirs, p. 170, Bentley Historical Library [bounty agents]; Roderick Gospero Shaw diary, entry for October 9, 1861, Florida State Archives, Tallahassee, Florida [profiteers]; Alfred A. Atkins to unknown, March 12, 1863, Georgia State Archives [copperheads]; Richard DeTreville, Jr., to friend Berwick, March 11, 1867, South Caroliniana Library [politicians]; Magnus Brucker to wife, September 18, 1864, Indiana Historical Library [traitors]; and Edgar Richardson to sister, January 18, 1862, Richardson Collection, Georgia State Archives [professional patriots].

3. Rice C. Bull, *Soldiering: The Civil War Diary of Rice C. Bull, 123rd New York Volunteer Infantry*, ed. K. Jack Bauer (San Rafael, Calif.: Presidio Press), p. 85 [how little]; William Watson, *Letters of a Civil War Surgeon*, ed. Paul Fatout (West Lafayette, Ind.: Purdue University Studies Humanities Series, 1961), pp. 23–24 [few at home]; Victor E. Comte to wife, Elise, April 20, 1864, Bentley Historical Library [impossible]; Joseph M. Rabb to sister, February 7, 1864, Indiana Historical Society [nobody at home]; Joseph M. Rabb to mother, March 5, 1865, Indiana Historical Society [debt]; David Ballenger to brother, May 13, 1863, South Caroliniana Library [hard times].

4. James C. Stephens diary, pp. 164–165, Indiana Historical Society.

5. Bull, *Soldiering*, pp. 240–241 [wild]; Nelson Stauffer, "Civil War Diary" (California State University, Northridge, Libraries, 1976), entry for April 12, 1865 [tears of joy]; James L. Cooper memoirs, p. 65, Confederate Collection, Tennessee State Archives [mirth].

6. George T. Ulmer, *Adventures and Reminiscences of a Volunteer, or a Drummer Boy from Maine* (1892), p. 76 [royal welcome]; Austin C. Stearns, *Three Years with Company K: Sergt. Austin C. Stearns, Company K, 13th Mass. Infantry (Deceased)*, ed. Arthur A. Kent (Rutherford, N.J.: Fairleigh Dickinson University Press, 1976), pp. 308–309 [Boston]; David Wiltsee diary, vol. III, entries for September 30 and October 8, 1865, Indiana Historical Library [Wabash]; Calvin Ainsworth diary, p. 99, Bentley Historical Library [wife].

7. Dixon Wecter, *When Johnny Comes Marching Home* (Westport, Conn.: Greenwood Press, 1944), pp. 125–128; Hermon Clarke, *Back Home in Oneida: Hermon Clarke and His Letters*, ed. Harry F. Jackson and Thomas F. O'Donnell (Syracuse: Syracuse University Press, 1965), p. 205 [hero].

8. Gervis D. Grainger, *Four Years with the Boys in Gray* (Dayton, Ohio: Morningside Press, 1972; originally published in 1902), p. 31 [Ulysses]; Newton Cannon memoirs, Confederate Collection, Tennessee State Archives [supper].

9. Carroll Henderson Clark memoirs, pp. 54 [mocked], 55 [couldn't vote], Confederate Collection, Tennessee State Archives; Nathaniel Francis Cheairs memoirs, p. 8, Confederate Collection, Tennessee State Archives [plantation wrecked]; Charles M. McGee, Jr., and Ernest M. Lander, Jr., eds., *A Rebel Came*

Home (Columbia: University of South Carolina Press, 1961), p. 92 [crushed]; Sarah Jane Johnston Estes diary, p. 17, Confederate Collection, Tennessee State Archives [wretchedness]; "Insanity in the South," *Nashville Daily Press,* July 16, 1865, p. 2 [dozens]. At the South Carolina State Archives, see the commitment papers of Harriet Bibb, July 3, 1863 [son killed]; Martha Harbin, March 28, 1864 [husband killed]; Alan F. Festner, February 18, 1868 [POW]; Pinckney Hogan, June 19, 1867 [POW]. Georgia state insane asylum records, Georgia State Archives; see cases (no numbers) for John C. Sharp, April 26, 1866 [Sherman POW]; John Smith, October 7, 1866 [loss of everything]; Hugh Lewis, August 25, 1868 [mind affected]; Captain William J. Dixon, May 4, 1869 [chagrined]; John B. Williams, August 21, 1871 [constantly frightened].

10. William Boston, *Civil War Diary* (privately published), p. 193 [splendid]; F. Schneider to Edwin J. March, June 21, 1865, Bentley Historical Library [everyone delighted]; John Milton Bancroft diary, p. 8, Bentley Historical Library [tedious]; Charles B. Haydon, *For Country, Cause, and Leader: The Civil War Journal of Charles B. Haydon,* ed. Stephen W. Sears (New York: Ticknor & Fields, 1993), p. 114 [fine sight]; Henry G. Noble to Ruth, May 26, 1865, Bentley Historical Library [much dreaded]; Jane S. Woolsey, *Hospital Days* (New York: D. Van Nostrand, 1970), pp. 176–177 [men disliked]; Melvin Jones, ed., *Give God the Glory: Memoirs of a Civil War Soldier* (privately published, 1979), p. 144 [chicken fixings]. For an account of a man falling ill from marching in a grand review at war's end, see federal pension file for William B. Daugherty [C 156 and I 134 Ind. Inf.], National Archives [declaration of October 27, 1887].

11. Abner R. Small, *The Road to Richmond: The Civil War Memoirs of Major Abner R. Small of the Sixteenth Maine Volunteers, Together with the Diary Which He Kept When He Was a Prisoner of War,* ed. Harold Adams Small (Berkeley: University of California Press, 1939), p. 183 [hard; parents]; Bull, *Soldiering,* p. 249; Carroll Henderson Clark memoirs, p. 53, Confederate Collection, Tennessee State Archives [tears].

12. William Henry Younts memoirs, pp. 98–100, Indiana Historical Society; Hillel Glover, "Survival Guilt and the Vietnam Veteran," *Journal of Nervous and Mental Disease,* 172 (7) (1984): 393–397.

13. Regarding prison commitments, see Edith Abbott, "Crime and the War," *Journal of the American Institute of Criminal Law and Criminology* (May 1918): 32–45; Betty B. Rosenbaum, "The Relationship between War and Crime in the United States," ibid., (January 1940): 722–740; and Willard Waller, *The Veteran Comes Back* (New York: Dryden Press, 1944), p. 125. "Annual Report of the Metropolitan Police Commissioners for the Year 1865," *New York Times,* January 5, 1866, p. 4 [rough material]; "Suicide of a Returned Veteran," *New York Times,* February 25, 1866, p. 5 [suicide]; "Burglary—John Delmont," *New York Times,* January 25, 1866, p. 8 [Confederate]; *Indianapolis Daily Herald,* January 13, 1866, p. 2 [attempted murder]; *Indianapolis Daily Herald,* March 23, 1866, p. 2 [insanity defense]; *Indianapolis Daily Herald,* January 29, 1866, p. 4 [Mars].

14. Kate Cumming, *The Journal of Kate Cumming; A Confederate Nurse, 1862–1865,* ed. Richard Harwell (Savannah, Ga.: Beehive Press, 1975), p. 269 [hanged

wife]; Charles M. McGee, Jr., and Ernest M. Lander, Jr., eds., *A Rebel Came Home* (Columbia: University of South Carolina Press, 1961), p. 94 [called out at night]; "Fiendish Outrages," *Nashville Daily Union*, September 8, 1865, p. 2 [castration; rape]; "More Guerrilla Operations. Robberies and Murders near Nashville. Stringent Measures Demanded Immediately," *Nashville Daily Union*, September 27, 1865, p. 6; "Disgraceful," *Southern Recorder* (Milledgeville, Ga.), May 9, 1865 [commissary stores]; "Reported Outrage," *Macon Daily Telegraph*, May 12, 1865, p. 1 [sacked]; "More Plundering," *Macon Daily Telegraph*, May 12, 1865, p. 2 [train]; "Violating Parole and Punishment," *Macon Daily Telegraph*, May 18, 1865, p. 1 [destruction of railroads]; "Killed," *Abbeville (S.Car.) Bulletin*, August 24, 1865 [Union soldier]. Newspaper headlines are from the *Macon Daily Telegraph*, for August 22, 1865, p. 3 ["A Night of Terror"], September 1, 1865, p. 2 ["Disorder in Alabama"], September 5, 1865 ["Guerillas in Mississippi"], and September 10, 1865, p. 2 ["Reign of Terror in East Tennessee"]. "The Reign of Violence," *Confederate Union* (Milledgeville, Ga.), December 12, 1865, p. 4. Diary of Clara W. Adger, entry for December 22, 1865, Adger and Bowen Families Papers, South Caroliniana Library [decent citizens]. Regarding violence in the South, see Dan T. Carter, *When the War Was Over: The Failure of Self-Reconstruction in the South, 1865–1867* (Baton Rouge, La.: Louisiana State University Press, 1985), p. 19.

15. Richard Maxwell Brown, *Strain of Violence; Historical Studies of American Violence and Vigilantism* (New York: Oxford University Press, 1975), pp. 9–12.

16. Without question the diagnostic picture of these men is complicated, and a full work-up within the DSM structure would result in multiple diagnoses; nonetheless, one suspects that if a retrospective examination were possible that PTSD would be an appropriate diagnosis in many of these cases.

17. Commitment no. 5039, August 30, 1872, Indiana Hospital for the Insane, Indiana State Archives; affidavits of Scott Boswell, May 9, 1895, and February 2, 1895, federal pension file of Elijah Boswell [B 68 Ind. Inf.], National Archives; inquest papers for Demarcus L. Hedges, commitment no. 9193, August 26, 1892, Indiana State Archives; inquest papers for Henry C. Carr, commitment no. 10588, April 1, 1898, Indiana State Archives [plan of defense]; inquest papers for Titus C. Jones, commitment no. 7949, August 14, 1888, Indiana State Archives; inquest papers for Leo C. Griffith, commitment no. 8308, September 15, 1889, Indiana State Archives; inquest papers for Hickman Dean, commitment no. 9376, August 16, 1893, Indiana State Archives [protection; threat to kill]; inquest papers for Michael Decamp, commitment no. 8454, April 2, 1890, Indiana State Archives [suicide attempt].

18. Affidavit of Jacob M. Shandy, January 9, 1889 (employer), federal pension file of William Dennis [E 6 Ind. Inf.], National Archives [axe]; affidavit of Harvey R. Benshan, June 5, 1894; federal pension file of John A. Cundiff [H 99 Ind. Inf.], National Archives [axe]; inquest papers of Squire Ridgeway, commitment no. 5414, May 29, 1882, Indiana State Archives [knife/axe]; inquest papers of Robert M. Higgins, commitment no. 5488, January 31, 1874, Indiana State Archives [slept with revolver] [nonsample]; inquest papers of Jacob Fink, commitment no. 5320, March 6, 1882, Indiana State Archives [fort]; affidavits of James Guile (guardian), March 5, 1895, and Anna Com-

stock (niece), April 5, 1895, federal pension file of William H. Guile [I 63 and H 128 Ind. Inf.], National Archives; inquest papers of Elias Hammon, commitment no. 6020, November 17, 1883, Indiana State Archives.

19. Affidavit of Anna Britton (wife), September 23, 1890; federal pension record of John C. Britton [F 10 Ind. Inf.], National Archives; inquest papers of Oliver Grayless, commitment no. 5458, June 27, 1882, Indiana State Archives [going out in fields]; affidavits of Logan Stanley (doctor), July 12, 1889, and Ren Carpenter (son), November 2, 1894, federal pension file of Rufus C. Carpenter [B 54 Ind. Inf.], National Archives; inquest papers of Lewis H. Chowning, commitment no. 8010, November 9, 1888, Indiana State Archives.

20. Affidavits of John McFetridge, May 11, 1895 [shunned], and Eli Williams (soldier/neighbor), May 11, 1895 [acquaintances]; affidavit of Harvey M. McCaskey and Andrew [Gemmill?], August 12, 1889; federal pension file of Jesse Downs [D 34 Ind. Inf.], National Archives [leave room]; federal pension file of Elijah Boswell [B 68 Ind. Inf.], National Archives; inquest papers of Arthur Brenton, commitment no. 10115, June 14, 1896, Indiana State Archives [utterly alone]; commitment ledger and inquest papers of Michael Cassidy, commitment no. 12334, July 24, 1903, Indiana State Archives; affidavit of M. L. Kellogg, September 1, 1887; federal pension file of Edwin Kellogg [H 129 Ind. Inf.], National Archives; inquest papers of Edwin Kellogg, commitment no. 6974, February 24, 1886, Indiana State Archives.

21. Affidavits of Thomas McMahon, February 1, 1888 [army incident], and Charlotte (wife), June 24, 1890 [trembling]; federal pension file of John Bumgardner [26th Ind. L.A.], National Archives.

22. Affidavits of Margaret Johns (wife), February 10, 1893 [fever and roof], Sarah A. Prichard, May 20, 1895 [brothers]; Benjamin Boren, July 16, 1896 [army], and Thomas D. Mills, June 6, 1898 [army]; federal pension file of Rany Johns [A 101 Ind. Inf.], National Archives.

23. See affidavits of James H. Boyd, August 5, 1896, W. S. Kincaid, August 5, 1896, and Hiram Corns, August 7, 1896; federal pension file of John Corns [D 10 Ind. Cav.], National Archives.

24. Affidavit of Dr. Levi Conner, June 24, 1889; federal pension file of Howard Creed [E 37 Ind. Inf.], National Archives [impending]; records for Howard Creed from the Northern Indiana Hospital for the Insane, Logansport, Indiana, commitment no. 375–397, February 10, 1889, Indiana State Archives [dire calamity]; papers pertaining to Ephraim H. Goss, commitment no. 8448, March 24, 1890, records of the Indiana Hospital for the Insane, Indiana State Archives [suicide].

25. Small, *The Road to Richmond*, p. viii; Joseph C. Carter, *Magnolia Journey: A Union Veteran Revisits the Former Confederate States*, arranged from letters of correspondent Russell H. Conwell to the *Daily Evening Traveller* (Boston, 1869) (University: University of Alabama Press, 1974), p. 23 [skeletons]; Judson L. Austin Papers, Nina Ness Collection, Bentley Historical Library.

26. Affidavits of Dr. Henry K. Deen, September 8, 1898 [brooding], and Jasper Inman, 9/8/98 [spells of despondency]; federal pension file of John Agnew [C 50 and E 144 Ind. Inf.], National Archives; federal pension file of Owen Flaherty [C 135 Ill. Inf.], National Archives; inquest papers of John W. Robin-

son, commitment no. 10450, October 1, 1897, Indiana Hospital for the Insane, Indiana State Archives [very much depressed].

27. Inquest papers of Henry Barnhart, commitment no. 7906, July 12, 1888, Indiana Hospital for the Insane, Indiana State Archives [cry at intervals]; inquest papers of John Emory Bastin, commitment no. 9047, December 6, 1891, Indiana Hospital for the Insane, Indiana State Archives [weeps bitterly]; inquest papers of Josiah Markey, commitment no. 8142, March 27, 1889, Indiana Hospital for the Insane, Indiana State Archives [weeps without cause].

28. Special examiner's summary, May 25, 1885 ["hystero-epileptic" spells], federal pension file of Ephram M. Goodwin [I 149 Ind. Inf.], National Archives; inquest papers of D.W. Kingery, commitment no. 8361, November 18, 1889, Indiana Hospital for the Insane, Indiana State Archives [Globus Hystericus]; inquest papers for John Agnew, commitment no. 7677, November 29, 1887, Indiana Hospital for the Insane, Indiana State Archives ["Wants to be always on the move"]; inquest papers for Robert S. Byers, commitment no. 8323, October 5, 1889, Indiana Hospital for the Insane, Indiana State Archives [very nervous and excitable]; affidavit of Benson Douglass, June 9, 1891 ["When excited He would shake with apparent Nervousness"], federal pension file of Lewis H. Chowning [I 43 Ind. Inf.], National Archives; affidavit of John Shelk, April 5, 1895 ["his knees shake and seems to shake all over"], federal pension file of William H. Guile [I 63 & H 128 Ind. Inf.], National Archives; report of medical board, May 6, 1885 ["gets to trembling and shaking"], federal pension file of Edwin Kellog [H 129 Ind. Inf.], National Archives; inquest papers of Ralph Platt, commitment no. 9057, December 21, 1891, Indiana Hospital for the Insane, Indiana State Archives [very nervous manner]; affidavit of Dr. J. H. Reynolds, November 16, 1888 [frantic], federal pension file of Dixon Irwin [B and D 13 Ind. Inf.], National Archives; pension claim of Lucian A. Gray [C 13 Ind. Cav.], National Archives [smothering spells].

29. Inquest papers for Alexander Blythe, commitment no. 5241, December 23, 1881, Indiana Hospital for the Insane, Indiana State Archives [corpse]; commitment of Thomas Dawson, commitment no. II/162, April 29, 1891, Northern Hospital for the Insane, Logansport, Indiana, Indiana State Archives [heinous]; inquest papers of Peter Reed, commitment no. 5460, June 27, 1862, Indiana State Hospital, Indiana State Archives [great crimes]; inquest papers of David Wiltsee, commitment no. 7756, March 6, 1888, Indiana Hospital for the Insane, Indiana State Archives [something terrible].

30. Affidavit of I. J. Hopper, M.D., March 1, 1899, federal pension file of William Churchill [F 59 Ind. Inf. & Com. Sgt. 59 Ind. Inf.], National Archives; William A. Ketcham memoirs, pp. 7 [glad], 12 [grateful], Indiana Historical Society.

31. Declaration by John C. Britton, January 14, 1888, federal pension file of John C. Britton [F 10 Ind. Inf.], National Archives; declaration by William Churchill, November 20, 1894 [bewilderment], federal pension file of William Churchill [F 59 Ind. Inf. & Com. Sgt. 59 Ind. Inf.], National Archives; affidavit of Nancy Gleason (widow), April 14, 1888 [will power], federal pension file of Newell Gleason [Col. 87 Ind. Inf.], National Archives. Affidavit of John E. Payne, n.d. [blank], federal pension record of William H. Guile [I 63 and H 128 Ind. Inf.], National Archives.

32. See commitment ledger for George Wood, commitment no. 4658, July 31, 1880, Indiana Hospital for the Insane, Indiana State Archives; pension medical board report, June 4, 1901 [plot], affidavits of Henry Wood, September 9, 1889 [failure in business; alcohol], Thomas Whitford, September 16, 1889 [sunstroke in service], John A. Kyle, September 17, 1889 [army experience], John N. Milburn, December 11, 1889 [teacher's license], Benjamin J. Grant, December 11, 1889 [arrests], John W. Curtis, December 13, 1889 [Franklin College, Harriet Diltz], Mary E. Wood, December 14, 1889 [eyes frightened her], George L. Cheek, December 16, 1889 [garret], federal pension file of George Wood [K 26 Ind. Inf.], National Archives. See also David Speigel, "Multiple Personality as a Post-Traumatic Stress Disorder," *Psychiatric Clinics of North America*, 7 (1) (March 1984): 101–110; and W. C. Young, "Emergence of a Multiple Personality in a Posttraumatic Stress Disorder of Adulthood," *American Journal of Clinical Hypnosis*, 29 (1987): 249–254.

33. Commitment no. 4248, May 16, 1870, Indiana Hospital for the Insane, Indiana State Archives; see affidavits from Dr. C. F. Bucklin, December 18, 1902 [need for "strong room"], medical board (Vevay), September 26, 1887 [insanity], Dr. P. C. Holland, September 28, 1887 [operation through window], Almena C. Gaither, November 29, 1887, and January 19, 1903 (letter) [wagon incident], S. R. Tinker, March 20, 1888 [shelling incident], Jeremiah Plew, January 30, 1890 ["off"], Thomas S. Robbins, March 20, 1890 [shell incident], John H. Murphy, September 23, 1887 [shell shock], James A. Works, October 28, 1887 [litigation], and the divorce proceedings in *Evelyn A. Wiley vs. Allen E. Wiley*, federal pension file of Allen E. Wiley [C 54 Ind. Inf.], National Archives.

34. See cases of Amos Farmer [committed to asylum in 1858; see commitment no. 2358, September 17, 1862, Indiana Hospital for the Insane, Indiana State Archives], Parke Freeman [committed to asylum in 1851; see inquest papers, commitment no. 4017, October 19, 1869, Indiana Hospital for the Insane, Indiana State Archives], Jeremiah Hayworth [uncle and father had both been committed to asylum; see commitment no. 2465, April 7, 1863, and commitment no. 3101, May 31, 1866, Indiana Hospital for the Insane, Indiana State Archives], William S. Hoover [had been in asylum in Stockton, California in 1856; see commitment no. 3159, August 15, 1866, Indiana Hospital for the Insane, Indiana State Archives], James Jenkins [had been in asylum in Pennsylvania in 1846; see certificate from Lancaster County Almshouse and Hospital, August 17, 1891, in federal pension file of James Jenkins (F 36 Ind. Inf.; D 167 Ohio Inf.), National Archives], Reuben Mason [commitment in 1860; see letter from Orpheus Everts, Supt., August 29, 1871, in federal pension file of Reuben L. Mason [H 35 Ind. Inf.], National Archives], John B. Avey [grandmother and mother were insane; see inquest and commitment records, commitment no. 2378, October 22, 1862, Indiana Hospital for the Insane, Indiana State Archives], and Franklin Bradley ["it was quite commonly thought in the Co. that he was crazy"; see affidavit of Jay D. Parkinson, June 13, 1900, in federal pension file of Franklin Bradley (A 12 Ind. Cav.), National Archives]. Of course, it is entirely possible that a person who had been committed to an asylum before the war could have recovered, and then been subjected to an entirely new traumatic experience in the Civil War; one must

also be extraordinarily cautious about assertions of hereditary insanity in nineteenth-century sources.

35. See commitment no. 3475, December 9, 1867, Indiana Hospital for the Insane, Indiana State Archives.

36. See affidavits of Dr. William W. Slaughter, April 26 and April 27, 1892 [incident in army], Larkin J. Smith, April 26, 1892 [laughing and crying spells], George W. Price, May 3, 1892 [dread of battle], William H. Wheeler, May 3, 1892 [coffin], federal pension file of William H. Smith [B 60 Ind. Inf.], National Archives.

37. Commitment of John Medsker, commitment no. 11566, April 16, 1901, Indiana Hospital for the Insane, Indiana State Archives; see declaration, December 19, 1865, and affidavits of S.H. Schofield, February 3, 1898 [description], and W.C. Pyatt, July 14, 1897 [spits up blood], federal pension file of John Medsker [F 10 and F 58 Ind. Inf.], National Archives. For Farr case, see medical board report (Gosport), April 20, 1904 [limitations], board report (Martinsville), November 15, 1899 [symptoms], and affidavits of Josiah L. Bunton, January 2, 1904, and Elizabeth Farr, January 2, 1904 [behavior], in federal pension file of James B. Farr [H 33 Ind. Inf.], National Archives. For Vietnam-era research on the relationship between gunshot wounds and PTSD, see Lawrence A. Palinkas and Patricia Coben, "Psychiatric Disorders among United States Marines Wounded in Action in Vietnam," *Journal of Nervous and Mental Disease*, 175 (5) (1987): 291–300; L. Buydens-Branchey, D. Noumair, and M. Branchey, "Duration and Intensity of Combat Exposure and Post-traumatic Stress Disorder in Vietnam Veterans," *Journal of Nervous and Mental Disease*, 178 (9) (1990): 582–587; and Roger K. Pitman, Bruce Altman, and Michael L. Macklin, "Prevalence of Posttraumatic Stress Disorder in Wounded Vietnam Veterans," *American Journal of Psychiatry*, 146 (5) (May 1989): 667–669. P. S. Ellis, "The Origins of the War Neuroses" (pt. I), *Journal of the Royal Naval Medical Services*, 70 (1984): 168–177, 172, cites Guion, in *Agents Provocateurs de l'Hysterie*, as briefly mentioning cases of soldiers wounded in the Franco-Prussian War in whom hysterical paralyses developed at periods varying from two and a half to fifteen years after these injuries.

38. Affidavit of Gabriel Schmuck, n.d. [broken down], federal pension file of John Donnelly [G 53 Ind. Inf.], National Archives; affidavit of Vardiamon Jewell, November 27, 1899 [total wreck], federal pension file of Lewis H. Chowning [I 43 Ind. Inf.], National Archives; affidavits of George Harris and Isaac Braner, March 9, 1883 [emaciated], federal pension file of John T. Blair [D 43 Ind. Inf.], National Archives; and affidavit of Francis M. Hancock, May 10, 1895 [dead man], federal pension file of Elijah Boswell [B 68 Ind. Inf.], National Archives.

39. Pension medical board reports, November 18, 1885 [cannot rest], and May 6, 1891 [sad countenance], federal pension file of Eli Bucher [Unass'd 83 and K 48 Ind. Inf.], National Archives; examining surgeon's certificate, March 6, 1884 [anemia], federal pension file of Charles D. Comptom [C 34 Ind. Inf.], National Archives; affidavits of Byron Love, October 30, 1900 [perfectly crazy], and Pryor Rigdon, July 11, 1900 [chronic diarrhea], federal pension file of Jesse Downs [D 34 Ind. Inf.], National Archives.

6. "Dying of Nostalgia"

1. Andrew Jackson Smith diary, December 25, 1864, Indiana Historical Society ["Have the blues"]; Alfred A. Atkins to parents, April 25, 1864, Georgia State Archives ["lonesome"]; Wash Vosburgh to Ella, April 24, 1864, Nina L. Ness Collection, Bentley Historical Library ["disheartened"]; Benjamin Franklin Wells to unknown, May 23, 1862, Bentley Historical Library ["down-hearted"]; S. Emma E. Edmonds, *Nurse and Spy in the Union Army: The Adventures and Experiences of a Woman in Hospitals, Camps, and Battle-Fields* (Hartford, Conn.: W. S. Williams & Co., 1865), p. 60 ["discouraged"]; Ferdinand Davis memoirs, p. 150, Bentley Historical Library ["demoralized"]; Charles H. Allen to Catherine, May 30, 1862, South Caroliniana Library ["I feel very nervous"]; Victor E. Comte to Elise, January 26, 1864, Bentley Historical Library ["played out"]; Charles B. Haydon, *For Country, Cause, and Leader: The Civil War Journal of Charles B. Haydon,* ed. Stephen W. Sears (New York: Ticknor & Fields, 1993), pp. 65, 38 ["used up"; "worn down"]; Benjamin Franklin Wells to Melissa, May 23, 1862, Bentley Historical Library ["anxious"]; Mary Boykin Chesnut, *A Diary from Dixie* (Gloucester, Mass.: Peter Smith, 1961; originally published in 1905), p. 241 ["awful depression"]; affidavit of Josiah Raush, June 28, 1872 ["rattled"], federal pension file of Emmanuel Gilbert [B 101 Ind. Inf.], National Archives ["By rattled I mean that he acted strange and queer and talked strange and extravagant things about what he could do and what the army could do"]; Joseph Dill Alison Diary, entry for May 17, 1863, P. K. Yonge Library of Florida History, University of Florida, Gainesville ["disspirited"]; John Johnston memoirs, p. 16, Confederate Collection, Tennessee State Archives ["intense sadness"]; Roderick Gospero Shaw to sister, January 28, 1864, Florida State Archives, Tallahassee, Florida ["melancholy"]; and Haydon, *For Country, Cause, and Leader,* p. 197 ["badly blown"].

2. John G. Perry, *Letters from a Surgeon of the Civil War,* ed. Martha Derby Perry (Boston: Little, Brown and Co., 1906), p. 164 [blue and homesick]; William Watson, *Letters of a Civil War Surgeon,* ed. Paul Fatout (West Lafayette, Ind.: Purdue University Studies Humanities Series, 1961), p. 38 [get the blues]; Orlando E. Carpenter diary, entry for December 7, 1864, Bentley Historical Library [too numerous]; Robert S. Robertson, *Diary of the War,* ed. Charles N. Walker and Rosemary Walker (Fort Wayne, Ind.: Allen County–Fort Wayne Historical Society, 1965), p. 91 [blue days]; Haydon, *For Country, Cause, and Leader,* p. 299 [rage].

3. Kate Cumming, *The Journal of Kate Cumming; A Confederate Nurse, 1862–1865,* ed. Richard Harwell (Savannah, Ga.: Beehive Press, 1975), pp. 63, 235 [Hood]; Joseph Dill Alison diary, entry for May 17, 1863, P. K. Yonge Library of Florida History, University of Florida, Gainesville [balance]; John H. Brinton, *Personal Memoirs of John H. Brinton* (New York: Neale, 1914), p. 219 [straggler].

4. Affidavit of Sanford Fortner, August 31, 1988, federal pension file of Gen. Newell Gleason [Col., 87 Ind. Inf.], National Archives ["rattled"]; Henry Albert Potter, "Account of the Battle of Chickamauga and Wheeler's Raid,"

p. 16, Bentley Historical Library ["played out"]; Haydon, *For Country, Cause, and Leader*, p. 197 ["badly blown"].

5. Nancy Tomes, *A Generous Confidence: Thomas Story Kirkbride and the Art of Asylum-Keeping, 1840–1883* (Cambridge: Cambridge University Press, 1985), pp. 55–85; John S. Haller, Jr., *American Medicine in Transition, 1840–1910* (Urbana: University of Illinois Press, 1981), pp. 5–11.

6. See Norman Dain, *Concepts of Insanity in the United States, 1789–1865* (New Brunswick, N.J.: Rutgers University Press, 1964), pp. 71–83; Erwin H. Ackerknecht, *A Short History of Psychiatry* (New York: Hafner Publishing Co., 1968), pp. 13–15; George Rosen, *Madness in Society: Chapters in the Historical Sociology of Mental Illness* (Chicago: University of Chicago Press, 1968), pp. 71–136; Gregory Zilboorg, *A History of Medical Psychology* (New York: W. W. Norton, 1941), pp. 36–92, 53; and, in general, Albert Deutsch, *The Mentally Ill in America: A History of Their Care and Treatment from Colonial Times* (Garden City, N.Y.: Doubleday, 1937).

7. *The War of the Rebellion: A Compilation of the Official Records of the Union and Confederate Armies . . .* , 70 vols. in 128 pts. (Washington, D.C., 1880–1901), hereafter *O.R.*, ser. III, vol. III, pp. 126, 137 (from act of March 3, 1863). For circulars providing amendments, see *O.R.*, ser. III, vol. III, p. 1071 (November 9, 1863); *O.R.*, ser. III, vol. IV, pp. 6–8 (January 5, 1864); and *O.R.*, ser. III, vol. IV, pp. 651ff. (September 1, 1864). For the rate of rejection, see *O.R.*, ser. III, vol. III, p. 1053 (November 5, 1863). For World War II rates, see Eli Ginzberg et al., *The Ineffective Soldier*, vol. 1, *The Lost Divisions* (New York: Columbia University Press, 1959), pp. 143, 145.

8. For general procedures for medical discharges from the Union Army, see *O.R.*, ser. III, vol. I, p. 310 (G.O. No. 39 from L. Thomas, Adjutant-General, July 1, 1861); *O.R.*, ser. III, vol. II, pp. 9–10 (G.O. 36, from L. Thomas, April 7, 1862); *O.R.*, ser. III, vol. IV, pp. 46–47 (Circular no. 11 from Adjutant-General's Office, January 26, 1864). For the Union Army's policy on discharge for insanity, see Roberts Bartholow, A.M., M.D., *A Manual of Instructions for Enlisting and Discharging Soldiers with Special Reference to the Medical Examination of Recruits, and the Detection of Disqualifying and Feigned Diseases* (Philadelphia: J. B. Lippincott and Co., 1863), p. 237 (this volume was adopted by the Surgeon-General for issue to medical officers of the army); for a copy of General Order no. 98 (November 13, 1861), setting forth the proper procedure for committing soldiers to the Government Hospital for the Insane, see William Grace, *The Army Surgeon's Manual, for the Use of Medical Officers, Cadets, Chaplains, and Hospital Stewards, containing the Regulations of the Medical Department, All General Orders from the War Department, and Circulars from the Surgeon-General's Office, from January 1st, 1861, to July 1st, 1864* (New York: Bailliere Brothers, 1864; reprinted by Norman Publishing, 1992), p. 35, and Lieutenant-Colonel George Patten, *Patten's Army Manual: Containing Instructions for Officers in the Preparation of Rolls, Returns and Accounts Required of Regimental and Company Commanders, and Pertaining to the Subsistence and Quartermasters' Departments, Etc., Etc.* (New York: J. W. Fortune, 1862), pp. 213–216. The proper procedure was for a regimental medical officer to provide a certificate describing the insanity; the commanding officer would

then issue an order providing for transportation of the man to Washington, D.C., and the Adjutant-General's Office in Washington reviewed applications, which in turn had to be approved by the Secretary of War. Discharges from the Government Hospital for the Insane were likewise approved by the Adjutant-General's Office. Note Circular no. 16 of September 12, 1863, which established the policy that no insane soldier could be discharged from the service on a mere surgeon's certificate of disability. The registers for the Government Hospital for the Insane are contained at the National Archives, Record Group 94, Entry 271.

    Also of interest is a U.S. Army medical register located in Record Group 94, Entry 544, Department Register 38 1/2, at the National Archives. This register contains a list of about 280 insane Civil War soldiers, who were placed at various facilities from August 26, 1863, to the end of April 1865. A small percentage of these men were sent to the Government Hospital for the Insane, but most were sent to other facilities, including forts, hospitals, army division hospitals, prisons, and several other facilities, including Fairfax Seminary, Georgetown Seminary, and Vienna, Virginia.

9. Regarding World War II, see Ginzberg et al., *The Ineffective Soldier*, vol. 1, *The Lost Divisions*; idem, *The Ineffective Soldier*, vol. 2: *Breakdown and Recovery*, and vol. 3, *Patterns of Performance* (New York: Columbia University Press, 1959); as well as Samuel A. Stouffer et al., *Studies in the Social Psychology of World War II*, 4 vols. (vol. 1, *The American Soldier: Adjustment during Army Life*) (Princeton: Princeton University Press, 1949). Regarding army policy in the Civil War era, see J. Theodore Calhoun, "Feigned Diseases," *Medical and Surgical Reporter*, 10 (17) (August 22, 1863): 229–230. For the circular on examination before battle, see Surgeon General Joseph K. Barnes, U.S. Army, ed., *The Medical and Surgical History of the War of the Rebellion (1861–1865)*, pt. III, Surgical Volume (Washington, D.C.: U.S. Government Printing Office, 1870), p. 911.

10. C. Macfarlane, *Reminiscences of an Army Surgeon* (Oswego, N.Y.: Lake City Print Shop, 1912), p. 40 [detective]; Major and Surgeon S. C. Gordon, "Reminiscences of the Civil War from a Surgeon's Point of View," in Military Order of the Loyal Legion of the United States, Maine Commandery, *War Papers* (Portland, Maine: Lefavor-Tower, 1898–1919), p. 143 [deadbeats]; Charles O. Leary, Medical Director, 6th Corps to [S. A. Hohman?], Medical Director [?], in U.S. Army of the Potomac, Medical Corps; Letterbook (1862–1865), Library of Congress [objective assessment]; Jane Augusta Gunn, *Memorial Sketches of Doctor Moses Gunn, by His Wife* (Chicago: W. T. Keener, 1889), p. 114 [duty]; disability discharge papers, June 16, 1862 [incapable of feigning], federal pension file of John F. Hutchings [F 40 Ind. Inf.], National Archives; affidavit of Estes H. Layman, July 17, 1886 [no object in "playing off"], federal pension file of Patrick McKinney [C 149 Ind. Inf.], National Archives. See also William W. Keen, S. Weir Mitchell, and George R. Morehouse, "On Malingering, Especially in Regard to Simulation of Diseases of the Nervous System," *American Journal of Medical Sciences*, 48 (July-October, 1864): 367–394, 367–368 [positively].

11. S. Weir Mitchell, "The Medical Department in the Civil War," *Journal of the*

American Medical Association, 62 (19) (May 9, 1914) [regret]. See also W. S. Chipley, "Feigned Insanity—Motives—Special Tests," *American Journal of Insanity,* 22 (July 1865): 1–24.

12. Darius Bateman, commitment no. 848, February 19, 1863; for an account of the battle, see *O.R.,* p. 341; see also affidavit of Alonza Willis, September 18, 1863 [talking funny], federal pension file of Darius Bateman [I 25 N.J. Inf.], National Archives.

13. For Weldon Railroad, see David Callaghan, commitment no. 1801, February 2, 1865, Government Hospital for the Insane, National Archives; see affidavit of Frederick Hutchins, January 17, 1888 [sunstroke], federal pension file of David Callaghan [G 32 Mass. Inf.], National Archives. For Vicksburg, see Thomas Farrell, commitment no. 750, November 6, 1862, Government Hospital for the Insane, National Archives, and army discharge papers, July 25, 1863, federal pension file of Thomas Farrell [B 9 Conn. Inf.], National Archives. For Gettysburg, see Samuel S. Garner, commitment no. 1058, August 26, 1863, Government Hospital for the Insane, National Archives. For the case of David Harper, see commitment no. 757, November 17, 1862, Government Hospital for the Insane, National Archives, and affidavit of Alfred E. Harper, April 2, 1867 [strangely], federal pension file of David Harper [E 111 Pa. Inf.], National Archives. For Xavier Hinderlet, see commitment no. 971, June 7, 1863, Government Hospital for the Insane, National Archives, and affidavit of F. B. Gregory, June 1, 1878 [windage], federal pension file of Xavier Hinderlet [G 1 N.Y. Art.], National Archives. For David Kells [B 1 Mich. Inf.], see commitment no. 1219, January 15, 1864, Government Hospital for the Insane, National Archives. For Francis Steck, see commitment no. 983, June 16, 1863, Government Hospital for the Insane, National Archives, and declaration in pension file for minor claim filed on his account [G 73 Pa. Inf.], National Archives.

14. For asylum records on Albert S. Green, see commitment record no. 1814, February 16, 1865, Government Hospital for the Insane, National Archives; affidavits of Jane Green, April 26, 1889 [screaming], James L. Sears, April 29 1889 [tied to tree], and Charles A. Waterhouse, May 8, 1889 [spent ball], federal pension file of Albert S. Green [F 7 Maine Inf.], National Archives. For asylum records on John G. Hildt, see commitment record no. 779, December 13, 1862, Government Hospital for the Insane, National Archives. See also pension medical board reports, July 27, 1888, and April 3, 1890, federal pension record of John G. Hildt [D 1 Mich. Inf.], National Archives.

15. See *Report of the Board of Visitors of the Hospital for the Insane* (Washington, D.C.: George W. Bowman, 1860), for the 1859 figures, and *Reports of the Board of Visitors and the Superintendent of Construction of the Government Hospital for the Insane* (Washington, D.C.: Gideon & Pearson, 1864), indicating a capacity of 278 in mid-1863.

16. See pension file of Daniel B. Kivett [A 33 Ind. Inf.], National Archives, especially the affidavit of Dr. Charles Seaton, April 7, 1869; affidavit of Joseph Whittaker, July 5, 1879 [Virginia asylum], federal pension file of John Donnelly [G 53 Ind. Inf.], National Archives; federal pension file of Samuel Long [K 86 Ind. Inf.], National Archives [Nashville, Tenn., asylum]; see affidavit

of Uriah Slagle, June 16, 1891, mother's claim of Julia Slagle, in the federal pension file of Francis Slagle [E 17 Ind. Inf.], National Archives; for Francis Slagle's commitment, see no. 2428, January 15, 1863, Indiana Hospital for the Insane, Indiana State Archives. The military records in the pension file of Jeremiah Hayworth [F 11 Ind. Cav] indicate that Maj. General Thomas of the Department of the Cumberland authorized his relatives to take him home; if this was not possible, then the man was to be sent to the Government Hospital for the Insane in Washington, D.C. For Confederate policy on the insane, see H. H. Cunningham, *Doctors in Gray: The Confederate Medical Service* (Gloucester, Mass.: Peter Smith, 1970), pp. 214–215.

17. For numbers committed to the Indiana Hospital for the Insane, see *Seventeenth Annual Report of the Commissioners, Superintendent and Steward of the Indiana Hospital for the Insane for the Year ending October 31, 1865. To the Governor*, vol. II, *Reports* (Indianapolis: Samuel M. Douglass, State Printer, 1866), p. 132. The following commitments are from the Indiana Hospital for the Insane, Indiana State Archives: Amos Farmer, commitment no. 2358, September 17, 1862, and William Daffin, commitment no. 2366, September 26, 1862 [committed directly from camp]; Anthony Bihler, commitment no. 2357, September 14, 1862 [Pea Ridge]; Thomas Bilderback, commitment no. 2370, October 1, 1862 [exposure in army]; Samuel Long, commitment no. 2436, February 4, 1863 [fright before a battle]; Solomon Winningham, commitment no. 2400, November 19, 1862 [war excitement]; William H. Smith, commitment no. 2874, May 12, 1865 [shock of battle]; Cornwell P. Meek, commitment no. 2715, July 7, 1864 [shell burst]; John H. Polk, commitment no. 2907, July 18, 1865 [the war]; Mary Jane Moore, commitment no. 2546, September 2, 1863 [death of son]; Mary Jane Sage, commitment no. 2552, September 9, 1863 [grieves]; Emily Kuipe, commitment no. 2681, April 29, 1864 [death of brother]; Hester A. Taylor, commitment no. 3449, November 6, 1867 [husband died in army]; and Nancy E. Donaldson, commitment no. 3545, March 21, 1868 [talked much].

18. Records of the Illinois State Hospital for the Insane at Jacksonville, Illinois State Archives, Springfield, Illinois: Albert E. Arnold, commitment no. 1490, October 29, 1861 [war excitement; from camp]; William A. Lynn, commitment no. 1591, April 11, 1862 [exposure]; Michael Dazey, commitment no. 1682, September 16, 1862 [sunstroke]; John J. Sargent, commitment no. 1710, November 8, 1862 [Pea Ridge]; John Hill, commitment no. 1773, March 13, 1863 [fatigue]; Christian Fasig, commitment no. 1795, April 24, 1863 [Perryville]; Charles H. Hall, commitment no. 3304, October 11, 1865 [overexertion]; John S. Taylor, commitment no. 3359, May 19, 1869 [return from army]; Millicent C. Loar, commitment no. 1653, July 11, 1862 [brothers]; Jane A. Brown, commitment no. 1765, February 17, 1863 [anxiety over son]; Maria Walsh, commitment no. 1943, February 10, 1864 [Mission Ridge]. For the Columbus Hospital for the Insane, pertaining to Morgan's raid, see Jesse Brokaw, commitment no. 4122, August 5, 1863; Christian Miller, commitment no. 4124, August 6, 1863; Lydia M. Shaw, commitment no. 4125, August 8, 1863; James Johnson, commitment no. 4156, October 10, 1863. For political prisoners subsequently committed at Longview Hospital in Cincinnati, see (no numbers) A. P. Chapman, June 13, 1863; and James B. Mason, August 6, 1863.

19. Ferdinand Davis memoirs, pp. 153–154, Bentley Historical Library [Norfolk]; Haydon, *For Country, Cause, and Leader,* p. 322 [hard labor]; Robertson, *Diary of the War,* pp. 102–103 [bucked and gagged].

20. Affidavits of Andrew Allen and Robert R. Scott, n.d. [army experience], Wesley Bell, October 17, 1891 [Rebel charge], George Hardy, October 9, 1891 [eyes], federal pension file of Daniel L. McElfresh [H 88 Ill. Inf.], National Archives.

21. Robertson, *Diary of the War,* p. 189 [court-martial at Spotsylvania Courthouse]; Macfarlane, *Reminiscences of an Army Surgeon,* p. 57 [men wandering]. For British policy in World War I, see Anthony Babington, *For the Sake of Example: Capital Courts-Martial, 1914–1920* (New York: St. Martin's Press, 1983), and Harry R. Kormos, "Nature of Combat Stress," in Charles R. Figley, ed., *Stress Disorders among Vietnam Veterans* (New York: Brunner/Mazel, 1978), pp. 3–22, 7.

22. See affidavit of Reuben A. Riley, April 8, 1870 [account], federal pension file of Cornwell P. Meek [A 4 Ind. Cav.], National Archives; for Meek's asylum record, see commitment no. 2715, July 7, 1864, Indiana Hospital for the Insane, Indiana State Archives. Court martial records, federal pension file of G. H. E. Bailey [F 5 Md. Inf.], National Archives.

23. Affidavit of Joseph Noble, August 29, 1889 [Shiloh], federal pension file of David Leaming [B 8 Ind. Cav.], National Archives; affidavit of James H. Kinnear, December 17, 1880 [weeks at a time], federal pension file of Dixon Irwin [B & D 13 Ind. Inf.], National Archives; affidavits of Lewis Campbell, June 23, 1906, and September 29, 1906, and Miles A. Barker, June 21, 1906, and William H. Young, December 9, 1905, federal pension file of James D. Campbell [C 99 Ind. Inf.], National Archives.

24. Rice C. Bull, *Soldiering: The Civil War Diary of Rice C. Bull, 123rd New York Volunteer Infantry,* ed. K. Jack Bauer (San Rafael, Calif.: Presidio Press, 1977), pp. 117, 62 [skulkers, stragglers]; Spencer Glasgow Welch, *A Confederate Surgeon's Letters to His Wife* (Marietta, Ga.: Continental Book Co., 1954; originally published in 1911), p. 107 [contemptible]; P. L. Ledford, *Reminiscences of the Civil War, 1861–1865* (Thomasville, N.C.: News Printing House, 1909), p. 63 [artful]; Carroll Henderson Clark memoirs, p. 47, Confederate Collection, Tennessee State Archives [o war]. For a challenge to the idea that mental breakdown or exposure to battle and disease were primary causes of desertion in the Civil War, see Bob Sterling, "Discouragement, Weariness, and War Politics: Desertions from Illinois Regiments during the Civil War," *Illinois Historical Journal,* 82 (4) (Winter 1989): 239–262; Richard Bardolph, "Confederate Dilemma: North Carolina Troops and the Deserter Problem," *North Carolina Historical Review,* 66 (1) (January 1989): 61–86; and Peter S. Bearman, "Desertion as Localism: Army Unit Solidarity and Group Norms in the U.S. Civil War," *Social Forces,* 70 (2) (December 1991): 321–342.

25. Letter of William Morris, May 16, 1887, and affidavit of John S. Benham, December 12, 1929, federal pension file of William Morris [B 68 Ind. Inf.], National Archives. See commitments of John William Gordon, no. 2780, October 31, 1864 [fear of being shot], no. 4091, January 7, 1870 [depression], no. 11505, February 2, 1901 [woods], Indiana Hospital for the Insane, Indiana State Archives.

26. See Donald Lee Anderson and Godfrey Tryggve Anderson, "Nostalgia and Malingering in the Military during the Civil War," *Perspect. Biol. Med.,* 28 (1) (Autumn 1984), 156–166; J. Theodore Calhoun, "Nostalgia as a Disease of Field Service," *Medical and Surgical Reporter,* 11 (February 27, 1864); DeWitt C. Peters, "Remarks on the Evils of Youthful Enlistments and Nostalgia," *American Medical Times* (February 14, 1863); George Rosen, "Nostalgia: A 'Forgotten' Psychological Disorder," *Clio Medica,* 10 (1) (1975), 28–51; and Albert Deutsch, "Military Psychiatry: The Civil War, 1861–1865," in J. Hall, G. Zilboorg, and H. Bunker, eds., *One Hundred Years of American Psychiatry* (New York: Columbia University Press, 1944), pp. 367, 374–375; Bartholow, *A Manual of Instructions for Enlisting and Discharging Soldiers,* pp. 21–22.

27. Judson L. Austin to wife, February 26, 1865, Nina L. Ness Collection, Bentley Historical Library; Wash Vosburgh to Ella, May 22, 1864, Nina L. Ness Collection, Bentley Historical Library [very lonely]; Victor E. Comte to Elise, January 8, 1864, Bentley Historical Library [unhappy]; *Abner R. Small, The Road to Richmond: The Civil War Memoirs of Major Abner R. Small of the Sixteenth Maine Volunteers, Together with the Diary Which He Kept When He Was a Prisoner of War,* ed. Harold Adams Small (Berkeley: University of California Press, 1939), p. 172 [dying of nostalgia]; Macfarlane, *Reminiscences of an Army Surgeon,* p. 73 [pluck].

28. Henry H. Bellamy to parents, n.d., Bentley Historical Library.

29. Shelby Foote, *The Civil War: A Narrative—Fort Sumter to Perryville* (New York: Random House, 1958), p. 344 [looks of terror]; report of John H. Brinton with the Army of the Tennessee, from February to June of 1862, Barnes, ed., *Medical and Surgical History,* pt. I, Medical Volume, Appendix, p. 33 [flocking on board]; the *Medical and Surgical History* itself reports 5,213 cases of nostalgia, 2.34 cases annually per thousand of strength, which increased to 3.3 per thousand in the second year of the war. For some reason, it does not extend its analysis to the third or fourth years of the war. The report of 5,213 cases is the reported number for the *entire* war, not just the first year (which is the implication as stated). Albert Graves to [Fitch?], December 11, 1862, Morris Fitch Correspondence, Nina L. Ness Collection, Bentley Historical Library [new fellers].

30. Henry Hartshorne, "On Heart Disease in the Army," *Summary of the Transactions of the College of Physicians of Philadelphia* (July 1864): 89–94; Charles F. Wooley, "From Irritable Heart to Mitral Valve Prolapse: World War I, the British Experience and James Mackenzie," *American Journal of Cardiology,* 57 (February 1986): 6; J. M. DaCosta, "On Irritable Heart: A Clinical Study of a Form of Functional Cardiac Disorder and Its Consequences," *The American Journal of the Medical Sciences,* 121 (January 1871): 20–21; pension bureau medical board report, February 18, 1891 [smothering spells], federal pension file of William S. Hoover [21st Ind. Light Artillery], National Archives.

31. See affidavit of Frederick Hutchins, January 17, 1888 [sunstroke], federal pension file of David Callaghan [G 32 Mass. Inf.], National Archives. For Vicksburg, see Thomas Farrell, commitment no. 750, November 6, 1862, Government Hospital for the Insane, National Archives, and army discharge papers, July 25, 1863, federal pension file of Thomas Farrell [B 9 Conn. Inf.], National

Archives. Barnes, ed., *Medical and Surgical History*, pt. III, Medical Volume, pp. 857–858.

32. Affidavits of Charles Adams, n.d. (1871?), and Capt. William C. Williams, n.d. (1871?), federal pension file of Charles Adams [G 44 Ind. Inf.], National Archives; see commitment of Charles Adams, commitment no. 4537, February 25, 1871, Indiana Hospital for the Insane, Indiana State Archives.

33. Affidavit of Eli Williams, May 11, 1895, federal pension file of Elijah Boswell [B 68 Ind. Inf.], National Archives; declaration of claimant, 1879 et seq., federal pension file of Joel H. Miller [E 129 Ind. Inf.], National Archives; affidavit of Charles W. Dillingham, February 24, 1885, federal pension file of Edward Strickland [B 8 Ky. Cav. and K 53 Ind. Inf.], National Archives.

34. John Q. Anderson, *A Texas Surgeon in the C.S.A.* (Tuscaloosa, Ala.: Confederate Publishing Co., 1957), pp. 39, 99 [poor emaciated men]; Barnes, ed., *Medical and Surgical History*, pt. I, Medical Volume, Appendix, p. 55 [pouring rain]; Barnes, ed., *Medical and Surgical History*, pt. II, vol. 1, p. 388 [dysentery].

35. For creation of the Invalid Corps and disqualifying conditions, see *O.R.*, ser. III, vol. III, pp. 205–208 (G.O. 130, May 15, 1863); for the battalion setup and additional disqualifications, see *O.R.*, ser. III, vol. III, pp. 474–478 (G.O. 212, July 9, 1863); regarding the new name of Veteran Reserve Corps, see *O.R.*, ser. III, vol. IV, p. 188 (G.O. 111, March 18, 1864); for the policy requiring that any man being discharged be considered for the VRC, see *O.R.*, ser. III, vol. IV, p. 218 (Circular no. 33, April 6, 1864); for assessment of the IC/VRC including numbers served, see *O.R.*, ser. III, vol. V, pp. 679ff.

36. In wars prior to the twentieth century, at least two, and sometimes as many as seven men died of disease for every battle death; World War I was the first major war in which deaths from disease (even in spite of the great influenza epidemic) were only a fraction of battle deaths, and subsequent wars of the twentieth century followed this trend. See G. H. Rice, "The Evolution of Military Medical Services, 1854 to 1914," *Journal of the Royal Army Medical Corps*, 135 (1989): 147–150; R. L. Blanco, "Medicine in the Continental Army, 1775–1781," *Bulletin of the N.Y. Academy of Medicine*, 57 (8) (October 1981): 677–704, 683, 688; and the discussion in the Conclusion.

7. "This Must End Sometime"

1. In general, see Gerald N. Grob, *Mental Institutions in America: Social Policy to 1875* (New York: Free Press, 1973); idem, "The Transformation of the Mental Hospital in the United States," *American Behavioral Scientist*, 28 (5) (May–June 1985): 639–654; Albert Deutsch, *The Mentally Ill in America: A History of Their Care and Treatment from Colonial Times* (New York: Columbia University Press, 1937); and Norman Dain, *Concepts of Insanity in the United States, 1789–1865* (New Brunswick, N.J.: Rutgers University Press, 1964). See Appendix C for a discussion of insane asylums and the law regarding involuntary commitment in the state of Indiana in the nineteenth century.

2. David J. Rothman, *The Discovery of the Asylum: Social Order and Disorder in the New Republic* (Boston: Little, Brown and Company, 1971), p. 131 [28 of 33 states]; Gerald N. Grob, *Mental Illness and American Society, 1875–1940*

(Princeton: Princeton University Press, 1983), p. 8 [1880]; Nancy Tomes, *A Generous Confidence: Thomas Story Kirkbride and the Art of Asylum-Keeping, 1840–1883* (Cambridge: Cambridge University Press, 1985), p. 141 [Kirkbride plan]. Debates surrounding the "rise of the asylum" have centered on three questions: (a) What forces (industrialization, urbanization, the spread of the market, an Enlightenment-derived desire to improve the care of the insane) were driving this development? (b) Was the emergence of the central insane asylum basically a good development in providing humane care for the insane in lieu of chains and ridicule in the local community, or were asylums intended to simply rid the local community of a "nuisance" and to provide new, more terrible "mind-forged manacles" or a model of "social control" as a way of maintaining order and establishing or vindicating bourgeois manners and values? And (c) because medical men were increasingly put in charge of insane asylums (with their substantial building funds, budgets, and growing patient populations) to what extent were doctors driving this development (asylum-centered health care) as a way of increasing their own professional power and influence—with the welfare of the insane patient being a decidedly secondary consideration?

For the conventional view of the insane asylum as an Enlightenment institution intended to benefit the insane, see Deutsch, *The Mentally Ill in America*. For the revisionist view that asylums were intended to expel from society disruptive elements which might impede a rapidly industrializing economy, see Rothman, *The Discovery of the Asylum*, and Michel Foucalt, *Madness and Civilization: A History of Insanity in the Age of Reason* (New York: Vintage Books, 1973). Gerald Grob in *Mental Institutions in America* takes a middle view, arguing that the original intentions of those who built the institutions were good, but that these institutions lapsed into custodial care and neglect of their patients in the latter half of the nineteenth century for a number of reasons.

3. Letter of George C. Durland, September 28, 1996 [strangers], federal pension file of William R. Durland [C 10 Ind. Cav.], National Archives; affidavit of Lizzie Dudley, April 5, 1895, federal pension file of William H. Guile [I 63 and H 128 Ind. Inf.], National Archives; affidavit of Elizabeth Farr, January 2, 1904 [constant watchfulness], federal pension file of James B. Farr [H 33 Ind. Inf.], National Archives.

4. Affidavit of Eliza J. Foster, September 25, 1906 [shut-up], federal pension file of James D. Campbell [C 99 Ind. Inf.], National Archives; affidavits of Moses Tomlinson and William N. Stone, Department of the Interior summary of evidence, May 2, 1887, federal pension file of Thomas G. Conaty [B 54 Ind Inf.; I 9 Ind. Cav.], National Archives; affidavit of Elizabeth Hacker, April 25, 1900 [committed], federal pension file of Ahab Killar Ball [15th Ind. L.A.], National Archives [nonsample]. Confinement in jail was apparently contemplated and approved by statute in nineteenth-century Indiana, in that spaces at the insane asylum were always limited, and not all mentally ill people in the state who posed a threat to local communities could be immediately hospitalized. See Appendix C.

5. Affidavits of Joseph A. Bridge, November 1, 1900 [jailer]; Henry K. Stauffer,

November 2, 1900 [threats to kill]; Charles O. Stansel, October 22, 1900 [insulted local women]; Thomas McDowell, November 2, 1900 [drinking]; Alfred J. Anderson, March 16, 1901 [poison]; and letter from Special Examiner to Commissioner, November 30, 1900 [character]; federal pension file of Clinton Anderson [E 116 Ind. Inf.], National Archives.

6. Inquest papers for Matthew L. Collett [vicious], November and December 1883, Indiana State Archives [no commitment resulted on these occasions]; for other Collett commitments, see commitment no. 4340, December 2, 1879, Indiana Hospital for the Insane, Indiana State Archives [acute mania], and commitment no. 236-204, Northern Hospital for the Insane [Logansport], Indiana State Archives [homicidal and confined in cell]; commitment ledger for Charles D. Compton [vigorous effort], commitment no. 671-701, Northern Hospital for the Insane [Logansport], Indiana State Archives. For the Leaming case, see affidavits of George Walter, August 30, 1889 [whipped horses], Albert R. Tucker, M.D., December 5, 1889 [God; dread], Dr. Lewis Starzman, August 30, 1889 [mind not right], Joseph Noble, August 29, 1889 [Shiloh], Barnhardt Gintert, November 25, 1889 [piano], Peter Case, December 17, 1889 [flighty spells], federal pension file of David Leaming [B 8 Ind. Cav.], National Archives; see also commitment no. 3536, February 20, 1877, Indiana Hospital for the Insane, Indiana State Archives.

7. For Jacob Defferen, see commitments nos. 5319 and 5963, March 4, 1882, and September 22, 1883, Indiana Hospital for the Insane, Indiana State Archives; for John J. Cameron, see commitments nos. 6084, 6185, and 8003, on January 26, 1884, May 7, 1884, and October 24, 1888, Indiana Hospital for the Insane, Indiana State Archives. For Daniel Kivett, see commitment no. 4653, June 27, 1871, Indiana Hospital for the Insane, Indiana State Archives. For Joseph McCann, see commitment no. 4105, January 18, 1870, Indiana Hospital for the Insane, Indiana State Archives; for Ephraim Maple, see commitments nos. 4058, 5675, 8989, 10255, 11179, dated April 4, 1879, January 9, 1883, October 12, 1891, February 13, 1897, and January 17, 1900, Indiana Hospital for the Insane, Indiana State Archives, in addition to commitment no. 212-170, August 11, 1888, Northern Hospital for the Insane (Logansport), Indiana State Archives. For causes of insanity assigned at the Iowa Hospital for the Insane, see Sharon E. Wood, " 'My Life Is Not Quite Useless': The Diary of an Asylum Bookkeeper," *Palimpsest*, 70 (1) (Spring 1989): 3–13, 5.

8. See commitment of Christian Weiler, commitment no. 321-334 [dance, work on ward], Northern Hospital for the Insane (Logansport), Indiana State Archives; commitment of Henry Sloan, commitment no. 4466, December 8, 1870, Indiana Hospital for the Insane, Indiana State Archives; pension bureau medical board report, June 20, 1892 [kitchen work, ward work], federal pension file of Julius M. McDonald [K 12 Ind. Cav., G 46 Ind. Inf.], National Archives; commitment of Horace Hobart [attacked attendants], commitment no. 5315, July 25, 1873, Indiana Hospital for the Insane, Indiana State Archives; affidavit of Cornelius Luther, June 19, 1897, federal pension file of Cornelius Luther [I 129 Ind. Inf.], National Archives; inquest papers of Edmond R. Floyd, commitment no. 11804, January 10, 1902, Indiana Hospital for the Insane, Indiana State Archives.

9. For an instance of bleeding employed in 1882, see inquest papers of General W. Kilgore, commitment no. 5363, April 14, 1882, Indiana Hospital for the Insane, Indiana State Archives; for use of morphine, see inquest papers of John M. Smith, commitment no. 4645, June 21, 1871, Indiana Hospital for the Insane, Indiana State Archives; for use of purgatives, see inquest papers of Shelby A. Bridgewater, commitment no. 5217, December 5, 1881, Indiana Hospital for the Insane, Indiana State Archives; for use of sedatives, see inquest papers of Henry Hild, commitment no. 6515, February 25, 1885, Indiana Hospital for the Insane, Indiana State Archives.

10. For instances of restraint at home, see doctors' statement in application for federal pension, November 25, 1885 [kept under lock and key at home], federal pension file of Jacob Fink [F 1 U.S. Cav.; D 5 Ind. Cav.], National Archives; inquest papers of Gabriel Lawson [restrained for several days at home], commitment no. 11537, March 11, 1901, Indiana Hospital for the Insane, Indiana State Archives; pension bureau medical board report, February 27, 1884 [confined in room], federal pension file of Benjamin Murphy [F 93 Ind. Inf; H 21 VRC], National Archives; affidavit of Dr. C. F. Bucklin, December 18, 1902 [strong room], federal pension file of Allen E. Wiley [C 54 Ind. Inf.], National Archives.

11. For instances of charity, poor relief, and the poorhouse, see guardian's declaration, September 28, 1891 [poorhouse, charity, alms], federal pension file of James H. Galbreath [F & H 135 Ind. Inf., H 19 U.S. Inf.], National Archives; for an instance of GAR relief, see affidavit of August Fagel, October 12, 1894, federal pension file of John H. Stotsunberg [A & F 76 Ind. Inf.], National Archives.

12. Willard Waller, *The Veteran Comes Back* (New York: Dryden Press, 1944), pp. 199, 219–220 [number of veterans; 1893 level]; William H. Glasson, *Federal Military Pensions in the United States* (New York: Oxford University Press, 1918), p. 266 [number in 1902]; George Hazzard, *The Democratic Party; The True Soldier's Best Friend; With Some Observations on Pensions and Pension Legislation by a Pensioner* (Tacoma, Wash.: Democratic Party Publication, 1890), p. 16 [number of invalid pensioners]. On Civil War veterans and the pension system, see (in addition to Waller and Glasson) John William Oliver, "History of the Civil War Military Pensions, 1861–1885," *Bulletin of the University of Wisconsin*, no. 844, History Series, vol. 4, no. 1 (1917): pp. 1–120; Gustavus A. Weber, *The Bureau of Pensions: Its History, Activities, and Organization* (Baltimore: Johns Hopkins University Press, 1923); Roger Burlingame, *Peace Veterans: The Story of a Racket and a Plea for Economy* (New York: Minton, Balch and Co., 1932); Knowlton Durham, *Billions for Veterans: An Analysis of Bonus Problems—Yesterday, Today, and Tomorrow* (New York: Brewer, Warren, and Putnam, 1932); Mary R. Dearing, *Veterans in Politics: The Story of the G.A.R.* (Baton Rouge, La.: Louisiana State University Press, 1952); William Pyrle Dillingham, *Federal Aid to Veterans* (Gainesville: University of Florida Press, 1952); Judith Gladys Cetina, "A History of Veterans' Homes in the United States, 1811–1930" (diss., Case Western University, 1977); and Theda Skocpol, *Protecting Soldiers and Mothers: The Political Origins of Social Policy in the United States* (Cambridge, Mass.: Harvard University Press, 1992).

13. John Harley Warner, *The Therapeutic Perspective: Medical Practice, Knowledge, and Identity in America, 1820–1885* (Cambridge, Mass.: Harvard University Press, 1986), pp. 1–7; Richard Harrison Shryock, *The Development of Modern Medicine: An Interpretation of the Social and Scientific Factors Involved* (Philadelphia: University of Pennsylvania Press, 1936), pp. 30–32, 152–157, 187–197; and John S. Haller, Jr., *American Medicine in Transition, 1840–1910* (Champaign: University of Illinois Press, 1981), pp. 5–11. See also Lester S. King, *Transformations in American Medicine: From Benjamin Rush to William Osler* (Baltimore: Johns Hopkins University Press, 1990); William G. Rothstein, *American Physicians in the Nineteenth Century: From Sects to Science* (Baltimore: Johns Hopkins University Press, 1972); and Paul Starr, *The Social Transformation of American Medicine: The Rise of a Sovereign Profession and the Making of a Vast Industry* (New York: Basic Books, 1982). Note that the asylum ledger at the Indiana Hospital for the Insane contained, as late as 1866, a blank for "temperament," for which the admitting clerk or physician was apparently to provide an answer in accordance with the classical system of humoral theory. See commitment for Leroy L. Smith, commitment no. 3230, November 20, 1866, Indiana Hospital for the Insane, Indiana State Archives. For contemporary medical treatises on insanity, see A. H. Bayles, "Mental Influences as Conducive to Health or Productive of Disease" (medical school thesis, University of Michigan, n.d.); William R. Berry, "Lucid Intervals in Insanity" (medical school thesis, University of Michigan, 1866); and Jacob Eton Bowers, "The History, Pathology and Treatment of Insanity" (medical school thesis, University of Michigan, 1869).

14. In general, see Erwin H. Ackerknecht, *A Short History of Psychiatry* (New York: Hafner Publishing Co., 1968), pp. 64–73, 75–82.

15. George C. Palmer, "Insanity" (medical school thesis, University of Michigan, 1865), p. 1.

16. Affidavit of Orange T. [Rumls?], M.D., September 2, 1897 [morbid conditions], federal pension file of Elmer Cady [B 132 Ind. Inf.], National Archives [nonsample]; affidavit of John M. Youart, M.D., December 29, 1881 [medulla oblongata], federal pension file of Horace Hobart [G 17 Ind. Inf.], National Archives; inquest papers of Jacob Seay, commitment no. 11289 [metastic], May 31, 1900, Indiana Hospital for the Insane, Indiana State Archives [nonsample]; affidavit of C. W. Shill, M.D., September 8, 1886 [general debility], federal pension file of Lafayette Hardesty [H 33 Ind. Inf.], National Archives [nonsample]; statement of Dr. A. E. Bell [re suicide], in the pension case of *Maggie Schweigert*, V, *Decisions of the Department of the Interior in Appealed Pension Claims* (1892), pp. 32–35. See also the cases of *Mary A. Buker*, I, *Decisions of the Department of the Interior in Appealed Pension Claims* (Washington, D.C.: U.S. Government Printing Office), p. 108 (1887); and *Margaret, Widow of Adam Mayer*, II, *Decisions of the Department of the Interior in Appealed Pension Claims* (1888), 203–204. Regarding the often arcane methods and rules of the Pension Bureau, see Bureau of Pensions, *Bureau of Pensions: Its Officers and Their Duties* (Washington, D.C.: U.S. Government Printing Office, 1890), p. 31–33 [rates]; Bureau of Pensions, *A Treatise on the Practice of the Pension Bureau* (Washington, D.C.: U.S. Government Printing Office, 1898), pp. 24–

25 [pathological sequence]; Pension Bureau, *Instructions to Examining Surgeons* (Washington, D.C.: U.S. Government Printing Office, 1882, 1886, 1889).

17. Commitment report of the Kansas State Insane Asylum, June 1, 1878 [open wound], federal pension file of Er Julian [A 30 Ind. Inf.], National Archives.

18. To a certain extent, this state of affairs was attributable to the basic requirement that *any* disability originate in the service and continue thereafter to be compensable, as well as an original prohibition against parole evidence. See William H. Glasson, *Federal Military Pensions in the United States* (New York: Oxford University Press, 1918), p. 165.

19. Affidavit of Fred H. Austin, M.D., February 12, 1894, federal pension file of Squire Ridgeway [G 147 Ind. Inf.], National Archives; see Pension Bureau decision concerning Sloan's claim for a service-related pension in 1886, federal pension file of Henry Sloan [C 5 Ind. Cav.], National Archives; Pension Bureau decision, March 25, 1911, federal pension file of John M. Smith [B 146 Ind. Inf.], National Archives.

20. Letter from W. D. Halfhill, to commissioner of pensions, July 31, 1888 [profligate], federal pension file of Jerome Asbury [D 31 Ind. Inf.], National Archives; affidavit of Samuel W. Curtis, September 2, 1890 [restlessness], federal pension file of John C. Britton [F 10 Ind. Inf.], National Archives. In general, see W. Andrew Achenbaum et al., "Patterns of Alcohol Use and Abuse among Aging Civil War Veterans, 1865–1920," *Bulletin of the New York Academy of Medicine*, 69 (1) (January-February 1993): 69–85.

21. See Pension Bureau decision of March 2, 1899, affidavits of James A. Clark, October 19, 1889 [spells after army], John Phifer, February 21, 1890 [sprees], Mrs. Lucy R. Ford, August 8, 1890 [excited at mention of army], letter of special examiner, August 18, 1890 [lantern], federal pension file of William R. Durland [C 10 Ind. Cav.], National Archives. Inquest papers for Samuel Spencer Goldsberry, commitment no. 10113, June 6, 1896, and commitment no. 11764, November 16, 1901, Indiana Hospital for the Insane, Indiana State Archives.

22. Inquest papers of Ephraim B. Maple, commitment no. 5675, January 9, 1883 [chronic masturbator], Indiana Hospital for the Insane, Indiana State Archives; L. J. Kahn, *Nervous Exhaustion; Its Cause and Cure, Comprising a Series of Eight Lectures on Debility and Disease, as Delivered Nightly at Dr. Kahn's Museum of Anatomy, with Practical Information on Marriage . . .* (New York, 1876), p. 7 [desolation]; inquest papers of Joseph Batson, commitment no. 3057, January 12, 1875 [exciting cause], Indiana Hospital for the Insane, Indiana State Archives, and Pension Bureau decision of May 12, 1890 [rejection based on masturbation], federal pension file of Joseph Batson [H 123 Ind. Inf.] National Archives; surgeon's certificate in army discharge papers, October 14, 1862, and Pension Bureau decision of February 11, 1892, federal pension file of Lewis Y. Crum [14th Ind. L.A.], National Archives. For contemporary medical theory on masturbation, see G. A. Brundage, "Spermatorrhoea" (medical school thesis, University of Michigan, 1876), p. 1; and Hayes French, "Spermatorrhaea" (medical school thesis, University of Michigan, 1865), p. 2 [incubus].

23. *O.R.*, ser. I, vol. 30, pt. I, p. 173 [casualties]; *O.R.*, ser. I, vol. 30, pt. I, p. 4

[Report of Col. Ferdinand Van Derveer, Thirty-Fifth Ohio Infantry, Commanding Third Brigade].

24. Affidavit of Sanford Fortner, August 31, 1888 [rattled], Charles E. Triplett, April 18, 1889 [So. Car.; D.C.], Milo D. Ellis, January 31, 1887 [D.C.], federal pension file of Newell Gleason [Col. 87 Ind. Inf.], National Archives.

25. Affidavits of George E. Woolsey, May 3, 1889 [Ellis brought him home], Charles E. Triplett, October 21, 1887 [mental prostration], Nancy Gleason, April 14, 1888 [condition], federal pension file of Newell Gleason [Col. 87 Ind. Inf.], National Archives; commitment of Newell Gleason, commitment no. 3029, November 28, 1874, Indiana Hospital for the Insane, Indiana State Archives; letter of Dr. George L. Andrew to Dr. O. Everts, superintendent of the Indiana Hospital for the Insane, November 30, 1874, inquest papers of Newell Gleason, see above.

26. Affidavit of William D. Biddle, November 11, 1887 [night before], and Nancy Gleason, n.d. [circumstances of suicide], Pension Bureau decision of 1889 [acceptance despite doubts], Eber L. Amis, n.d. [coroner], George L. Andrews, M.D., October 21, 1887 [hardships], federal pension file of Newell Gleason [Col. 87 Ind. Inf.], National Archives.

27. The *Medical and Surgical History of the War of the Rebellion*, Medical History, pt. I, vol. I, ed. Barnes, indicates that for Union troops (white and black), there were 236,912 cases of gunshot wounds and 33,949 deaths; 32,209 Union soldiers were discharged on account of gunshot wounds, and another 6,159 were discharged on account of amputations (see pp. 641, 712, 648, 718). The total number of amputations for Union soldiers in the war is usually placed at about 30,000 (see introduction to index by James I. Robertson, Jr., p. x). For the Agnew case see affidavits of Jasper Inman, September 8, 1898 [despondent], Richard L. Adams, September 8, 1898 [talk of suicide], Dr. Henry K. Deen, September 8, 1898 [brooding], Pension Bureau medical board report, July 8, 1880 [sleepless], and coroner's report of Rolla E. Kirk, J.P., from Harrison Co., Ind., June 14, 1898, federal pension file of John Agnew [C 50 and E 144 Ind. Inf.], National Archives.

28. Affidavits of S. Davis, M.D., April 28, 1867 [walk, manual labor], James C. Burt, M.D., April 26, 1869 [exact injury], Solomon W. Biddinger, M.D., June 1, 1877 [insanity due to wound], W.J. Elstum, M.D., January 20, 1879 [suicide attempt], Jobe Shirk, January 4, 1866 [growing worse], Thomas A. Shirk, January 21, 1886 [crying], Pension Bureau Medical Examiner, September 30, 1886 [suicide due to gunshot wound], Pension Bureau Legal Reviewer, L.E. [Deckey?], February 19, 1887 [mind shattered by 1870], federal pension file of Logan P. Herod [H 12 Ind. Inf.], National Archives.

29. Paul E. Steiner, *Disease in the Civil War: Natural Biological Warfare in 1861–1865* (Springfield, Ill.: Charles C. Thomas, 1968).

30. Soldier's declaration, October 22, 1886 [army experience], Pension Bureau medical board report, June 17, 1996 [emaciated, vertigo, etc.], Dr. T. C. Light, June 18, 1904 [certified suicide], George M. Beaman, December 25, 1902 [suicide], Otto W. Ruble, December 26, 1903 [prior attempt], federal pension file of Joshua Jordan [E 149 Ind. Inf.], National Archives.

31. Affidavit of James O. Huston, February 2, 1891 [victuals], federal pension

file of John W. Robinson [B 66 Ind. Inf.], National Archives; inquest papers of John W. Robinson, commitment no. 10450, October 1, 1897, Indiana Hospital for the Insane, Indiana State Archives. Affidavits of J. Marshall Barkley, M.D., June 8, 1889 [last visit], John H. Jackson, April 29, 1887 [depressed, brooding], Robert J. Simpson (doctor?), May 13, 1887 [melancholia], Joseph M. Pearce, J.P. for Pleasant Twp., Switzerland Co., April 21, 1887 [suicide], federal pension file of Benjamin Welch [B 140 Ind. Inf.], National Archives. For a consideration of the cause of widespread chronic diarrhea in Civil War soldiers, see Alfred Jay Bollet, "Scurvy and Chronic Diarrhea in Civil War Troops: Were They Both Nutritional Deficiency Syndromes?" *Journal of the History of Medicine*, 47 (January 1992): 49–67.

32. George Rosen, "History in the Study of Suicide," *Psychological Medicine*, 1 (1971), 267–85; Michael MacDonald, "The Medicalization of Suicide in England: Laymen, Physicians, and Cultural Change, 1500–1870," *Milbank Quarterly*, 67 (Supp. 1) (1989): 69–91.

33. Affidavits of Mary J. Shearer, n.d., Nancy Janes Phillips, May 17, 1895 [poison], Elizabeth Davis, May 17, 1895 [melancholy, poison], John M. Phillips, May 22, 1895 [poison], federal pension file of Daniel Shearer [59 Ind. Inf.], National Archives. Affidavit of W. J. Elstum, M.D., January 20, 1879 [suicide attempt—reflex action], federal pension file of Logan P. Herod [H 12 Ind. Inf.], National Archives.

34. Soldier's declaration, October 11, 1883 [fall as accident], army disability discharge papers, January 23, 1863 [shotgun injury], Martha M. Soper, June 2, 1884 [hallucination], federal pension file of Lineas Risley [D 18 Ind. Inf.], National Archives. Commitment of Lineas Risley, commitment no. 2442, February 11, 1863, Indiana Hospital for the Insane, Indiana State Archives.

35. *Hannah McClellan (Dependent Mother)*, 4, *Decisions of the Department of the Interior in Appealed Pension Claims* (1891), pp. 117–120; *Elizabeth Penman, now Fulmer (as Widow)*, 12, *Decisions of the Department of the Interior in Appealed Pension and Bounty-Land Claims* (1901–02; 9/10/1902), pp. 459–464.

8. "Tramping by Night and Day"

1. See service record [court-martial] and medical board report, April 6, 1870 [sensitivity to alcohol], federal pension file of John W. Blake [Col. 40 Ind. Inf.], National Archives; inquest papers for John W. Blake, commitment no. 7613, September 19, 1887, Indiana Hospital for the Insane, Indiana State Archives. Sar A. Levitan and Karen A. Cleary, *Old Wars Remain Unfinished: The Veteran Benefits System* (Baltimore: Johns Hopkins Press, 1973), p. 9 [1.9 million Union veterans].

2. Inquest papers of Alfred Modlin [choke], commitment no. 5908, August 7, 1883, Indiana Hospital for the Insane, Indiana State Archives; inquest papers of Martin M. Ring [threat to kill], commitment no. 6149, April 5, 1884, Indiana Hospital for the Insane, Indiana State Archives; inquest papers of Josiah Gossett [assaults], commitment no. 1-673, November 3, 1892, Eastern Hospital for the Insane (Richmond), Indiana State Archives; inquest papers of Robert Lash [destroys furniture], commitment no. 11618, June 13, 1901, Indiana Hos-

pital for the Insane, Indiana State Archives; inquest papers of John J. Cameron, commitment no. 6084 and no. 6185C, January 26, 1884, and May 7, 1884, Indiana Hospital for the Insane, Indiana State Archives; affidavits of Catherine Knorr, November 30, 1881 [Chickamauga], and Peter Fisher, December 6, 1881 [whipping], federal pension file of Frank Knorr [1st Lt. D 32 and Capt. H 32 Ind. Inf.], National Archives; affidavit of John P. Jaehring, March 6, 1888 [bowling ball], federal pension file of John Kirk [Unass'd 79 Ind. Inf. and H 13 Ind. Inf.], National Archives; inquest papers of Manville Russell [peace bond], commitment no. 8420, February 14, 1890, Indiana Hospital for the Insane, Indiana State Archives.

3. Affidavit of John H. Russe, December 2, 1881 [thumbs], federal pension file of Frank Knorr [1st Lt. D 32 and Capt. H 32 Ind. Inf.], National Archives; inquest papers of Arthur Brenton, commitment no. 10115, June 14, 1896, Indiana Hospital for the Insane, Indiana State Archives; inquest papers of Jacob Fink, commitment no. 3281, January 10, 1876, Indiana Hospital for the Insane, Indiana State Archives; inquest papers of Samuel M. Martin, commitment no. 9775, April 4, 1895, Indiana Hospital for the Insane, Indiana State Archives; inquest papers of Leonard C. Griffith [homicidal impulse], commitment no. 8308, September 15, 1889, Indiana Hospital for the Insane, Indiana State Archives.

4. Inquest papers of Henry Hild [drove family away], commitment no. 6515, February 25, 1885, Indiana Hospital for the Insane, Indiana State Archives; affidavit of Lyman B. Wilcox, January 24, 1905 [Nancy Hoover], federal pension file of William S. Hoover [21 Ind. L.A.], National Archives; affidavit of Ellen McKinney, December 1, 1890, federal pension file of Patrick McKinney [C 149 Ind. Inf.], National Archives; inquest papers of John C. Britton, commitment no. 5925, August 25, 1883, and commitment report for commitment no. 6873, November 28, 1885, Indiana Hospital for the Insane, Indiana State Archives; inquest papers of Ephraim B. Maple, commitments no. 10255 [niece] and no. 11179 [threat to kill], February 13, 1897, and January 17, 1900, Indiana Hospital for the Insane, Indiana State Archives.

5. Inquest papers of Martin V. Toney [refuses to talk], commitment no. 13398, October 26, 1906, Indiana Hospital for the Insane, Indiana State Archives; physicians' statements of D. F. Davis and John E. Fetzer [shot to death], n.d., federal pension file of William H. Hobson [A 38 and A & B 24 Ind. Inf.], National Archives; for rude behavior, see affidavit of Jacob A. Horner, November 21, 1894 [swearing at ladies], federal pension file of William Churchill [F 59 Ind. Inf. & Com. Sgt. 59 Ind. Inf.], National Archives; and inquest papers for William H. Guile [insulting ladies on the street], commitment no. 4970, May 14, 1881, Indiana Hospital for the Insane, Indiana State Archives; for attempted rape, see inquest papers of Elias Bickerton, commitment no. 8960, August 18, 1891, Indiana Hospital for the Insane, Indiana State Archives.

6. Commitment report of Joseph S. Valentine, commitment no. 12688, July 22, 1904, Indiana Hospital for the Insane, Indiana State Archives [nonsample; probably a case of senile dementia, and excluded from sample on that account]; inquest papers of John A. M. Cox, commitment no. 7190, August 31, 1886, Indiana Hospital for the Insane, Indiana State Archives; inquest papers

of Leonard C. Griffith, commitment no. 8308, September 15, 1889, Indiana Hospital for the Insane, Indiana State Archives; inquest papers of George Barter, commitment no. 4998, June 7, 1881, Indiana Hospital for the Insane, Indiana State Archives.

7. Affidavit of Maggie Glover, July 28, 1919 [spree], federal pension file of William J. Glover [C 1 Ind. H.A.; C 21 Ind. Inf.], National Archives [nonsample]; affidavit of Catherine Knorr, November 30, 1881, and letter of Clay Lemmon to Catherine Knorr, January 28, 1887, federal pension file of Frank Knorr [1st Lt. D 32 and Capt. H 32 Ind. Inf.], National Archives.

8. Affidavit of Robert Walsh, July 7, 1892, federal pension file of Robert Walsh [B 4 Ind. Cav; I 16 Ind. Inf.], National Archives; commitment ledger of Robert D. Commons, commitment no. 5658, July 4, 1874, Indiana Hospital for the Insane, Indiana State Archives; inquest papers of Jacob Mann, commitment no. 8392, December 27, 1889, Indiana Hospital for the Insane, Indiana State Archives; commitment ledger for Joel J. Porter, commitment no. 4115, June 3, 1879, Indiana Hospital for the Insane, Indiana State Archives; affidavit of John R. Virden, March 18, 1991 [profligacy], and report of W. S. Neely (Pension Bureau official), December 18, 1990, federal pension file of Robert B. Vance [3 Ind. L.A.], National Archives; and commitment ledger of Robert B. Vance [worthless vagabond], commitment no. 6466, January 9, 1885, Indiana Hospital for the Insane, Indiana State Archives.

9. Letters of Perry B. Bowser, April 24, 1896, and September 23, 1897, federal pension file of Perry B. Bowser [F 12 Ind. Cav; E 9 Ill. Cav.; D 9 Ind. Inf.], National Archives [nonsample]; affidavit of Dr. V. E. Delashmutt, June 7, 1892, federal pension file of Lewis Chowning [I 43 Ind. Inf.], National Archives; inquest papers of George A. C. Gooch, commitment no. 6973, February 24, 1886, Indiana Hospital for the Insane, Indiana State Archives; affidavit of Franklin W. Hays, July 25, 1896, federal pension file of Samuel M Martin [Band 18 Ind. Inf.], National Archives; inquest papers of William H. Bradley, commitment no. 8118 [Dr. J. R. Houston], March 12, 1889, and inquest papers of June 7, 1890 (recommitment number not available), Indiana Hospital for the Insane, Indiana State Archives.

10. Gerald Grob notes in *Mental Illness and American Society, 1875–1940* (Princeton: Princeton University Press, 1983), p. 8, that by 1880 there were 140 mental institutions in the United States with 41,000 patients; these hospitals ranged in capacity from small (139) to large (1,254), with the average patient population being 544. From 1880 census data, Grob estimates that 45 percent of the insane in the United States were in hospitals, 45 percent were cared for at home, and the remaining 10 percent were kept in almshouses. See Appendix C.

11. For disability rates, see W. H. H. Terrell, *Report of the Adjutant General of the State of Indiana,* vol. I (Indianapolis: Alexander H. Conner, 1869), Statistics and Documents, p. 115; *O.R.,* ser. III, vol. V, p. 668 (Washington, D.C.: U.S. Government Printing Office, 1900); Paul E. Steiner, *Disease in the Civil War: Natural Biological Warfare in 1861–1865* (Springfield, Ill.: Charles C. Thomas, 1968), pp. 8–9. For desertion rates, see Terrell, p. 115, and *O.R.,* p. 668.

12. This outcome can possibly be explained by two factors. First, information on

nativity for members of the Indiana Sample was derived from military and asylum records; for men who were committed to the asylum in the 1880s or 1890s, nativity might have been reported as "Indiana" because these men had lived in the state for an extended period of years by that time, even though they had actually been born out of state. In such cases, if actual place of birth had been recorded as place of nativity, then perhaps the numbers for this Indiana Sample would be more in line with the numbers for all Indiana volunteers during the Civil War. Second, in the absence of Social Security numbers and other definitive data on identity, one way of matching nineteenth-century record groups is to find a link between men claiming an obscure crossroads town as their hometown; this is to say that if a "John Smith" of the 60th Indiana Regiment hailed from Oolitic, Indiana, and a "John Smith" from Oolitic, Indiana, was committed to the insane asylum in 1880, and the age otherwise seemed to match in the two records, this is a strong indication that these John Smiths were one and the same person. It becomes much more difficult to declare such a match when one is dealing with dozens of John Smiths from huge metropolitan areas such as Indianapolis. Hence, there was probably a bias in the Indiana Sample toward men who came from small villages and who had been born in Indiana. This possible bias would hold true if one could assume that men immigrating to Indiana from other states would tend to settle in larger cities—which is not necessarily a valid assumption.

13. B. Kathleen Jordan et al., "Lifetime and Current Prevalence of Specific Psychiatric Disorders among Vietnam Veterans and Controls," *Archives of General Psychiatry*, 48 (3) (March 1991): 207–215 [high levels of war zone stress]; Josefina J. Card, "Epidemiology of PTSD in a National Cohort of Vietnam Veterans," *Journal of Clinical Psychology*, 43 (1) (January 1987): 6–7 [27 percent versus 19 percent].

14. For officers, the mean death rate was 9.94 percent, whereas this rate was 12.52 percent for enlisted men.

15. For the Regimental Data, the differences between infantry and cavalry casualty indices were not statistically significant for the officer casualty (percentage died in war) index [$t(27.8) = 1.7857$, $p = 0.0851$, two tails], for the casualty index for enlisted men [$t(27.3) = 0.9276$, $p = 0.3618$, two tails], or the total casualty index [$t(27.3) = 0.9839$, $p = 0.3338$, two tails]. Owing to unbalanced classes (infantry companies = 205; cavalry companies = 28, heavy artillery companies = 2, and light artillery companies = 8), an ANOVA test is not appropriate, and glm tests indicated no significant differences on casualty indices per branch of service, including the battle index on which there seemed to be the greatest difference (4.285 percent for infantry, 3.33 percent for heavy artillery, 2.5 percent for cavalry, and 1.62 percent for light artillery).

16. On the basis of the Company Sample data, all indices were higher by statistically significant margins for volunteers than for recruits: battle casualties [$t(484) = -3.6238$, $p = 0.0003$, two tails], death rate [$t(484) = -5.2223$, $p = 0.000$, two tails], disability rate [$t(484) = -7.716$, $p = 0.000$, two tails], and total casualty (death + disability) rate [$t(484) = -7.9403$, $p = 0.000$, two tails].

17. For Regimental Data, higher rates in the western theater for enlisted men [$t(136) = -2.8997$, $p = 0.0044$, two tails] and total (officers + enlisted men) death indices [$t(136) = -2.8675$, $p = 0.0048$, two tails] were statistically significant; the rates for officer casualties were also higher [$t(136) = -1.3718$, $p = 0.1724$, two tails] in the western theater, but not statistically significant. For the Company Sample, death [$t(234) = -3.9763$, $p = 0.0001$, two tails], disability [$t(234) = -2.0850$, $p = 0.0382$, two tails], and total casualty [$t(234) = -3.2853$, $p = 0.0012$, two tails] indices were higher by statistically significant margins for units operating in the western theater; the battle casualty index was higher for units fighting in the eastern theater, but not by a statistically significant margin [$t(37.1) = 0.1241$, $p = 0.9019$, two tails].

18. This data relates to the issues of dissent during the Civil War: the first, second, third, and fourth districts are in southern Indiana along the Ohio River or south of Indianapolis; the ninth, tenth, and eleventh districts are in northern Indiana, the eleventh being the site of Huntington County, the home of notorious Copperheads such as Lambdin Milligan.

19. Battle [(number killed in action + number died of wounds + number discharged due to wounds)/number in company], Battles per month [the above number divided by the number of months the company was actually in service], Death [(number died of disease + number killed in battle)/number in company], Deaths per month [previous number divided by the number of months the company was actually in service], Disability [number discharged for disability/number in company], Disabilities per month [previous number divided by the number of months the company was actually in service], Total [Death + Disability rates combined], Total per month [previous number divided by the number of months the company was actually in service], Desertion [rate of desertion], Reenlistment [for units in service over twenty-four months, the rate of reenlistment as veterans].

20. For the Indiana Sample, the mean equaled .12326, compared with a mean of .1111 for the Company Sample [$t(533) = -1.5138$, $p = 0.1307$, two tails].

21. The major problems with this approach are threefold. First, casualty indices for non-Indiana units were not available, so men who served in such units were excluded from the analysis; only 249 men were included in this analysis, rather than the 291 men in the Indiana Sample. Second, men who were separated from the military for a disability would have an artificially low index because their months in the military were limited, whereas in fact they should represent the highest index possible for disability. Third, the comparison in effect compares apples and oranges, since the individual experience of the Indiana Sample is compared with the unit averages of the Company Sample. A better method would be to compare the Indiana Sample with a similar number of individual soldiers in a control group.

22. The differences were statistically significant for three of the indices: for battle [$t(9247) = -2.0799$, $p = 0.0386$, two tails], disability [$t(62) = -3.0143$, $p = 0.0037$, two tails], and total [$t(59.7) = -2.0983$, $p = 0.0401$, two tails].

9. "I Am Glad I Served My Country"

1. "Vietnam Veterans' Readjustment," hearings before the Committee on Veterans' Affairs, United States Senate, 96th Cong., 2nd sess., February 21,

March 4, and May 21, 1980, Washington, D.C., Pt. 2 (Washington, D.C.: U.S. Government Printing Office, 1980), p. 869 [home loans]; for benefits available to Civil War veterans [mainly bounty land, artificial limbs, and pensions], see Dixon Wecter, *When Johnny Comes Marching Home* (Westport, Conn.: Greenwood Press, 1944), pp. 186–214.

2. *Myths and Realities: A Study of Attitudes toward Vietnam Era Veterans,* report submitted by the Veterans' Administration to the Committee on Veterans' Affairs, U.S. House of Representatives (Washington, D.C.: U.S. Government Printing Office, 1980), pp. xl and 52 [public doesn't blame Vietnam vets], xxxix [pride], and 39 [friendly reception]. For evidence that Vietnam veterans themselves feel that the war improved or strengthened them as people, see James Webb, "Viet Vets Didn't Kill Babies and They Aren't Suicidal," *Washington Post,* April 6, 1986, p. C1a; "Poll Finds Veterans Are at Home Again; Most Have Joined Mainstream America," *Washington Post,* April 14, 1985, p. A1a [homeowners]; Michael Norman, "For Us, the War Is Over," *New York Times Magazine,* March 31, 1985, pp. 64–71; Jonathan Borus, "Reentry I. Adjustment Issues Facing the Vietnam Returnee," *Archives of General Psychiatry,* 28 (April 1973): 501, 503–504, notes that 90 percent of the veterans in his study stated that they were not sorry they had served in Vietnam. They felt useful and productive in their roles in Vietnam, and described being part of a "family" or "team." The majority did not feel let down by the general society upon their return, nor did they feel that civilians were uncaring about them; William Goldsmith and Constantine Cretekos, "Unhappy Odysseys: Psychiatric Hospitalizations Among Vietnam Returnees," *Archives of General Psychiatry,* 20 (January 1969): 78–83, 83: "There was no expression of bitterness by any patient about the dissension in the United States concerning the war."

3. P. S. Prescott, review of *Home from the War,* by Robert Jay Lifton, in *Newsweek,* June 18, 1973, pp. 106–107 [antiwar investigator]; R. J. Lifton, "Scars of Vietnam," *Commonweal,* February 20, 1970, pp. 554–556 [psychological crucible].

4. For allegations of disproportionate minority casualties in Vietnam, see "The War That Has No Ending," *Discover,* June 1985, p. 46; and "Veterans of the Wrong War: The Vertigo of Homecoming," *Nation,* December 17, 1973, pp. 646–649. For class warfare allegations, see "Who Really Died in Vietnam," *Saturday Review,* November 18, 1972 [fought for us by our "servants"]; "Vietnam Vet," *Commonweal,* March 10, 1972, pp. 12–14; "Who Really Died in Vietnam? The Cost in Human Lives," *Saturday Review,* November 18, 1972, pp. 40–43; and James Fallows, "What Did You Do in the Class War, Daddy?" *Washington Monthly,* 7, 8 (1975): 5–20. For studies on the socioeconomic and racial composition of casualties, see "Toll of the War," *U.S. News and World Report,* Dec. 18, 1972, p. 27 [indicates that nearly 13 percent of the war dead (7,178) were black, about the same as black strength in the services]. M. Zeitlin, K. G. Lutterman, and J. W. Russell, "Death in Vietnam: Class, Poverty, and the Risks of War," *Politics and Society,* 3 (3) (1973): 313–328 [27.2 percent of Vietnam war casualties came from poor families; not a "class war"]; Gilbert Badillo and G. David Curry, "The Social Incidence of Vietnam Casualties; Social Class or Race?" *Armed Forces and Society,* 2 (3) (1976): 397–406 [social class, not race, was the factor most responsible for disproportion-

ate casualties borne by "certain American communities"]; Sue E. Berryman, *Who Serves? The Persistent Myth of the Underclass Army* (Boulder, Col.: Westview Press, 1987), pp. 37–42; R. Martin and G. Boulanger, "Who Went to War?" in *Vietnam Veterans: Facts and Fictions of Their Psychological Adjustment*, ed. G. Boulanger and C. Kadushin (Mahwah, N.J.: Lawrence Erlbaum, 1985), p. 27 [that race, class, and predisposition can be ruled out as determining the amount of combat to which a man was exposed]; Allan Mazur, "Was Vietnam a Class War?" *Armed Forces & Society*, 21 (3) (Spring 1995): 455–459 [not a class war]; and Thomas C. Wilson, "Vietnam-Era Military Service: A Test of the Class-Bias Thesis," *Armed Forces & Society*, 21 (3) (Spring 1995): 461–471 [not an equal-opportunity war, but not a "class war" either].

5. "The War and the Arts: There Has Been a Cultural Turnaround on the Subject of Vietnam," *New York Times Magazine*, March 31, 1985, pp. 51, 55 [changing images]; Kevin Phillips in *Post-Conservative America: People, Politics, and Ideology in a Time of Crisis* (New York: Random House, 1982), p. 165; *Washington Post*, February 25, 1981, p. 2 [Reagan].

6. Lisa M. Heilbronn, "Coming Home a Hero: The Changing Image of the Vietnam Vet on Prime Time Television," *Journal of Popular Film and Television*, 13 (1) (1985): 25–30 [survivor-hero]; Colman McCarthy, "Veterans Owed Apologies, Not Parades," *Washington Post*, June 29, 1986, p. G10d [criticism of parades].

7. For the idea that the military has learned from Vietnam, see James Kitfield, *Prodigal Soldiers: How the Generation of Officers Born of Vietnam Revolutionized the American Style of War* (New York: Simon & Schuster, 1995).

8. "The Vietnam-Veteran Blues," *New York Times*, March 29, 1974, p. 35:2 [billions]; Willard Waller, *The Veteran Comes Back* (New York: Dryden Press, 1944), p. 189; Craig Kubey et al., *The Viet Vet Survival Guide: How to Cut Through the Bureaucracy and Get What You Need—And Are Entitled To* (New York: Ballantine Books, 1985), p. 15 [bank].

9. For the size of the VA budget, work force, and hospital system, see "Whatever Happened to the Vietnam Veteran?" *Nation's Business*, Dec. 1978, pp. 74–77; "War's Relentless Cost; It Doesn't End When the Shooting Stops," *U.S. News and World Report*, October 25, 1982, pp. 80–81; Veterans Administration, *Annual Report, 1984* (Washington, D.C.: U.S. Government Printing Office, 1985), pp. xvi, 13; and "Hearing before the Committee on Veterans' Affairs," *Fiscal Year 1989 Budget for Veterans' Programs and S. 2049, The Veterans' Home Loan Program Improvements Act of 1988*, U.S. Senate, 100th Cong., 2nd sess. (Washington, D.C.: U.S. Government Printing Office, 1988), p. 559. For the cost of veterans' benefits, see Series Y849–855, "Estimates of Total Cost of U.S. Wars," U.S. Bureau of the Census, *Historical Statistics of the United States, Colonial Times to 1970*, Pt. 2 (Washington, D.C.: U.S. Government Printing Office, 1975), p. 1140; no. 546, "Estimates of Total Dollar Costs of American Wars," and no. 569, "Veterans Benefits—Expenditures from Appropriated Funds, by War: Total and 1940 to 1988," in U.S. Bureau of the Census, *Statistical Abstract of the United States, 1990,* (Washington, D.C.: U.S. Government Printing Office, 1990), pp. 336, 345; and the statement of James L. Clayton, University of Utah, at "Hearings before the Subcommittee on Economy in

Government," U.S. Congress, Joint Economic Committee, *The Military Budget and National Economic Priorities*, pt. I, 91st Cong., 1st sess. (Washington, D.C.: U.S. Government Printing Office, 1969), pp. 143–150. Regarding payment of veterans' benefits into the next century, Maris A. Vinovskis, in "Have Social Historians Lost the Civil War? Some Preliminary Demographic Speculations," *Journal of American History*, 76 (1) (June 1989), notes that in 1987, sixty-six Civil War widows remained on the pension rolls (p. 52). "Veterans Rights Appear Safe," *Washington Post*, June 16, 1978, p. C-2-1C [veterans as 50 percent of federal work force].

10. "Memorial Day," *Washington Post*, May 28, 1979, p. A-20-1E [attack on Carter administration for inadequate *increases*]; "O'Brien Assails President on Aid to War Veterans," *New York Times*, May 30, 1970, p. 19:3 [attack on Nixon administration]; "The Vets: Heroes as Orphans," *Newsweek*, March 5, 1973, p. 22 +; "Help for Vietnam Veterans," *Washington Post*, September 11, 1978, p. A-26–1E [fight over disability benefit levels]; Causey, "Veterans Rights Appear Safe"; "Veterans' Group Ends 19-Day Sit-In; Disabled Servicemen Meet V.A. Head in Los Angeles and Voice Complaints," *New York Times*, March 3, 1974, p. 12:1 [bungling]; "The Discarded Army; When Fighting Men Lose Equal Rights," *New York Times*, March 31, 1974, section VII, p. 20 [bloated]; "An Advocate for Vietnam Veterans," *Washington Post*, February 10, 1978, p. A-15-2C [Vietnam vet advocacy]; "Vietnam Veterans in Congress," *Washington Post*, May 8, 1978, editorial [same].

11. Sar A. Levitan and Karen A. Cleary, *Old Wars Remain Unfinished: The Veteran Benefits System* (Baltimore: Johns Hopkins Press, 1973), p. ix.

12. Robert H. Fleming, "Post Vietnam Syndrome: Neurosis or Sociosis?" *Psychiatry*, 48 (2) (1985): 122–139, 128.

13. Christina Hoff Sommers, "Once a Soldier, Always a Dependent," *Hastings Center Report* 16 (4) (August 1986): 15–17.

14. John Keegan, *The Face of Battle* (New York: Dorset Press, 1976), pp. 27, 34.

15. "Vietnam, a Convert, Pursues Capitalism Devoutly," *New York Times*, April 5, 1996, p. A4; Daniel Hallin, *The "Uncensored War"* (New York: Oxford University Press, 1986), pp. 176–178.

16. For the argument of a central role for the media in undermining the will to wage war in Vietnam, see Robert Elegant, "How to Lose a War: Reflections of a Foreign Correspondent," *Encounter*, August 1981, pp. 73–90; Samuel P. Huntington, *American Politics: The Promise of Disharmony* (Cambridge, Mass.: Harvard University Press, 1981); and the discussion in Hallin, *The "Uncensored War."* Michael Mandelbaum, in "Vietnam: The Television War," *Daedalus*, 111 (4) (1982): 157–169, analyzes and rejects the conventional wisdom of a decisive role for television in Vietnam.

17. On the one hand, the "objective journalism" model would not pertain exactly, because the question was not necessarily a political one and government sources were not "managing" the news. On the other hand, much of what Hallin says about the media not taking the initiative to frame an issue for fear of appearing biased may relate to the delayed reaction on this issue.

18. For exceptions, see NBC, May 25, 1971, and a commentary by Eric Sevareid on CBS, April 21, 1971. Television news, of course, did cover specific issues

such as Vietnam vet drug abuse, unemployment, or incidents of criminal conduct, but was largely responding to statistics released by the government and covering extensive congressional committee hearings. It did not seem to be focusing on drumming up interest in the image of a uniquely troubled and scorned Vietnam veteran.

19. For dissenting views on the matter of the Vietnam veteran (that is, that his problems have been exaggerated) in the print media, see Anne Keegan, "GI's Vietnam Was Bittersweet Plum," *Chicago Tribune*, January 31, 1983, p. 15, C:1 [story of a Vietnam vet who was not assigned to combat and had a good time in Vietnam]; "Victims of Our Noble Cause," *Progressive*, February 1983 [calls the obsession with Vietnam veterans a "freak show"]; Fred Reed, "Jello Writers," *Harpers*, December 1980 [recounts the excitement of the war zone, and ridicules the writers who couldn't begin to understand or put the experience in perspective]; "The Forgotten Warriors," *Time*, July 13, 1981 [mentions that many men who fought in Vietnam loved the action, never feeling so wildly alive before or since]; "Vietnam Veterans' Nonstop Con Game," *New York Times*, March 10, 1986, I, 19:2 [that Vietnam has become an excuse]; James Webb, "Viet Vets Didn't Kill Babies and They Aren't Suicidal," p. C1a; and William K. Lane, Jr., "Enough of Vietnam Sob Stories," *Indianapolis Star*, November 11, 1988, p. A-25 (reprinted from *Wall Street Journal*).

20. Occasionally, in the midst of a segment on Vietnam veteran problems, a veteran would be interviewed and contend that he was not bitter (CBS, March 20, 1985) or a doctor would be quoted maintaining that Vietvets were "resilient" (CBS, May 25, 1987), but the foregone conclusion presented by most television shows was that the Vietnam veteran was in a crisis, that the government was to blame, that the government wasn't doing anything about it, and if it was, it was too late. For portrayals of agony, see CBS, May 30, 1979 [flashing back]; CBS, October 17, 1981 [pushed under the rug]; CBS, November 14, 1982 [too late for me]; CBS, January 11, 1984 [weapons of war]; ABC, April 30, 1985 [betrayed]; CBS, March 5, 1986 [women and children]; ABC, September 29, 1987 [can't shake it]; CBS, May 12, 1988 [fought and struggled].

21. Neil Postman, *Amusing Ourselves to Death: Public Discourse in the Age of Show Business* (New York: Penguin Books, 1985); James Fallows, *Breaking the News: How the Media Undermine American Democracy* (New York: Pantheon, 1995).

22. "Looking at War's Brutality through Vietnamese Eyes," *New York Times*, May 15, 1995, p. B1; "Vietnamese Psychics Joint Hunt for Missing," *New York Times*, Dec. 14, 1995, p. A21.

23. For rare media accounts of suffering by Cambodians, Vietnamese, or ARVN veterans, see "They Cried Until They Could Not See," *New York Times*, June 23, 1991, section 6, p. 25 [Cambodians who were tortured]; "Immigrants Face New Life, New Stresses: Many Suffer Mental Torment from Uprooting, Experts Say," *Newsday*, February 9, 1992, p. 69 [Cambodians]; "Decades Old U.S. Bombs Still Killing Laotians," *New York Times*, August 10, 1995, p. A12 [Laos]; "Vietnam Asylums: War Never Ends; Ill Veterans Relive Traumas in Impoverished Surroundings," *Washington Post*, October 23, 1993, p. A17; "A Long and Lonely Struggle with Bitterness," *Los Angeles Times*, April 24, 1995, pt. A, p. 3 [ARVN veterans].

24. See George L. Priest, "The Invention of Enterprise Liability: A Critical History of the Intellectual Foundations of Modern Tort Law," *Journal of Legal Studies*, 14 (3) (Dec. 1985): 461–528; Mary Ann Glendon, *Rights Talk: The Impoverishment of Political Discourse* (New York: Free Press, 1991); Abigail M. Thernstrom, *Whose Votes Count? Affirmative Action and Minority Voting Rights* (Cambridge, Mass.: Harvard University Press, 1987); Mary Douglas and Aaron Wildavsky, *Risk and Culture: An Essay on the Selection of Technical and Environmental Dangers* (Berkeley: University of California Press, 1982); and Charles Krauthammer, *Cutting Edges: Making Sense of the Eighties* (New York: Random House, 1985); Wendy Kaminer, *I'm Dysfunctional, You're Dysfunctional: The Recovery Movement and Other Self-Help Fashions* (New York: Vintage Books, 1993), p. xii; Philip K. Howard, *The Death of Common Sense: How Law Is Suffocating America* (New York: Random House, 1994); and Charles J. Sykes, *A Nation of Victims: The Decay of the American Character* (New York: St. Martin's Press, 1992).

25. Regarding the right of veterans to sue the federal government (and the "Feres Doctrine"), see Howard Ball, "The U.S. Supreme Court's Glossing of the Federal Tort Claims Act: Statutory Construction and Veterans' Tort Actions," *Western Political Quarterly*, 41 (3) (September 1988): 529–552.

26. Thomas L. Friedman, "The No-Dead War," *New York Times*, August 23, 1995, p. A21; "The Military's Getting Queasier about Death," *New York Times*, August 6, 1995, p. E5 ["the public is intolerant of casualties"].

27. Substance abuse [CDC Vietnam Experience Study, "Health Status of Vietnam Veterans, 1: Psychosocial Characteristics," *JAMA*, 259 (1988), 2701–2707 (39 percent); F. S. Sierles, J. J. Chen, R. E. McFarland, and M. A. Taylor, "Posttraumatic Stress Disorder and Concurrent Psychiatric Illness: A Preliminary Report," *American Journal of Psychiatry*, 140 (1983) (84 percent)]; depression [Michael R. Hryvniak and Richard B. Rosse, "Concurrent Psychiatric Illness in Inpatients with Post-Traumatic Stress Disorder," *Military Medicine*, 154 (8) (August 1989), 399–401 (36.5 percent); and Thomas R. Kosten, Victor Wahby, Earl Giller, Jr., and John Mason, "The Dexamethasone Suppression Test and Thyrotropin-Releasing Hormone Stimulation Test in Posttraumatic Stress Disorder," *Biological Psychiatry*, 28 (8) (October 15, 1990): 657–664 (50 percent)]; anxiety disorders [J. R. T. Davidson, H. S. Kudler, W. B. Saunders, R. D. Smith, "Symptom and Morbidity Patterns in World War II and Vietnam Veterans with Post-Traumatic Stress Disorder," *Comparative Psychiatry*, 31 (1990): 1882–1870 (47 percent generalized anxiety disorder)]; antisocial personality [Bonnie L. Green, Jacob D. Lindy, and Mary C. Grace, "Posttraumatic Stress Disorder: Toward DSM-IV," *Journal of Nervous and Mental Disease* 173 (7) (1985): 406–411 (14 percent)]; free-standing [Michael R. Hryvniak and Richard B. Rosse, "Concurrent Psychiatric Illness in Inpatients with Post-Traumatic Stress Disorder," *Military Medicine*, 154 (8) (August 1989), 399–401 (1.6 percent)]. Bonnie L. Green, "Chronic Posttraumatic Stress Disorder and Diagnostic Comorbidity in a Disaster Sample," *Journal of Nervous and Mental Disease*, 180 (12) (1992): 760–766; F. Suzanne Talbert et al., "MMPI Profiles in PTSD as a Function of Comorbidity," *Journal of Clinical Psychology*, 50 (4) (July 1994): 529–536. For overviews of PTSD, see David A. Tomb, "The Phenom-

enology of Post-Traumatic Stress Disorder," *Psychiatric Clinics of North America*, 17 (2) (June 1994): 237–250; Charles R. Figley, *Stress Disorders among Vietnam Veterans: Theory, Research, and Treatment* (New York: Brunner/Mazel, 1978), pp. xiii–xxiv; and the discussion in Chapter 2.

28. Susan D. Solomon and Glorisa J. Canino, "Appropriateness of DSM-III-R Criteria for Posttraumatic Stress Disorder," *Comprehensive Psychiatry*, 31 (3) (May/June 1990): 227–237 [that "ordinary stress" may be equally traumatic]; Green, Lindy, and Grace, "Posttraumatic Stress Disorder: Toward DSM-IV" [notes anomaly of etiologic-specificity]; Naomi Breslau and Glenn C. Davis, "Posttraumatic Stress Disorder: The Stressor Criterion," *Journal of Nervous and Mental Disease*, 175 (5) (May 1987): 255–276 [definition of PTSD is imprecise; questions legitimacy of measuring "objective" stress, argues that individual and social factors are important in onset]; Laura M. Davidson and Andrew Baum, "Chronic Stress and Posttraumatic Stress Disorders," *Journal of Consulting and Clinical Psychology*, 54 (3) (1986): 303–308 [studies role of chronic stress in causing PTSD]; Howard P. Parette, Jr., Bobby J. Farrow, Jonelle M. Farrow, and Michael Hazelwood, "The Aging War Veteran and Alcohol Abuse: An Emerging Relationship?" *Perceptual and Motor Skills*, 68 (1989): 985–986, at 986 [empirical vacuum]. For varying estimates on the percentage of Vietnam veterans with PTSD, see Richard A. Kulka et al., *Trauma and the Vietnam War Generation: Report of Findings from the National Vietnam Veterans Readjustment Study* (New York: Brunner/Mazel, 1990), p. xvii [NVVRS (National Vietnam Veteran Readjustment Study) based on a total sample of 2,348 veterans estimated a current case rate in male theater veterans of 15.2 percent, additional symptomatology in another 11.1 percent males, and lifetime prevalence for male theater vets of 30.6 percent]; and John E. Helzer et al., "Post-Traumatic Stress Disorder in the General Population," *New England Journal of Medicine*, 26 (Dec. 24, 1987): 1630–1634 [study of 2,493 people; estimates rate of 1 percent in general U.S. population and rate of 3.5 percent for general Vietnam veteran population (similar to rate for civilians exposed to physical attack), but rate of 20 percent in Vietnam vets wounded in the war]; J. P. Wilson, "Identity, Ideology and Crisis: The Vietnam Veteran in Transition," pt. 1 (Cleveland State University, 1977) [50 percent]; Charles Figley, ed., *Stress Disorders among Vietnam Veterans: Theory, Research, and Treatment* (New York: Brunner/Mazel, 1978), pp. xiii–xxvi [50 percent].

29. For instance, see L. C. Kolb, "A Neuropsychological Hypothesis Explaining Posttraumatic Stress Disorders," *American Journal of Psychiatry*, 144 (1987): 989–995; Roger K. Pitman et al., "Psychophysiologic Assessment of Posttraumatic Stress Disorder Imagery in Vietnam Combat Veterans," *Archives of General Psychiatry*, 44 (November 1987): 970–975; Rosalind Ramsay, "Invited Review: Post-Traumatic Stress Disorder: A New Clinical Entity?" *Journal of Psychosomatic Research*, 34 (4) (1990): 355–365; Bernard Lerer et al., "Platelet Adenylate Cyclase and Phospholipase C Activity in Posttraumatic Stress Disorder," *Biological Psychiatry*, 27 (7) (April 1, 1990): 735–740; Miles E. McFall et al., "Autonomic Responses to Stress in Vietnam Combat Veterans with Posttraumatic Stress Disorder," *Biological Psychiatry*, 27 (10) (May 15, 1990):

1165–1175; and Steven M. Southwick et al., "Psychobiologic Research in Post-Traumatic Stress Disorder," *Psychiatric Clinics of North America,* 17 (2) (June 1994): 251–264. Gregory L. Belenky, "Varieties of Reaction and Adaptation to Combat Experience," *Bulletin of the Menninger Clinic,* 51 (1) (1987): 64–79 [suggests usefulness of discussing *combat reaction spectrum disorder* (CRSD) because symptoms blend imperceptibly into one another]; George Henry Savage, *The Increase of Insanity* (New York: Cassell, 1907), p. 11 ["I still believe"].

30. Landy Sparr and Loren D. Pankratz, "Factitious Posttraumatic Stress Disorder," *American Journal of Psychiatry,* 140 (8) (August 1983): 1016–1019, 1017 [case study], 1016 [easily simulated]; Edward J. Lynn and Mark Belza, "Factitious Posttraumatic Stress Disorder: The Veteran Who Never Got to Vietnam," *Hospital and Community Psychiatry,* 35 (7) (July 1984): 697–701; J. DeVance Hamilton, "Pseudo-Posttraumatic Stress Disorder," *Military Medicine,* 150 (July 1985): 353–356; and Lee Hyer et al., "Vietnam Veterans: Overreporting versus Acceptable Reporting of Symptoms," *Journal of Personality Assessment,* 52 (3) (1988): 475–486.

31. For the extent of typical verification, see Thomas A. Mellman et al., "Phenomenology and Course of Psychiatric Disorders Associated with Combat-Related Posttraumatic Stress Disorder," *American Journal of Psychiatry,* 149 (11) (November 1992): 1568–74; for problems of retrospective bias, see Norman Q. Brill and Gilbert W. Beebe, "Follow-Up Study of Psychoneuroses; Preliminary Report," *American Journal of Psychiatry* 108 (December 1951), 417–425 [variance between histories given in military and at follow-up]; Robert S. Laufer et al., "War Stress and Trauma: The Vietnam Veteran Experience," *Journal of Health and Social Behavior,* 25 (March 1984): 65–85 [retrospective bias]; Samuel Futterman and Eugene Pumpian-Mindlin, "Traumatic War Neuroses Five Years Later," *American Journal of Psychiatry,* 108 (December 1951): 401–408 [tendency of veterans to exaggerate the importance of trauma, and to idealize their prewar past]; L. Buydens-Branchey et al., "Duration and Intensity of Combat Exposure and Posttraumatic Stress Disorder in Vietnam Veterans," *Journal of Nervous and Mental Disease,* 178 (9) (1990): 582–587 [discussion]. Wecter, *When Johnny Comes Marching Home,* p. 365 [dignity]; Guenther Lewy, *America in Vietnam* (New York: Oxford University Press, 1978), p. 321 [Moskos]; George Rosen in *Madness in Society: Chapters in the Historical Sociology of Mental Illness* (Chicago: University of Chicago Press, 1968) [mass psychosis]; and Robert H. Fleming, "Post Vietnam Syndrome: Neurosis or Sociosis?" *Psychiatry,* 48 (2) (1985): 122–139 [problem of embellishment]; Joel Osler Brende and Erwin Randolph Parson, *Vietnam Veterans: The Road to Recovery* (New York: Signet Books, 1985), pp. 185–186 [instance of therapist convincing a patient to place Vietnam in its "proper place" as central and the rest of his problems as derivative].

32. Gerald Goldstein et al., "Survivors of Imprisonment in the Pacific Theater during World War II," *American Journal of Psychiatry,* 144 (9) (September 1987): 1210–1213 [World War II POWs]; William Henry Younts memoirs, p. 100, Indiana Historical Society; for a rare analysis in the psychiatric literature of veterans viewing combat as a positive experience, see Samuel L.

Bradshaw, Jr., et al., "The Love of War: Vietnam and the Traumatized Veteran," *Bulletin of the Menninger Clinic*, 55 (1) (Winter 1991): 96–103.

33. Jonathan F. Borus, "Incidence of Maladjustment in Vietnam Returnees," *Archives of General Psychiatry*, 30 (April 1974): 554 [overstepped their data]; R. H. Fleming, "Post Vietnam Syndrome: Neurosis or Sociosis?" *Psychiatry*, 48 (2) (1985): 122–139 [foster rage]. Chaim Shatan led the movement which approached the APA Task Force on Nomenclature and requested inclusion of PTSD as a category. Figley and Wilson served on the Subcommittee which developed the definition of PTSD for the DSM-III. See relevant discussion in Chapter 2.

34. See Wilbur J. Scott, "PTSD in DSM-III: A Case in the Politics of Diagnosis and Disease," *Social Problems*, 37 (3) (August 1990): 294–310.

35. Charles E. Rosenberg, "The Place of George M. Beard in Nineteenth-Century Psychiatry," *Bulletin of the History of Medicine*, 36 (1962): 245–259; David J. Rothman, *The Discovery of the Asylum: Social Order and Disorder in the New Republic* (New York: Little, Brown and Co., 1971); Carroll Smith-Rosenberg, "The Hysterical Woman: Sex Roles and Role Conflict in Nineteenth-Century America," *Social Research*, 39 (1972): 652–678; Andrew Scull, "From Madness to Mental Illness: Medical Men as Moral Entrepreneurs," *European Journal of Sociology*, 16 (1975): 219–261; Barbara Sicherman, "The Uses of a Diagnosis: Doctors, Patients, and Neurasthenia," *Journal of the History of Medicine and Allied Sciences*, 32 (1) (January 1977): 33–54; Elaine Showalter, *The Female Malady: Women, Madness, and English Culture, 1830–1980* (New York: Penguin Books, 1985); Ian Dowbiggin, "Degeneration and Hereditarianism in French Mental Medicine, 1840–90," in W. F. Bynum, Roy Porter, and Michael Shepherd, eds., *The Anatomy of Madness: Essays in the History of Psychiatry*, vols. 1–2 (New York: Tavistock Publications, 1985); Jan Goldstein, *Console and Classify: The French Psychiatric Profession in the Nineteenth Century* (Cambridge: Cambridge University Press, 1987); Nancy Tomes, "The Anatomy of Madness: New Directions in the History of Psychiatry," *Social Studies of Science*, 17 (1987): 358–371; Gerald N. Grob, "World War II and American Psychiatry," *Psychohistory Review*, 19 (Fall 1990): 41–69.

36. See Andrew J. Polsky, *The Rise of the Therapeutic State* (Princeton: Princeton University Press, 1991).

37. This gendered view of psychopathology emerges when one reviews contemporary psychiatric theory, which dealt at length with the role of shock and fright in producing insanity, but almost never discussed the military experience as a possible source of such shock or fright. See the following medical theses from the 1860s and 1870s, which make no mention of war as a condition or environment that might produce insanity: A. H. Bayles, "Mental Influences as Conducive to Health or Productive of Disease" (medical school thesis, University of Michigan, 1860s?), p. 3 [shock of severe mental impression]; E. P. Jennings, "Hysteria" (medical school thesis, University of Michigan, 1853), pp. 1–2 [hysteria, but no mention of war; primarily a female problem]; Levi O. Johnson, "Mental Influences" (medical school thesis, University of Michigan, 1868), p. 14 [terror]. For an exception to this tendency, see Mary J. Forsyth, "Mental Derangement" (medical school thesis, University of

Michigan, 1876), p. 30 ["The writer has seen a number bereft of reason, through the lapses and misfortunes of the late war"].

38. *Carolina Spartan*, April 5, 1866, "Advice to Young Men," p. 1 [South Carolina Library].

39. "Reduced Gentlewomen," *Daily South Carolinian*, December 22, 1865 [commiseration]; "The Young Men of the South," *Daily South Carolinian*, February 24, 1866, p. 2 [despondency as unmanly]; "Adversity—How to Bear It," *Macon Daily Herald*, May 8, 1865, p. 2 [fate and manly fortitude]; David Wiltsee diary, entries for January 30, 1862, and February 9, 1862, Indiana Historical Society [more like a woman]; "Voice of a Disabled Soldier," *Soldier's Friend*, April 1866, p. 2 [unmans energy]; "The Battle of Life," *Soldier's Friend*, December 1864, p. 2 [stand up manfully]. In general, see George M. Fredrickson, *The Inner Civil War: Northern Intellectuals and the Crisis of the Union* (New York: Harper & Row, 1965), pp. 169–175.

40. For typical sentimental or ironic accounts of the Civil War, see the various stories in *The Soldier's Friend* and *The Veteran* (Library of Congress); Washington Davis, *Camp-Fire Chats of the Civil War; Being the Incident, Adventure, and Wayside Exploit of the Bivouac and Battle Field, as Related by Veteran Soldiers Themselves. Embracing the Tragedy, Romance, Comedy, Humor, and Pathos in the Varied Experiences of Army Life* (Lansing, Mich.: P. A. Stone, 1889); Louisa May Alcott, *Hospital Sketches* (Boston: James Redpath, 1863), in *The History of American Nursing: Civil War Nursing*, ed. Susan Reverby (New York: Garland, 1984), pp. 63–65.

41. Stephen Crane, *The Red Badge of Courage* (Rutland, Vt.: Charles E. Tuttle, Everyman Edition, 1992), pp. 24 [blood-swollen], 31 [monster], 38 [fierce and cruel god], 90 [dark pit], 73 [debauch], 48 [machine], and 78 [wisdom]; Ambrose Bierce, *Ambrose Bierce's Civil War* (Washington, D.C.: Regnery Gateway, 1956). Regarding Civil War literature, see Daniel Aaron, *The Unwritten War: American Writers and the Civil War* (New York: Knopf, 1973); Frederickson, *The Inner Civil War;* and Edmund Wilson, *Patriotic Gore: Studies in the Literature of the American Civil War* (Boston: Northeastern University Press, 1962).

42. Gaines M. Foster, "Coming to Terms with Defeat: Post-Vietnam America and the Post-Civil War South," *Virginia Quarterly Review*, 66 (1) (1990): 17–35.

43. In general, see Gaines M. Foster, *Ghosts of the Confederacy: Defeat, the Lost Cause, and the Emergence of the New South* (New York: Oxford University Press, 1987), and Charles Reagan Wilson, *Baptized in Blood: The Religion of the Lost Cause, 1865–1920* (Athens: University of Georgia Press, 1980). For early accounts of ceremonies centering on cemeteries, see Joseph C. Carter, *Magnolia Journey: A Union Veteran Revisits the Former Confederate States,* arranged from letters of correspondent Russell H. Conwell to the *Daily Evening Traveller* (Boston, 1869) (University: University of Alabama Press, 1974), pp. 93–94.

44. Charles M. McGee, Jr., and Ernest M. Lander, Jr., eds., *A Rebel Came Home* (Columbia: University of South Carolina Press, 1961), pp. 114–115 [procession].

45. See the United Daughters of the Confederacy–Atlanta Chapter Scrapbooks, Georgia State Archives; "Expression of Deathless Gratitude," Lee Davis Lodge, Address to Reunion of the UCV of South Carolina, in Chester, S.C.,

on June 23, 1909, South Caroliniana Collection, South Caroliniana Library [ardent wish]; John E. Hobeika, *A Tribute to the Confederate Soldier: An Address Before Anne Fulmore Harllee Chapter United Daughters of the Confederacy, Dillon, S.C.* (1930; South Caroliniana Library), p. 6 [Confederate soldier].

46. Thomas C. Leonard, *Above the Battle: War-Making in America from Appomattox to Versailles* (New York: Oxford University Press, 1978), pp. 1–39.

47. In general, see Robert J. Keehn et al., "Twenty-Four Year Mortality Follow-Up of Army Veterans with Disability Separations for Psychoneurosis in 1944," *Psychosomatic Medicine,* 36 (1) (January-February 1974): 27–46.

48. For analysis of the problems of returning veterans of earlier American wars, see Willard Waller, *The Veteran Comes Back* (New York: Dryden Press, 1944); Wecter, *When Johnny Comes Marching Home;* and Gerald F. Linderman, *Embattled Courage: The Experience of Combat in the American Civil War* (New York: Free Press, 1987). For attitudes on parades, see Wecter, pp. 129, 302, 317; and Robert J. Havighurst et al., *The American Veteran Back Home: A Study of Veteran Readjustment* (New York: Longmans, Breen and Co., 1951), pp. 69–70. See also Wecter, pp. 183 [Civil War soldiers hiding service record], and 188 [unemployment]. For crime, see Colin Wilson, *A Criminal History of Mankind* (New York: Granada, 1984), p. 540; Waller, p. 125. For suicide, see Wecter, p. 399 [that the *American Legion Weekly* after World War I suggested a high suicide rate of two per day in veterans]. For images of violent veterans, see "Heroes for Sale" (1933), and "They Gave Him a Gun" (1937) [World War I veterans], Foster Hirsch, *The Dark Side of the Screen: Film Noir* (New York: A. S. Barnes, 1981) [World War II]; and *The Blue Dahlia* (1946; Paramount), *Crossfire* (1947; RKO), and *Criss Cross* (1949; Universal-International) [World War II].

49. Davis R. B. Ross, *Preparing for Ulysses: Politics and Veterans during World War II* (New York: Columbia University Press, 1969); for a pattern of neglect, see Waller, *The Veteran Comes Back,* p. 15.

50. Thomas C. Leonard, in *Above the Battle: War-Making in America from Appomattox to Versailles* (New York: Oxford University Press, 1978), argues that war making in America had a dreamlike, unreal quality ("above the battle") *until* the World War I experience, when war was seen for what it is, destructive and horrible. Dixon Wecter, *When Johnny Comes Marching Home,* also documents the tendency of World War I veterans to remain silent on their war experience, a reluctance to glorify their "exploits" that often puzzled civilians.

51. Robert Weldon Whalen, *Bitter Wounds: German Victims of the Great War, 1914–1939* (Ithaca, N.Y.: Cornell University Press, 1984) [Weimar Germany].

52. *Veterans' Benefits in the United States: Findings and Recommendations* (A Report to the President by the President's Commission on Veterans' Pensions, April 1956) [Bradley]; Ross, *Preparing for Ulysses,* p. 18.

Conclusion

1. Of Mexican War volunteers, a nineteenth-century physician noted: "Thousands . . . returned home to die among their friends from the effects of diseases contracted in camp. For some time after the war, volunteers

formed a noted proportion of the inmates of civil hospitals, and the chronic diseases under which they were laboring were with great difficulty controlled." Julian John Chisolm, *A Manual of Military Surgery: For the Use of the Surgeons in the Confederate States Army; with an Appendix of the Rules and Regulations of the Medical Department of the Confederate Army* (San Francisco: Norman Publishing, 1989; originally published in 1861 by West & Johnston of Richmond, Virginia), p. 22.

2. George W. Adams, *Doctors in Blue: The Medical History of the Union Army in the Civil War* (Dayton, Ohio: Morningside Press, 1985), p. 3 [two deaths from disease for every battle death in the Civil War]. The *Army Almanac* (Harrisburg, Pa.: Stackpole Books, 1959] indicates that death from disease (per thousand men) for the following wars was as follows: Mexican War (102); Civil War (Union troops) (62); Spanish-American War (25.6); World War I (16.5); World War II (0.6); and Korean War (0.5). The figure for the Civil War can reasonably be adjusted upward, perhaps to as high as 100 per thousand soldiers, in that many men enlisted several times, and therefore any statistic calculated per enlistment will understate overall deaths. G. H. Rice, "The Evolution of Military Medical Services, 1854 to 1914," *Journal of the Royal Army Medical Corps*, 135 (1989): 147–150, estimates that the ratio of disease deaths to battle deaths in the Crimean War was 3:1 for the French and 4:1 for the British. Hospital mortality rates for the wounded, which had been as high as 39 percent in the Crimean, War were 1.81 percent in the Vietnam War. William Caldwell, "Address of Retiring President of the Northwestern Ohio Medical Association," *Cleveland Medical Gazette*, 4 (4) (February 1889): 139–151, 142, suggested that the Civil War had shortened the lives of its soldiers by an average of twenty-one years. A. Newman, "A Comparison of the Mortality from Disease in Armies with That of Men of Military Ages in Civil Life, Showing the Groups of Diseases Chiefly Concerned in Causing the Excess of Mortality in Armies," *Leavenworth M. Herald*, 3 (1869–1870): 241, 304, 242, found a mortality rate for civilian men of military age (15–50) in 1860 to be 6.3 per thousand, compared with mortality rates of 232 per thousand [British Army, 1809]; 450 per thousand [British army in Burma]; 232 per thousand [British Crimean army]; 103.8 per thousand [Mexican War]; 48.7 per thousand [first year of Civil War]; 65.2 per thousand [second year of Civil War]. Morris Janowitz, *The Professional Soldier: A Social and Political Portrait* (New York: Macmillan, 1960, 1971), p. 65 [over 90 percent in Civil War had purely military occupation specialties]; Eli Ginzberg et al., *The Ineffective Soldier*, vol. 3: *Patterns of Performance* (New York: Columbia University Press, 1959) [30 percent of World War II American soldiers in combat]; Francis C. Steckel, "Morale and Men: A Study of the American Soldier in World War II" (diss., Temple University, 1990), pp. 122–123 [37 percent of World War II troops overseas experienced combat]; Robert H. Fleming, "Post Vietnam Syndrome: Neurosis or Sociosis?" *Psychiatry*, 48 (2) (1985): 122–139, 128 [15 percent in Vietnam in combat]. See also Louis C. Duncan, *The Medical Department of the United States Army in the Civil War* (Washington, D.C.: Department of Defense, 1917) [estimates disease:battle death ratio at 4:1 for Napoleonic Wars, 7:1 for Mexican War].

3. For the trend toward viewing American veterans as victims or as having been badly used, see Richard Severo and Lewis Milford, *The Wages of War: When America's Soldiers Came Home—From Valley Forge to Vietnam* (New York: Simon and Schuster, 1989), p. 15.

4. In general, see James M. McPherson, *Ordeal by Fire: The Civil War and Reconstruction* (New York: McGraw-Hill, 1992), pp. 248–250 [paradox]. James L. Cooper memoirs, p. 22 [excitement], Confederate Collection, Tennessee State Archives; Samuel L. Bradshaw, Jr., et al., "The Love of War: Vietnam and the Traumatized Veteran," *Bulletin of the Menninger Clinic*, 55 (1) (Winter 1991): 96–103.

5. "U.S.S. Intrepid: The Story of the 'Fighting I' " (A&E Television Networks, 1995) [McCain]; Elizabeth A. Paul, "Wounded Healers: A Summary of the Vietnam Nurse Veteran Project," *Military Medicine*, 150 (11) (November 1985): 571–576, 575 ["For some, it was an uplifting, challenging, rewarding, and a memorable time in their lives"]; William H. Sledge et al., "Self-Concept Changes Related to War Captivity," *Archives of General Psychiatry*, 37 (April 1980): 430–443; Raina E. Eberly and Brian E. Engdahl, "Prevalence of Somatic and Psychiatric Disorders among Former Prisoners of War," *Hospital and Community Psychiatry*, 42 (8) (August 1991): 807–813 ["Many POWs used their ordeal as a springboard toward greater psychological health"]; Theodore Van Putten and Joel Yager, "Posttraumatic Stress Disorder: Emerging from the Rhetoric," *Archives of General Psychiatry*, 41 (April 1984): 411–413; and Jonathan Borus, "Reentry I: Adjustment Issues Facing the Vietnam Returnee," *Archives of General Psychiatry*, 28 (April 1973); Glen H. Elder, Jr., and Elizabeth C. Clipp, "Wartime Losses and Social Bonding: Infuences across Forty Years in Men's Lives," *Psychiatry*, 51 (1988): 177–197 [intense combat and social loss can either promote *or* thwart enduring ties with service mates]; Glen H. Elder, Jr., and Elizabeth Colerick Clipp, "Combat Experience and Emotional Health: Impairment and Resilience in Later Life," *Journal of Personality*, 57 (2) (June 1989): 311–341 [heavy combat veterans from World War II became more resilient and less helpless over time when compared with other men; benefits associated with military experience].

6. Josephine King Evans, "Nostalgia for a Nickel: the *Confederate Veteran*," *Tennessee Historical Quarterly*, 48 (4) (Winter 1989): 238–244 [maiden issue in 1893]; Louise Rosenfield Noun, "The Iowa Soldiers' and Sailors' Monument," *Palimpest*, 67 (3) (May–June 1986): 80–93 [idea in 1888; construction began in 1894]; Gaines M. Foster, *Ghosts of the Confederacy: Defeat, the Lost Cause, and the Emergence of the New South* (Oxford University Press, 1987); Charles Reagan Wilson, *Baptized in Blood: The Religion of the Lost Cause, 1865–1920* (Athens: University of Georgia Press, 1980).

7. Mary R. Dearing, *Veterans in Politics: The Story of the GAR* (Baton Rouge: Louisiana State University Press, 1952), pp. 57–65, 115, and 149–181; David Montgomery, *Citizen Worker* (Cambridge: Cambridge University Press, 1993), pp. 95–98. See also Stuart McConnell, *Glorious Contentment: The Grand Army of the Republic, 1865–1900* (Chapel Hill: University of North Carolina Press, 1992), pp. 206–238; and Gerald F. Linderman, *Embattled Courage: The Experience of Combat in the American Civil War* (New York: Free Press, 1988), pp. 275–297.

8. Peter W. Huber, *Liability: The Legal Revolution and Its Consequences* (New York: Basic Books, 1988); Peter H. Schuck, "Multi-Culturalism Redux: Science, Law, and Politics," *Yale Law & Policy Review,* 11 (1) (1993): 1–46; idem, *Agent Orange on Trial: Mass Toxic Disasters in the Courts* (Cambridge, Mass.: Harvard University Press, 1986).

9. This wall has been the subject of dozens of stories reported in the media over the years. See, for instance, "A Wall for the Fallen," *Southern Living,* January 1988, pp. 28, 30; "The Wall: Monument to a Nation's Sacrifice," *McCall's,* June 1988, pp. 42, 45; " 'We Touch the Wall and the Wall Touches Us,' " *TV Guide,* May 28/June 3, 1988, pp. 2–4; "Woman of the Wall," *U.S. New and World Report,* March 7, 1988, p. 13 [monument for women Vietnam vets]; Elizabeth McGowan, "The Wringing at the Wall: Washington's Controversial Vietnam Veterans Memorial," *Travel Holiday,* April 1989, p. 11 + ; "Voices at the Wall: For Everyone Who Visits and Reflects on It, the Vietnam Memorial Takes on Personal Meaning," *New York Times Magazine,* May 27, 1990, pp. 16–19 [cover story]; "Asking Questions at the Vietnam Memorial," *People Weekly,* January 28, 1991, p. 42; "Facing the Wall: Ten Years after the Dedication of the Vietnam Memorial, the Events of a Typical Day Show That Its Power Has Not Diminished," *Life,* November 1992, pp. 24–29 + ; "Along the Wall, Gifts from the Heart: The Humble Offerings Strewn by the Vietnam Memorial Speak of Love and Devotion," *People Weekly,* June 1, 1992, p. 109; "Remembering Bert: Visiting Washington's Vietnam Memorial, Bill Clinton Pays Homage to a Fallen Buddy," *People Weekly,* June 21, 1993, p. 48; "Another Vietnam Memorial," *U.S. News and World Report,* November 15, 1993, p.21.

10. See "Pentagon's Haiti Policy Focuses on Casualties," *New York Times,* October 6, 1994, p.A5: "The American intervention in Haiti offers a case study of an important shift in the Pentagon's concept of military planning: a casualty-free operation. . . . 'It is impossible to overestimate how the experience of Vietnam lodged itself in the psyche of American military leaders.' " Thomas L. Friedman, "The No-Dead War," *New York Times,* August 23, 1995, p. A21; "The Military's Getting Queasier about Death," *New York Times,* August 6, 1995, p. E5 ["the public is intolerant of casualties"].

11. For a discussion of Civil War historiography, including the "Blundering Generation" interpretation of James G. Randall and Avery Craven, see note 10 in the Introduction.

Appendix C

1. Louis B. Ewbank and Dorothy L. Riker, eds., *The Laws of Indiana Territory, 1809–86* (Indianapolis: Indiana Historical Bureau, 1934).

2. See, for instance, "An act Authorizing Asylums for the Poor in the Counties of Washington and Dearborn," *Laws of the State of Indiana,* 14th session, December 1829 (Indianapolis: Smith and Bolton, 1830), pp. 7–8.

3. *Fourth Biennial Report of the Board of Control and Medical Superintendent of the Eastern Indiana Hospital for the Insane, at Easthaven, Near Richmond, for the Biennial Period Ending October 31, 1896. To the Governor* (Indianapolis: William B. Burfurd, 1896), p. 14.

4. See Henry M. Hur et al., *The Institutional Care of the Insane in the United States and Canada*, vol. 2 (Baltimore: Johns Hopkins Press, 1916); the yearly reports of the relevant asylum, for example, *Report on the Subject of Hospitals for the Insane, by John Evans, M.D., Made to the Commissioners of the Lunatic Asylum of Indiana, June 22, 1845* (Indianapolis: J. P. Chapman, State Printer, 1845); Barbara Brandon, "The State Care of the Insane in Indiana, 1840–1890" (M.A. thesis, University of Chicago, 1938); and Mary Hammond Houk, "The State Care of the Insane in Indiana, 1891–1938" (M.A. thesis, University of Chicago, 1939).

5. "An Act for the government of the Indiana Hospital for the Insane," *General Laws of the State of Indiana*, 32nd session, 1847 (Indianapolis: John D. Defrees, 1848), pp. 83–95.

6. "An ACT defining who are persons of unsound mind, and authorizing the appointment of guardians for such person. . . ," *Revised Statutes of the State of Indiana*, 36th session, 1852, vol. 2 (Indianapolis: J. P. Chapman, 1852).

7. "An ACT to provide for the confinement of person insane and dangerous when suffered to run at large, and for the compensation of him to whom the custody of such insane person is committed," *Laws of the State of Indiana*, 38th session, 1855 (Indianapolis: Austin H. Brown, 1855), pp. 133–136.

8. "An ACT to provide for the care and treatment of the incurable insane of the State of Indiana, and matters properly connected therewith," *Laws of the State of Indiana*, 1865 (Indianapolis: Samuel M. Douglass, 1866), pp. 199–200.

9. "An ACT regulating insanity inquests, and the committal of insane persons to hospitals for the insane, and their discharge therefrom," *Laws of the State of Indiana*, 52nd session, 1881 (Indianapolis: Carlon & Hollenbeck, 1881), pp. 545–555.

Appendix D

1. Dr. Richard C. Smith, White Stone, Va., "How the Insanity Ruse Worked," in *Confederate Veteran*, 23 (4) (April 1915): 169–171.

2. In general, see Judith Gladys Cetina, "A History of Veterans' Homes in the United States, 1811–1930," (unpublished diss., Case Western University, 1977), pp. 235–249.

Index